Mia's MATH SERIES

ALGEBRA 2

Mia's Algebra 2

발 행	2023년 4월 25일 초판 1쇄
	2024년 9월 25일 초판 2쇄

저 자	소미혜
발행인	최영민
발행처	헤르몬하우스
주 소	경기도 파주시 신촌로 16
전 화	031-8071-0088
팩 스	031-942-8688
전자우편	hermonh@naver.com
출판등록	2015년 3월 27일
등록번호	제406-2015-31호

ⓒ 소미혜 2023, Printed in Korea.

ISBN   979-11-92520-43-8 (53410)

- 책 값은 뒤 표지에 있습니다.
- 헤르몬하우스는 피앤피북의 임프린트 출판사입니다.
- 이 책의 어느 부분도 저작권자나 발행인의 승인 없이 무단 복제하여 이용할 수 없습니다.
- 파본 및 낙장은 구입하신 서점에서 교환하여 드립니다.

✤ 저자직강 인터넷 강의는 SAT, AP No.1 인터넷 강의 사이트인 마스터프랩 (www.masterprep.net) 에서 보실 수 있습니다.

'이해하기 쉬운 개념 + 다양한 example 문제 + 심화응용문제'

삼중 그물망구조로 Algebra 2에 필요한 모든 토픽 및 개념과 실전 능력을 한 번에 잡는다!

지난 10년간 결과로 증명된 학교 GPA관리용 최적의 교재!

이해하기 쉽고 친근한 이미지를 활용하여 어려운 수식을 빠르게 이해!

1. '이해하기 쉬운 개념 + 다양한 example문제 + 심화응용문제'

   그 동안의 Algebra 2교재에서는 볼 수 없었던 삼중 그물망구조로 Algebra 2에 필요한 모든 토픽 및 개념과 실전 능력을 한 번에 잡는다!

2. 스스로 빈칸을 채워가며 개념을 꼼꼼히 공부할 수 있도록 설계한 교재

3. 그저 그런 교재가 아니다!

   지난 13년간 현장에서 수많은 학생들에게 결과로 증명된 학교 GPA 최적의 교재!

Preface

Algebra 2는 미국고등수학에서 가장 먼저 배우는 과목이고, 미국고등수학의 뼈대를 세우는 과목입니다. 실제로 Algebra 2에서의 내용을 잘 마스터 해야만 이 다음단계의 수학 Precalculus, Calculus(미적분학), Statistics(통계학)를 순조롭게 이수할 수 있습니다. 또한, 미국의 대학 수학능력시험인 SAT, ACT시험에서 수학파트 문제 대부분이 Algebra2에서 출제되고 있으며, AMC, AIME 등과 같은 미국고등수학경시대회들은 Algebra 2를 시험범위에 포함시키고 있습니다. 이 때문에 저자는 Algebra 2가 미국고등수학의 'backbone(척추)'과 같다고 생각합니다. 이를 위해 학생들이 쉽고 재미있게 공부하면서 기본기를 다질 뿐만 아니라 기본기를 확장시켜서 다양한 심화문제에 응용하는 연습을 할 수 있는 나만의 Algebra 2교재를 제작하기 시작했습니다.

교재 제작을 위해 수 많은 Algebra 2 textbook들의 내용들과 문제들을 연구하였습니다. 그리고 학원 및 개인지도를 통해 알게 된 국내외 많은 국제학교/외국인학교에 재학중인 학생들의 Algebra 2를 지도하면서 각 학교 선생님들의 가르치는 방식과 내용들을 벤치마킹(Benchmarking) 하였습니다. 또한 학생들이 어려워하는 부분들을 분석하고, 학생들의 의견들을 참고하며 교재를 지속적으로 개선하며 교재수준을 향상시켰습니다. 이렇게 완성된 교재를 통해 매년 많은 학생들이 Algebra 2 학교수학시험에서 A이상을 맞는 성과를 얻을 수 있었습니다.

이 책을 통해 학생들이 Algebra 2라는 과목이 충분히 doable하다는 것을 깨닫고, 문제를 해결했을 때의 즐거움을 느끼며, 깊이 있는 문제들을 다루면서 사고력과 응용력이 한층 더 깊어지길 바랍니다.

마지막으로 이 책을 함께 만들기 위해 애써준 사랑하는 남편TY와 잘생긴 아들 주원이, 그 동안 함께해 준 고마운 학생들, 그리고 헤르몬 하우스 관계자 여러분과 마스터프렙의 권주근 대표님께 감사의 마음을 드립니다. 그리고 무엇보다도 소중한 기회를 주신 하나님께 감사와 찬양을 올려드립니다.

Mia Mihye So

Mia's Algebra 2의 특징

1. 교재 내용, 문제에 대한 쉽고 명쾌한 Mia쌤의 설명, 해설강의는 유학 인터넷 강의 전문 사이트인 마스터프렙 (www.masterprep.net)에 마련되어 있습니다.

2. '이해하기 쉬운 개념 + 다양한 example 문제 + 심화 응용 문제' 삼중 그물망 구조로 개념과 실전연습을 한번에 잡아줍니다. 어려운 개념들을 쉽게 배우고 다양한 example 문제로 연습을 한 뒤, 배운 개념에 대한 심화 응용 문제까지 연습함으로 완벽한 개념정리를 완성시킬 수 있습니다.

3. 각 단원 마지막의 Expand Knowledge(심화응용문제)를 통해 일반 미국교과서에서는 접하기 힘들지만 Algebra2 다음단계의 수학 Precalculus, Calculus(미적분학)을 배우는데 도움이 되는 심화문제 또는 심화개념을 공부할 수 있습니다. Expand Knowledge(심화응용문제)는 학생의 공부방향에 따라 선택적으로 공부하면 됩니다.

4. 스스로 빈칸을 채워가며 개념을 꼼꼼하게 공부할 수 있게 설계하였습니다. 빈칸의 답은 페이지하단에 배치하여 학생들이 필요 시 바로 참고할 수 있습니다.

5. 이해하기 쉽고 친근한 이미지를 활용하여 어려운 수식을 빠르게 이해할 수 있도록 작성하였습니다. 꼭 암기해야 할 개념, 공식은 shade박스 안에 정리하였습니다.

◆ 기호 정리

* (star): 심화 응용 문제

$\mathbb{R}$: Real numbers
$\mathbb{Z}$: Integers
$\mathbb{N}$: Natural numbers
$\cup$: or
$\cap$: and

$\emptyset$: empty set (no solution)
∞ : infinity
$\therefore$: Therefore
$\because$: Since

저자 소개

Mia(소미혜) 선생님은 지난 13년 이상을 유학 수학 현장에서 다양한 학생들과 호흡하면서 최적화된 미국 수학 및 국제학교 수학에 대한 솔루션을 제공해온 수학 전문가이다.

압구정 미국수학 전문강사라는 타이틀이 위의 노력들을 통해서 자연스럽게 얻게 된 선생님의 별칭이다.

미국에서 인증된 수학전문강사(Texas 8-12 미국수학교사자격증 content exam + PPR exam 통과)로 관련된 전문자격증을 소지하고 있으며, 특히, 해외 엄마들 사이에 입 소문난 실력파 강사이다.

Precalculus, AP calculus AB BC, AP Statistics, SAT 1 2 math, IB Math 등에서 13년 이상의 경력을 가지고 있다. 또한 한국 수능수학 강의 경력도 4년 이상을 가지고 있어서 한국 수학과 미국/국제학교 수학에 대해서 모두 정통한 수학 전문가이다.

- 8-12 Texas Mathematics Teacher Certificate (content exam + PPR exam 통과)
- (현) No.1 유학 인터넷 강의 사이트 마스터프렙(www.masterprep.net) 수학강사
- (전) IBAdvance IB, sat 수학대표강사
- (전) 해커스유학 미국수학강사
- (전) PSU Edu AP, SAT 수학강사
- 미국텍사스고등학교, 국내국제고등학교 수학교사 경력 6년.
- 수능수학강의 경력 4년
- 용인외대부고 , 경기외고 , KIS, 제주KIS, SIS, 청라달튼, 브랭섬홀, 일본, 싱가포르, 베트남 국제학교 등의 학생들의 온라인/오프라인 개인지도
- College Board certification for AP Calculus AB, BC
- College Board certification for AP Statistics

Contents

1. Functions and Linear

1.1 Function and Relations 12
1.2 Transformation... 22
1.3 The Slope of a Line.. 37
1.4 Graphs of Linear Functions................................. 42
1.5 Finding an Equation of the Line 49
1.6 Two linear Graphs.. 55
1.7 Piecewise Function.. 60
1.8 Absolute value function 64
1.9 Absolute Value equations and Inequalities 71

2. Systems and Matrices

2.1 Systems of Linear Equations.............................. 80
2.2 Word Problems about System............................ 90
2.3 Systems of Inequalities 104
2.4 Linear Programming 109
2.5 Algebra of Matrices 114
2.6 Inverse and Matrix Equation............................... 121

3. Factoring and Expanding Polynomials

3.1 Law of Exponents.. 128
3.2 Polynomials... 136
3.3 Multiplying Polynomials 139
3.4 Factoring using GCF 151
3.5 Factoring Quadratic 155
3.6 Factoring Polynomials 164
3.7 Solving Polynomial Equations............................ 173

3.8 Word Problems about Polynomial Equation 179
3.9 Solving polynomial Inequalities 188

4. Quadratic Function

4.1 Imaginary Numbers 194
4.2 Complex numbers... 199
4.3 Graphing Quadratic Functions 208
4.4 Vertex of Quadratic Graphs 217
4.5 Word Problems about Optimization 228
4.6 Finding Zeros by Factoring 238
4.7 Finding Zeros by Completing the Square 243
4.8 Quadratic Formula.. 248
4.9 Solving Equations in Quadratic Form.................. 253
4.10 Quadratic Inequalities using graphs.................. 258
4.11 Discriminant... 266
4.12 Sum and product of the roots 276

5. Polynomials

5.1 Graphing Polynomials.. 284
5.2 Dividing Polynomials.. 290
5.3 The Remainder and Factor Theorems................. 297
5.4 Theorems about Roots of Polynomial 302
5.5 Complex Roots of Polynomial function 308

6. Rational Expressions

6.1 Rational Expressions.. 314
6.2 Multiplying and Dividing Rational Expressions..... 321

Contents

    6.3 Sums and Differences of Rational Expressions 324
    6.4 Complex Fractions 330
    6.5 Rational Equations and Word Problems 336
    6.6 Graph of Rational Functions 346

7. Radicals

    7.1 Roots of Real Numbers 354
    7.2 Properties of Radicals 365
    7.3 Operations of Radicals 372
    7.4 Radical Equations 382
    7.5 Graph of Radical Function 388
    7.6 Rational and Real Exponents 392

8. Exponential and Logarithm

    8.1 Composite Function 406
    8.2 Inverse Function 410
    8.3 Exponential Function 420
    8.4 Definition of Logarithms 426
    8.5 Laws of Logarithms 435
    8.6 Log and Exp Equations 443
    8.7 The Natural Logarithm Function 451
    8.8 Exponential Growth and Modeling 459

9. Sequence and Series

    9.1 Sequence and Series 466
    9.2 Arithmetic Sequence and Series 475
    9.3 Geometric Sequence and Series 482

9.4 Infinite Geometric Series 488

10. Coordinate Geometry

10.1 Distance and midpoint Formulas 496
10.2 Equation of Circle.. 501
10.3 Basics of Conic Sections 510

11. Basic Statistics

11.1 Measuring Center of Data................................. 522
11.2 Measuring Spread of Data 531
11.3 Probability 541
11.4 Independent and dependent Event................... 549

Answers... 559

Part 1

Functions and Linear

1.1 Function and Relations

1.2 Transformation

1.3 The Slope of a Line

1.4 Graphs of Linear Functions

1.5 Finding an Equation of the Line

1.6 Two linear Graphs

1.7 Piecewise Function

1.8 Absolute value function

1.9 Absolute Value equations and Inequalities

Mia's Algebra 2
1.1 Function and Relations

1. Relation

Let's say we have a box that squares a number and add 1.
If we put -1 and 0 into the box;

※ **Relation**

A ③_____ is a set of pairs of input and output values.

It ④_____ the x(**input**) to y(**output**).

Input (=⑤_____ = ⑥_____ variable) is the set of X.

Output (=⑦_____ = ⑧_____ variable) is the set of Y.

Blank : ① 2   ② 1   ③ relation   ④ relates   ⑤ domain   ⑥ independent   ⑦ range   ⑧ dependent

You can write a relation in many ways..such as

| Mapping | Table | Order Pairs | Graph |

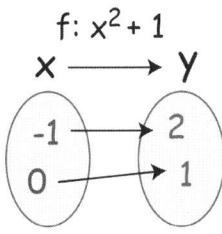

x	y
-1	2
0	1
1	2

$(x, y) = \{(-1,2), (0,1)\}$

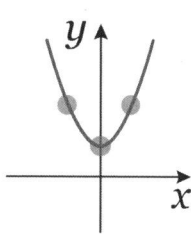

2. Function

A **function** is a specific kind of relation.

※ **Function**

A **function** is a special relation

where ① _____ input has ② _____ output.

※ **Function or not?**

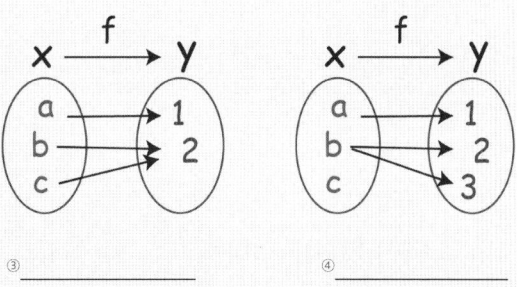

③ _____   ④ _____

Easy way to check if a relation is a function?

① _____ different ⑤ _____ coordinate

② _____ ⑥ _____ test

Blank : ① each   ② one   ③ function   ④ Not a function   ⑤ x   ⑥ vertical line

Part 1 Functions 13

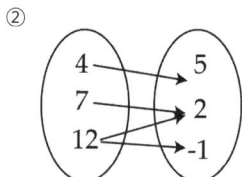

Not a function !　　　　Function !

If a vertical line crosses the curve twice or more, then it is NOT a function.

EXAMPLE 1. Determine whether each relation is a function or not.

①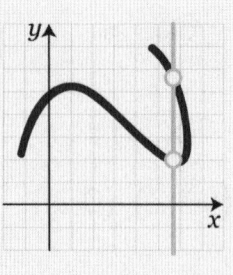

②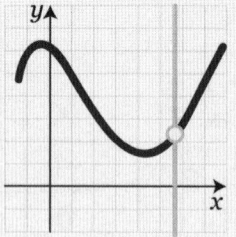

③ $\{(2,-3),(-1,4),(3,5),(8,-11)\}$

④ $\{(-1,3),(0,1),(2,-3),(-1,0)\}$

⑤ $\{(0,2),(-1,3),(12,-30),(0,4),(2,3)\}$

⑥ $\{(1,2),(2,1),(4,4),(0,4),(3,4)\}$

⑦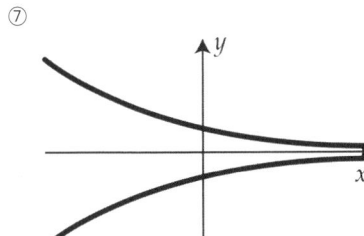

⑧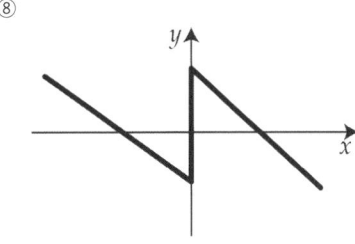

⑨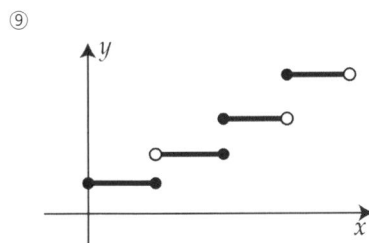

⑩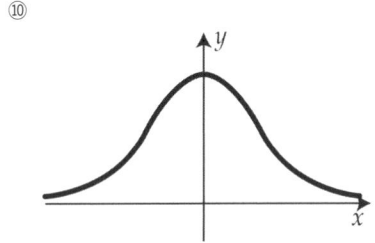

⑪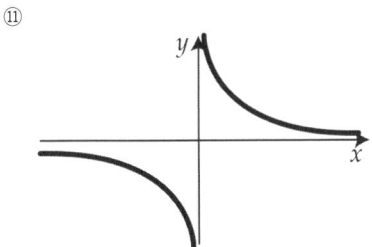

⑫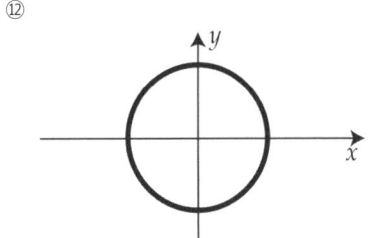

Part 1 Functions 15

3. Domain

※ Finding Domain

When you have	$\dfrac{f(x)}{g(x)}$	$\sqrt{f(x)}$
domain is	① _____	② _____

EXAMPLE 2. Find the domain of each function.

① $f(x) = \dfrac{3}{x(x-5)}$

② $h(x) = \dfrac{2}{(x-1)(x+1)}$

③ $g(x) = \dfrac{5}{x^2+1}$

④ $H(x) = \sqrt{x+6}$

⑤ $h(x) = \sqrt{3x+2}$

⑥ $f(x) = \dfrac{2}{x^2-4}$

Blank : ① g(x) ≠ 0   ② f(x) ≥ 0

⑦ $K(x) = x^2 + 4$ ⑧ $G(x) = x - 1$

⑨ $f(x) = \sqrt{x^2 + 1}$

4. Evaluating Functions

※ **Evaluating Function** (*e-value-ating* : finding the value)

$$f(x) = x^2 + 1$$

$$f(input) = (input)^2 + 1$$

$$f(2x) = (2x)^2 + 1$$

$$f(♥) = ♥^2 + 1$$

"x" is Just a Place-Holder

☺ $(2x)^2 \neq 2x^2$

EXAMPLE 3. Find each value if

$$f(x) = \frac{5}{x+2}, \quad g(x) = -2x+3, \quad h(x) = x^2+2$$

① $f(3)$ ② $g(-4)$

③ $h(-1)$ ④ $f(0)$

⑤ $g(m+2)$ ⑥ $f(a-2)$

⑦ $f(g(-2))$ ⑧ $g(h(1))$

⑨ $h\left(\dfrac{1}{f(2)}\right)$

⑩ $h\left(\dfrac{1}{g(2)}\right)$

⑪ $\dfrac{g(x+a)-g(x)}{a}$

⑫ $g(a+1)-g(a)$

5. Expand Knowledge*

EXAMPLE 4. * If $f(x)=\dfrac{6}{x}$ $f\left(\dfrac{1}{2}\right)=a$, and $f(-2)=b$, then what is $f(a+b)$?

EXAMPLE 5.   * If $f(x) = \{$Remainder when we divide x by 3$\}$, what is
$$f(1)+f(2)+f(3)+\ldots+f(30) \ ?$$

※ **Finding Range** (What can come OUT from the function?)

When you have	$\sqrt{f(x)} = ?$	$f(x)^2 = ?$	$2^{f(x)} = ?$
range is	① _____	② _____	③ _____

EXAMPLE 6.   * If $f(x) = (-x+3)^2 + 3$, then which of the following is NOT in the range of $f(x)$? (Choose. There can be more than one answer.)

　　　　　　　　I. 5　　　II. 3.5　　　III. 2　　　IV. 0

Blank : ① $y \geq 0$　② $y \geq 0$　③ $y > 0$

EXAMPLE 7. * If $g(x) = 2^x$, then which of the following is NOT in the range of $g(x)$?

(Choose. There can be more than one answer.)

        I. 3   II. 0.5   III. 0   IV. -0.5

EXAMPLE 8. * If $f(x) = 2 + \sqrt{4x-3}$, which of the following is NOT a value of $f(x)$?

(Choose. There can be more than one answer.)

        I. 5   II. 3.5   III. 2   IV. 0

Mia's Algebra 2
1.2 Transformation

1. Six Basic Functions

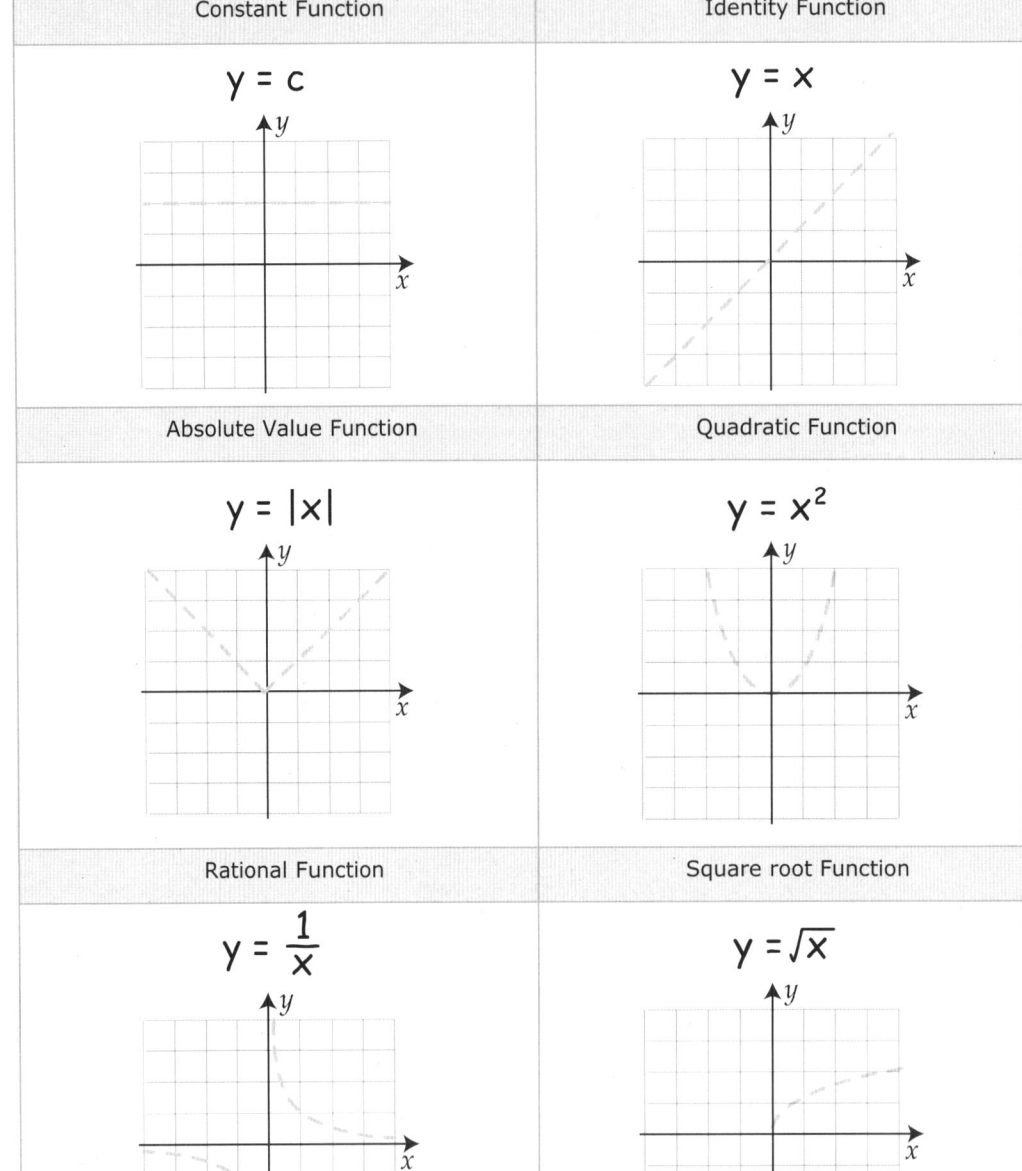

2. Transforming Functions

1) Shifted Up or Down

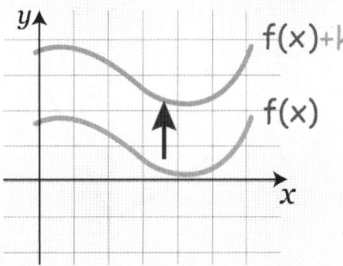

$$y = f(x) + k$$

: Vertically Shifted ① _____

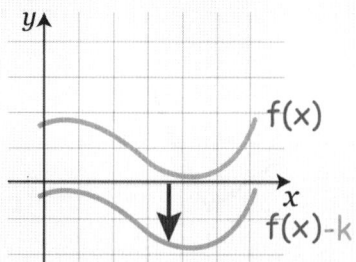

$$y = f(x) - k$$

: Vertically Shifted ② _____

2) Shifted Right or Left

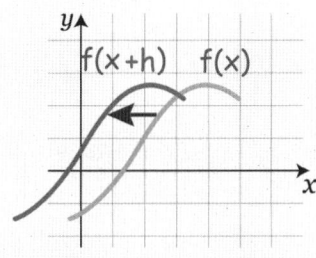

$$y = f(x + h)$$

: Horizontal Shift to the ③ _____

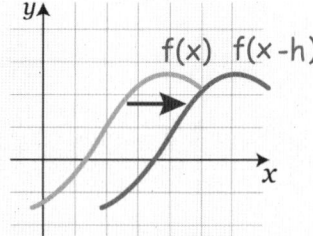

$$y = f(x - h)$$

: Horizontal Shift to the ④ _____

Blank : ① up k units ② down k units ③ left h units ④ right h units

EXAMPLE 1. Graph of $f(x)$ is given. Graph the following function.

① $y = f(x+1)$

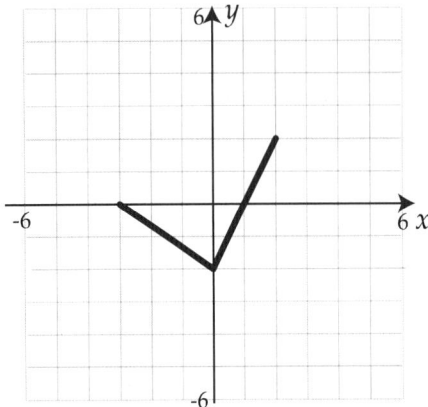

② $y = f(x-3)$

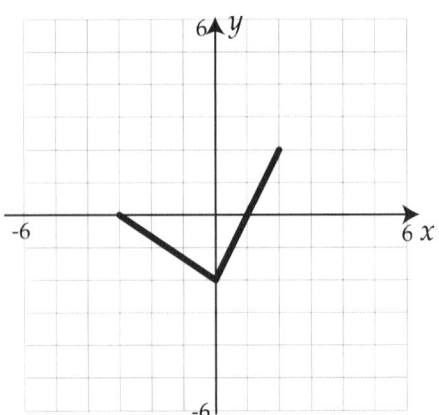

③ $y = f(x) - 3$

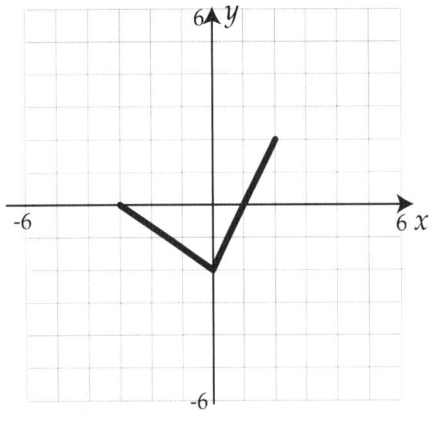

④ $y = f(x) + 2$

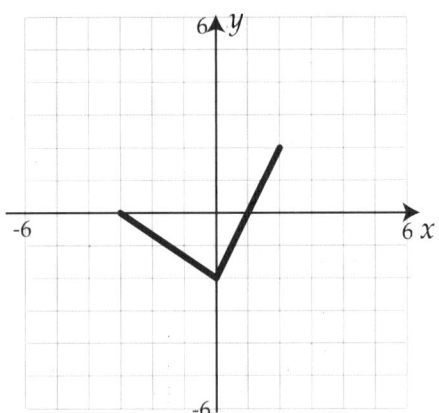

⑤ $y = 1 + f(x-2)$ ⑥ $y = f(x+2) - 1$

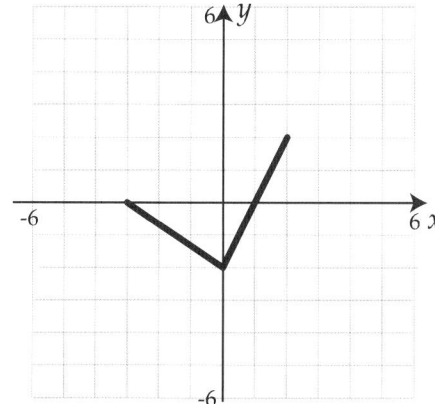 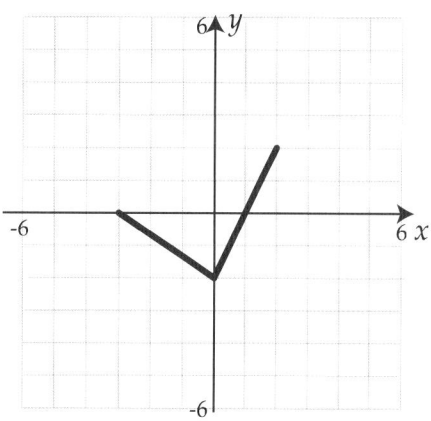

3) Reflection

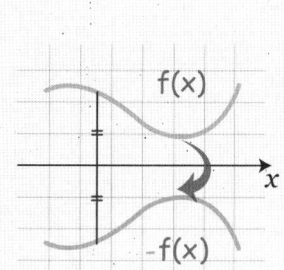

$y = -f(x)$

: reflected over ① ____ -axis

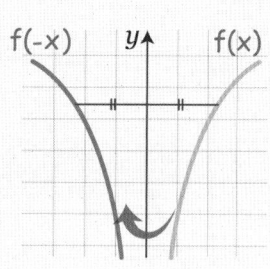

$y = f(-x)$

: reflected over ② ____ -axis

Blank : ① x   ② y

EXAMPLE 2. Graph of $f(x)$ is given. Graph the following function.

① $y = f(-x)$

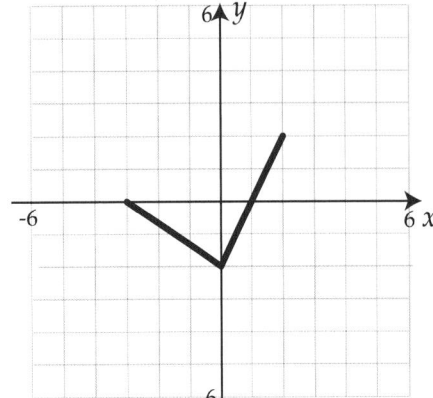

② $y = -f(x) - 1$

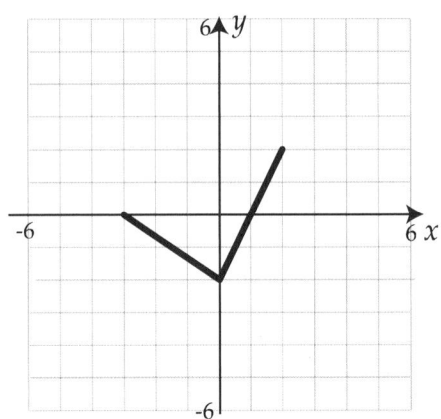

③ $y = -f(x) + 2$

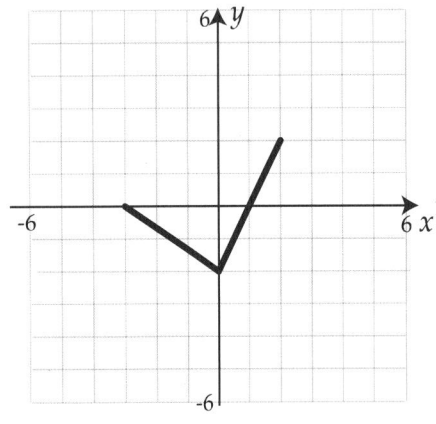

④ $y = -f(-x)$

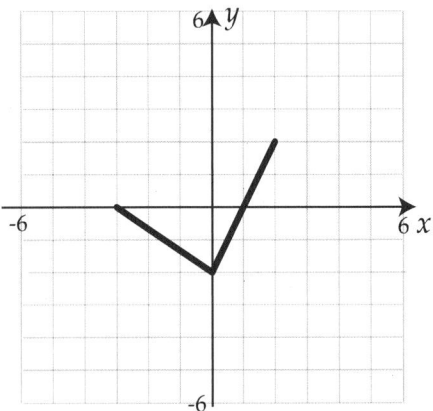

4) Vertical Stretch or Compression

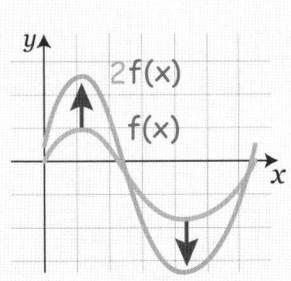

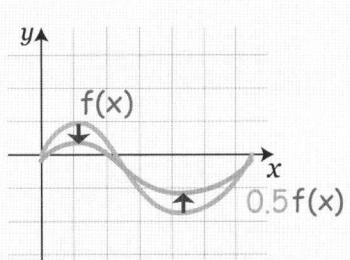

$y = 2f(x)$

: Vertical ①_____

by the factor of 2

(it makes it ②_____)

$y = 0.5f(x)$

: Vertical ③_____

by the factor of 0.5

(it makes it ④_____)

5) Horizontal Stretch or Compression

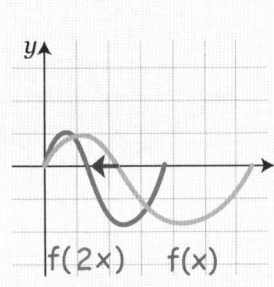

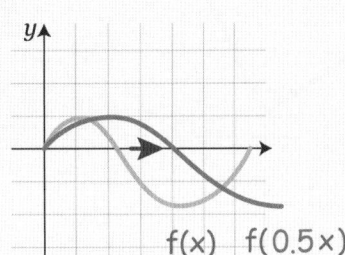

$y = f(2x)$

: Horizontal ⑤_____

by the factor of ⑥_____.

$y = f(0.5x)$

: Horizontal ⑦_____

by the factor of ⑧_____.

Blank : ① stretch ② steeper ③ shrink ④ wider ⑤ shrink ⑥ $\frac{1}{2}$ ⑦ stretch ⑧ 2

EXAMPLE 3. Graph of $f(x)$ is given. Graph the following function.

① $y = \dfrac{f(x)}{2}$

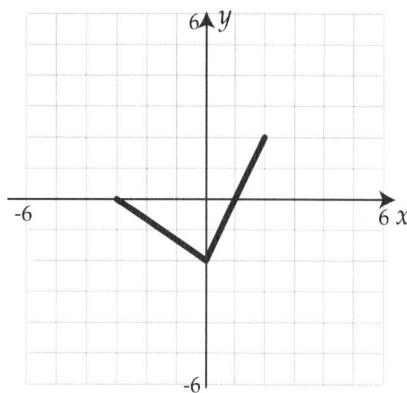

② $y = f(3x)$

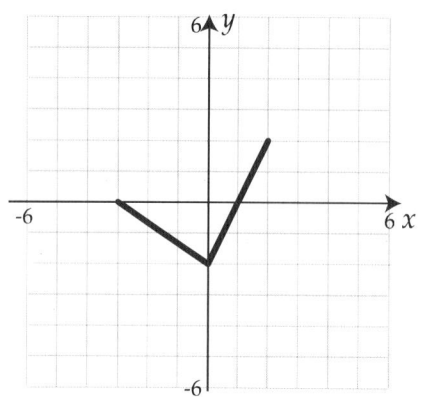

③ $y = f(2x)$

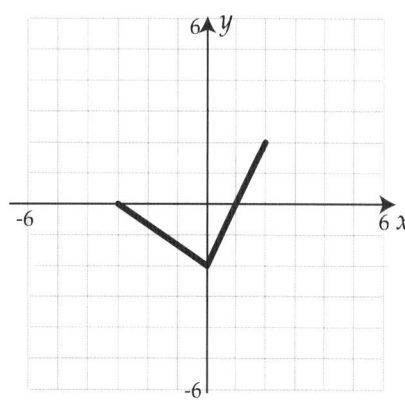

④ $y = 2f(x)$

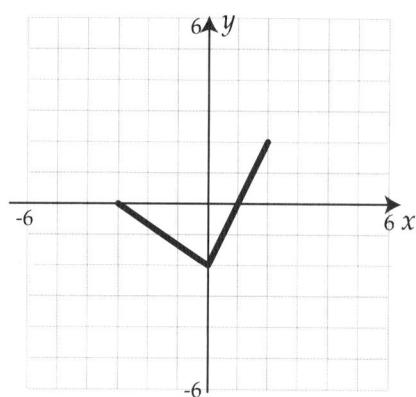

⑤ $y = -2f(x)$

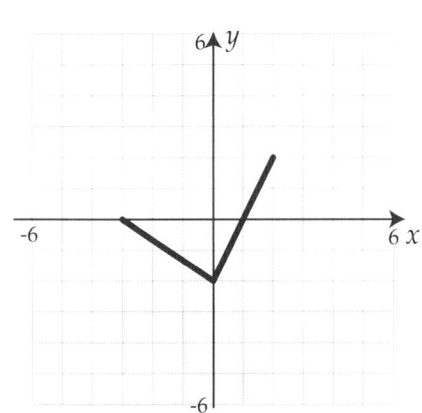

⑥ $y = f\left(\dfrac{x}{2}\right) - 1$

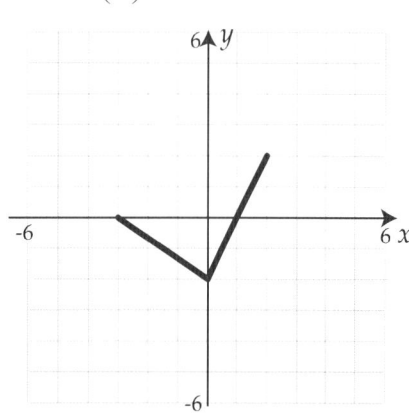

3. Combined Transformation

Y = f(x)	original function (parent function)
y= f(x) + k	Vertically Shifted ①_____ k units
y= f(x) - k	Vertically Shifted ②_____ k units (k>0)
y= f(x + h)	Horizontal Shift to the ③_____ h units
y= f(x - h)	Horizontal Shift to the ④_____ h units (h>0)
y= - f(x)	reflected over ⑤____-axis ('x'caped)
y= f(-x)	reflected over ⑥____-axis
y= af(x), a > 1	vertically ⑦_____ by the factor _____
0<a<1	vertically ⑧_____ by the factor _____
y= f(bx), b > 1	horizontally ⑨_____ by the factor _____
0<b<1	horizontally ⑩_____ by the factor _____

★ Order of Transformation is determined by order of operations.
Reflect or stretch or compress → translation (shifting)

Blank : ① up ② down ③ left ④ right ⑤ x ⑥ y ⑦ stretch, a ⑧ shrink, a ⑨ shrink, $\dfrac{1}{b}$ ⑩ stretch, $\dfrac{1}{b}$

EXAMPLE 4. Graph of $f(x)$ is given. Graph the following function.

① $y = 2f(x-1)-2$ ② $y = -f(x+1)+3$

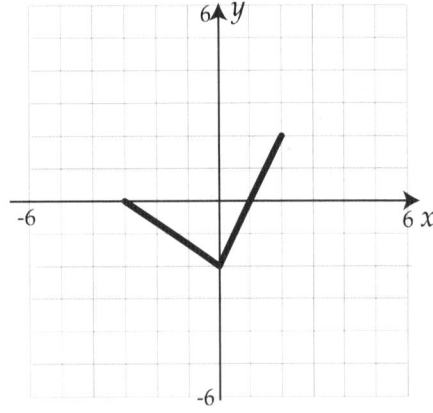
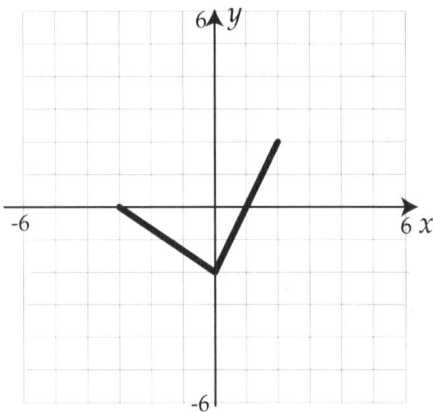

③ $y = 1 - f(2+x)$ ④ $y = 2f(3+x)$

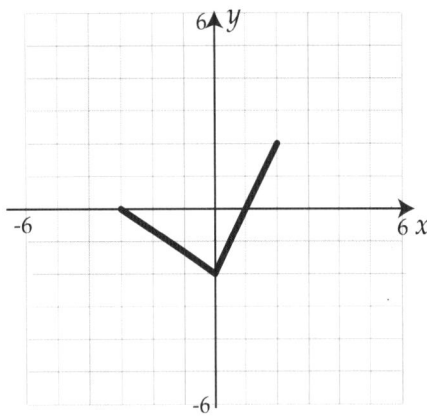
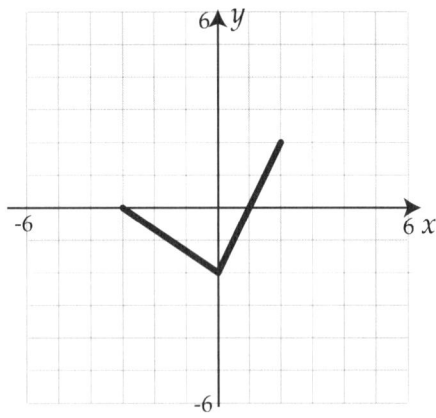

⑤ $y = f(0.5x) + 1$

⑥ $y = 1 - f(2x)$

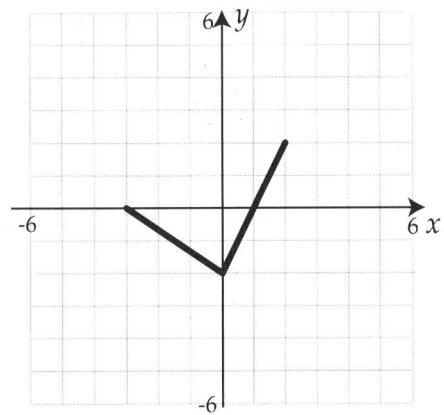

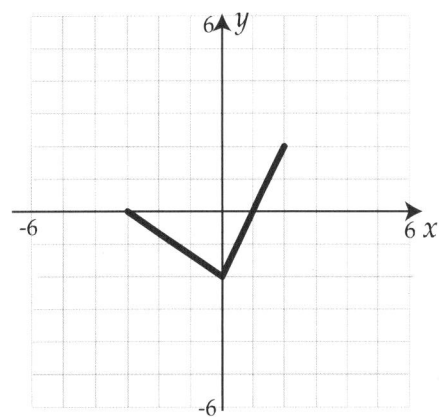

EXAMPLE 5. Graph the function using the six basic functions.

① $y = -|x+2| - 1$

② $y = -\dfrac{|x|}{2} + 3$

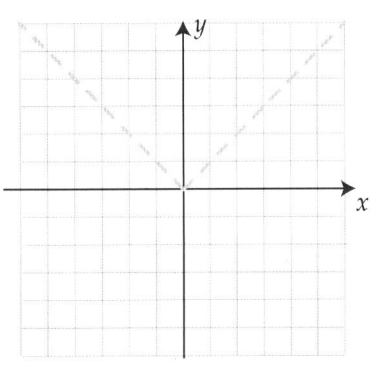

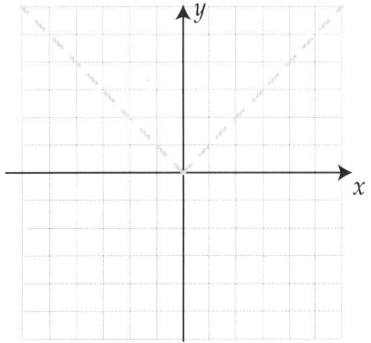

③ $y = -2|x| + 2$

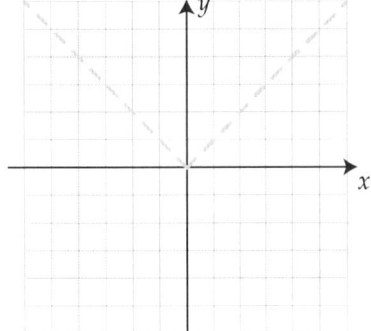

④ $y = -|-x| + 1$

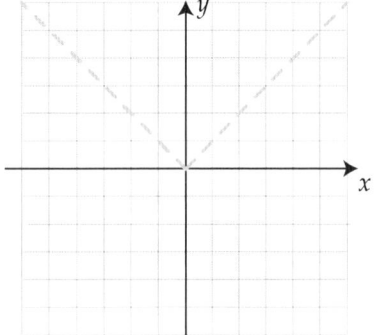

⑤ $y = 0.5(x+1)^2 + 1$

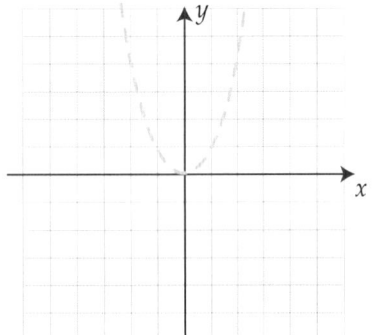

⑥ $y = -(x-3)^2 - 2$

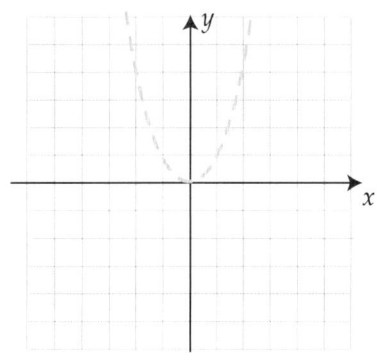

⑦ $y = -\sqrt{x-1} + 2$

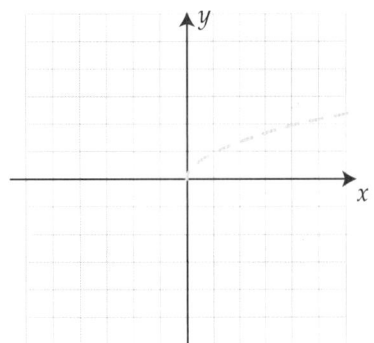

⑧ $y = -2\sqrt{x-2}$

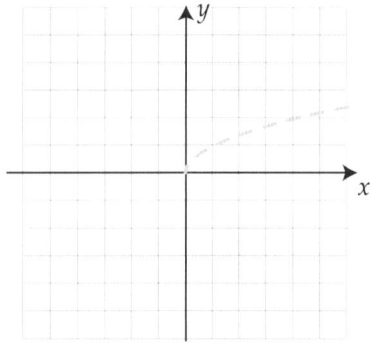

⑨ $y = -\dfrac{1}{x-2} + 1$

⑩ $y = \dfrac{1}{x+1} - 3$

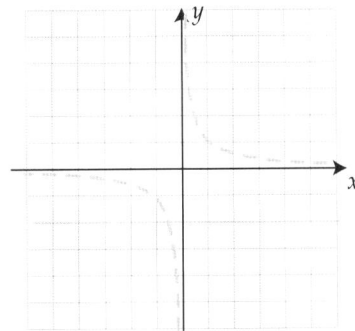

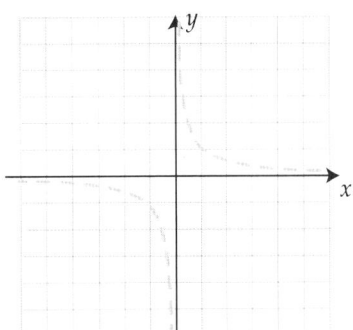

4. Expand Knowledge*

★ Few things to Remember

1) Order of Transformation is determined by order of operations.
   Reflect or stretch or compress → translation (shifting)

2) When you have a f(bx+c) + d? ① _____

   ex) $y = f(-x+1) + 2$ ⇒ $y = f(-(x-1)) + 2$
   : Reflect over y axis → Shift right 1 → Shift up 2

Blank : ① factor out b from bx+c (change to $y = af\left[b\left(x + \dfrac{c}{b}\right)\right] + d$)

EXAMPLE 6. *Graph of $f(x)$ is given. Graph the following function.

① $y = f(-x-1)$

② $y = f(-x+2)$

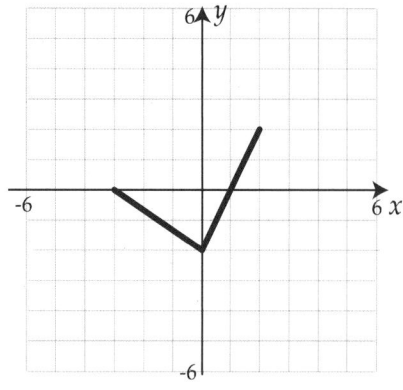

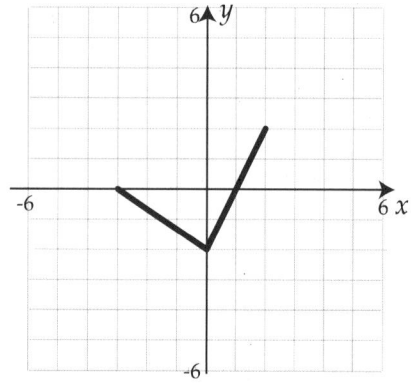

③ $y = -f(-x+1) - 2$

④ $y = 2 - f(-x-3)$

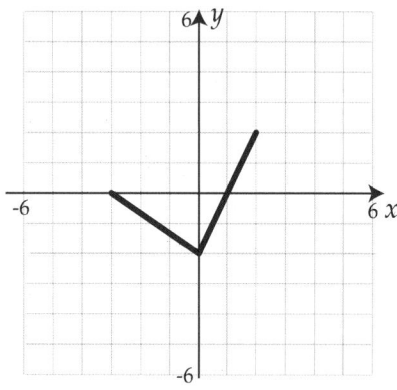

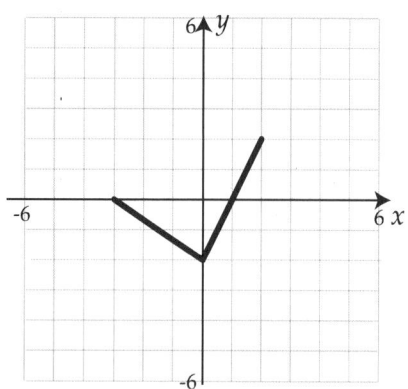

⑤ $y = f(2x-4)$

⑥ $y = f(2x+2)$

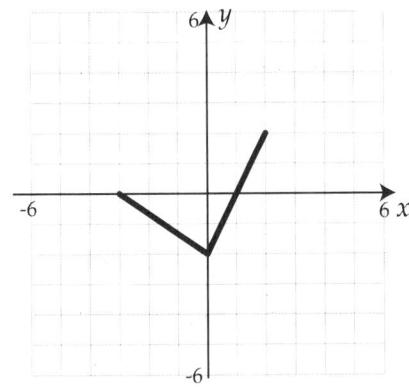

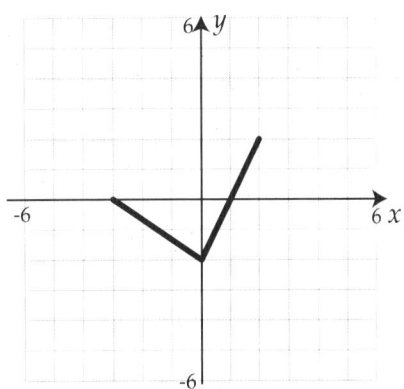

EXAMPLE 7. *Graph the function using the six basic functions.

① $y = |-x-5|$

② $y = |-x+3|+1$

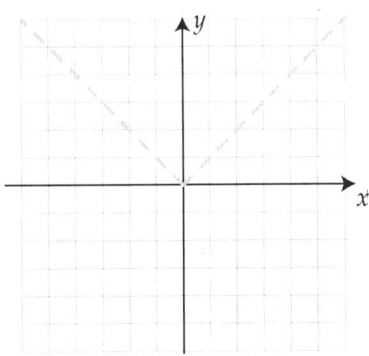

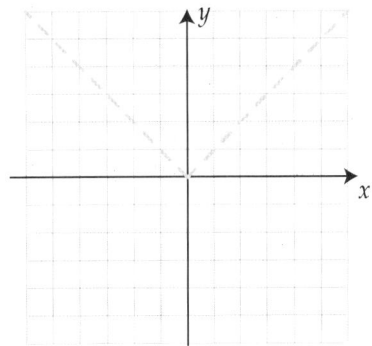

③ $y = \sqrt{1-x}$

④ $y = \sqrt{-x-2}$

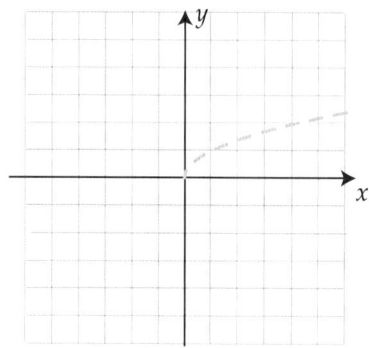

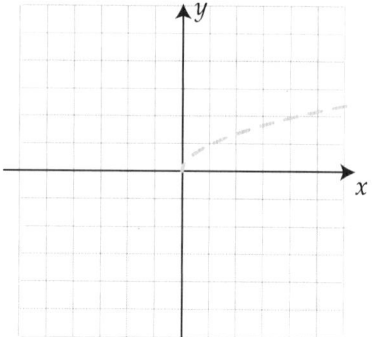

⑤ $y = \dfrac{1}{1-x}$

⑥ $y = \dfrac{1}{-x-2}$

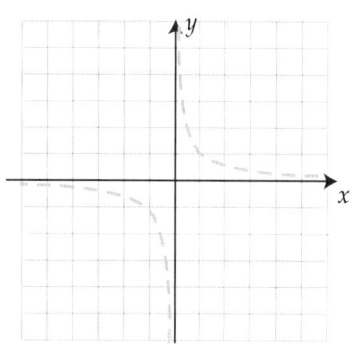

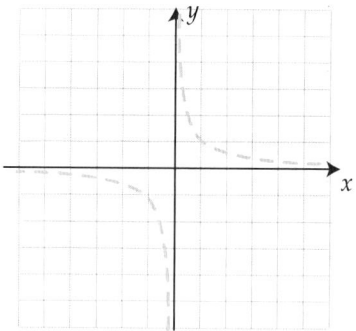

Mia's Algebra 2
1.3 The Slope of a Line

1. Rate of Change

※ **Slope** shows the ①_____ of a line.

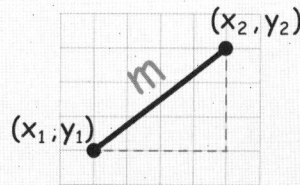

$$\text{slope} = \boxed{②} \text{ of change} = \frac{\text{rise}}{\text{run}} = \frac{\Delta y}{\Delta x} = \boxed{③} = \frac{f(b)-f(a)}{b-a}$$

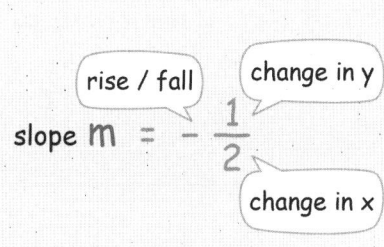

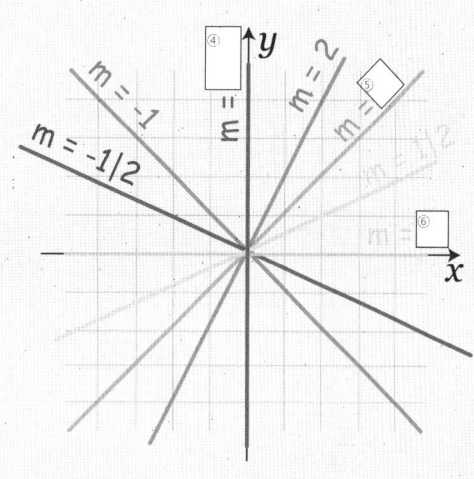

☺ Symbols m: slope
            Δx : increments (= difference) of x

Blank : ① steepness   ② rate   ③ $\frac{y_2 - y_1}{x_2 - x_1}$ ④ undefined   ⑤ 1   ⑥ 0

EXAMPLE 1. Find the slope of the line.

①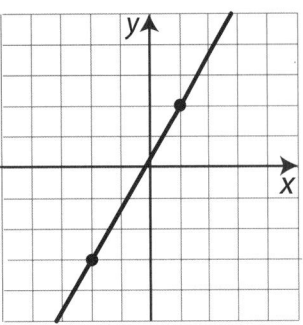

②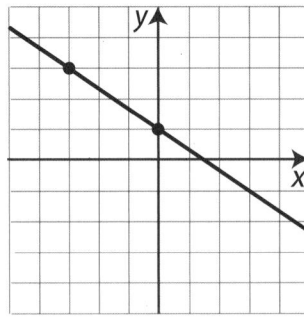

③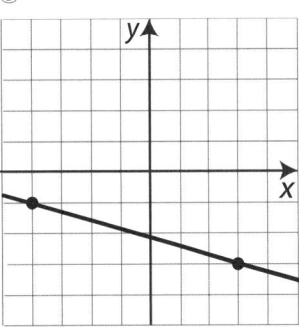

④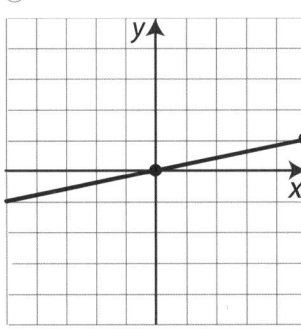

⑤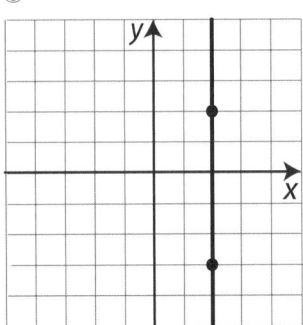

⑥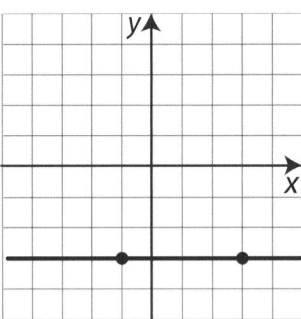

⑦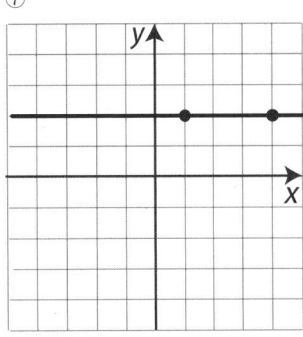

EXAMPLE 2. Find the slope of the line that passes through each pair of points.

☺ Tip: Make sure to subtract in the *same order*
in the numerator and the denominator

① $(1,5), (-1,-3)$

② $(1,9), (0,6)$

③ $(0,2), (3,0)$

④ $(8,-5), (4,-2)$

⑤ $\left(-\dfrac{5}{2}, -4\right), (1,2)$

⑥ $(2,-3), \left(\dfrac{3}{2}, -4\right)$

⑦ $(5,2), (-3,2)$

⑧ $(8,2), (8,-1)$

EXAMPLE 3. Graph the line passing through the given point with the given slope.
① $(0,4), m = 2$ ② $(2,-3), m = 3$

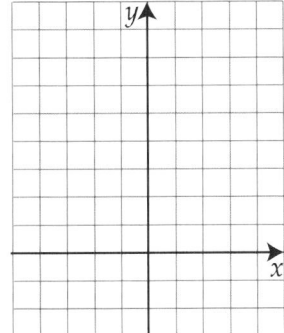
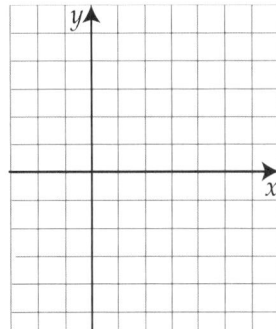

③ $(-2,-1), m = -4$

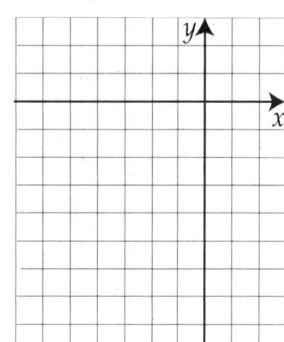

④ $(-3,-5), m = -\dfrac{1}{3}$

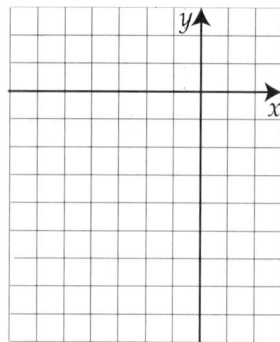

⑤ $(2,-1), m = \dfrac{3}{4}$

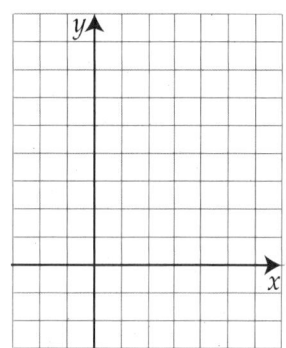

⑥ $(0,-1), m = \dfrac{5}{4}$

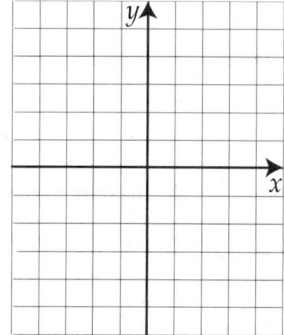

⑦ $(0,2), m = 0$

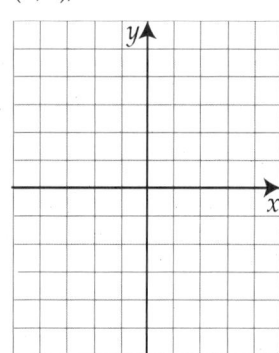

⑧ $(0,-3), m = undefined$

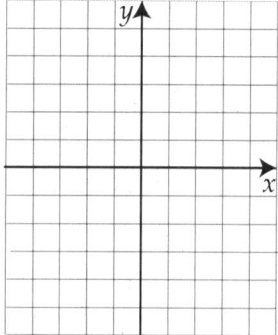

⑨ $(3,1), m = undefined$

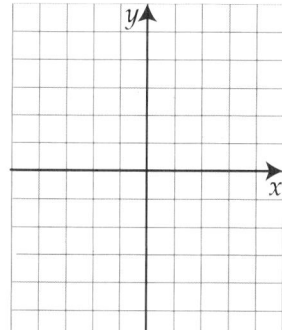

⑩ $(-5,2), m = 0$

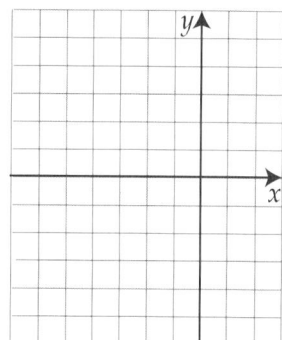

2. Expand Knowledge*

EXAMPLE 4. * In the figure, if the area of the shaded region is 3, what is the slope of the line l?

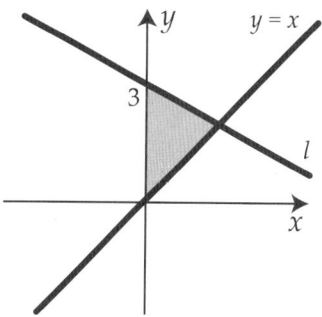

EXAMPLE 5. * Three points $(2a, 3), (a+3, -2)$, and $(a, 8)$ are collinear. Find a.

☺ Tip: Collinear means the points are in the same line (⇒ same ①_____)

Blank : ① slope

Mia's Algebra 2

1.4 Graphs of Linear Functions

1. Identifying Linear Function

※ How to Identify Linear Function

If a function is in the form ①_____ the function is linear function.

(A and B not both 0)

or

When a quantity grows by the same amount during each unit of time.

x	-1	0	1	2
y	2	5	8	11

+3 ② ③

EXAMPLE 1. State whether each equation or function is linear.

① $y = \dfrac{x}{2} - 1$ 　　　　　② $y = -2x + 6$

③ $2x + \dfrac{1}{y} = 10$ 　　　　④ $-\dfrac{3}{x} + y = 10$

⑤ $y = 4x^2 - 5$ 　　　　　⑥ $\dfrac{1}{3}x = y + 8$

⑦ $y = 8$ 　　　　　　　　⑧ $y = \sqrt{x} + 2$

Blank : ① Ax + By = C 　② +3 　③ +3

42 Mia's Algebra 2

EXAMPLE 2. State whether each equation or function is linear. If it is linear, find the slope.

①

x	y
2	0.5
5	3
8	18
11	108

②

x	y
-2	0.1
-1	0.01
0	0.001
1	0.0001

③

x	y
-2	0
0	4
2	8
4	12

④

x	y
0	3
3	8
6	13
9	18

2. Standard form of Linear Function

The **standard form** of a linear equation is

$$Ax + By = C$$

where A, B are not both 0.

☺ Vocabulary

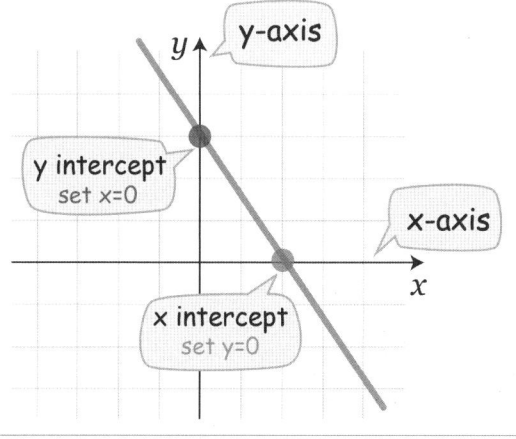

x intercept : Where a line crosses the x-axis of a graph

To find the x intercept, you set ① _____

then solve for x

y intercept : Where a line crosses the y-axis of a graph

To find the y intercept, you set ② _____

then solve for y

Blank : ① y = 0   ② x = 0

EXAMPLE 3. Find the x-intercept and the y-intercept of the graph of each equation. Then graph the equation.

① $5y - 2x = 10$

② $2x + 7y = 14$

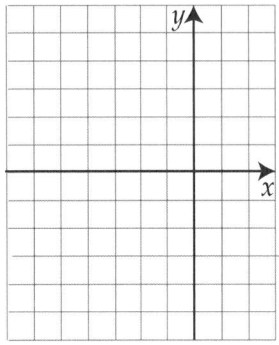

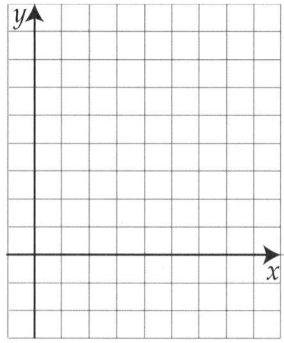

③ $2y = 3x - 6$

④ $y = 2x + 4$

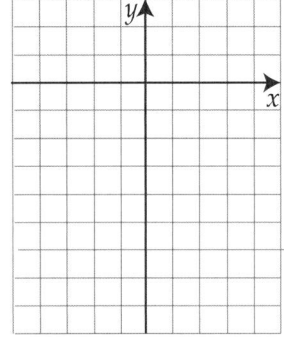

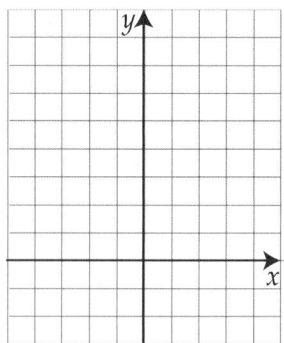

⑤ $\dfrac{3}{4}y = \dfrac{2}{3}x + 6$

⑥ $\dfrac{2}{5}x + \dfrac{1}{3}y = 2$

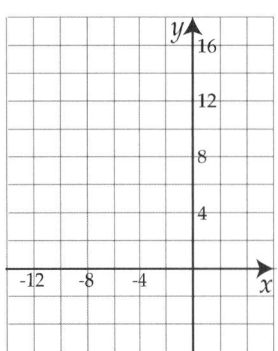

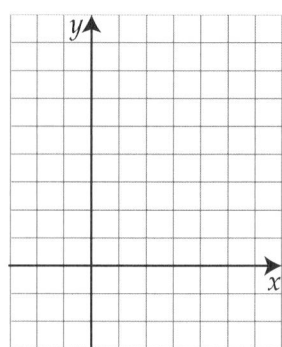

⑦ $y = -2x$

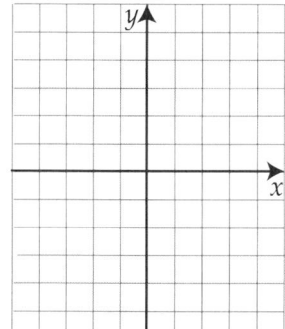

⑧ $x + y = 0$

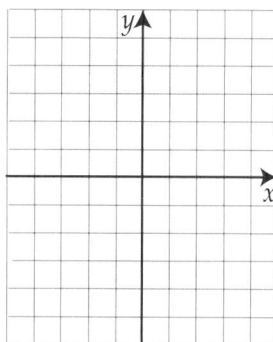

The slope of the line of $Ax + By = C$ is ①_____.

EXAMPLE 4. Find the slope of each line.

① $2x - 7y = 4$

② $x - y - 3 = 0$

③ $3y + 2 = 9x$

④ $-x = y - 6$

⑤ $\dfrac{x}{3} - \dfrac{y}{2} = 1$

⑥ $\dfrac{x}{4} + \dfrac{y}{6} = 1$

Blank : ① $-\dfrac{A}{B}$

3. Special lines

※ Special Lines

hOrizontal Line	(hori) $y = c$	slope is ① ____	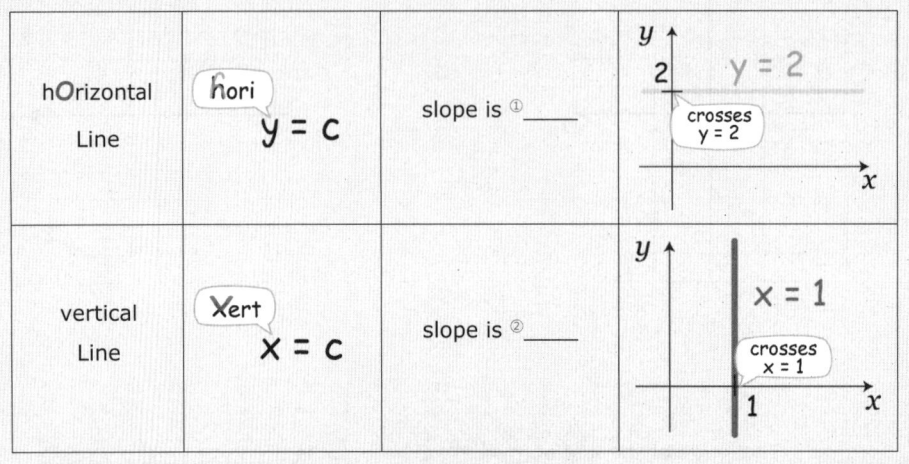
vertical Line	(Xert) $x = c$	slope is ② ____	

EXAMPLE 5. Graph the following.

① $x = 2$

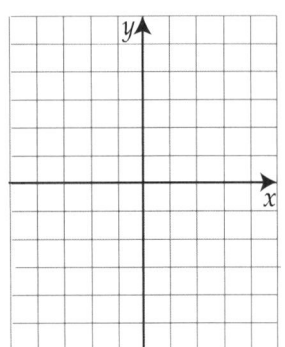

② $x + 1 = 0$

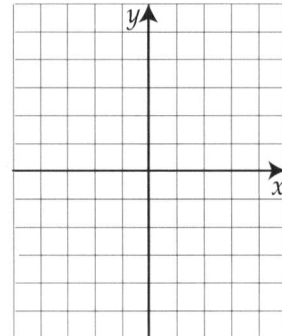

Blank : ① 0   ② undefined

③ $y=-2$

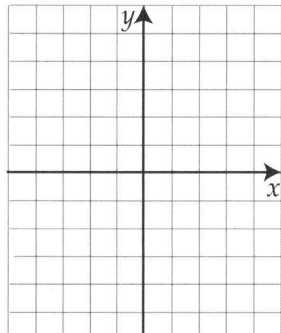

④ $y-4=0$

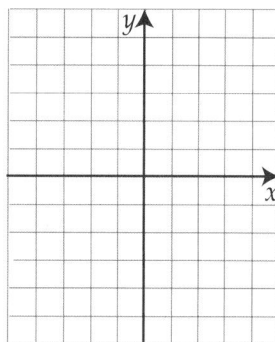

EXAMPLE 6. Find the equation of the line described.

① Horizontal line that contains (4.5, 2.3)

② Vertical line that contains (5, 2)

③ passes (5, 1), no slope

④ (-4, -2), zero slope

⑤ passes (3, -2), zero slope

⑥ (-2, 0), undefined slope

4. Expand Knowledge*

EXAMPLE 7. * Find the area of the region in the first quadrant that is enclosed by the graphs $x+2y=6$ and $y=-x+1$ of as shown.

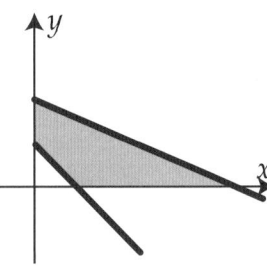

EXAMPLE 8. * What is an equation of the points that are equidistant from the two points $(-3,-4)$ and $(-3,0)$.

> ☺ Tip: Points that equidistant from two points A, B forms a
> ① _____ of line AB.

Blank : ① perpendicular bisector

Mia's Algebra 2

1.5 Finding an Equation of the Line

1. Slope-Intercept Form

※ **Slope-Intercept Form**

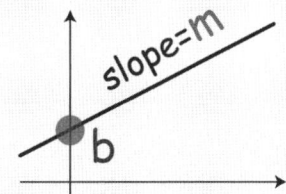

slope   y intercept

$y = mx + b$

EXAMPLE 1. State the slope and y-intercept of the graph of each equation.

① $y = 3x - 5$

② $y = -\dfrac{3}{5}x + 2$

③ $y = -\dfrac{2}{3}x$

④ $3y + 5 = 0$

⑤ $5y = 4x - 7$

⑥ $3x - 2y + 6 = 0$

⑦ $2x - y = -1$

⑧ $2y = 6 - 5x$

EXAMPLE 2. Write an equation in slope-intercept form for each graph.

①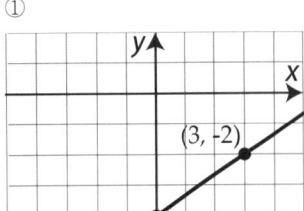

②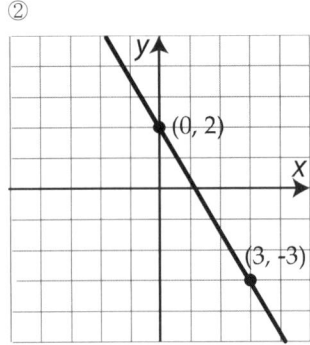

③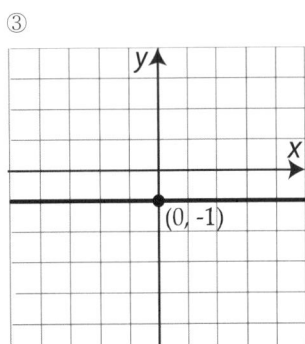

④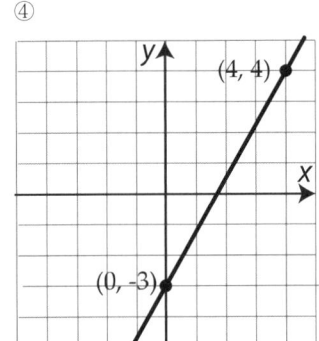

⑤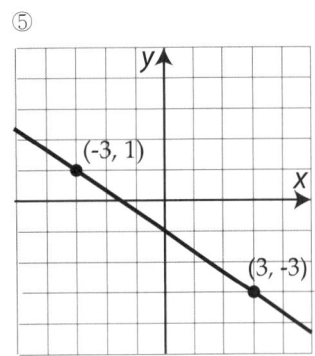

⑥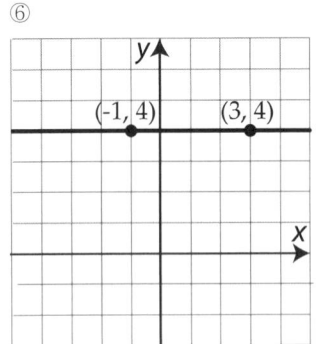

2. Point-slope Form

※ **Point-slope Form**

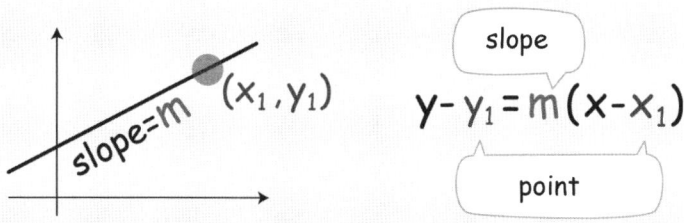

☺ Remember

What do you need to find the equation of the line?

Always we need ①_____ and ②_____

EXAMPLE 3. Write an equation in slope-intercept form ($y = mx+b$) that passing through the given point with the given slope.

① $(1,4), m = 2$ ② $(2,-3), m = -1$

③ $(-2,-1), m = -2$ ④ $(-3,-5), m = 2$

Blank : ① slope   ② point

⑤ $(2,-1), m=-\dfrac{3}{4}$ ⑥ $(0,-1), m=\dfrac{5}{4}$

EXAMPLE 4. Write an equation in slope-intercept form ($y = mx+b$) for the line that satisfies each set of conditions.

① passes through (2,-3), (1, 4)   ② passes through (-4, 6), (2, 3)

③ passes through (-1, -2) and (3, -5)   ④ passes through (-2, -4) and (1, 0)

⑤ x intercept 3, y intercept -4   ⑥ x intercept $\dfrac{5}{2}$, y intercept 3

3. Expand Knowledge*

EXAMPLE 5.   * A square is inscribed inside the region bounded by $y = -\frac{3}{2}x + 3$, x axis, and the y axis as shown. What is the area of the square?

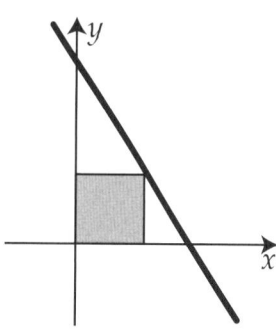

EXAMPLE 6.   * A square is inscribed inside the region bounded by $y = x$, $y = -2x + 12$ and the x axis as shown. What is the area of the square?

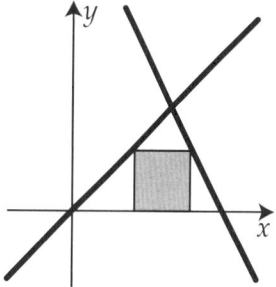

EXAMPLE 7.   * A line passes through (-1, 3) and (5, 9). After the line is shifted up 3 units, it contains the point $(k, 1)$. What is the value of k?

EXAMPLE 8. * The line $y=(2k+3)x-(k+1)$ does not pass through 4th quadrant. What is the range of the value of k?

EXAMPLE 9. * Which of the linear function intersects the line $y=2x-4$ on the third quadrant?

I. $y=-0.5x+2$ II. $y=-2x+1$ III. $y=4x-2$ IV. $y=x-2$ V. $y=x-5$

Mia's Algebra 2

1.6 Two linear Graphs

1. Two Linear Graphs

   ※ **Parallel Line and Perpendicular Line**

   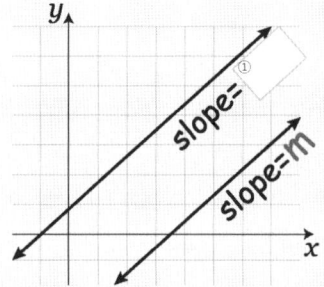 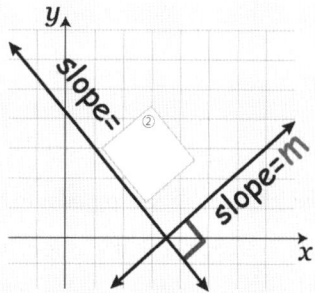

   Parallel Line has the ③_____ slope!

   Perpendicular Line has ④_____ & _____ slope!

   So if two lines are perpendicular, the product of their slope is ⑤_____.

   EXAMPLE 1. Write an equation in slope-intercept form ($y = mx + b$) for the line that satisfies each set of conditions.

   ① Passes through (7, -5), perpendicular to the $y = \dfrac{1}{2}x + 3$

   ② Passes through (8, -5), perpendicular to the $y = -4x + 7$

Blank : ① m ② $-\dfrac{1}{m}$ ③ same ④ opposite & reciprocal ⑤ -1

Part 1 Functions 55

③ Passes through (1, 5), perpendicular to the line that passes through (3, 4) and (-2, 2)

④ Passes through (1, -1), perpendicular to the line that passes through (-2, 1) and (4, -8)

⑤ Passes through (2, 5), parallel to the line with x intercept -2 and y intercept 5.

⑥ Passes through (-2, 3), parallel to the line $2x - y = 4$

EXAMPLE 2. Sketch the graph and find the equation of the line described.

① Passes through (7, -5), parallel to the y-axis

② Passes through (-5, 8), perpendicular to the x-axis

③ Passes through (-1, 3),

perpendicular to the y-axis

④ Passes through (2, -4),

parallel to the y-axis

⑤ Passes through (2, -3),

parallel to the $x = 4$

⑥ Passes through (-2, 3),

perpendicular to the $x = 8$

⑦ Passes through (0, 4),

perpendicular to the $x = -1$

⑧ Passes through (2, -1),

parallel to the $y = 0$

2. Expand Knowledge*

EXAMPLE 3.   * A line $y = -ax + 3$ is parallel to $y = -3x + 1$ and intersects the line $y = bx + 2$ on the x axis. What is the value of a and b?

EXAMPLE 4.   * What is the equation of the points that are equidistant from $(1, 5)$ and $(-3, 7)$?

> ☺ Tip: Points that equidistant from two points A, B forms a ①_____ of line AB.
>
> ☺ Tip: midpoint of (x_1, x_2) and (y_1, y_2) is $\left(\dfrac{x_1 + x_2}{2}, \dfrac{y_1 + y_2}{2} \right)$

Blank : ① perpendicular bisector

EXAMPLE 5. * Triangle ABC with sides AB, BC, and BA is given above. What is the product of the slopes of these three lines?

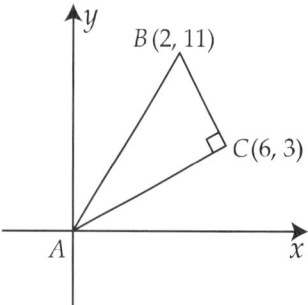

EXAMPLE 6. * If the vertices of a triangle are $A(0, 3)$, $B(5, 7)$, and $C(8, -3)$, then what is the equation of the line that contains the altitude from C to side AB?

Mia's Algebra 2
1.7 Piecewise Function

1. Piecewise-defined Functions

※ **Piecewise-defined Functions**
(= Piecewise function)
: a function made up in pieces.

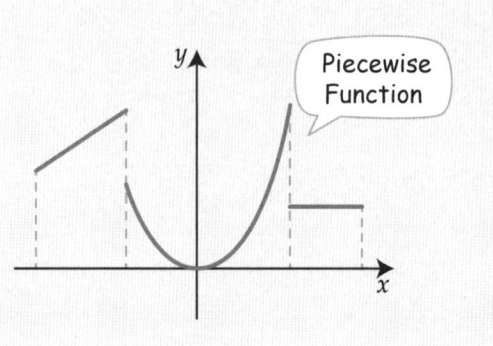

☺ Vocabulary:

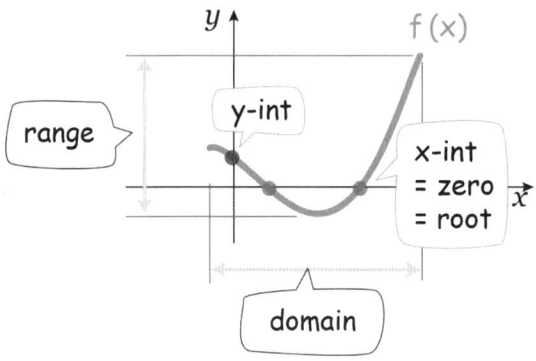

Domain : the set of possible x values
range : the set of possible y values

EXAMPLE 1. Graph the functions. Identify the domain and range.

① $f(x) = \begin{cases} x, & x < 0 \\ 3, & x \geq 0 \end{cases}$

② $h(x) = \begin{cases} -4, & x < 0 \\ x-2, & x \geq 0 \end{cases}$

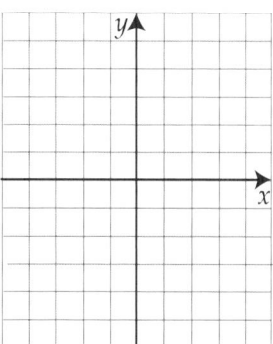

③ $h(x) = \begin{cases} x+2, & x < 1 \\ -x+2, & x \geq 1 \end{cases}$

④ $f(x) = \begin{cases} -x, & x < -2 \\ 2x+2, & x \geq -2 \end{cases}$

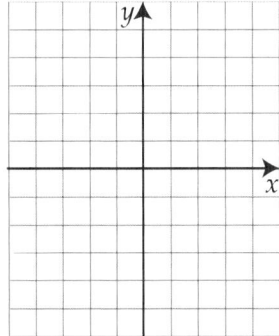

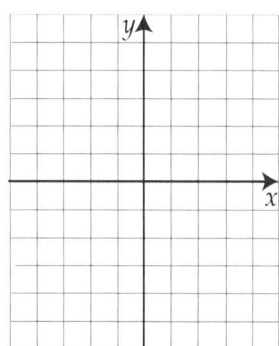

⑤ $h(x) = \begin{cases} \dfrac{x}{2} & , x \leq 0 \\ 2x - 3 & , 0 < x < 2 \\ 1 & , x \geq 2 \end{cases}$

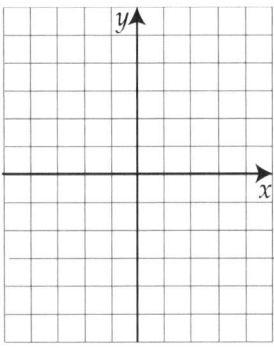

EXAMPLE 2. Give a rule for the piecewise-defined function.

①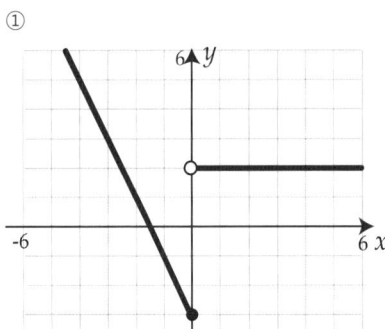

②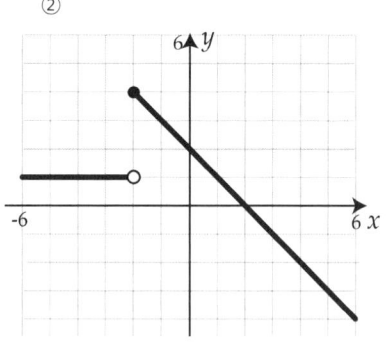

③ 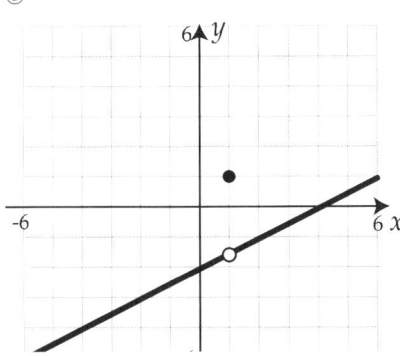   ④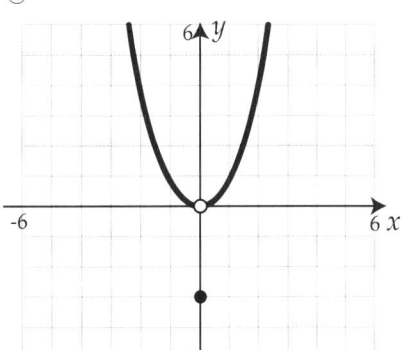

EXAMPLE 3. Evaluate the function.

① Find $f(0)$, $f(1)$, and $f(3)$ if $f(x) = \begin{cases} 2, & \text{if } x \leq 1 \\ x, & \text{if } x > 1 \end{cases}$

② Find $g(9)$, $g(-2)$, and $g(0)$ if $g(x) = \begin{cases} \dfrac{1}{x}, & \text{if } x < 0 \\ \sqrt{x}, & \text{if } x \geq 0 \end{cases}$

③ Find $f(-4)$, $f(1)$, and $f(2)$ if $f(x) = \begin{cases} -2x+1, & \text{if } x < 1 \\ 2, & \text{if } x = 1 \\ x^2, & \text{if } x > 1 \end{cases}$

Mia's Algebra 2

1.8 Absolute value function

1. y = |x| versus y = [x]

※ **Absolute Value Function** $y=|x|$

Absolute Value means **how far** a number is from ①_____.

ex) -2 is ②____ units from 0, so we write ③_____

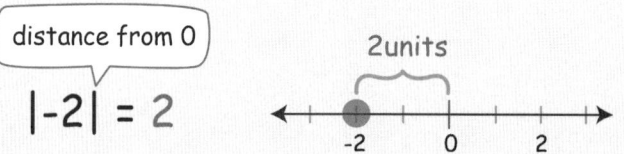

※ **Greatest Integer Function** $y=[x]$ (=step function)

: the greatest integer that is less than or equal to x.

ex) [2.5] = ④____

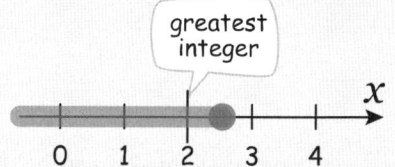

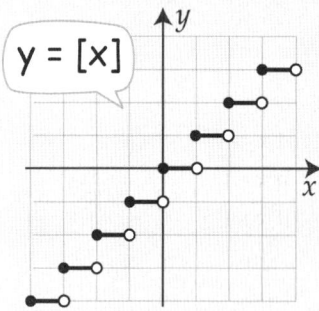

x	[x]
1	⑤
1.2	⑥
1.5	⑦
1.9	⑧
2	⑨
2.2	⑩

Blank : ① origin ② 2 ③ |-2| = 2 ④ 2 ⑤ 1 ⑥ 1 ⑦ 1 ⑧ 1 ⑨ 2 ⑩ 2

EXAMPLE 1. Find the value.

① a) $|5.1|$ b) $[5.1]$

② a) $|-3.2|$ b) $[-3.2]$

③ a) $|-0.5|$ b) $[-0.5]$

④ a) $|0.5|$ b) $[0.5]$

⑤ a) $|7|$ b) $[7]$

⑥ a) $|5|$ b) $[5]$

⑦ a) $|-3|$ b) $[-3]$

⑧ a) $|-2|$ b) $[-2]$

2. Definition of Absolute Value

※ **Absolute Value definition**

$$|x| = \left\{ \begin{array}{l} \boxed{①} \ , \ x \geq 0 \\ \boxed{②} \ , \ x < 0 \end{array} \right\} = \sqrt{x^2}$$

"flip back to positive"

It's because $|2| = 2$ (x itself when x ≥ 0),
$|-2| = 2 = -(-2)$ (opposite of x when x < 0)

Blank : ① x   ② -x

EXAMPLE 2. Simplify using the Absolute value definition.

☺ Tip: When you simplify the absolute value $|a-b|$, you check the sign of $a-b$.

If $a > b \Rightarrow a - b > 0$, then $|a-b| = a - b$

If $b > a \Rightarrow a - b < 0$, then $|a-b| =$ ① _____

① $|x|$, $x \geq 0$

② $|y|$, $y < 0$

③ $|x-1|$, $x \geq 1$

④ $|u+2|$, $u < -2$

⑤ $|2-c|$, $c \geq 2$

⑥ $|1-2x|$, $x > \dfrac{1}{2}$

Blank : ① $-(a-b) = b - a$

⑦ $|a-b|+|b-a|, \quad a \geq b$

⑧ $|x-y|-|y-x|, \quad x \leq y$

⑨ $|a-1|+|a|+|1-a|, \quad 0 < a < 1$

⑩ $|x-2|-|x|+|2-x|, \quad 0 < x < 2$

⑪ $|x-2|+|x-4|, \quad 2 < x < 4$

⑫ $|x|+|x-5|, \quad 0 < x < 5$

⑬ $|x-1|-|x+1|$, $-1<x<1$ 　　　　⑭ $|x+2|-|x+7|$, $-7<x<-2$

EXAMPLE 3. Write the Absolute Value Function into a piecewise function and graph it.

① $g(x)=2|x|$ 　　　　② $f(x)=|x|+2$

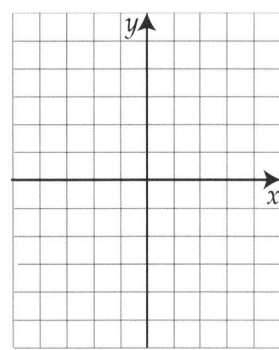
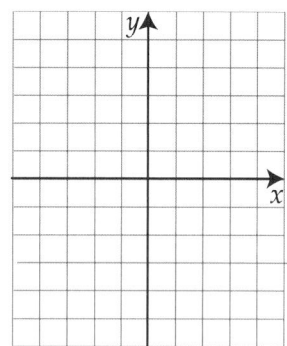

③ $g(x) = |x+3|$

④ $f(x) = |x-2|$

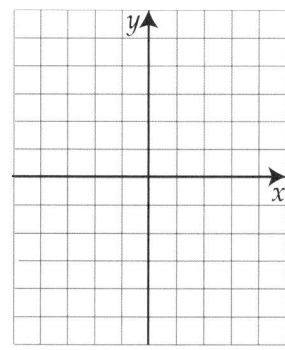

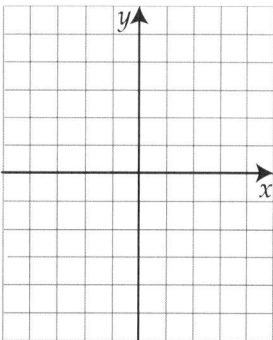

⑤ $h(x) = |2x-1|$

⑥ $g(x) = -2|x|$

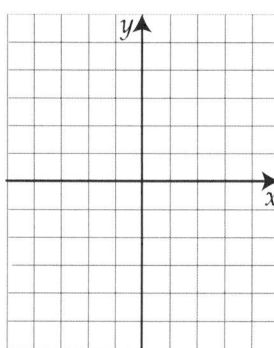

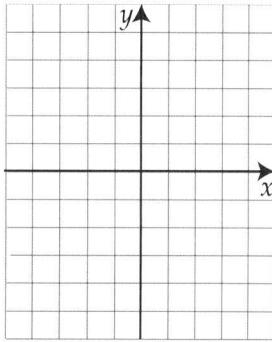

3. Expand Knowledge*

EXAMPLE 4. *Graph $|y|=|x|$.

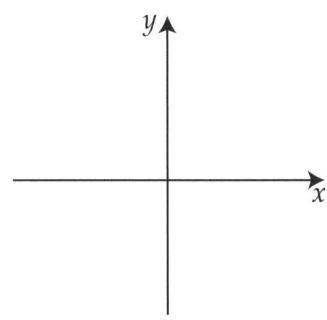

EXAMPLE 5. *Graph $|x|+|y|=4$.

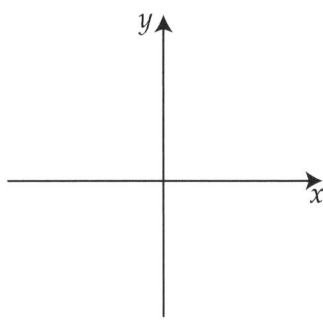

Mia's Algebra 2

1.9 Absolute Value equation & Inequality

1. Absolute Value Equations and Inequalities

※ **Absolute equation and inequalities**

$|x|=2$	$|x|<2$	$|x|>2$
Find x where the distance from origin is 2	Find x where the distance from origin is less than 2	Find x where the distance from origin is more than 2

$x = -2$ or $x = 2$

① _____   ② _____

☺ Shortcut:

If the question is 'less than...', then ③ _____ of ± (NUMBER)

If the question is 'greater than...', then ④ _____ of ± (NUMBER)

EXAMPLE 1. Solve the equations.

① $|n-2|=10$ ② $|x-13|=2$

③ $7=|1-c|$ ④ $|2a-1|=\dfrac{1}{2}$

Blank : ① -2<x<2   ② x<-2 or x>2   ③ inside   ④ outside

⑤ $4|6-y|-1=11$

⑥ $\dfrac{|4d-5|+3}{2}=2$

⑦ $2\left|\dfrac{2x-1}{3}\right|-3=5$

⑧ $4\left|\dfrac{2y-5}{2}\right|+5=9$

⑨ $|p-7|=-11$

⑩ $\left|\dfrac{1}{3}x-3\right|=-2$

⑪ $-3|4x-9|+3=27$

⑫ $-5|2d-3|=1$

⑬ $2|4-x| = -4x$ ⑭ $|8+p| = 2p-4$

⑮ $|4x-1| = x+3$ ⑯ $|5r-1| = 3r+2$

☺ Remember: $|something|$ must be always ①_____

EXAMPLE 2. Solve the inequalities.

① $|y+5| \leq 2$ ② $|x-8| \geq 8$

Blank : ① positive or 0 (≥0)

③ $|h+1|+1 \geq 5$

④ $2|2z-1|-2 \leq 6$

⑤ $\dfrac{7-|x-5|}{2} \geq 2$

⑥ $2\left|\dfrac{3x-5}{3}\right|+4 > 6$

⑦ $11-3|2x+1| < 2$

⑧ $\dfrac{4-|3x+1|}{3} \geq 1$

⑨ $|4b-6| \leq -3$

⑩ $|3x+2| \leq 0$

⑪ $\left|\dfrac{x}{2} - 5\right| \geq 0$

⑫ $|p + 2| \leq -3$

⑬ $|3f - 11| > -7$

⑭ $|a + 9| \geq -1$

⑮ $|10 - 2k| \leq 0$

⑯ $\left|\dfrac{c}{2} - 5\right| > -3$

2. Expand Knowledge*

EXAMPLE 3. * What is the domain of the function $f(x) = \dfrac{x+1}{|x+1|-1}$?

EXAMPLE 4. * Solve the equation $\big||x|-1|-2\big| = 3$.

EXAMPLE 5. * Solve the equation $|2x-|x-5|| = x$.

EXAMPLE 6. * How many integers are in the solution set of the inequality $\left|2-|1+3x|\right|<5$.

EXAMPLE 7. * Two points $(1,k)$ and $(4,|k|)$ has a slope of 2. Find k.

Part 2
Systems and Matrices

2.1 Systems of Linear Equations

2.2 Word Problems about System

2.3 Systems of Inequalities

2.4 Linear Programming

2.5 Algebra of Matrices

2.6 Inverse and Matrix Equation

Mia's Algebra 2

2.1 Systems of Linear Equations

1. Systems of equations

    ※ **System of Linear Equations**

    A system of Equations is when we have *two or more* equations working together. You can solve it by;
    $$\begin{cases} y = x+2 \\ y = -2x+5 \end{cases}$$

    ① substitution
    $$\begin{cases} x - y = -6 \\ y = -4x + 1 \end{cases}$$

    ② elimination
    $$\begin{cases} 4x - 2y = 7 \\ x + 2y = 3 \end{cases}$$

    ③ by Graphing
    The solutions to a system of equations are the intersection points.

    ※ **Special Cases**

When the equation ends up:	$\# \cdot x = \#$ (number)	$0 \cdot x = 0$	$0 \cdot x = \#$
Solution:	②	③	④

Blank : ① +   ② one solution   ③ infinite solution (= all real numbers $\mathbb{R}$)   ④ no solution (= ∅)

EXAMPLE 1. Solve the system of equation by substitution.

① $\begin{aligned} m+n &= 20 \\ m &= n-4 \end{aligned}$
② $\begin{aligned} x+3y &= -3 \\ 4x &= 6-3y \end{aligned}$

③ $\begin{aligned} x-y &= 1 \\ 2x+3y &= 12 \end{aligned}$
④ $\begin{aligned} 2w+z &= 4 \\ 3w+2z &= 1 \end{aligned}$

⑤ $\begin{aligned} a+3b &= 8 \\ \tfrac{1}{3}a+b &= 9 \end{aligned}$
⑥ $\begin{aligned} r-2h &= \tfrac{1}{2} \\ 2h &= 5+r \end{aligned}$

EXAMPLE 2. Solve the system of equation by elimination.

① $\begin{aligned} 2x-y &= 5 \\ 3x+y &= 5 \end{aligned}$
② $\begin{aligned} 3p+q &= 2 \\ 2p-q &= 3 \end{aligned}$

③ $\begin{aligned} y &= 2x - 1 \\ x + 2y &= 3 \end{aligned}$

④ $\begin{aligned} 2m + 3n &= 9 \\ m - n &= 2 \end{aligned}$

⑤ $\begin{aligned} 6a + 3b &= 6 \\ 8a + 5b &= 12 \end{aligned}$

⑥ $\begin{aligned} 2x - 3y &= 9 \\ 3x - 2y &= 1 \end{aligned}$

⑦ $\begin{aligned} \frac{1}{3}a - \frac{1}{2}b &= \frac{1}{6} \\ \frac{3}{5}a - \frac{3}{10}b &= \frac{13}{10} \end{aligned}$

⑧ $\begin{aligned} \frac{2}{3}x - \frac{y}{3} &= 1 \\ x + \frac{1}{5}y &= \frac{11}{5} \end{aligned}$

⑨ $\begin{aligned} 3x - 4y &= 12 \\ \frac{1}{3}x - \frac{4}{9}y &= \frac{4}{3} \end{aligned}$

⑩ $\begin{aligned} 2x + 6y &= 11 \\ \frac{1}{2}x + \frac{3}{2}y &= 11 \end{aligned}$

⑪ $\begin{array}{l} -4x+2y=6 \\ 2x-y=-4 \end{array}$

⑫ $\begin{array}{l} 2f+4g=6 \\ -f-2g=-3 \end{array}$

EXAMPLE 3. Solve the system.

> ☺ Tip: When you have system as A = B = C ;
> set A = B, B = C

① $2x+y=3x+2y+2=x-2y-3$

② $\dfrac{x+3}{2}=\dfrac{4x+3y}{5}=\dfrac{-2y+5}{3}$

2. Type of Solutions of Systems of equations

※ Type of solution

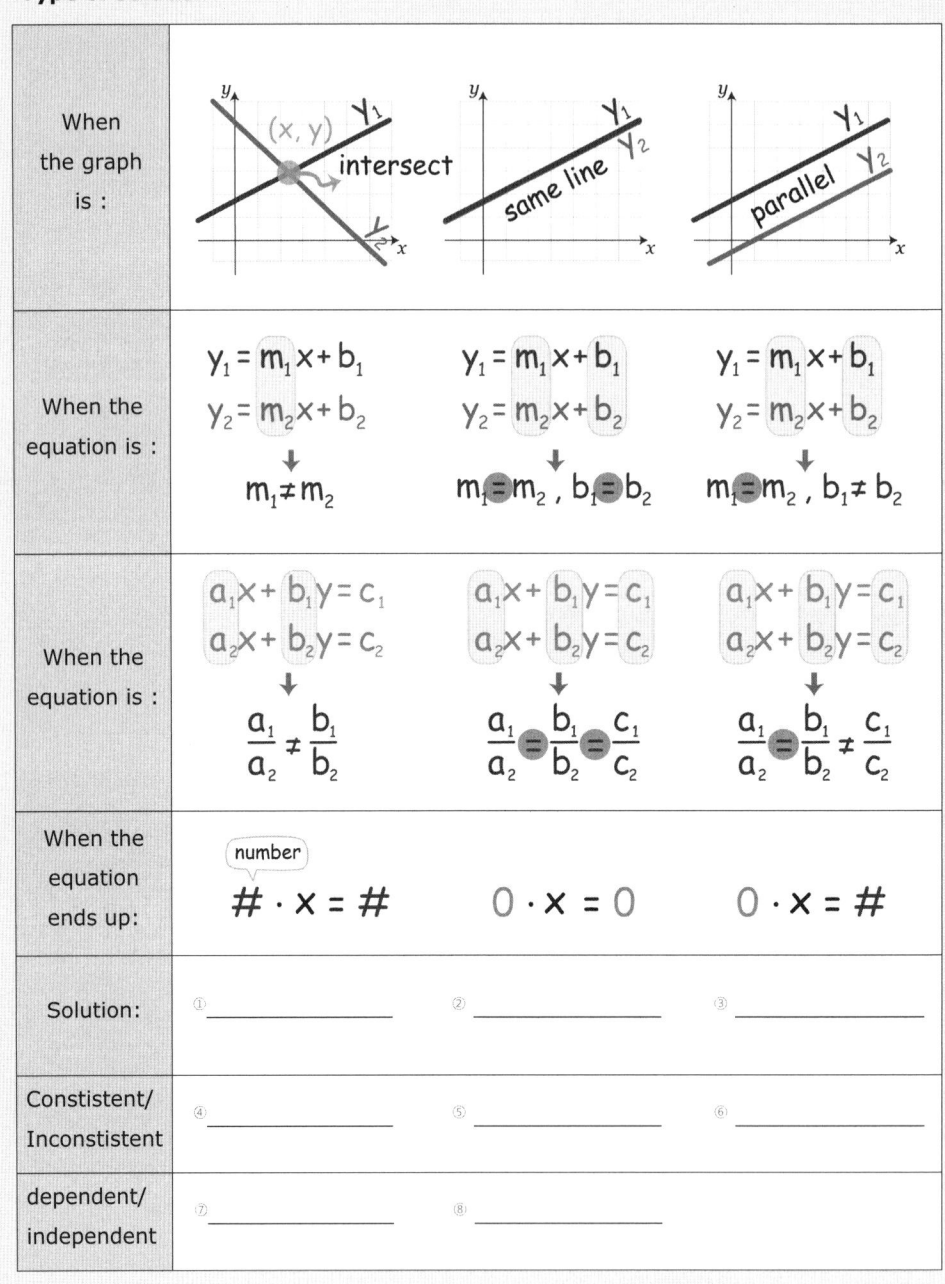

When the graph is:	intersect	same line	parallel
When the equation is:	$y_1 = m_1 x + b_1$ $y_2 = m_2 x + b_2$ ↓ $m_1 \neq m_2$	$y_1 = m_1 x + b_1$ $y_2 = m_2 x + b_2$ ↓ $m_1 = m_2 , b_1 = b_2$	$y_1 = m_1 x + b_1$ $y_2 = m_2 x + b_2$ ↓ $m_1 = m_2 , b_1 \neq b_2$
When the equation is:	$a_1 x + b_1 y = c_1$ $a_2 x + b_2 y = c_2$ ↓ $\frac{a_1}{a_2} \neq \frac{b_1}{b_2}$	$a_1 x + b_1 y = c_1$ $a_2 x + b_2 y = c_2$ ↓ $\frac{a_1}{a_2} = \frac{b_1}{b_2} = \frac{c_1}{c_2}$	$a_1 x + b_1 y = c_1$ $a_2 x + b_2 y = c_2$ ↓ $\frac{a_1}{a_2} = \frac{b_1}{b_2} \neq \frac{c_1}{c_2}$
When the equation ends up:	# · x = # (number)	0 · x = 0	0 · x = #
Solution:	① _____	② _____	③ _____
Constistent/ Inconstistent	④ _____	⑤ _____	⑥ _____
dependent/ independent	⑦ _____	⑧ _____	

Blank : ① one solution   ② infinite solution (= all real numbers $\mathbb{R}$)   ③ no solution (= ∅)
④ consistent   ⑤ consistent   ⑥ inconsistent   ⑦ independent   ⑧ dependent

☺ Vocabulary

"Consistent" means that we have at least one point of *intersection* of two graphs.
"Inconsistent" means that we have *no* points *intersects*.

"Independent" means that they are *different* equation.
"Dependent" means that they are *same* equation.

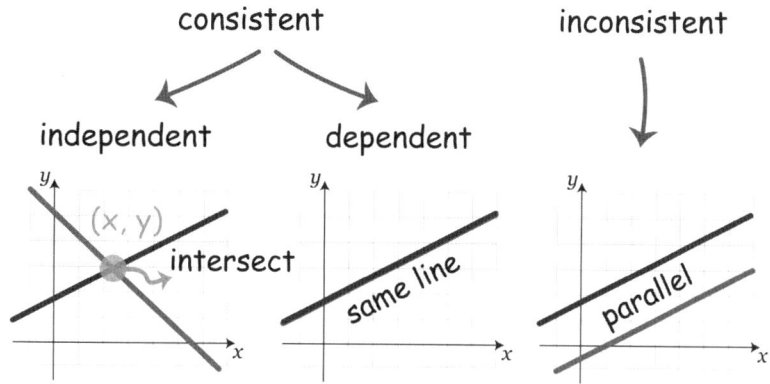

EXAMPLE 4. State the number of solution and describe it as consistent and independent, consistent and dependent, or inconsistent.

① $\begin{array}{l} 3a+b=-2 \\ 6a+2b=10 \end{array}$

② $\begin{array}{l} 3m-15=-6n \\ m+2n=5 \end{array}$

③ $\begin{array}{l} x + 2y = 4 \\ 2x - y = 3 \end{array}$

④ $\begin{array}{l} 4x - 6y = 4 \\ 2x - 3y = 0 \end{array}$

⑤ $\begin{array}{l} 4g + h = -2 \\ 2g + \dfrac{h}{2} = -1 \end{array}$

⑥ $\begin{array}{l} 3a - b = 2 \\ a + b = 6 \end{array}$

⑦ $\begin{array}{l} y = -x - 2 \\ y = -x + 1 \end{array}$

⑧ $\begin{array}{l} 2y - 8 = x \\ y = \dfrac{1}{2}x + 4 \end{array}$

EXAMPLE 5.

$$-ax - 12y = 15$$
$$4x + 3y = -3$$

If the system of equations above has no solution, what is the value of a?

EXAMPLE 6.

$$3x - 4y = 8$$
$$mx + ny = 32$$

In the system of equations above, m and n are constants. If the system has infinitely many solutions, what is the value of $m + n$?

3. Expand Knowledge*

EXAMPLE 7. * Find an equation that is parallel to y axis and contains the intersection point of $3x - y = 2$ and $y = x - 1$.

EXAMPLE 8. * Solve the system.

$$\begin{cases} (x+y) - 2(x-y) = 3 \\ 3(x+y) + 2(x-y) = 1 \end{cases}$$

☺ Tip: Using Substitution helps

EXAMPLE 9. *

$$2a + b + c = 6$$
$$a + 2b + c = 11$$
$$a + b + 2c = 7$$

Based on the system equation above, what is the value of mean (average) of a, b, and c ?

EXAMPLE 10. *

$$x = a - b + 3$$
$$x = b - c - 1$$
$$x = c - d + 5$$
$$x = d - a + 1$$

Based on the system of equation above, what is the value of $a - d$?

2.2 Word Problems about System

Mia's Algebra 2

* Translating English into algebra

+	−	×	÷	=
plus	minus	times	divide by	equal,
sum of	difference of	multiplied by	quotient	is,
combined	decreased by	product	'each'	was,
exceed	diminish	'of'	'per'	will be,
increase	drop	triple	ratio of A to B	has,
greater than	*fewer than	double	'out of'	costs,
higher than	*less than	twice		gets to,
larger than	*subtract from			is the same as,
more than	lower than			becomes,
totals to	smaller than			yields
added to				
	(for *careful with the order)			

ex)

a certain number	
The product of two numbers is	
The sum of two numbers is	
The difference between two numbers is	
15 less a number	
15 less than a number	
3 decreased by a number	
The difference of 15 and a number	
3 subtracted from a number	
3 subtract a number	
5 times a number	

Pat ate 5 candies for every 2 that Marvin ate	
A runs 5 feet for every 1 feet that B walks	
The difference between Sara's salary and Pat's salary is $100	
Peter is 4 years older than Susan	
The price increased by 10%	
The discount is 10% off	
sides are in ratio 2: 3: 5	
3 consecutive integers	
3 consecutive odd integers	
3 consecutive even integers	
There are twice as many girls as boys	
It is four times as long as it is wide	
Karan drove twice as many miles as Sam	
Victor has five more than twice as many peanuts as walnuts.	
is less than 2 is fewer than 2	
is more than 2 is greater than 2	
is less than or equal to 2 is no more than 2	
is greater than or equal to 2 is no less than 2	
is at most 2	
is at least 2	
x is between a and b	
x is between a and b, inclusive	

1. Problem Solving Using Systems

1) Digits

> ☺ Tip: When we let ten's digit number = x, unit digit number = y,
> the number will be $10x + y$.

EXAMPLE 1. The sum of the digit of a two-digit number is 11. The difference of the number and a number obtained by reversing its digit is 45. What is the original number?

EXAMPLE 2. In a two digit number, the unit's digit is twice the ten's digit. If 27 is added to the number, the digit interchange their places. Find the number.

2) General (price, numbers,..)

EXAMPLE 3. An algebra2 test contains 38 problems. Some of the problems are 2 points each. The rest are 3 points each. A perfect score is 100 points. How many problems are worth 2 points?

EXAMPLE 4. Tickets for the Senior Prom cost $25 for a single ticket and $40 for a couple. Ticket sales totaled $3800 and 110 tickets were sold. How many tickets of each type were sold?

EXAMPLE 5. A cashier had to give Sarah $3.45 in change but he had only quarters and dimes in the cash register. If he gave her 15 coins, how many dimes did she receive?

3) Age

> ☺ Tip: When someone is x years old,
>
> $$\text{age after } a \text{ years} = x + a$$
>
> $$\text{age } b \text{ years ago} = x - b$$

EXAMPLE 6. Jay is 8 years older than Albert. After 5 years, Jay's age is 10% more than Albert's age. How old is Albert now?

EXAMPLE 7. 5 years ago, Sally's father was 3 times as old as Sally. 2 years from now, Sally's father will be seven more than twice as old as Sally. How old are they this year?

4) With Interests

> ☺ Tip: When interest rate is r%
>
> Interest = investment money x r%

EXAMPLE 8. Sam has a total of $ 10,000 invested in two accounts. The older account pays 8%, while the new one pays 10%. How much does he have invested in each account in his total account interest income is $ 850?

EXAMPLE 9. Mary invested a certain amount of money at 12% interest rate and 2000$ more than that at 10% interest rate. Her total yearly interest earned is 1300$. How much did she invest at each rate?

5) Mixtures

☺ Tip: When you have mixture problem:

When we mix two salt (or acid...) solution,

(amount of solution A) + (amount of solution B) = (amount of solution mixture)
(amount of salt in A) + (amount of salt in B) = (amount of salt is mixture)

EXAMPLE 10. Jeff adds a 70% acid solution to 12 milliliters of a solution that is 20% acid. How much of the 70% acid solution should be added to create a solution that is 60% acid?

EXAMPLE 11. How many gallons of a 30% fruit juice solution must be added to 80% fruit juice solution to make 50 gallons of a 40% fruit juice solution?

6) Motions

☺ Tip:
Step 1: Draw a diagram to represent the relationship between the distances involved in the problem.
Step 2: Set up a 'DRT table' based on the formula
: distance = rate × time
Step 3: Use the chart to set up one or more equations.
Step 4: Solve the equations.

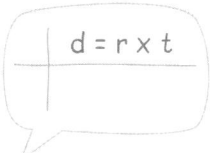

(1) When (distance of A) = (distance of B)

EXAMPLE 12. At 2 P.M. a freight train leaves Chicago traveling at 40 miles per hour. At 6 P.M., a passenger train leaves the same station traveling in the same direction at 60 miles per hour. How long will it take the passenger train to overtake the freight train?

EXAMPLE 13. Sam starts travelling at 5 km/h from a campsite 8 hours ahead of Ray, who travels 9 km/h in the same direction. How many hours will it take for Ray to catch up to Sam?

(2) When (distance of A) + (distance of B) = (Total distance)

EXAMPLE 14. A freight train left a station at noon, going north at a rate of 50 miles per hour. At 1:00 P.M. a passenger train left the same station, going south at a rate of 60 miles per hour. At what time were the trains 380 miles apart?

EXAMPLE 15. Tom traveled 260 miles east of St. Louis. For most of the trip he averaged 60 mph, but for one period of time he was slowed to 20 mph due to a traffic jam. If the total time of travel was 7 hours, how many miles did he drive at the reduced speed?

EXAMPLE 16. Two trains start at the same time from the same place and travel in opposite directions. If the rate of one is 6 km/h more than the rate of the other and they are 168 kilometers apart at the end of 4 hours, what is the rate of each?

(3) Other Motions

EXAMPLE 17. * A freight train and a passenger train start toward each other at the same time from two towns that are 500 miles apart. After 3 hours, the trains are still 80 miles apart. If the average rate of speed of the passenger train is 20 miles per hour faster than the average rate of speed of the freight train, what is the average rate of speed, in miles per hour, of the freight train?

EXAMPLE 18. *When Any starts to run, Britney starts to walk in the same direction but starting at the point 20 feet ahead of Any. Any runs 5 feet for every 1 feet that Britney walks. What is the distance that Britney needs to walk to catch up with Any?

7) Tail wind and Head wind

Aircraft speed The speed of an aircraft in still air.
Ground speed The speed of the aircraft relative to the ground.
Wind speed The speed of the wind.
Tail wind A wind blowing in the *same direction* as the path of the aircraft.
Head wind A wind blowing in the *direction opposite* to the path of the aircraft.

With a tail wind: ground speed = aircraft speed ① _____ wind speed.

With a head wind: ground speed = aircraft speed ② _____ wind speed.

EXAMPLE 19. An airplane travels 1200 mi in 4 hours with the wind. The same trip takes 5 hours against the wind. What is the speed of the plane in still air?

Blank : ① +   ② −

EXAMPLE 20. A crew team rowed 18 mi in 12 hours going with the current. Traveling against the current, it rowed 8 miles in the same amount of time. Find the speed of the crew in still water.

EXAMPLE 21. With the wind, a small plane traveled 420 miles in 1 hour and 30 minutes. The return trip against the same wind took 30 minutes longer. Find the wind speed and the aircraft speed of the plane.

8) Circular Track

☺ Tip: Running around Circular Track

in opposite direction: distance of A + distance of B = length of track

in same direction: distance of A - distance of B = length of track

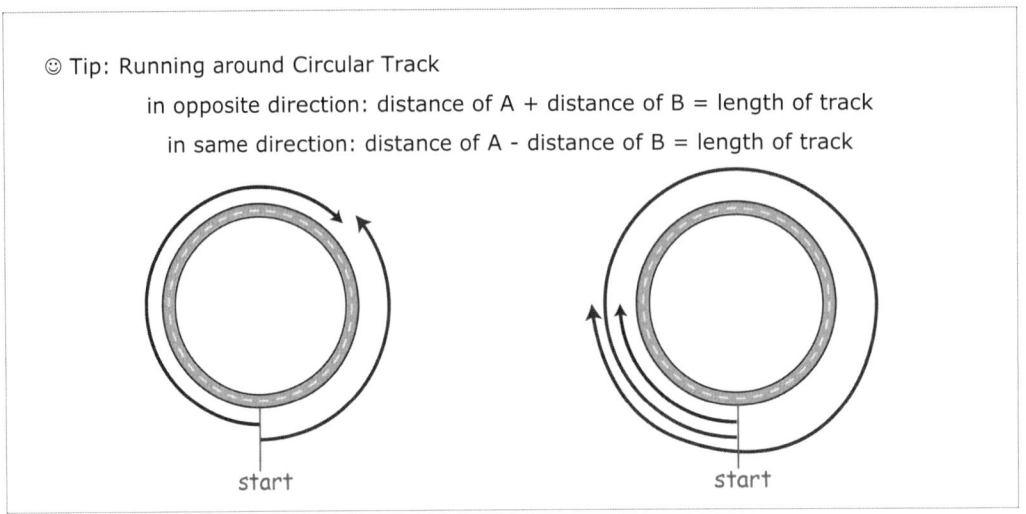

EXAMPLE 22. Runner A and B is running around a 1.5 km circular track in a constant speed. If they run in opposite direction, they meet after 3 minutes for the first time. If they run in the same direction, they meet after 15 minutes for the first time. Find their speed.

9) Others

EXAMPLE 23. Henry has twice as many candies as Ross. Even though Henry gives Ross 10 candies Henry still has 15 more than Ross. How many candies does Henry have in the beginning?

EXAMPLE 24. * A teacher is figuring out seating charts. If she assigns 2 people to each table, she needs 3 extra tables. If she assigns 4 people to each table, she has 3 empty tables. How many students are there in the class?

EXAMPLE 25. * A group of friends wants to split the cost of renting car equally. If each person pays 10$ they will have 30$ more than the cost of renting. If each friend pays 8$ they will have 20$ less. How much does it cost for renting car?

Mia's Algebra 2

2.3 Systems of Inequalities

1. Systems of Inequalities

※ **Solving each system of inequalities**

1. Graph y=   with

... equal to

$y \geq$ $y \leq$ solid line

$y >$ $y <$ dotted line

2. Then shade.

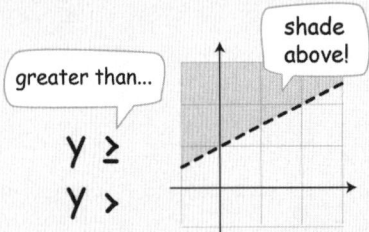

greater than...

$y \geq$
$y >$

shade above!

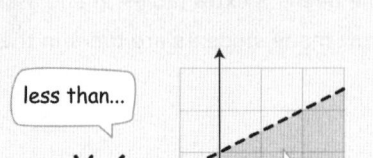

less than...

$y \leq$
$y <$

shade below!

If you have 'greater than..'

,then shade ①_____ the line.

If you have 'less than..'

,then shade ②_____ the line.

☺ Tip: Or we can pick a test point (usually (0, 0)) and test it in the inequality.
Shade the region that satisfies inequalities.

Blank : ① above   ② below

EXAMPLE 1. Solve each system of inequalities by graphing.

① $y \geq x$
$y > -x$

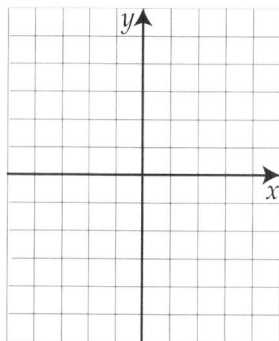

② $y < -4x$
$y \geq 3x - 2$

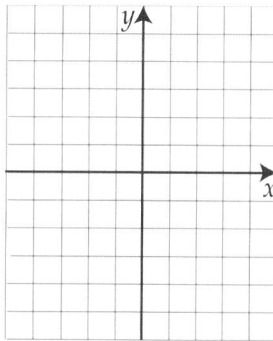

③ $x - y \geq -1$
$3x + y < 3$

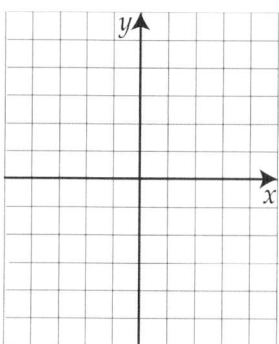

④ $x - y \geq 4$
$2x + y > 4$

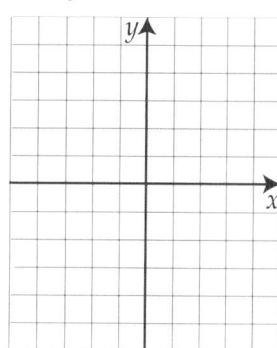

⑤ $x < 1$
$y \leq -2$

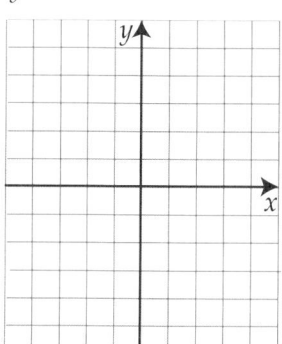

⑥ $x \geq -2$
$y < 4$

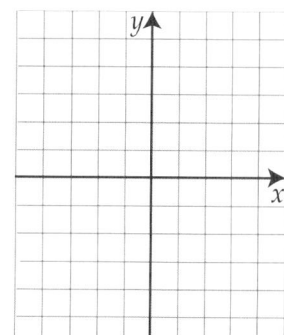

⑦ $y + 1 < 2x$
$x \geq 2$

EXAMPLE 2. Solve each system of inequalities by graphing.

① $|x - 2| \leq 1$

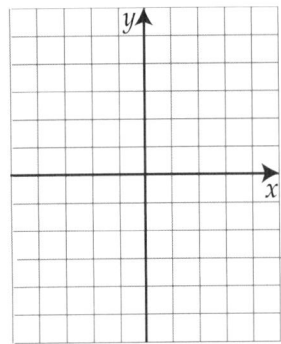

② $|y + 2| < 2$

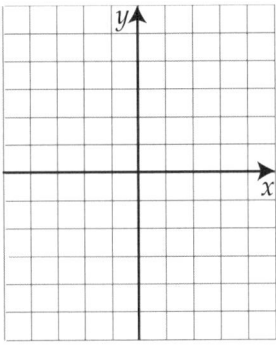

③ $|x| \leq 1$
$|y| < 3$

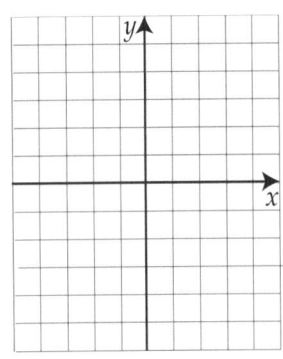

④ $|x + 1| \leq 2$
$|y| < 1$

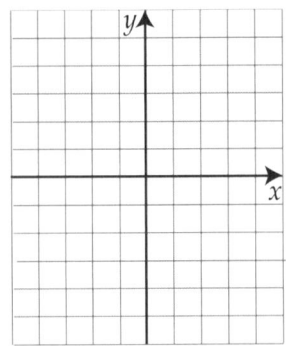

EXAMPLE 3. Write the system of linear inequalities that will produce the shaded region as its solution.

①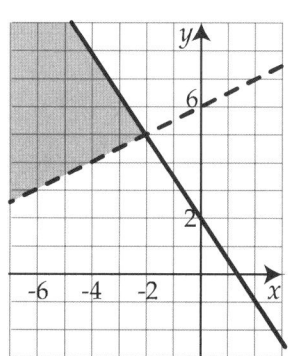

②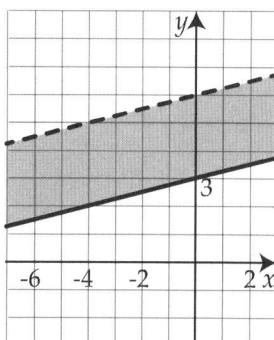

③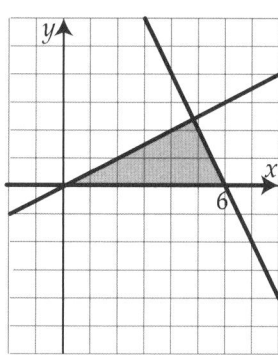

④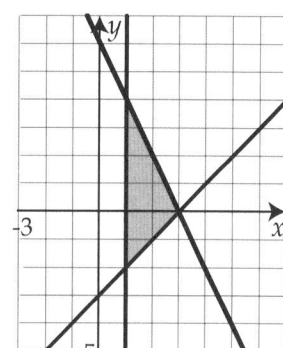

2. Expand Knowledge

EXAMPLE 4. * Which of the following could be the region of $xy > 0$

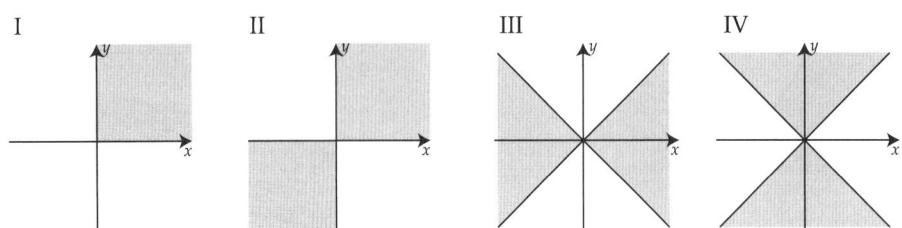

I II III IV

EXAMPLE 5. * What is the area bounded by $0 \leq y \leq x \leq 1$?

EXAMPLE 6. * What is the area bounded by $|x| + |y| \leq 1$.

Mia's Algebra 2

2.4 Linear Programming

1. Linear Programming

※ Linear Programming

This linear programming includes questions on finding constraints, and finding the maximum and minimum profit or cost for the constraints given.

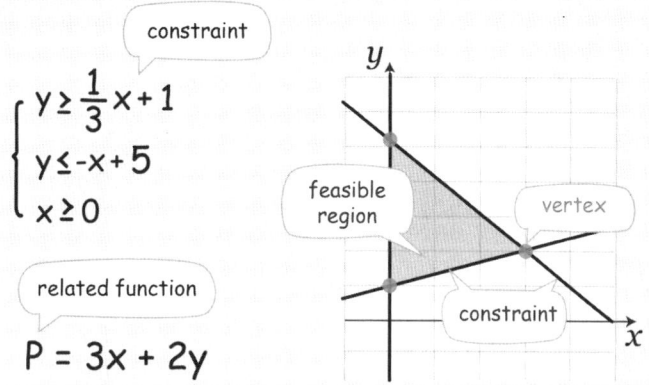

constraint
$$\begin{cases} y \geq \frac{1}{3}x + 1 \\ y \leq -x + 5 \\ x \geq 0 \end{cases}$$

related function
$$P = 3x + 2y$$

Feasible region is the region enclosed by the constraints.
The **maximum and minimum** of the related function always occurs at the ①_____ of the feasible region.

Blank : ① vertices

EXAMPLE 1. Graph each system of inequalities. Name the coordinates of the vertices of the feasible region. Find the maximum and minimum values of the given function for this region.

① $\begin{cases} x \geq 1 \\ y \leq 6 \\ y \geq x \end{cases}$

Min and Max for $P = x - 2y$

② $\begin{cases} x + 2y \leq 6 \\ x \geq 2 \\ y \geq 1 \end{cases}$

Min and Max for $C = 3x + 4y$

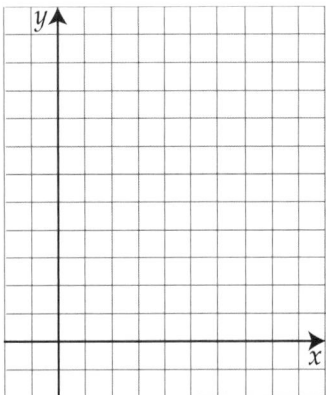

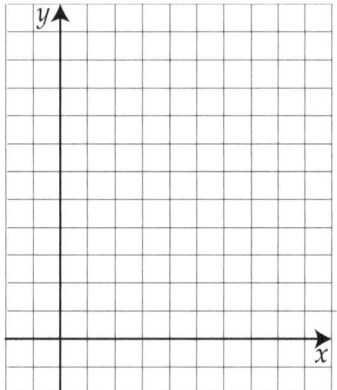

③ $\begin{cases} x + y \leq 10 \\ x + 2y \leq 16 \\ x \geq 0, \ y \geq 0 \end{cases}$

Min and Max for $P = x + 3y$

④ $\begin{cases} x + y \leq 8 \\ x + 5y \leq 20 \\ x \geq 0, \ y \geq 2 \end{cases}$

Min and Max for $C = 3x + 4y$

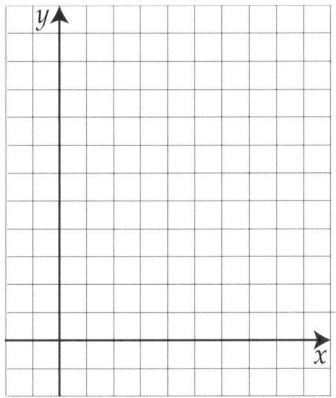

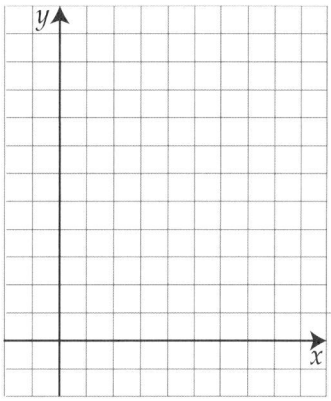

⑤ $\begin{cases} x \geq 2 \\ x \leq 5 \\ y \geq 1 \\ y \leq 4 \end{cases}$

Min and Max for $P = x + 2y$

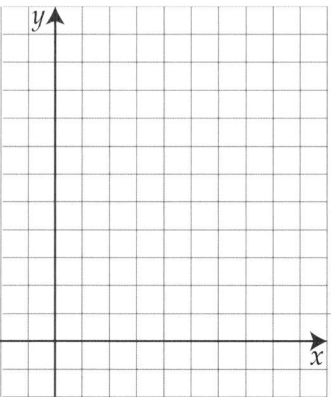

EXAMPLE 2. Gordon makes banana bread and nut bread to sell. A loaf of banana bread needs 2 cups of flour and 2 eggs. A loaf of nut bread takes 3 cups of flour and 1 egg. He has 12 cups of flour and 8 eggs on hand. He makes 3$ profit per loaf of banana bread and $2 per loaf of nut bread. To maximize the profit, how many loaves of each type does he bake?

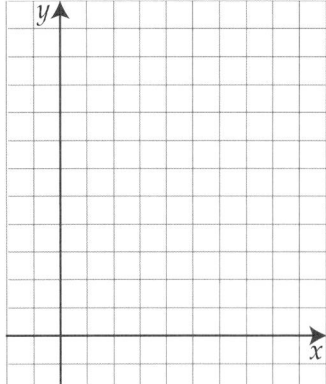

EXAMPLE 3. A biologist needs at least 40 mice for her experiment. She cannot use more than 25 white mice or more than 30 brown mice. Each white mouse cost $5 and brown mouse cost $3. How many of each mouse should she use to minimize the cost?

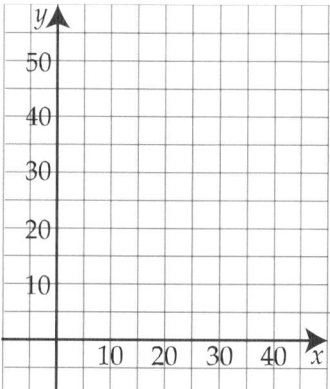

EXAMPLE 4. A potter can form 8 simple vases or 2 elaborate vases in a day. For no more than 8 days, the potter must form at least 40 vases. If the potter makes a profit of 20$ per day worked on the simple vases and 30$ per day worked on the elaborate vases, find the numbers of days the potter should spend on each type of vases to maximize the profit. What is the maximum profit?

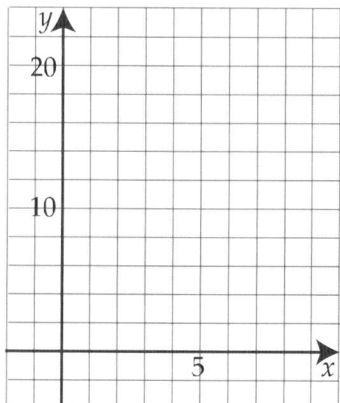

Mia's Algebra 2

2.5 Algebra of Matrices

1. Matrix

※ A **Matrix** is an array of numbers (plural: Matrices)

※ **Order of Matrix** (=Dimension of Matrix =① _____ of Matrix)

To show how many rows and columns a matrix has we often write

numbers of ② _____ × numbers of ③ _____.

$$\begin{bmatrix} 6 & 4 & 24 \\ 1 & -9 & 7 \end{bmatrix}$$ (2 rows, 3 columns) 2 X 3

$$\begin{bmatrix} 2 & 3 \\ 0 & 4 \\ 3 & -1 \end{bmatrix}$$ ④

$$\begin{bmatrix} -1 & -3 \\ 2 & 4 \end{bmatrix}$$ ⑤

※ Each element is shown by a lower case letter with a "subscript" of row, column:

$$A = \begin{bmatrix} a_{11} & a_{12} & a_{13} \\ a_{21} & a_{22} & a_{23} \end{bmatrix}$$

a_{rc} (row, column)

2. Operation of Matrices

※ To **add** or **subtract** two matrices: add the numbers in the matching positions.

$$\begin{bmatrix} 2 & -5 \\ 1 & 9 \end{bmatrix} - \begin{bmatrix} 1 & 3 \\ -2 & -4 \end{bmatrix} = \begin{bmatrix} 1 & -8 \\ 3 & 13 \end{bmatrix}$$

2−1=1

Blank : ① size ② row ③ column ④ 3 x 2 (3 by 2) ⑤ 2 x 2 (2 by 2)

※ We can **multiply** a matrix **by some value**:

$$3 \times \begin{bmatrix} 1 & 3 \\ -2 & -4 \end{bmatrix} = \begin{bmatrix} 3 & 9 \\ -6 & -12 \end{bmatrix}$$

$3 \times 1 = 3$

EXAMPLE 1. Find the sum or difference of the matrix, if possible.

① $\begin{bmatrix} -1 & 5 \\ 2 & 4 \end{bmatrix} + 2 \begin{bmatrix} 2 & 8 \\ -4 & 5 \end{bmatrix}$

② $\begin{bmatrix} 1 & 5 & 7 \\ -4 & 0 & 5 \end{bmatrix} - 2 \begin{bmatrix} 7 & -1 & 4 \\ -2 & 4 & 4 \end{bmatrix}$

③ $-\begin{bmatrix} 2 & -3 \\ 4 & -1 \\ 8 & 7 \end{bmatrix} - 3 \begin{bmatrix} 0 & 8 \\ 4 & -2 \\ 3 & 4 \end{bmatrix}$

④ $\begin{bmatrix} 1 & 4 & 0 \end{bmatrix} + 2 \begin{bmatrix} 4 \\ -3 \\ 1 \end{bmatrix}$

⑤ $2 \begin{bmatrix} 2 & 3 \\ -8 & 2 \end{bmatrix} + 3 \begin{bmatrix} 2 & 4 \\ 4 & -2 \\ 5 & 7 \end{bmatrix}$

EXAMPLE 2. Solve the equation.

① $\begin{bmatrix} 2 & 6 \\ 3 & 1 \end{bmatrix} + X = \begin{bmatrix} 4 & 7 \\ 0 & 9 \end{bmatrix}$

② $\begin{bmatrix} 0 & 3 & 9 \\ -1 & 5 & -3 \end{bmatrix} - X = \begin{bmatrix} 2 & -11 & 6 \\ 3 & 4 & 8 \end{bmatrix}$

※ But to **multiply** a matrix A **by another matrix B**

$$\begin{bmatrix} 2 & 4 & -1 \\ 1 & -9 & 7 \end{bmatrix} \times \begin{bmatrix} 2 & 3 \\ 0 & 4 \\ 3 & -1 \end{bmatrix} = \begin{bmatrix} 1 & \\ & \end{bmatrix}$$

$2\cdot 2 + 4\cdot 0 + (-1)\cdot 3$

$$\begin{bmatrix} 2 & 4 & -1 \\ 1 & -9 & 7 \end{bmatrix} \times \begin{bmatrix} 2 & 3 \\ 0 & -1 \\ 3 & -2 \end{bmatrix} = \begin{bmatrix} 1 & 4 \\ & \end{bmatrix}$$

$2\cdot 3 + 4\cdot (-1) + (-1)\cdot (-2)$

$$\begin{bmatrix} 2 & 4 & -1 \\ 1 & -9 & 7 \end{bmatrix} \times \begin{bmatrix} 2 & 3 \\ 0 & -1 \\ 3 & -2 \end{bmatrix} = \begin{bmatrix} 1 & 4 \\ 23 & \end{bmatrix}$$

$1\cdot 2 + (-9)\cdot 0 + 7\cdot 3$

$$\begin{bmatrix} 2 & 4 & -1 \\ 1 & -9 & 7 \end{bmatrix} \times \begin{bmatrix} 2 & 3 \\ 0 & -1 \\ 3 & -2 \end{bmatrix} = \begin{bmatrix} 1 & 4 \\ 23 & ① \end{bmatrix}$$

EXAMPLE 3. Find the product, if possible.

① $\begin{bmatrix} -1 & 0 \\ 2 & 4 \end{bmatrix} \times \begin{bmatrix} 2 & 8 \\ -4 & 1 \end{bmatrix}$

② $\begin{bmatrix} -1 & 3 \\ 3 & 2 \end{bmatrix} \times \begin{bmatrix} -2 & 0 \\ -1 & 3 \end{bmatrix}$

Blank : ① -2

③ $\begin{bmatrix} -2 & 3 & 5 \end{bmatrix} \times \begin{bmatrix} 0 & 1 \\ -1 & 2 \\ 2 & 3 \end{bmatrix}$

④ $\begin{bmatrix} 0 & -3 & 1 \\ 5 & -1 & 0 \end{bmatrix} \times \begin{bmatrix} 1 & 2 \\ 0 & 1 \\ 1 & -1 \end{bmatrix}$

⑤ $\begin{bmatrix} 0 & 7 \\ 2 & 1 \end{bmatrix} \times \begin{bmatrix} -4 & 3 & 0 \\ 4 & 2 & -2 \end{bmatrix}$

⑥ $\begin{bmatrix} -6 & 2 & 9 \end{bmatrix} \times \begin{bmatrix} 4 \\ 0 \\ -3 \end{bmatrix}$

⑦ $\begin{bmatrix} -4 & 1 & -5 \\ 0 & 0 & 4 \end{bmatrix} \times \begin{bmatrix} 0 & 2 & -5 \\ 1 & 3 & 7 \end{bmatrix}$

⑧ $\begin{bmatrix} 2 & -8 \\ -1 & 3 \\ 2 & -6 \end{bmatrix} \times \begin{bmatrix} 5 & 0 \\ -1 & 7 \\ 2 & 1 \end{bmatrix}$

※ **Product of Matrices**

$$\text{Matrix product: } A \times B = AB$$
$$\text{size: } m \times n \quad n \times p \quad m \times p$$

Product of Matrices AB is defined
only when the number of columns in A is equal to the number of rows in B.

EXAMPLE 4. If matrices A, B, C, D and E have dimensions of 2 x 3, 2 x 3, 3 x 2, 2 x 2, and 3 x 3, respectively, what are the dimensions of following operations?

① BA

② AEC

③ BCD

④ $D(A - 3B)$

⑤ $BC + 2D$

⑥ $(AE - B)C$

⑦ $(BC - D)A$

EXAMPLE 5. Which of the following matrices can be multiplied by themselves?

$$A=\begin{bmatrix} 1 & 1 \\ 3 & 1 \\ 1 & 2 \end{bmatrix} \quad B=\begin{bmatrix} 3 & -1 & 1 \\ 1 & -1 & 2 \\ 2 & 1 & -3 \end{bmatrix} \quad C=\begin{bmatrix} 1 & 1 & 4 \end{bmatrix} \quad D=\begin{bmatrix} 1 & 0 \\ 0 & 1 \end{bmatrix}$$

3. Properties of Matrices

※ Properties of Matrix

(AB)C = A(BC)   Association Property

C(A + B) = CA + CB
                       Distributive Property
(A + B) C = AC + BC

BUT Matrix Multiplication is *NOT Commutative*!

AB ≠ BA

EXAMPLE 6. If A and B are two matrices, find $(A+B)^2$.

EXAMPLE 7. If A and B are two matrices, find $(A+B)(A-B)$.

4. Identity Matrix

The "Identity Matrix" is the matrix equivalent of the number "1":

$$I_3 = \begin{bmatrix} 1 & 0 & 0 \\ 0 & 1 & 0 \\ 0 & 0 & 1 \end{bmatrix}$$

(3 x 3 Identity Matrix)

It is "square" matrix (has same number of rows as columns),

It has 1s on the diagonal and 0s everywhere else.

Its symbol is the capital letter I.

It is a special matrix, because when we multiply by it, the original is unchanged:

$$AI = IA = A$$

EXAMPLE 8. Find the product.

① $\begin{bmatrix} -1 & 0 \\ 2 & 4 \end{bmatrix} \times \begin{bmatrix} 1 & 0 \\ 0 & 1 \end{bmatrix}$

② $\begin{bmatrix} 1 & 0 & 2 \\ 0 & 2 & -4 \\ 3 & -5 & 4 \end{bmatrix} \times \begin{bmatrix} 1 & 0 & 0 \\ 0 & 1 & 0 \\ 0 & 0 & 1 \end{bmatrix}$

Mia's Algebra 2

2.6 Inverse and Matrix Equation

1. Determinant of Matrices

The ①_____ of a matrix is a special number that can be calculated from a **square matrix**(=Matrix with same number of rows and columns, ex) 2x2, 3x3,..).

※ **Determinant of 2x2 Matrix**:

$$|A| = \begin{vmatrix} a & b \\ c & d \end{vmatrix} = ad - bc$$

Determinant of Matrix A

EXAMPLE 1. Find the determinant.

① $\begin{vmatrix} 7 & 3 \\ 5 & 2 \end{vmatrix}$ ② $\begin{vmatrix} 2 & 3 \\ -1 & 2 \end{vmatrix}$

③ $\begin{vmatrix} 4 & 5 \\ -1 & 1 \end{vmatrix}$ ④ $\begin{vmatrix} 12 & -7 \\ -4 & 3 \end{vmatrix}$

⑤ $\begin{vmatrix} 2 & 2 \\ 5 & 5 \end{vmatrix}$ ⑥ $\begin{vmatrix} 2 & -4 \\ 3 & -6 \end{vmatrix}$

Blank : ① determinant

※ **Determinant of 3x3 Matrix:**

$$|A| = \begin{vmatrix} a & b & c \\ d & e & f \\ g & h & i \end{vmatrix} \begin{matrix} a & b \\ d & e \\ g & h \end{matrix}$$

$$= aei + bfg + cdh - gec - hfa - idb$$

EXAMPLE 2. Find the determinant.

① $\begin{vmatrix} 1 & -1 & 5 \\ -4 & 2 & -4 \\ -1 & -2 & 3 \end{vmatrix}$
② $\begin{vmatrix} 4 & 1 & 1 \\ 3 & 6 & 1 \\ 2 & 5 & 2 \end{vmatrix}$

③ $\begin{vmatrix} 1 & 2 & 4 \\ 2 & 2 & 5 \\ 1 & 2 & 4 \end{vmatrix}$
④ $\begin{vmatrix} 1 & 0 & 2 \\ 0 & 2 & -4 \\ 3 & -5 & 4 \end{vmatrix}$

2. Inverse of Matrices

When you multiply a Matrix by its ①_____ matrix, you get the Identity Matrix.

$$A \times A^{-1} = A^{-1} \times A = I$$

※ **Inverse of a Matrix of 2 x 2**

$$A^{-1} = \begin{bmatrix} a & b \\ c & d \end{bmatrix}^{-1} = \frac{1}{|A|} \begin{bmatrix} d & -b \\ -c & a \end{bmatrix}$$

(switch! negative~)
(Determinant)

$$= \frac{1}{ad-bc} \begin{bmatrix} d & -b \\ -c & a \end{bmatrix}$$

If determinant of **A** ≠ 0, then **A**$^{-1}$ exists

If determinant of **A** = ②_____ , then **A**$^{-1}$ does not exist.

EXAMPLE 3. Find the inverse, if it exists, for the matrix.

① $\begin{bmatrix} 5 & 3 \\ 3 & 2 \end{bmatrix}$ ② $\begin{bmatrix} 10 & 1 \\ -1 & 0 \end{bmatrix}$

③ $\begin{bmatrix} -5 & -1 \\ 6 & 0 \end{bmatrix}$ ④ $\begin{bmatrix} -2 & 4 \\ 4 & -4 \end{bmatrix}$

Blank : ① inverse   ② 0

⑤ $\begin{bmatrix} 4 & -8 \\ 3 & -6 \end{bmatrix}$ ⑥ $\begin{bmatrix} -2 & 4 \\ 1 & -2 \end{bmatrix}$

3. Matrices and Systems of Equations

EXAMPLE 4. You have Matrix A and B, find Matrix X when $AX = B$

EXAMPLE 5. You have Matrix A and B, find Matrix X when $XA = B$

EXAMPLE 6. Solve the system by using the inverse of the coefficient matrix.

① $\begin{aligned} 3x + 5y &= -10 \\ -3x - 6y &= 9 \end{aligned}$ ② $\begin{aligned} x + 3y &= -8 \\ -14x - 4y &= -2 \end{aligned}$

4. Cramer's Rule

Given that
$$ax + by = p$$
$$cx + dy = q$$

then

$$x = \frac{\begin{vmatrix} p & b \\ q & d \end{vmatrix}}{\begin{vmatrix} a & b \\ c & d \end{vmatrix}} \quad y = \frac{\begin{vmatrix} a & p \\ c & q \end{vmatrix}}{\begin{vmatrix} a & b \\ c & d \end{vmatrix}}$$

(replace with p,q)

EXAMPLE 7. Solve the system by using the cramer's rule.

① $\begin{aligned} 2x + 6y &= 2 \\ 2x - y &= -5 \end{aligned}$

② $\begin{aligned} -5x + 3y &= 8 \\ 3x - 6y &= -30 \end{aligned}$

Part 3
Factoring and Expanding Polynomials

3.1 Law of Exponents

3.2 Polynomials

3.3 Multiplying Polynomials

3.4 Factoring using GCF

3.5 Factoring Quadratic

3.6 Factoring Polynomials

3.7 Solving Polynomial Equations

3.8 Word Problems about Polynomial Equation

3.9 Solving polynomial Inequalities

Mia's Algebra 2

3.1 Law of Exponents

1. Properties of Exponents

If a and b are positive numbers,

$$x^a \cdot x^b = x^{a+b} \quad \text{(add)}$$

Multiplication Law

ex) $x^3 \cdot x^2 = (x \cdot x \cdot x)(x \cdot x) = x^5$

$$\frac{x^a}{x^b} = x^{a-b} \quad \text{(subtract)}$$

Division Law

ex) $\dfrac{x^3}{x^2} = \dfrac{x \cdot x \cdot x}{x \cdot x} = x$

$$(x^a)^b = x^{ab} \quad \text{(multiply)}$$

Power Law

ex) $(x^3)^2 = (x \cdot x \cdot x)(x \cdot x \cdot x) = x^6$

$$(xy)^a = x^a y^a$$

Power of a Product Law

ex) $(x^2 y^3)^3 = (x^2)^3 \cdot (y^3)^3 = x^6 y^9$

$$\left(\frac{x}{y}\right)^a = \frac{x^a}{y^a}$$

Power of a Quotient Law

ex) $\left(\dfrac{x^3}{y^2}\right)^4 = \dfrac{(x^3)^4}{(y^2)^4} = \dfrac{x^{12}}{y^8}$

☺ Be careful! $(x+y)^a \neq x^a + y^a \quad (x-y)^a \neq x^a - y^a$

$$(-1)^n \begin{cases} = \underline{\quad ① \quad}, & \text{when } n \text{ is odd} \\ = \underline{\quad ② \quad}, & \text{when } n \text{ is even} \end{cases}$$

Blank : ① -1   ② 1

EXAMPLE 1. Simplify.

① $a^3 \cdot a^2$

② $c^4 \cdot c^3$

③ $(a^3)^2$

④ $(c^4)^3$

⑤ $(-x^2)^5$

⑥ $(-a^3)^4$

⑦ $(-x^5)^2$

⑧ $(-a^4)^3$

⑨ $(-2mn^2)^4$

⑩ $(-4x^2y^3)^2$

⑪ $(-3r^3s^2)^3$

⑫ $(-2r^2s^3)^5$

⑬ $(-6mn^3)(2m^3n^4)$

⑭ $(-p^3)(p^4q^3)(-p^3q)$

⑮ $(-a^2)(-a)^3(-a)^4$

⑯ $(-m^2)(-m^3)(-m)^6$

⑰ $(-x^2y)^3(2x^3y^4)^3$

⑱ $(4mn^3)^2(-m^2n^6)^5$

⑲ $\dfrac{x^5}{x^3}$ ⑳ $\dfrac{t^9}{t^5}$

㉑ $\dfrac{5a^2}{a^7}$ ㉒ $\dfrac{2a^4}{8a^{10}}$

㉓ $\dfrac{24ab^5c^4}{56b^2c^6}$ ㉔ $\dfrac{5u^2v^6}{15u^3v^8w^2}$

㉕ $\dfrac{(-x^4yz^5)^2}{x^3y^8z}$ ㉖ $\dfrac{(-pq^2r^4)^3}{(p^3q^4r^2)^2}$

EXAMPLE 2. Simplify.

① $a^{n-2} \cdot a^{n+2}$ ② $c^t \cdot c^{t+1}$

③ $(a^{n+1})^n$ ④ $(c^m)^{m-2}$

⑤ $(r^{m+2})^2 r^{m-1}$

⑥ $p \cdot (p^{2k-1})^3 \cdot p^{k-1}$

⑦ $p^n(p^{m+1} + p^{m-n})$

⑧ $r^m(r^{1-m} - r^{m+n})$

⑨ $\dfrac{x^{m-1}}{x^{m+2}}$

⑩ $\dfrac{y^{n+2}}{y^{1-n}}$

⑪ $\dfrac{(a^{2m}b^m)^3}{(ab^4)^m}$

⑫ $\dfrac{(p^n q^{n-1})^3}{p^{n-1}q^n}$

⑬ $\dfrac{(x^m)^2}{x^m \cdot x^2}$

⑭ $\dfrac{t^{n+1} \cdot t^{n-1}}{t^{1-n}}$

2. Zero or Negative Exponent

If a and b are positive numbers,

zero exponent

$$x^0 = 1$$

*Note that 0^0 is undefined.

negative exponent

$$x^{-a} = \frac{1}{x^a}, \quad \frac{1}{x^{-a}} = x^a$$

ex) $\dfrac{x^{-2}}{y^{-3}} = \dfrac{1}{x^2 y^{-3}} = \dfrac{y^3}{x^2}$

$$\left(\frac{x}{y}\right)^{-a} = \left(\frac{y}{x}\right)^a$$

ex) $\left(\dfrac{x^3}{y^2}\right)^{-4} = \left(\dfrac{y^2}{x^3}\right)^4 = \dfrac{y^8}{x^{12}}$

EXAMPLE 3. Simplify.

☺ Tip: Make sure the answer has no negative exponents.

① $(-2)^0$

② -3^0

③ -2^0

④ $-6^0 \cdot (-5)^0$

⑤ $a^{-1} \cdot b^2 \cdot c^{-2}$

⑥ $u^2 \cdot v^{-1} \cdot w^{-3}$

⑦ $\dfrac{x^{-1}y^{-4}}{x^{-2}y^{0}}$

⑧ $\dfrac{9ab^{-2}}{-3a^{-3}b^{-1}}$

⑨ $\left(\dfrac{x^{-2}y}{x^{2}y^{-1}}\right)^{-2}$

⑩ $\left(\dfrac{3pq^{-1}}{p^{-2}q}\right)^{-1}$

⑪ $4z(2y^{2}z^{-1})^{-2}$

⑫ $3x^{2}(3x^{-1}y)^{-3}$

⑬ $\dfrac{(2a^{-1})^{-3}}{2(a^{-1})^{-2}}$

⑭ $\dfrac{3(a^{-1})^{-2}}{(3a^{-3})^{-1}}$

⑮ $\left(\dfrac{x^{3}}{y^{-1}}\right)^{-2}\left(\dfrac{y^{3}}{x^{-2}}\right)^{2}$

⑯ $\left(\dfrac{c^{2}}{d^{-4}}\right)^{2}\left(\dfrac{c^{-5}}{d^{-1}}\right)^{-1}$

EXAMPLE 4. Fill in the blanks.

① $2^{3+m} = \underline{\hspace{1cm}} \cdot 2^m$

② $3^{m+2} = \underline{\hspace{1cm}} \cdot 3^m$

③ $b^{n-1} = b^n \cdot \underline{\hspace{1cm}}$

④ $b^{3n-2} = b^{3n} \cdot \underline{\hspace{1cm}}$

⑤ $25^m = (5^{\underline{\hspace{0.5cm}}})^2$

⑥ $27^x = (3^3)^{\underline{\hspace{0.5cm}}}$

⑦ $b^{2n} = b^n \cdot \underline{\hspace{1cm}}$

⑧ $b^{3n} = b^n \cdot \underline{\hspace{1cm}}$

⑨ $\dfrac{6^m}{3^m} = \underline{\hspace{1cm}}$

⑩ $\dfrac{8^a}{2^{2a}} = \underline{\hspace{1cm}}$

3. Expand Knowledge*

※ **Adding a^n a times**

$$\underbrace{a^n + a^n + a^n + \cdots + a^n}_{\text{add 'a' times}} = a \cdot a^n = a^{1+n}$$

EXAMPLE 5. * Find a.

a) $5^3 + 5^3 + 5^3 + 5^3 + 5^3 = 5^a$

b) $4^2 \times 4^2 \times 4^2 \times 4^2 = 2^a$

c) $3^x + 3^x + 3^x = 3^{a+x}$

d) $2^{10} + 2^{10} + 2^{10} + 2^{10} = 2^a$

EXAMPLE 6. * Simplify the following.

$$\frac{2^4 \times 2^4}{4^2 + 4^2 + 4^2 + 4^2} + \frac{3^3 \times 3^3 \times 3^3}{3^5 + 3^5 + 3^5}$$

Mia's Algebra 2

3.2 Polynomials

1. Polynomial

poly- means ①_____   -nomial means ②_____

※ **Polynomial** : an expression with *many terms* (but it can also be one term)

ex) $3x^3 + 2x - 7$, xy , $xy^3 - 2x^2y + x - yz$ ...

※ **Degree** of Polynomial: highest power that appears

Leading coefficient -2   Degree ③   Constant Term 7

$$-2x^4 - x^3 + 3x^2 + 7$$

Leading term $-2x^4$ Coefficient -2, -1, 3, 7

☺ Note that degree of $x^4 - 2x^2y^3 + 6y - 11$ is ④_____.

※ **Naming Polynomials** by terms

$3x^3$ $-x^2 + 3x$ $-2x^4 - x^3 + 7$

monomial   **bi**nomial   **tri**nomial

※ **Naming Polynomials** by degree

$4x - 1$ $-x^2 + 3x$ $3x^3$ $-2x^4 - x^3 + 7$

linear   quadratic   cubic   quartic

Blank : ① many ② terms ③ 4 ④ 2 + 3 = 5

※ Polynomial or not?
- Coefficients are ①_____.
- Exponents can only be 0, 1, 2, 3,... (no ②_____, no ③_____ Exponents)

  ex) $\dfrac{1}{x}+2x$, $\sqrt{x}+1$ is not a polynomial

EXAMPLE 1. Determine whether each expression is a polynomial. If it is a polynomial, state the degree of the polynomial.

① $5x^3+2x^4-7x+1$

② $25x^3y-x\sqrt{7}$

③ $12a^2b^5-a\sqrt{b}$

④ $-\dfrac{4}{3}x^5+\dfrac{x}{3}+\dfrac{1}{3}$

⑤ $\dfrac{5}{c}+c-4$

⑥ $\dfrac{5}{x}-\dfrac{4}{y}$

⑦ $27+3xy^3-12x^2y^4-\sqrt{10}y^5$

⑧ $\dfrac{10}{\sqrt{x}}+\sqrt[3]{x}+1$

⑨ $(3x^2+2x+1)(4x^3+5x-3)$

⑩ $(x+2)(4x^2+2x-1)$

Blank : ① all real numbers ($\mathbb{R}$)   ② negative   ③ fraction   (no fraction exponents means no $\sqrt{x}$)

2. Operations of Polynomial

Like terms have the same variables to the same power.
When we add or subtract polynomials we should **combine the like terms.**

$$a^2 + 2ab + 3a^2 - 5ab$$
$$= 4a^2 - 3ab$$

Combine the like terms

EXAMPLE 2. Add and subtract the polynomial.

① $(3mn^2 + 2n - 4m) + (n - 2m - mn^2)$

② $(6w - 11w^2s + 5) + (4s - 12w^2s - 3)$

③ $(5m^2 - 2mp - 6p) - (5mp - 3m + p)$

④ $(5t^2 - 7ts + 3s^2) - (5ts - 4s^2 + 6)$

⑤ $5ab + 3b - \{ab + b - (4a - 5ab)\}$

⑥ $-2mp - \{3m^2 + p^2 - 3(2p^2 - mp)\}$

⑦ $3x^2y - \{3x - 1 - 2(x^2y + 2x) - x^2y\}$

⑧ $2(uv - 4) - \{6 + 3u^2 - (5u^2 - 3uv)\}$

Mia's Algebra 2

3.3 Multiplying Polynomials

1. Multiplying Polynomial (Expanding)

※ **(Monomial) x (Polynomial)**

$$a(b + c + d) = ab + ac + ad$$

(distribute)

※ **(Polynomial) x (Polynomial)**

$$(a + b)(c + d) = ac + ad + bc + bd$$

(FOIL)

This is called the 'FOIL' method,
since we multiply the **F**irst, **O**uter, **I**nner, and **L**ast terms.

EXAMPLE 1. Multiply.

① $-5a^2b(a^3b - ab^4)$

② $c^3d^2(c^2d^5 - 3c^4d^3 + 7d^2)$

③ $2x^3(x^2 + xy - 2y^2)$

④ $\dfrac{2}{3}a^3bc^2(15a^2b - 6ac)$

⑤ $(x+2)(x-6)$

⑥ $(y-6)(y-10)$

⑦ $(a+2)(3a-4)$

⑧ $(z-4)(5z+1)$

⑨ $(r+2s)(2r-s)$

⑩ $(4x-3y)(x-3y)$

⑪ $(3m-2n)(2m+3n)$

⑫ $(2b+3a)(3b+2a)$

⑬ $(a+3)(a^2+3a-1)$

⑭ $(t-2)(t^2+3t+4)$

⑮ $(z^4+2z^2-1)(z^2+3)$

⑯ $(3-y^2-y^4)(2-y^2)$

※ **Special Product**

Special product	Pattern and Example
$(a+b)^2 = a^2 + 2ab + b^2$	$(\bullet + \bigstar)^2 = \bullet^2 + 2\bullet\bigstar + \bigstar^2$ 2 × product ex) $(2x+3y)^2 = (2x)^2 + 2(2x)(3y) + (3y)^2$ $= 4x^2 + 12xy + 9y^2$
$(a-b)^2 = a^2 - 2ab + b^2$	$(\bullet - \bigstar)^2 = \bullet^2 - 2\bullet\bigstar + \bigstar^2$ 2 × product ex) $(2x-3y)^2 = (2x)^2 - 2(2x)(3y) + (3y)^2$ $= 4x^2 - 12xy + 9y^2$
$(a+b)(a-b) = a^2 - b^2$	$(\bullet + \bigstar)(\bullet - \bigstar) = \bullet^2 - \bigstar^2$ sum difference ex) $(2x+3y)(2x-3y) = (2x)^2 - (3y)^2$ $= 4x^2 - 9y^2$

※ Careful!

$$(a+b)^2 \neq a^2 + b^2 \qquad (a-b)^2 \neq a^2 - b^2$$

※ Useful Formula

$$(-a-b)^2 = [-(a+b)]^2 = (a+b)^2$$
$$(-a+b)^2 = [-(a-b)]^2 = (a-b)^2$$
$$(-a+b)(-a-b) = [-(a-b)][-(a+b)] = (a-b)(a+b)$$

EXAMPLE 2. Multiply.

① $(x+2)^2$ ② $(t-1)^2$

③ $(y-5)^2$ ④ $(n+6)^2$

⑤ $(2a-3)^2$ ⑥ $(4z-5)^2$

⑦ $(-4-3h)^2$ ⑧ $(-5-7m)^2$

⑨ $(-3+x\sqrt{2})^2$ ⑩ $(-4+x\sqrt{3})^2$

⑪ $(a+2)(a-2)$ ⑫ $(z-4)(z+4)$

⑬ $(4r+5s)(5s-4r)$

⑭ $(4x-3y)(3y+4x)$

⑮ $(8t+1)(1-8t)$

⑯ $(2x-4y)(4y-2x)$

⑰ $(5-3t)(3t-5)$

EXAMPLE 3. Multiply.

① $(x^2-2)(x^2+4)$

② $(x^3+3)(x^3-7)$

③ $(x^2-5)^2$

④ $(5t^3-1)^2$

⑤ $(s^3 - t^3)^2$ 	⑥ $(2p - 3q^2)^2$

⑦ $\left(x + \dfrac{1}{x}\right)^2$ 	⑧ $\left(x - \dfrac{1}{x}\right)^2$

⑨ $\left(\dfrac{2}{a} - a\right)^2$ 	⑩ $\left(\dfrac{5}{z} + z\right)^2$

⑪ $m^2(m^3 + 4)^2$ 	⑫ $n^2(2n + 1)(2n - 7)$

⑬ $(x^{3n} + 1)^2$ 	⑭ $(p^m - q^{2n})^2$

⑮ $(p^n - q^n)(p^n + q^n)$ ⑯ $(x^m + 1)(x^m - 1)$

⑰ $(x^2 + 8y^4)(8y^4 - x^2)$ ⑱ $(2a^3 + 7b^5)(7b^5 - 2a^3)$

⑲ $(y+1)(y-1)(y^2+1)$ ⑳ $(a+b)(a-b)(a^2+b^2)(a^4+b^4)$

㉑ $(x^n - 1)(x^n + 1)(x^{2n} + 1)(x^{4n} + 1)(x^{8n} + 1)$

※ Special Product

Special product	Pattern and Example
$(a+b)^3$ $= a^3 + 3a^2b + 3ab^2 + b^3$	$(\bullet + \star)^3$ (3,2,1 power) $= \bullet^3 + 3\bullet^2\star + 3\bullet\star^2 + \star^3$ (1,2,3 power) ex) $(2x+3y)^3 = (2x)^3 + 3(2x)^2(3y) + 3(2x)(3y)^2 + (3y)^3$ $= 8x^3 + 36x^2y + 54xy^2 + 27y^3$
$(a-b)^3$ $= a^3 - 3a^2b + 3ab^2 - b^3$	$(\bullet - \star)^3$ (3,2,1 power) $= \bullet^3 - 3\bullet^2\star + 3\bullet\star^2 - \star^3$ (1,2,3 power) ex) $(2x-3y)^3 = (2x)^3 - 3(2x)^2(3y) + 3(2x)(3y)^2 - (3y)^3$ $= 8x^3 - 36x^2y + 54xy - 27y^3$

EXAMPLE 4. Multiply.

① $(x+2)^3$ ② $(x+3)^3$

③ $(y-4)^3$ ④ $(5-t)^3$

⑤ $(2m-3n)^3$ ⑥ $(4p+q)^3$

2. Expand Knowledge*

※ Square of sum formula and Square of difference formula

$$(a+b)^2 = a^2 + 2ab + b^2 \qquad (a-b)^2 = a^2 - 2ab + b^2$$

※ Sum of Squares formula

Sum of squares

$$a^2 + b^2 = (a+b)^2 - 2ab = (a-b)^2 + 2ab$$

EXAMPLE 5.   * When $x+y=2$ and $xy=-5$, then what is x^2+y^2 ?

EXAMPLE 6.   * When $x-y=5$ and $xy=3$, then what is x^2+y^2 ?

EXAMPLE 7. * Multiply.

> ☺ Tip: Sometimes 'making a substitution' would help!

① $(x^2+x-1)(x^2+x+2)$ ② $(y^2-2y+1)(y^2-y+1)$

③ $(z^2-3z+2)(z^2-z+2)$ ④ $(a^2-a)(a^2-a+2)$

⑤ $(x+2y-3)(x+2y+3)$ ⑥ $(3a^2+b-4)(3a^2+b+4)$

⑦ $(x+y+z)(x-y+z)$ ⑧ $(x+y+z)(x+y-z)$

EXAMPLE 8.   * Find the given term.

☺ Tip: Do not FOIL everything! Only multiply the terms we need!

① Find xy term from $(2x-y-1)(x+y+3)$

② Find x term from $(x+y-1)(2x-3y+7)$

③ Find x^2y term from $(2x^2-3x+2y-7)(-x^2+4xy-8y+10)$

④ Find x^3 term from $(3x^3+4x^2-7x-4)(5x^2+4x-2)$

EXAMPLE 9.   * Find the coefficient of x^3 from $(1+x+2x^2+3x^3+\ldots+100x^{100})^2$.

*All in one: Multiplying Techniques

Multiplying Technique	Formula or Examples
(Monomial) x (Polynomial)	$4a^2b(ab - 2) = 4a^3b^2 - 8a^2b$
(Polynomial) x (Polynomial) (FOIL Method)	$(a + b)(x + y) = ax + bx + ay + by$
(Sum) x (difference)	$(a - b)(a + b) = a^2 - b^2$
Square of sum	$(a + b)^2 = a^2 + 2ab + b^2$
Square of difference	$(a - b)^2 = a^2 - 2ab + b^2$
cube of sum	$(a + b)^3 = a^3 + 3a^2b + 3ab^2 + b^3$
cube of difference	$(a - b)^3 = a^3 - 3a^2b + 3ab^2 - b^3$
Sum of Squares*	$a^2 + b^2 = (a + b)^2 - 2ab$ $= (a - b)^2 + 2ab$

Mia's Algebra 2

3.4 Factoring using GCF

1. Using Prime Factorization

※ **GCF and LCM**

Greatest Common Factor (GCF) : Greatest common factor (GCF) of a polynomial is the largest monomial that divides evenly into each term.

ex) The GCF of 8 and 12 is ①_____

The GCF of $8xy^3z$ and $12x^2y^2$ is ②_____

($\rightarrow$ common variable factors with the ③_____ power)

$$8xyyyz$$
$$12xxyy$$
$$4 \quad x \quad y^2$$

Least Common Multiple (LCM) : Least common multiple (LCM) of a polynomial is the smallest monomial that is divisible by all terms.

ex) The LCM of 8 and 12 is ④_____

The LCM of $8xy^3z$ and $12x^2y^2$ is ⑤_____

($\rightarrow$ All variable factors with the ⑥_____ power)

EXAMPLE 1. Find (a) the GCF and (b) the LCM of the following monomials.

① $12x^2y, 15xy^2$ ② $49pq^2, 56q^3$

③ $-48mn^3, 84m^4n^2$ ④ $42xy, -70yz$

Blank : ① 4   ② $4xy^2$ ③ lowest   ④ 24   ⑤ $24x^2y^3z$ ⑥ highest

⑤ $60a^2b^3c$, $240a^3bd$

⑥ $108p^2q$, $144pq^3r^2$

⑦ $10rs^4$, $12rst$, $14r^2st^2$

⑧ $22xyz^2$, $33xy$, $44y^2z$

⑨ $16xy$, $24xz$, $32yz$

⑩ $7a^3b^2c$, $14abc^3$, $28ac^2d$

2. Factoring using GCF

Now we are going to learn factoring techniques.

$$(x + 1)(x + 2) = x^2 + 3x + 2$$

Factors — Factoring — Multiplying

When you are factoring a polynomial, then the first thing you have to do is 'Factoring out the greatest common Factor(GCF)'

$$4x^2 + 28x = 4x(x + 7)$$

(4x, 4x → factor out GCF)

EXAMPLE 2. Factor.

① $16y^3 + 4y^2$ 　　　　　　　② $4x - 28x^2$

③ $3x^4 - 6x^3 + 12x^2$ 　　　　④ $6x^2 - 8x^4 - 10x^5$

⑤ $8a^3b - 12a^2b^2 + 16a^4b$ 　⑥ $11a^3b - 22a^2b^2 + 55ab^3$

3. Expand Knowledge*

EXAMPLE 3. * Fill in the ( ) by a polynomial to make the expression true.

① $3x^5 - 10x^7 + 4x^8 = 3x^5($ _____ $)$ 　(factor $3x^5$ out)

② $4x^4 - 8x^6 + 11x^{11} = 4x^4($ _____ $)$

③ $\frac{1}{2}x^2 - 4x + \frac{1}{3} = \frac{1}{2}(\underline{\hspace{3cm}})$

④ $\frac{2}{3}x^2 + 6x - \frac{8}{3} = \frac{2}{3}(\underline{\hspace{3cm}})$

⑤ $\frac{1}{x^7} + \frac{5}{x^5} - \frac{8}{x^3} = \frac{1}{x^7}(\underline{\hspace{3cm}})$

⑥ $\frac{6}{x^3} - \frac{3}{x^5} - \frac{5}{4x^2} = \frac{1}{x^5}(\underline{\hspace{3cm}})$

Mia's Algebra 2
3.5 Factoring Quadratic

1. Factoring Quadratic

※ **Factoring Quadratic**

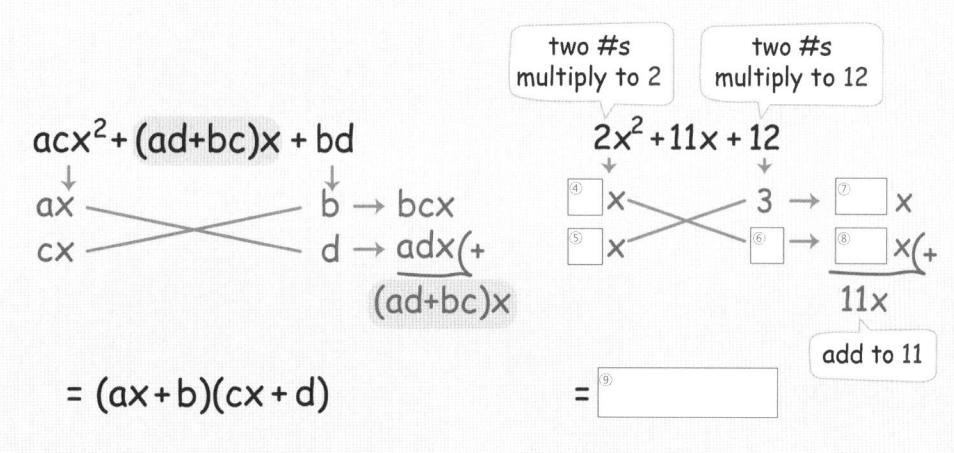

Blank : ① -4   ② 3   ③ (x−4)(x+3)   ④ 2   ⑤ 1   ⑥ 4   ⑦ 3   ⑧ 8   ⑨ (2x+3)(x+4)

EXAMPLE 1. Factor. Write prime, if it is not factorable.

① $x^2 + 7x + 12$ ② $z^2 + 5z + 6$

③ $k^2 - 7k + 6$ ④ $a^2 - 11a + 24$

⑤ $s^2 + 9s - 22$ ⑥ $p^2 + 2p + 3$

⑦ $a^2 - 11a - 60$ ⑧ $b^2 - 5b - 14$

⑨ $a^2 - 19a - 18$ ⑩ $x^2 + x - 72$

⑪ $6r^2 + 17r + 12$ ⑫ $3a^2 + 31a + 56$

⑬ $2y^2 - 9y - 5$ ⑭ $7x^2 - 36x + 32$

⑮ $2x^2 + 3x + 9$

⑯ $3t^2 + 5t - 6$

⑰ $9t^2 - 18t + 8$

⑱ $15g^2 + 8g - 16$

⑲ $25x^2 - 30xy - 16y^2$

⑳ $10m^2 - 11mn - 6n^2$

㉑ $10m^2n^2 + 41mn + 40$

㉒ $2x^2y^2 - 4xy - 70$

㉓ $2k^3 - 2k^2 - 112k$

㉔ $5z^3 - 25z^2 + 30z$

㉕ $27x^4 + 48x^3 - 12x^2$

㉖ $36x^4 + 60x^3 + 24x^2$

2. Factoring Specials Quadratic

※ **Factoring Perfect Square Trinomial** and **Difference of Square**

Factoring Techniqe	Pattern and Example
$a^2 + 2ab + b^2 = (a+b)^2$	$\bullet^2 + 2\bullet\star + \star^2 = (\bullet+\star)^2$ ex) $4x^2 + 12x + 9 = (2x)^2 + 2(2x)(3) + (3)^2$ $= (2x+3)^2$
$a^2 - 2ab + b^2 = (a-b)^2$	$\bullet^2 - 2\bullet\star + \star^2 = (\bullet-\star)^2$ ex) $4x^2 - 12x + 9 = (2x)^2 - 2(2x)(3) + (3)^2$ $= (2x-3)^2$
$a^2 - b^2 = (a+b)(a-b)$	$\bullet^2 - \star^2 = (\underbrace{\bullet+\star}_{\text{sum}})(\underbrace{\bullet-\star}_{\text{difference}})$ ex) $4x^2 - 9 = (2x)^2 - (3)^2$ $= (2x+3)(2x-3)$

※ Be careful!

$$a^2 + b^2 \neq (a+b)(a-b)$$

※ Vocabulary

$a^2 + 2ab + b^2$ or $a^2 - 2ab + b^2$ is called 'perfect square trinomial'.

EXAMPLE 2. Factor. Write prime, if it is not factorable.

① $x^2 + 10x + 25$ ② $z^2 - 16z + 64$

③ $4k^2 - 12k + 9$ ④ $4a^2 + 28a + 49$

⑤ $25x^2 + 20xy + 4y^2$ ⑥ $9p^2 - 6pq + q^2$

⑦ $3x^2 + 12x + 12$ ⑧ $5a^3 + 30a^2b + 45ab^2$

⑨ $x^2 - 49$ ⑩ $u^2 - 100$

⑪ $4y^2 - 25$ ⑫ $9x^2 - 64$

⑬ $x^2y^2 - y^2$

⑭ $x^3 - 100x$

⑮ $81rp^2 - 49rq^2$

⑯ $4x^2y - 36y$

⑰ $4x^2 + y^2$

⑱ $1 + 4x^2y^2$

EXAMPLE 3. Factor.

① $m^4n^2 - 14m^2n + 49$

② $x^4 - 6x^2y + 9y^2$

③ $x^4 - 10x^2 + 9$

④ $x^4 - 13x^2 + 36$

⑤ $a^4 - b^4$

⑥ $16k^4 - 1$

⑦ $x^4 - 81$

⑧ $m^4 n^4 - 1$

⑨ $(5x-y)^2 - (3x+2y)^2$

⑩ $(a-1)^2 - (b-1)^2$

⑪ $(x^2+3x+3)^2-(x^2+2x-6)^2$ ⑫ $(x^2-2x-4)^2-(x^2+2x-4)^2$

3. Expand Knowledge*

EXAMPLE 4.   * Factor. Assume that n represents a positive integer.

① $x^{2n}-1$ ② $x^{2n}+2x^n+1$

③ $x^{2n}+4x^n y^n+4y^{2n}$ ④ $x^{2n}-6x^n y^n-7y^{2n}$

⑤ $x^{4n} - x^{2n}y^{2n}$ ⑥ $x^{4n} + 2x^{2n}y^n + y^{2n}$

⑦ $x^{8n} - y^{8n}$

EXAMPLE 5. * Factor $x^4 + x^2 + 1$.
[Hint: Add and subtract x^2]

Mia's Algebra 2

3.6 Factoring Polynomials

1. Factoring Polynomials

   ※ **Factoring Sum or Difference of Cube**

Factoring Technique	Pattern and Example
$a^3 + b^3$ $= (a+b)(a^2 - ab + b^2)$	$\bullet^3 + \star^3 = (\bullet + \star)(\bullet^2 - \bullet\star + \star^2)$ same sign / opposite sign ex) $x^3 + 27 = (x)^3 + (3)^3$ $= (x+3)(x^2 - 3x + 9)$
$a^3 - b^3$ $= (a-b)(a^2 + ab + b^2)$	$\bullet^3 - \star^3 = (\bullet - \star)(\bullet^2 + \bullet\star + \star^2)$ same sign / opposite sign ex) $x^3 - 27 = (x)^3 - (3)^3$ $= (x-3)(x^2 + 3x + 9)$

EXAMPLE 1. Factor.

① $x^3 + 1$ 　　　　　　　　② $t^3 + 125$

③ $64 - y^3$

④ $1000 + r^3$

⑤ $5y^5 + 135y^2$

⑥ $16r^3m^2 - 2000m^2$

⑦ $24x^5 + 3x^2y^3$

⑧ $54x^5 - 128x^2y^3$

⑨ $x^6 + y^3$

⑩ $z^6 - 64$

⑪ $64x^6 - y^6$

⑫ $128p^6 - 2q^6$

2. Factoring using Substitution

Sometimes 'making a substitution' would help!

EXAMPLE 2. Factor.

① $a(b+2)-3(b+2)$

② $m(n+1)-(n+1)$

③ $p(q-2)-(2-q)$

④ $a(b-1)+(1-b)$

⑤ $(2x+1)^2 - 6(2x+1) + 8$

⑥ $(x-3)^2 - 7(x-3) + 12$

⑦ $(a+b)^2 - 3(a+b)c + 2c^2$

⑧ $(x-y)^2 - (x-y)z - 2z^2$

⑨ $(x-2y)(x-2y+2) + 1$

⑩ $2(x+y)(x+y+1) - 24$

3. Factoring Polynomials with at least 4 terms

If you have a polynomial with 4 terms, use GROUPING.
1) group into two binomials.

$$x^3 + x^2 + x + 1 = x^2(x+1) + (x+1)$$
$$= (x+1)(x^2+1)$$

(common factor)

2) group into perfect-square trinomial and a monomial

$$x^2 + 4x + 4 - 16y^2 = (x+2)^2 - 16y^2$$
$$= (x+2-4y)(x+2+4y)$$

If you have a polynomial with more than 4 terms, also use GROUPING.

EXAMPLE 3. Factor.

① $x^3 + x^2 - x - 1$

② $c^4 + c^3 - c^2 - c$

③ $20x^3 - 5x^2 + 8x - 2$

④ $10a^3 + 10a^2 + 3a + 3$

⑤ $9a^2b - 8a^2 - 9b + 8$

⑥ $5x^2y - 7x^2 - 7 + 5y$

⑦ $u^2 - v^2 - 2u - 2v$

⑧ $a^2 - b^2 + a + b$

⑨ $x^3 + y^3 + x^2y + xy^2$

⑩ $x^3 - y^3 - x^2y + xy^2$

⑪ $x^2 - 8x + 16 - 16y^2$

⑫ $z^2 + 10z + 25 - w^2$

⑬ $x^2 - y^2 - 6y - 9$

⑭ $a^2 - b^2 + 8b - 16$

⑮ $x^2y^3 - 3xy^3 + 2y^3 + x^2z^3 - 3xz^3 + 2z^3$ ⑯ $s^3t^2 + 6s^3t + 9s^3 + t^2p^3 + 6tp^3 + 9p^3$

4. Expand Knowledge*

EXAMPLE 4. * Factor. Assume that n represents a positive integer.

① $x^{3n} - y^{3n}$ ② $x^{6n} - y^{6n}$

③ $(x+y)^3 - (x-y)^3$ ④ $(a-b)^3 + (a+b)^3$

⑤ $(x+y)^4 - (x-y)^4$

⑥ $(x+y)^6 - (x-y)^6$

*All in one: Factoring Techniques

Number of terms	Factoring Technique	Formula or Examples
any number	GCF	$4a^3b^2 - 8a^2b = 4a^2b(ab - 2)$
two	Difference of squares	$a^2 - b^2 = (a - b)(a + b)$
two	Sum of Cubes	$a^3 + b^3 = (a + b)(a^2 - ab + b^2)$
two	Difference of Cubes	$a^3 - b^3 = (a - b)(a^2 + ab + b^2)$
three	perfect square trinomials	$a^2 + 2ab + b^2 = (a + b)^2$ $a^2 - 2ab + b^2 = (a - b)^2$
three	General trinomials	$acx^2 + (ad + bc)x + bd = (ax + b)(cx + d)$
four or more	grouping	$ax + bx + ay + by = (a + b)(x + y)$ $a^2 + 2ab + b^2 - c^2 = (a+b+c)(a+b-c)$

Mia's Algebra 2

3.7 Solving Polynomial Equations

1. Solving Polynomial Equations

    ☺ Vocabulary

    coefficient — variable
    $2x - 4 = 10$
    operater — constant

    equation: $2x - 4 = 10$ (expression)
    terms

    Expression : : a group of terms (separated by + or - signs)

    Equation: says two expressions are ① _____ .

    ex) $x^2 + 5x - 6 = 0$ or $x^2 = 6 - 5x$

    Zero-product property We use zero product property to find the solution of the equations.

    $AB = 0$ if and only if $A =$ ② ____ or $B =$ ③ ____

    ex) To find the roots of $x^2 + 5x - 6 = 0$
    $(x+6)(x-1) = 0$
    $x + 6 = 0$ or $x - 1 = 0$
    $x = -6$ or $x = 1$

    Root (solution) of an equation A value that satisfies the equation.

    ex) - 6 and 1 are the roots of $x^2 + 5x - 6 = 0$ because

    $(-6)^2 + 5(-6) - 6 = 0$ and $(1)^2 + 5(1) - 6 = 0$.

Blank : ① equal   ② 0   ③ 0

Double root A root of an equation that arises from a factor that occurs twice.

ex) 2 is a double root of the equation $(x - 2)(x - 2) = 0$.

EXAMPLE 1. Factor and solve the equation. Identify all double roots.

① $(x-2)(x+3)=0$ 　　　　　　　② $(x+4)(x-9)=0$

③ $(2x-5)(3x+1)=0$ 　　　　　　④ $(4x+7)(2x-9)=0$

⑤ $x(5-x)(5x+7)=0$ 　　　　　　⑥ $x(x+1)(2x-3)=0$

⑦ $(x-2)^2(x+4)=0$ 　　　　　　⑧ $(2-x)^2(2+x)=0$

⑨ $x^2 + 6x = 27$

⑩ $x^2 - 5x = 14$

⑪ $x + 1 = 6x^2$

⑫ $7 = 3x^2 + 20x$

⑬ $x^2 = 4x$

⑭ $5x^2 = 45x$

⑮ $x^2 = 4$

⑯ $5x^2 = 45$

⑰ $x^2 + 25 = 10x$ ⑱ $4x^2 = 4x - 1$

⑲ $x^2 = 4x^3$ ⑳ $x^3 = 18x - 7x^2$

㉑ $(x-2)(x-3) = 2$ ㉒ $(x+1)(x-5) = 7$

EXAMPLE 2. Factor and solve the equation. Identify all double roots.

① $x^4 - 13x^2 + 36 = 0$ 　　　　　　② $x^4 - 8x^2 + 16 = 0$

③ $t^6 + 16t^2 = 17t^4$ 　　　　　　④ $x^2(x^4 + 25) = 26x^4$

⑤ $(x-2)^3 = (x-2)^2$ 　　　　　　⑥ $(x-3)^3 = (x-3)^2$

⑦ $(x-2)^3 = (x-2)$ 　　　　　　⑧ $(x-3)^3 = (x-3)$

Part 3 Factoring and Expanding Polynomials

⑨ $(x^2 - 100)^2 = 0$ ⑩ $(x^2 - 8x - 9)^2 = 0$

⑪ $(x^2 - 2)^2 - 4(x^2 - 2) + 4 = 0$ ⑫ $(x^2 - 2)^2 - 9(x^2 - 2) + 14 = 0$

Mia's Algebra 2
3.8 Word Problems about Poly Equation

1. Problem Solving using Polynomial Equations

1) Numbers

> ☺ Tip: 3 consecutive integers : ①_____
>
> 3 consecutive odd integers : ②_____
>
> 3 consecutive even integers : ③_____

EXAMPLE 1. The sum of the squares of two consecutive negative even integers is 20. What are the numbers?

EXAMPLE 2. The sum of the squares of three consecutive positive odd integers is 371. What are the integers?

EXAMPLE 3. The difference between two positive numbers is 10. If their product is 144, find the smaller number.

Blank : ① x−1, x, x+1   ② x−2, x, x+2   ③ x−2, x, x+2

2) Ages

> ☺ Tip: When someone is x years old,
>
> age after a years $= x + a$
>
> age b years ago $= x - b$

EXAMPLE 4. The product of the ages of Sam and Katy is 100 less than the product of their ages in 5 years. If Sam is 3 years older than Katy, what are their current ages?

EXAMPLE 5. The product of the ages of Tim and Joey now is 114 more than the product of their ages 2 years ago. If Tim is 5 years older than Joey, what are their current ages?

3) Geometry

☺ Vocabulary:

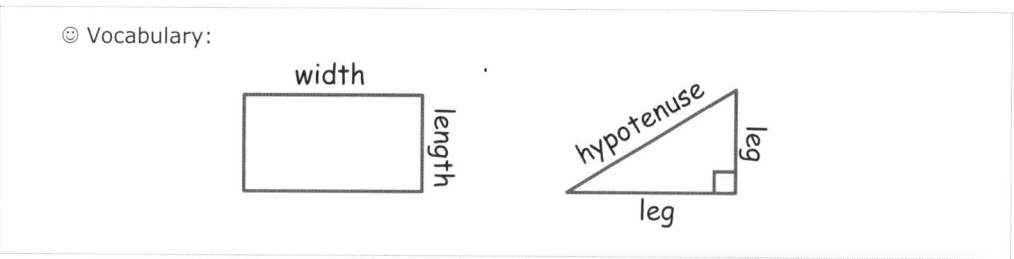

EXAMPLE 6. The area of a right triangle is 96 m². The length of one leg is 8 m less than twice the length of the other. Find the length of each leg.

EXAMPLE 7. A rectangle is 5 m longer than it is wide, and its area is 84 m². Find its dimensions.

EXAMPLE 8. An rectangle is inscribed in a circle with diameter 10cm. If the perimeter of the rectangle is 24cm, then what is the area of the rectangle?

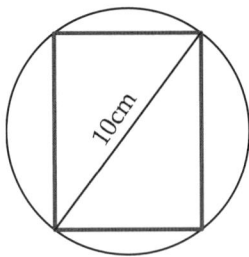

EXAMPLE 9. A rectangular lot has perimeter 46 ft and the diagonal of 17 ft. Find the area of the lot.

4) Changing Areas

> ☺ Tip: increased by 10: ① _____
>
> increased by 10%: ② _____

EXAMPLE 10. A farmer has a rectangular field that measures 100 feet by 80 feet. He plans to increase the area of the field by 50%. He will do this by increasing the length and the width by the same amount, x. What is the value of x?

EXAMPLE 11. If the length of each side of a square is increased by 6, the area is multiplied by 16. Find the length of one side of the original square

---

Blank : ① x + 10   ② (1+0.1)x = 1.1x

5) Border around Rectangle

EXAMPLE 12. A garden measuring 9 meters by 6 meters is to have a pedestrian pathway installed all around it. The pedestrian pathway area, *excluding the garden*, is 100 square meters. What will be the width of the pathway?

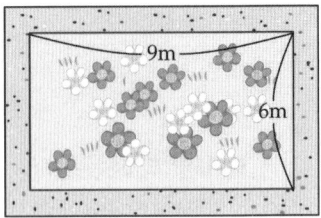

EXAMPLE 13. A wall painting is to be painted on a wall that is 9 m long and 10 m high. A border of uniform width is to surround the wall painting. If the wall painting is to cover 80% of the area of the wall, how wide must the border be?

EXAMPLE 14. A rectangular patio measures 20 meters by 12 meters. A walk of uniform width surrounds the patio. The total area of the patio and the walk is 560 m². How wide is the walk?

6) Making Box from Cardboard

EXAMPLE 15. You have to make a square-bottomed, unlidded box with a height of 3 inches and a volume of 48 cubic inches. You will be taking a piece of square cardboard, cutting 3 inches squares from each corner and folding up the edges. What should be the dimensions of the cardboard?

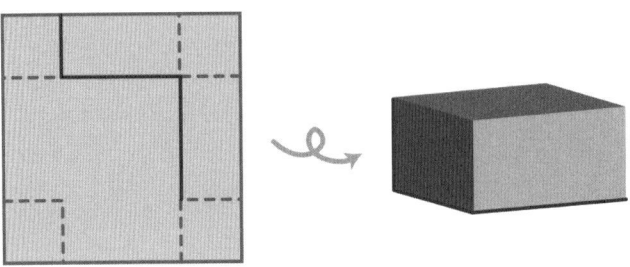

EXAMPLE 16. Tom cuts little squares with side 5 cm from the four corners of a square cardboard, and folds up the sides to form a cuboid box with no top. If the volume of the box is 500 cm³, what is the length of the side of the square cardboard?

7) Others

EXAMPLE 17. * A 10 inch x 2 inch x 2 inch rectangular prism with a square base is given in the figure. The vase has a solid base of height of 2 inches and the sides are each x inches thick. If the vase of the volume is 22 in³, then what is x?

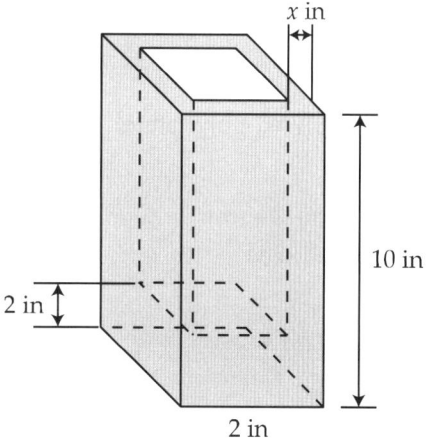

EXAMPLE 18. * Cube with length of $(x + 1)$cm is given. After a hole in the shape of rectangular prism with a dimension x, x, $x + 1$ is drilled through the cube in two sides as shown in the figure, the volume becomes 5 cm³. What is the value of x?

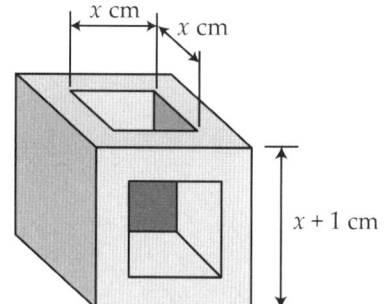

Mia's Algebra 2

3.9 Solving polynomial Inequalities

1. Solving polynomial Inequalities

   Sign diagram or **Sign graph** : A graph used to help find the solution set of a polynomial inequality.

   ※ How to solve polynomial inequalities
   ① Rearrange the terms and make f(x) > 0 form. (or <0, ≥0, ≤0)
   ② Find the roots of f(x) = 0 and label on the number line.
   ③ Pick a *test number* between every pair of roots.
   ④ Decide whether the polynomial is positive or negative between every pair of roots.

   ex)

   $(x-2)(x-5) < 0$

   $(1-x)(x+3) \leq 0$

   EXAMPLE 1. Solve the inequalities using the sign diagram.

   ☺ Tip: Usually around the double root, the sign does not change.

① $(x+1)(x-5) \geq 0$

② $(x-1)(x+7) \leq 0$

③ $b^2 - 4 < 0$

④ $t^2 - 3t < 0$

⑤ $3x^2 - 4x - 7 > 0$

⑥ $2x^2 - 7x - 9 \geq 0$

⑦ $x^2 - 10x + 25 \leq 0$

⑧ $4x^2 - 12x + 9 \leq 0$

⑨ $9x^2 + 24x + 16 > 0$ ⑩ $x^2 + 24x + 144 \geq 0$

⑪ $t(t-2)(t+3) < 0$ ⑫ $y(y-2)(y+2) \geq 0$

⑬ $t(t-2)^2(t+3) < 0$ ⑭ $y^2(y-2)(y+2)^2 \geq 0$

⑮ $x^4 - 9x^2 \geq 0$ ⑯ $x^3 - 16x^2 < 0$

⑰ $t^2 - 5t^3 < 0$

⑱ $x^2 - 4x^4 > 0$

⑲ $(x^2 + 1)(x^2 + x) < 0$

⑳ $(x^2 - 1)(x^2 - x) \geq 0$

㉑ $x^2(x^2 + 1) \leq 2x^3$

㉒ $x^2(x^2 + 25) \leq 10x^3$

Part 4
Quadratic Function

4.1 Imaginary Numbers

4.2 Complex numbers

4.3 Graphing Quadratic Functions

4.4 Vertex of Quadratic Graphs

4.5 Word Problems about Optimization

4.6 Finding Zeros by Factoring

4.7 Finding Zeros by Completing the Square

4.8 Quadratic Formula

4.9 Solving Equations in Quadratic Form

4.10 Quadratic Inequalities using graphs

4.11 Discriminant

4.12 Sum and product of the roots

Mia's Algebra 2

4.1 Imaginary Numbers

1. Imaginary Numbers

※ **Imaginary Number**

Try squaring some numbers and see if we can get a **negative1**:

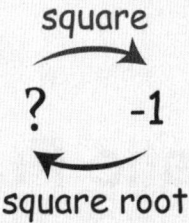

We **imagine** that there is such a *number*
which could multiply by itself (=square it) to get **-1**.
We will let that number as *i* (from '*i*'maginary number).

$$-1 = i^2 \qquad \sqrt{-1} = i$$

EXAMPLE 1. Simplify.

☺ Remember: $\sqrt{A}\sqrt{B} = \sqrt{AB}$ only when $A \geq 0, B \geq 0$.

① $\sqrt{-36}$ ② $\sqrt{-121}$

③ $\sqrt{-12}$ ④ $\sqrt{-20}$

⑤ $3\sqrt{-18}$

⑥ $5\sqrt{-27}$

⑦ $\sqrt{6}\sqrt{-12}$

⑧ $\sqrt{-14}\sqrt{7}$

⑨ $\sqrt{-5}\cdot\sqrt{-10}$

⑩ $\sqrt{-3}\sqrt{-15}$

⑪ $2i \cdot 5i$

⑫ $(-3i)\cdot 5i$

⑬ $(3i)^2$

⑭ $(-4i)^2$

⑮ $(i\sqrt{5})^2$

⑯ $(i2\sqrt{3})^2$

⑰ $(3i)(-i)^2(4i)$

⑱ $(-2i)(5i)(3i)^2$

⑲ $-\dfrac{3}{2i}$

⑳ $\dfrac{7}{3i}$

EXAMPLE 2. Simplify

① a) $\sqrt{-16} + \sqrt{-25}$ 　　　　　　　　b) $\sqrt{-16} \cdot \sqrt{-25}$

② a) $\sqrt{-2} + \sqrt{-8}$ 　　　　　　　　　b) $\sqrt{-2} \cdot \sqrt{-8}$

③ a) $3\sqrt{-18} + \sqrt{-8}$ 　　　　　　　b) $3\sqrt{-18} \cdot \sqrt{-8}$

④ a) $i\sqrt{32} - \sqrt{-50}$ 　　　　　　　　b) $i\sqrt{32} \cdot \sqrt{-50}$

2. Power of i

※ **Powers of** i

If we raise i by positive integer power;

$i^1 =$ ____ ①　　$i^2 =$ ____ ②　　$i^3 =$ ____ ③　　$i^4 =$ ____ ④

$i^5 =$ ____ ⑤　　$i^6 =$ ____ ⑥　　$i^7 =$ ____ ⑦　　$i^8 =$ ____ ⑧ ...

We can notice that imaginary number i "cycles" through 4 different values each time you multiply:

$i^{4k} = 1 \qquad i^{4k+1} = i \qquad i^{4k+2} = -1 \qquad i^{4k+3} = -i$

(multiples of 4)

EXAMPLE 3. Simplify.

> ☺ Tip: Let's say we divide n by 4, we have quotient Q and reminder R.
> Then we can say $n = $ ⑨_____   ex) $35 = 4 \cdot 8 + 3$

① i^6

② i^{16}

③ i^{37}

④ i^{22}

⑤ i^{63}

⑥ i^{87}

⑦ i^{916}

⑧ i^{132}

⑨ $i^{1000} + i^{1001} + i^{1002} + i^{1003}$

⑩ $i^{2019} + i^{2020} + i^{2021} + i^{2022}$

Blank : ① i ② -1 ③ -i ④ 1 ⑤ i ⑥ -1 ⑦ -i ⑧ 1 ⑨ 4Q + R

Part 4 Quadratic Function 197

3. Expand Knowledge*

EXAMPLE 4. * Simplify $i + i^2 + i^3 + \ldots + i^{2001}$

EXAMPLE 5. * Simplify $i + 2i^2 + 3i^3 + 4i^4 \ldots + 100i^{100}$.

EXAMPLE 6. * Simplify $\dfrac{1}{i} + \dfrac{1}{i^2} + \dfrac{1}{i^3} + \ldots + \dfrac{1}{i^{200}}$.

Mia's Algebra 2

4.2 Complex numbers

1. Complex Number

※ **Complex Number**

A complex Number is a combination of a ①_____ number and an ②_____ number.

Usually we use z to represent $a + bi$.

$$z = \underbrace{a + bi}_{\text{complex number}}$$

- real part: a
- imaginary part: bi ($\sqrt{-1}$)

2. Number System

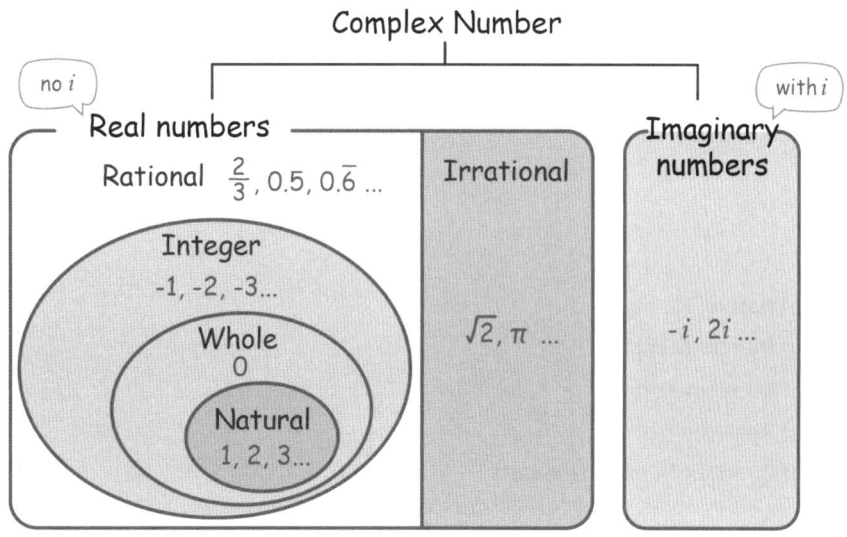

Blank : ① real   ② imaginary

Natural Numbers	1, 2, 3, 4...
Whole Numbers	①____, 1, 2, 3, . . .
Integer	. . . , -3, -2, -1, 0, 1, 2, 3, . . .
	= ②_____ + _____ + _____
Rational Number	numbers which can be written in ③_____
	ex) 2, 0.5, $\frac{1}{4}$, $-0.\bar{2}$ $(=-0.22222... = -\frac{2}{9})$
Irrational Number	numbers which is NOT rational
	ex) ④_____
Real Number	numbers in the number line
	= ⑤_____ + _____
Imaginary Number	numbers with i
Complex Number	$a + bi$

☺ Symbols

　　$\mathbb{N}$: Set of Natural Numbers

　　$\mathbb{Z}$: Set of Integer Numbers

　　$\mathbb{Q}$: Set of Quotient Numbers

　　$\mathbb{R}$: Set of Real Numbers

　　$\mathbb{C}$: Set of Complex Number Numbers

Blank : ① 0　　② negative + 0 + positive　　③ fraction　　④ $\sqrt{2}, \pi...$　　⑤ rational + irrational

EXAMPLE 1. Consider the numbers

$$\sqrt{-8},\ -22,\ \frac{0}{3},\ \frac{1}{2},\ \sqrt{21},\ 0.\overline{3},\ 0.3,\ i+5,\ \pi$$

a) Which of the numbers is a rational number?

b) Which of the numbers is an irrational number?

c) Which of the numbers is a real number?

d) Which of the numbers is a complex number?

3. Operation of Complex Number

※ **Equivalent complex number**

If $a + bi = c + di$, then ① _____.

※ **Conjugate of Complex number**

Conjugate of $a + bi$ is ② _____.

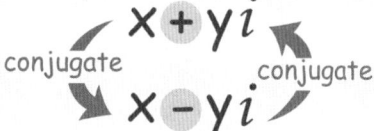

ex) Conjugate of $3 - 7i$: ③ _____

Conjugate of $i - 2$: ④ _____

Blank : ① $a = c,\ b = d$ ② $a - bi$ ③ $3 + 7i$ ④ $-i - 2$

EXAMPLE 2. Find the values of m and n that make each equation true.

① $15 - 28i = 4ni + (2m+1)$

② $(6-3m) + 3ni = 27i - 12$

③ $3m + 3i + 4 - ni = 16 - 3i$

④ $7 - 10i + n + 4mi = 3 - 6i$

EXAMPLE 3. Simplify.

① $(7-5i) + (-12+6i)$

② $(-5+3i) + (7i-12)$

③ $(10-4i) - 3(8-3i)$

④ $2(10+11i) - (17-21i)$

⑤ $i(2-5i)$

⑥ $2i(3i-4)$

⑦ $(2+i)(2+3i)$

⑧ $(3+i)(2-5i)$

⑨ $(2+i)(2-i)$

⑩ $(i+3)(3-i)$

⑪ $(-2+7i)(2+7i)$

⑫ $(4i-6)(6+4i)$

⑬ $(2+5i)^2$

⑭ $(3+4i)^2$

⑮ $(-1+\sqrt{3}i)^2$

⑯ $(-6-i)^2$

⑰ $(1+i)^2(1-i)^2$

⑱ $(\sqrt{5}+2i)^2(\sqrt{5}-2i)^2$

⑲ $(\sqrt{7}-3i)^2(\sqrt{7}+3i)^2$

⑳ $(7+i)^2(7-i)^2$

The product of complex conjugates is
a ①_____ number

Blank : ① real

EXAMPLE 4. Simplify.

> ☺ Tip: To make the denominator as a real number,
> we multiply ①_____ of the denominator on top and the bottom.

① $\dfrac{5}{3+i}$

② $\dfrac{3}{4-i}$

③ $\dfrac{2i+3}{i+2}$

④ $\dfrac{5+2i}{1-2i}$

⑤ $\dfrac{3-2i}{2i+3}$

⑥ $\dfrac{2-i}{i+2}$

Blank : ① conjugate

⑦ $\dfrac{-3+i\sqrt{5}}{-3-i\sqrt{5}}$ ⑧ $\dfrac{-4-i\sqrt{2}}{-4+i\sqrt{2}}$

EXAMPLE 5. Find the reciprocal of

① $-\sqrt{2}+3i$ ② $-\sqrt{5}-i\sqrt{3}$

4. Expand Knowledge*

EXAMPLE 6. * Simplify $(i-1)^{200} - (i+1)^{200}$.

☺ Tip: Use $(i+1)^2 = $ ①_____ and $(i-1)^2 = $ ②_____

EXAMPLE 7. * Simplify $\left(\dfrac{1+i}{1-i}\right)^{200} - \left(\dfrac{1-i}{1+i}\right)^{200}$.

☺ Tip: Use $\dfrac{1+i}{1-i} = $ ③_____ and $\dfrac{1-i}{1+i} = $ ④_____

Blank : ① 2i ② -2i ③ i ④ -i

Mia's Algebra 2

4.3 Graphing Quadratic Functions

1. Quadratic Functions

   ※ **Quadratic Functions**

   "*quad-*" means ① _____ ,

   so in quadratic functions the variable has degree of ② _____

   $$y = a\underline{x^2} + \underline{bx} + \underline{c}$$

   - square → x^2
   - ③ _____ Term
   - linear Term
   - ④ _____ Term

   a, b and c are known values. a can't be ⑤ _____ .

   ☺ Vocabulary

   A quadratic Function has a shape of ⑥ _____ .

   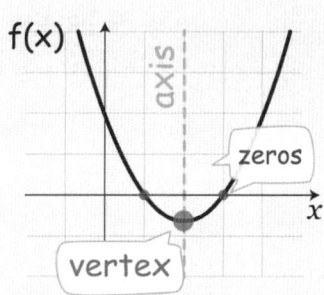

   The curve is symmetrical (mirror image) about the

   ⑦ _____ of symmetry.

   The very lowest (or very highest) point, called the

   ⑧ _____ .

Blank : ① square   ② 2   ③ quadratic   ④ constant   ⑤ 0   ⑥ parabola   ⑦ axis   ⑧ vertex

2. Three Forms of Quadratic Functions

※ **Standard Form** :

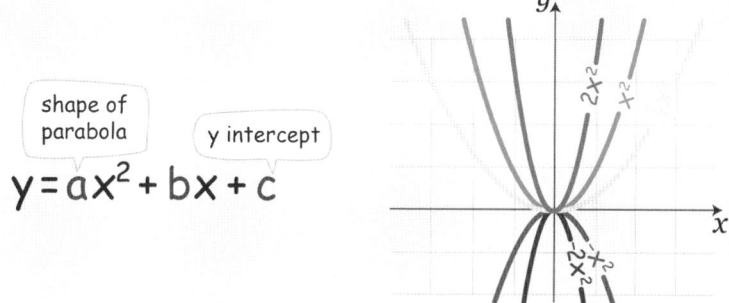

$$y = ax^2 + bx + c$$

(shape of parabola) (y intercept)

a determines the ① _____ of the parabola

(when $a > 0$: concave up, $a < 0$: concave down)

c determines ② _____ (when $x = 0$)

※ **Vertex Form** : vertex at ③ _____

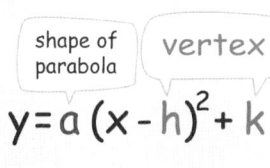
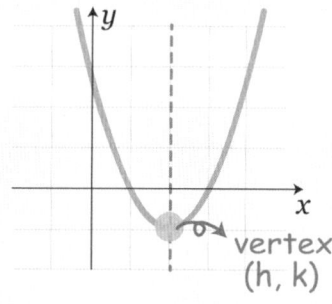

$$y = a(x - h)^2 + k$$

(shape of parabola) (vertex)

vertex (h, k)

※ **Factored Form** : zeros (=④ _____ =⑤ _____) at ⑥ _____

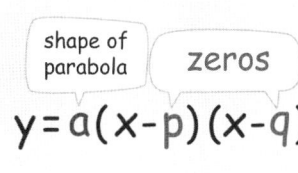
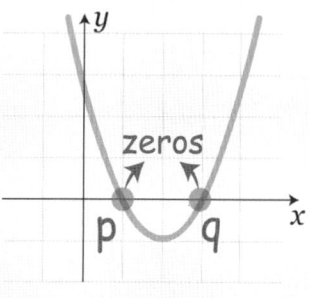

$$y = a(x-p)(x-q)$$

(shape of parabola) (zeros)

Blank : ① shape   ② y intercept   ③ (h, k)   ④ roots   ⑤ x intercepts   ⑥ x = p, x = q

EXAMPLE 1. Graph the function briefly. If you have vertex form, label the vertex. If you have factored form, label the zeros.

① $y = \dfrac{1}{2}(x-5)^2 + 3$

② $y = 5(x-3)^2 - 2$

③ $y = -\dfrac{3}{2}(x+1)^2 - 2$

④ $y = -\dfrac{5}{2}(x+5)^2 + 12$

⑤ $y = 6(x-4)^2$

⑥ $y = -0.2(x+0.6)^2$

⑦ $y = -7(x+1)(x-5)$

⑧ $y = 8(x-3)(x-1)$

⑨ $y = 0.4(x - 0.2)(x + 0.8)$

⑩ $y = -\dfrac{4}{3}(x + 0.5)(x + 0.7)$

3. Standard Form → Vertex Form (method 1)

※ How to change standard form $y = ax^2 + bx + c$ to vertex form $y = a(x - h)^2 + k$

1) Use the formula $x = -\dfrac{b}{2a}$ (☞in this chapter)

2) Complete the square

3) Find the midpoint of the x intercept

※ **Changing standard form to vertex form I** ($ax^2 + bx + c \to a(x-h)^2 + k$)

1) Use formula $x = -\dfrac{b}{2a}$

$y = ax^2 + bx + c$ has the axis of symmetry at

① _____.

And use $x =$ ② _____, and plug into quadratic to find y.

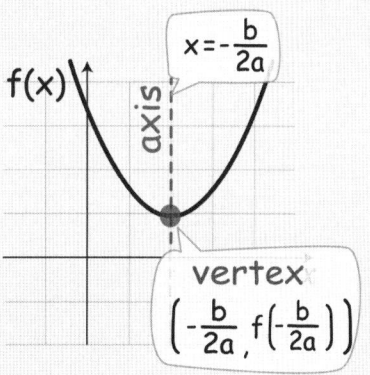

Blank : ① $x = -\dfrac{b}{2a}$ ② $-\dfrac{b}{2a}$

EXAMPLE 2. Solve the problem.

a. Find the equation of the axis of symmetry, and the vertex using $-\dfrac{b}{2a}$.

b. Use this information to graph the function and label the vertex, y intercept.

① $f(x) = x^2 + 6x + 8$

② $f(x) = -x^2 - 2x + 2$

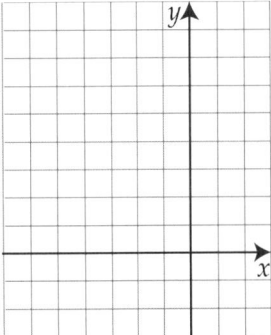

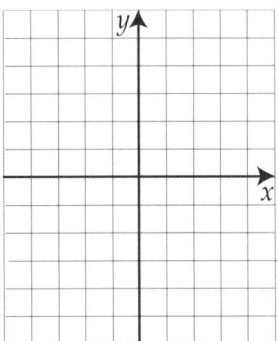

③ $f(x) = 2x^2 - 4x + 2$

④ $f(x) = x^2 - 4x + 4$

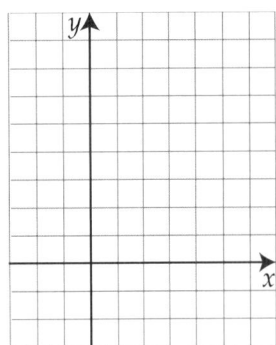

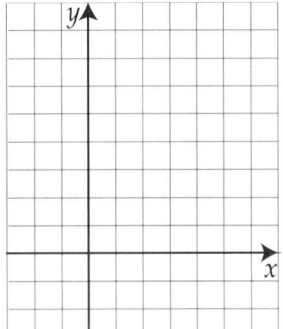

※ Maximum and Minimum of Quadratic

The minimum or the maximum of a quadratic $y = ax^2 + bx + c$ occurs at the

①_____.

When $a > 0$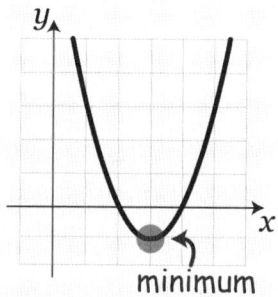

When $a < 0$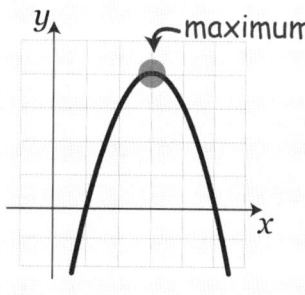

☺ Careful! Make sure you answer ②_____ for the max/min value.

EXAMPLE 3. Find the maximum or minimum value using $x = -\dfrac{b}{2a}$.

① $f(x) = x^2 + 4x - 7$

② $f(x) = -x^2 + 6x - 4$

Blank : ① vertex   ② y value

③ $f(x) = 10 + 6x - x^2$

④ $f(x) = 16 + 4x - 2x^2$

⑤ $f(x) = -5x^2$

⑥ $f(x) = 10x^2 + 3$

⑦ $f(x) = -2x^2 + 6x$

⑧ $f(x) = x^2 - 7x$

EXAMPLE 4. Match each graph with the description of the constant in the equation $y = ax^2 + bx + c$.

I.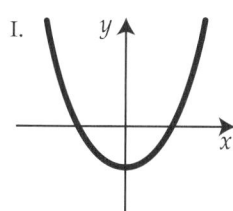
II.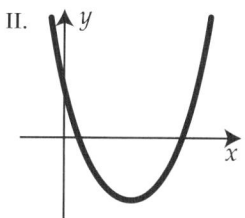
III.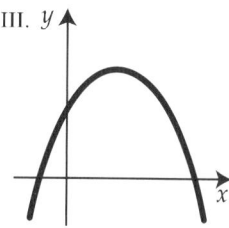

VI.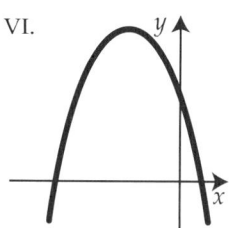
V.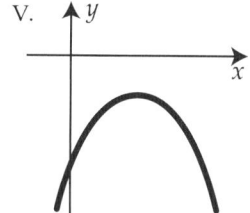
IV.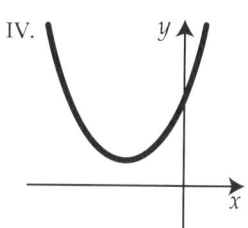

① $a > 0, b < 0, c > 0$

② $a < 0, b > 0, c < 0$

③ $a > 0, b = 0, c < 0$

④ $a > 0, b > 0, c > 0$

⑤ $a < 0, b > 0, c > 0$

⑥ $a < 0, b < 0, c > 0$

4. Expand Knowledge*

EXAMPLE 5. * Graph of two quadratic function $y = 5x^2$ and $y = 8ax^2$ is given as shown. What could be the interval of the value of a?

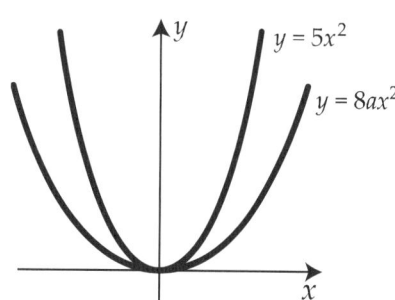

EXAMPLE 6. * In the xy-plane, find the equation of the line that intersects the graph of $y = \frac{1}{2}x^2$ at a point $(-2, p)$ and $(q, 8)$ where $q < 0$.

EXAMPLE 7. * Quadratic function $y = (x-h)^2 + k$ passes through a point $(2, 0)$ and the vertex passes through the line $y = -x$. Find the value of h and k. $(k < -1)$

Mia's Algebra 2

4.4 Vertex of Quadratic Graphs

1. Completing the square

  ※ How to '**complete the square**'? (= making perfect square trinomial)
  Take ① _____ and ② _____ the number in front of x!

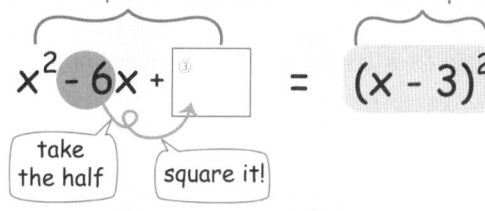

EXAMPLE 1. Find the value of c that makes each a perfect square trinomial. Then write the trinomial as a perfect square.

① $x^2 + 10x + c$

② $x^2 - 12x + c$

③ $x^2 - 22x + c$

④ $x^2 + 18x + c$

⑤ $x^2 + 3x + c$

⑥ $x^2 - x + c$

Blank : ① the half ② square ③ 9

⑦ $x^2 - 0.8x + c$ ⑧ $x^2 + 2.2x + c$

⑨ $x^2 + \dfrac{3}{5}x + c$ ⑩ $x^2 - \dfrac{x}{2} + c$

2. Standard Form → Vertex Form (method 2)

※ How to change standard form $y = ax^2 + bx + c$ to vertex form $y = a(x-h)^2 + k$

① Use the formula $x = -\dfrac{b}{2a}$

② Complete the square (☞ in this chapter)

③ Find the midpoint of the x intercept

※ **Changing standard form to vertex form II** ($ax^2 + bx + c \to a(x-h)^2 + k$)

2) Complete the square

① When the number in front of x is 1 ($a = 1$)

$y = x^2 + 2x + 3$

$ = x^2 + 2x \;\boxed{①}\;\boxed{②}\; + 3$ i) complete the square

$ = (x+1)^2 - 1 + 3$ ii) factor the perfect square trinomial

$ = (x+1)^2 + 2$ iii) Simplify

Blank : ① +1   ② −1

EXAMPLE 2. Write each quadratic function in vertex form and find the vertex. Then graph the function and label the vertex.

① $y = x^2 - 10x + 22$

② $y = x^2 + 8x + 7$

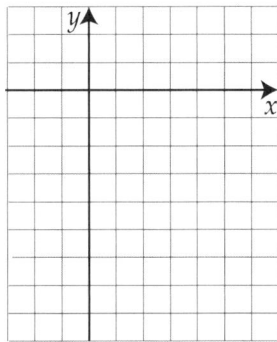

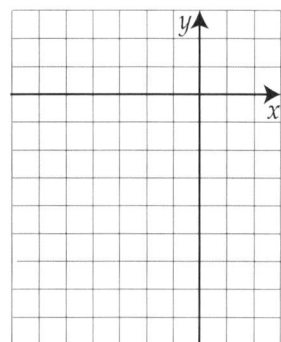

③ $y = 6x + x^2$

④ $y = -10x + x^2$

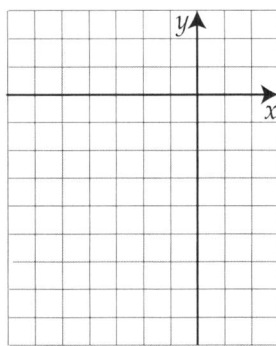

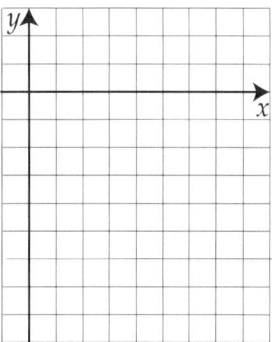

⑤ $y = x + x^2 + 4$ ⑥ $y = x^2 - 5x + 5$

② When the number in front of x is not 1 ($a \neq 1$)

$y = \underbrace{-2x^2 + 4x}_{\text{factor out } -2} + 3$

$= -2(x^2 - 2x \; \boxed{①} \; \boxed{②}) + 3$ i) Factor the a from the first two terms
　　　　　　　complete　　　　　　　　ii) complete the square

$= -2(\;(x-1)^2 \; \boxed{③}\;) + 3$ iii) factor the perfect square trinomial

$= -2(x-1)^2 \; \boxed{④} \; + 3$ iv) distribute a

$= -2(x-1)^2 + 5$ v) Simplify

Blank : ① +1   ② −1   ③ −1   ④ +2

EXAMPLE 3. Write each quadratic function in vertex form and find the vertex. Then graph the function and label the vertex.

① $y = -x^2 + 6x - 5$

② $y = 3x^2 - 12x + 7$

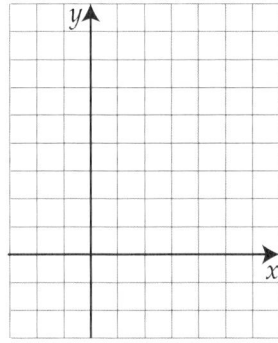
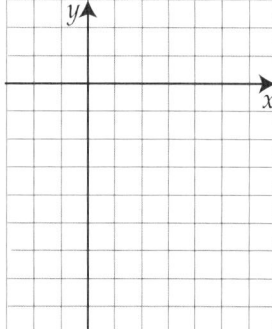

③ $y = -4x^2 + 16x - 13$

④ $y = -5x^2 - 10x + 7$

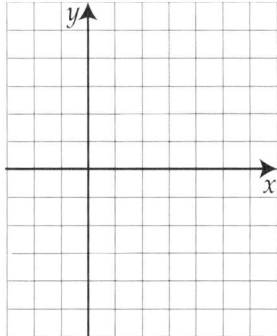
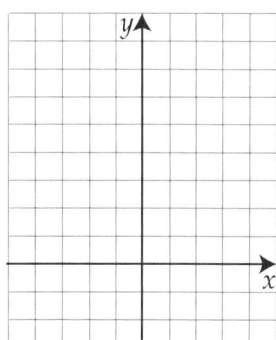

⑤ $y = 4x^2 + 8x$

⑥ $y = -4x^2 + 16x$

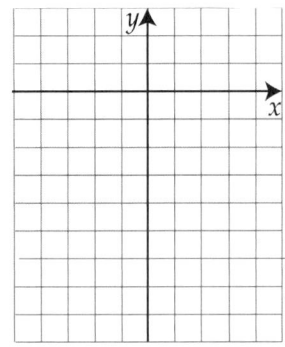

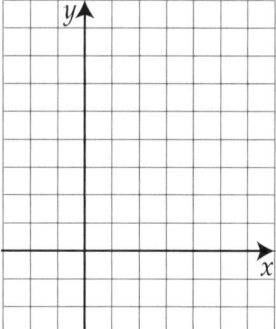

⑦ $y = 3x^2 - 3x + 1$

⑧ $y = 4x^2 + x + 3$

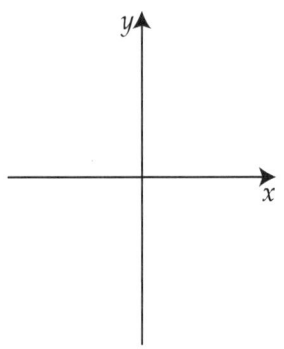

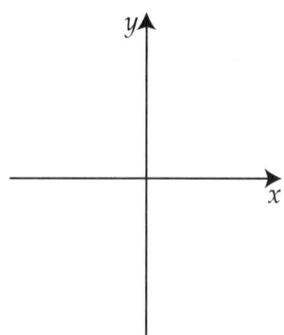

⑨ $y = 2x^2 - x + 10$ 　　　　　⑩ $-x^2 + 5x + 2$

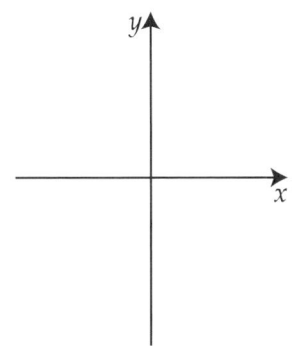
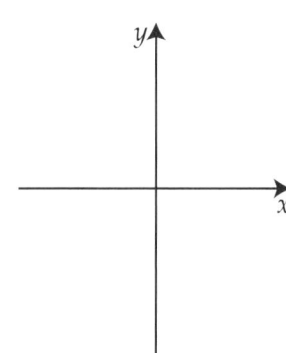

EXAMPLE 4. Find the maximum or minimum value by completing the square.

① $f(x) = 13 + 8x + 2x^2$ 　　　　② $f(x) = x^2 + 12x + 18$

③ $f(x) = -3x^2 + 4x - 1$ 　　　　④ $f(x) = 1 + 4x - 2x^2$

⑤ $f(x) = 10x^2 - 5x + 2$

EXAMPLE 5. Write an equation for the parabola *in vertex form* with the given information or graph.

①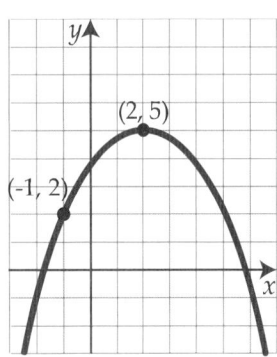

②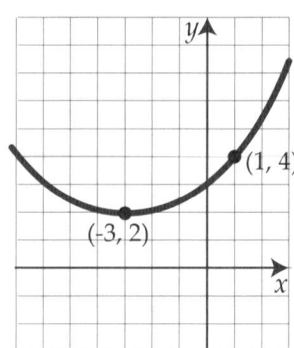

③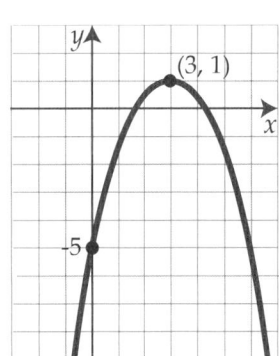

④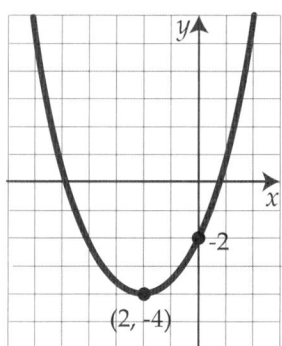

⑤ Vertex is at (-1, 7), pass through the point (-2, 4)

⑥ Vertex is at (4, 5), has x intercept at 2

EXAMPLE 6. Match each graph with the description of the constant in the equation $y = a(x-h)^2 + k$.

I.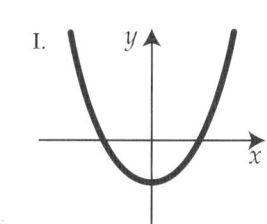

II.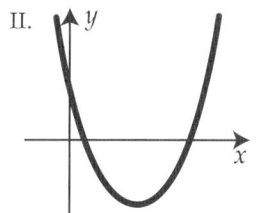

III.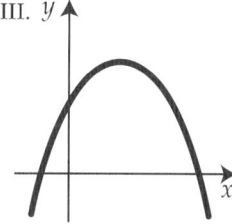

VI.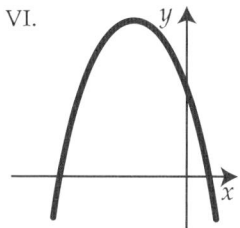

V.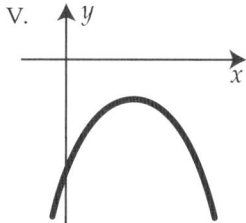

IV.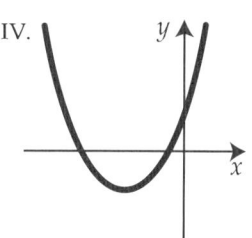

① $a < 0, h > 0, k > 0$

② $a < 0, h < 0, k > 0$

③ $a > 0, h = 0, k < 0$

④ $a > 0, h < 0, k < 0$

⑤ $a > 0, h > 0, k < 0$

⑥ $a < 0, h > 0, k < 0$

EXAMPLE 7. Which step is incorrect?

$$y = -\frac{1}{2}x^2 + 2x + 3 \qquad \text{I}$$

$$= -\frac{1}{2}(x^2 - 4x) + 3 \qquad \text{II}$$

$$= -\frac{1}{2}(x^2 - 4x + 4 - 4) + 3 \qquad \text{III}$$

$$= -\frac{1}{2}(x-2)^2 - 4 + 3 \qquad \text{IV}$$

$$= -\frac{1}{2}(x-2)^2 - 1$$

3. Expand Knowledge*

EXAMPLE 8. * If the graph of $y = a(x-b)^2 + c$ pass through the first, third and fourth quadrant, then what is the sign of a, b and c?

EXAMPLE 9.* Quadratic Function $y = 2(x-1)^2 + 3$ is shifted to the right 3 units, down 2 units, and reflected over x axis. What is the new quadratic function after the transformation?

EXAMPLE 10. * If a quadratic function has an axis of symmetry at $x = -3$ and passes through the point $(0, 2)$, $(-4, -6)$, and $(2, p)$, then what is the value of p?

EXAMPLE 11. * Quadratic function $y = kx^2 + 8x - 3$ has a minimum value p at $x = -1$. What is the value of k and p?

EXAMPLE 12. * Find the maximum value of $\dfrac{1}{(x^2 - 8x + 26)^4}$.

Mia's Algebra 2

4.5 Word Problems about Optimization

1. Optimization

In Optimization problem, we look for maximum or minimum.

☺ Reminder: Maximum or minimum of quadratic function occurs at the ①_____.

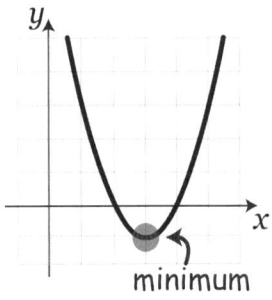
minimum

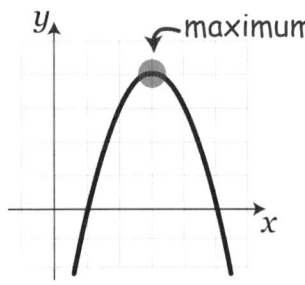
maximum

※ **How to find maximum or minimum of f**

i) First, find the quadratic function of f. (in terms of one variable)

ii) Second, find the vertex of f using $-\dfrac{b}{2a}$ or by completing the square.

iii) Third, careful what you have to answer. Is it x? Or is it y(=max/min value)?

Blank : ① vertex

1) Height of the Ball

EXAMPLE 1. The height h meters of a baseball t seconds after being hit is given by $h(t) = -16t^2 + 80t + 3$.

a) At what time does the ball reaches its maximum height?

b) What is the maximum height that the baseball reaches?

EXAMPLE 2. We are standing on the top of a 720 ft tall building and throw a small object upward. The object's distance from the ground, measured in feet, after t seconds is $h(t) = -16t^2 + 192t + 720$. At what time does the ball reaches its maximum height?

2) Perimeter and Area

EXAMPLE 3. The perimeter of a rectangle is 20 inches. Find the dimensions and the maximum area of a rectangle.

EXAMPLE 4. Jenny is constructing a garden and is using a wall as one side of the garden. If she has 16 m of fencing and wants to use it all, what is the largest possible area of the garden she could make?

EXAMPLE 5. A farmer with 100 ft of fencing wants to enclose a rectangle flower garden. He has 3 different kinds of flowers to plant so he will use part of the fencing to build two fences in the middle to divide into 3 sections as shown in the figure. Find the dimension that maximizes the area of the garden.

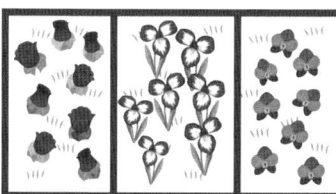

EXAMPLE 6. Two rectangular pens are to be made from 600 yards of fencing as seen below. Determine the dimensions that will produce the maximum area.

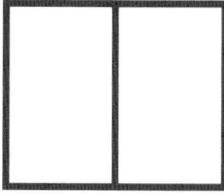

EXAMPLE 7. * An Athletic field with a perimeter of 40 mile consists of a rectangle with a semicircle at each end, as shown below. Find the radius of the semicircle that yield the greatest area of the Athletic field.

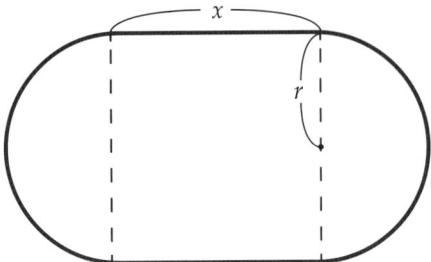

3) Inscribed Rectangle

EXAMPLE 8. A rectangle is bounded by the x-axis and the y-axis with a vertex on line $y = -2x + 4$ as shown.

a) Write a function for the area of the rectangle in terms of x.

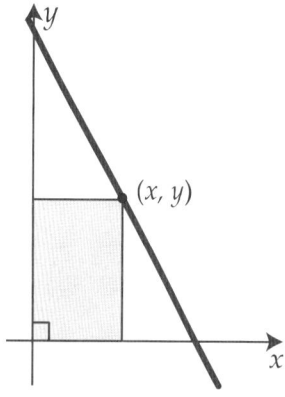

b) What is the largest area of the rectangle and the dimension?

EXAMPLE 9. A right isosceles triangle ABC with hypotenuse (longest side) 36cm is given. A rectangle is inscribed as shown. What is the largest area of the rectangle?

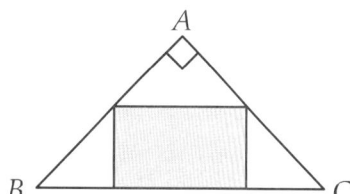

EXAMPLE 10. A rectangle is inscribed with its base on the x axis and upper corners on the parabola $y = -x^2 + 5$. What is the largest perimeter of the rectangle?

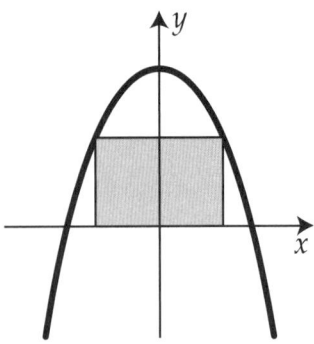

EXAMPLE 11. * A rectangle is inscribed with its base on the x axis and upper corners on the parabola $y = -x^2 + 4x + 5$. What is the largest perimeter of the rectangle?

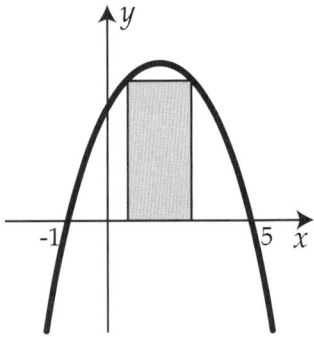

4) Max or Min Distance

EXAMPLE 12. What is the minimum vertical distance between $y = x^2 + 1$ and $y = x - x^2$?

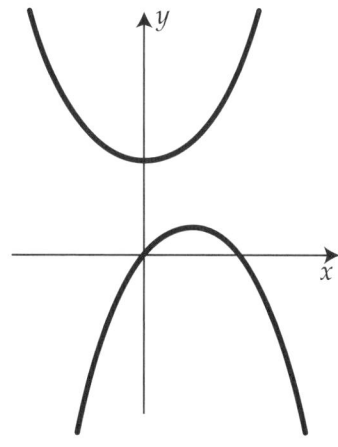

EXAMPLE 13. What is the minimum vertical distance between the line $y = x$ and the parabola $y = x^2 + 3$?

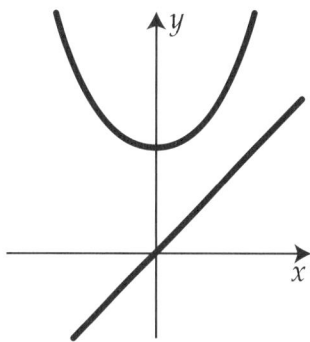

5) Maximum Profit

> Revenue = (Price) x (Number of items sold)

EXAMPLE 14. * A company finds that if they price their product at $60, they can sell 600 items of it. For $5 increase in the price, the number of items sold will decrease by 10.

a) Let x be the number of price increase from $60. Find a formula for the revenue R(x).

b) Find the price of the item that guarantees the maximum revenue.

c) Find the maximum revenue.

EXAMPLE 15. * A shop sells about 100 t-shirts each month for $8 each. The shop owner estimates that for each $2 increase in the price, he will sell about 10 fewer t-shirts per month. How much should the owner charge for each mug in order to maximize the monthly income from their sales?

Mia's Algebra 2

4.6 Finding Zeros by Factoring

1. Factored form of Quadratic

   ※ **Factored Form of Quadratic**

   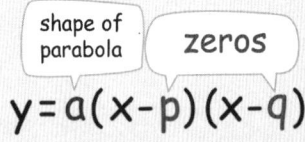

   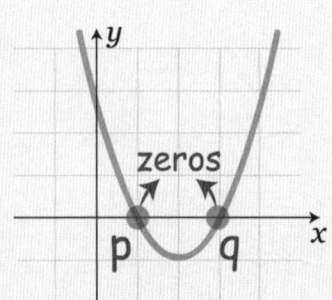

   EXAMPLE 1. Write a quadratic equation with the given zeros. Write the equation in the form $ax^2 + bx + c$ with integer coefficient.

   ① 3, −4

   ② −8, −2

   ③ 1, 6

   ④ 10, 5

   ⑤ −4

   ⑥ 2

⑦ $-\dfrac{1}{3}, 2$ ⑧ $3, \dfrac{4}{5}$

⑨ $\dfrac{2}{7}, -\dfrac{1}{3}$ ⑩ $-\dfrac{4}{3}, -\dfrac{3}{4}$

2. x-intercept of Quadratic Equation

To find the x intercept of a quadratic function $y = ax^2 + bx + c$, then we set $ax^2 + bx + c = $ ①_____ and find the solution.

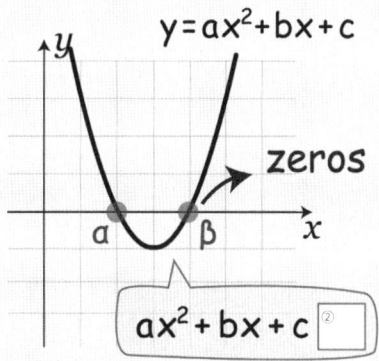

☺ Easy way to remember:
x intercept = root = zero = solution

※ We can solve $ax^2 + bx + c = 0$ using three methods
① By factoring (☞in this chapter)
② By completing the square
③ Using Quadratic Formula

Blank : ① 0 ② = 0

EXAMPLE 2. Write each quadratic function in factored form. Then graph the function and label the x intercept, y intercept.

① $y = -x^2 - 10x - 24$

② $y = -4x^2 + 8x$

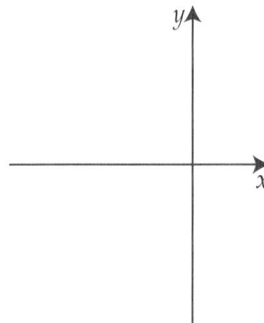
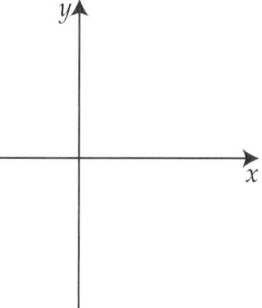

③ $y = 2x^2 + 12x$

④ $y = x^2 + x - 30$

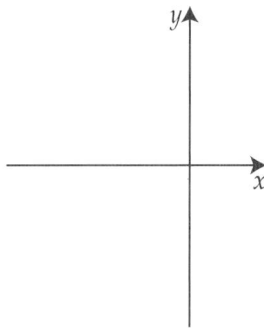
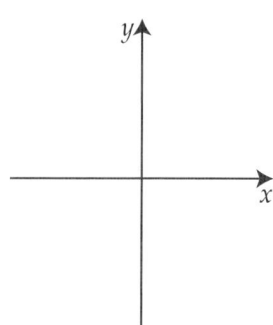

⑤ $y = 2x^2 - 7x - 9$

⑥ $y = 3x^2 - 4x - 7$

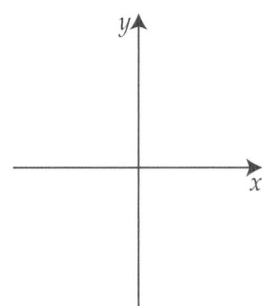
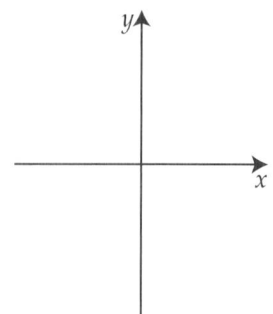

⑦ $y = -x^2 - 24x - 144$ ⑧ $y = -x^2 + 6x - 9$

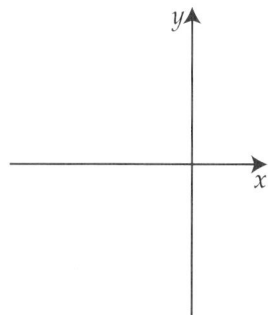
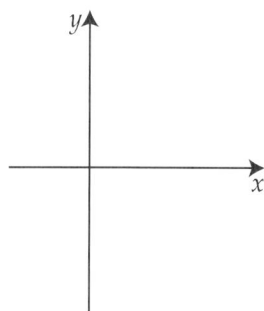

EXAMPLE 3. Write an equation for the parabola with the given information or graph.

①
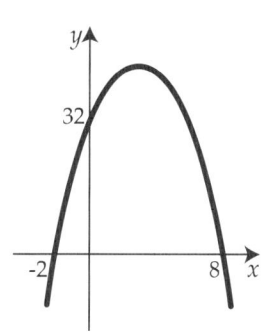

②
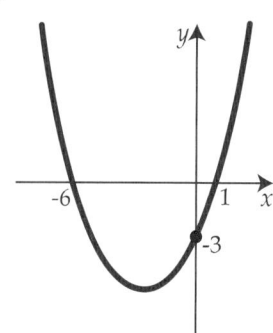

③
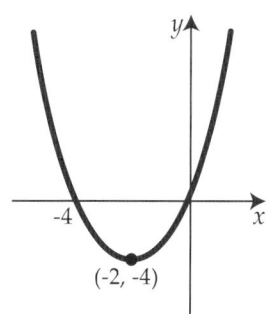

④
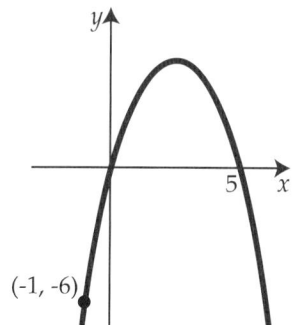

3. Expand Knowledge*

EXAMPLE 4. * For the graph of $y = -x^2 + 6x + 16$, let the x intercepts as A, B and y intercept as C. Then what is the area of the triangle ABC?

EXAMPLE 5. *A quadratic function passes through the point $(a-2, 0)$ and $(a+6, 0)$. Find the x coordinate of the vertex in terms of a.

Mia's Algebra 2

4.7 Finding Zeros by Completing Square

1. Square root property

   ※ **Square Root Property**

   $$x^2 = k \implies x = \pm\sqrt{k}$$

   Where k is a constant.

   ☺ Careful! $x^2 = 4 \implies x = \boxed{①} \implies x = \pm 2$

   But $\sqrt{4} = \boxed{②}$ (since $\sqrt{}$ means principal square root (=positive square root))

   EXAMPLE 1. Solve the equation by using the Square Root Property.

   ☺ Tip: Remember, $\sqrt{-k} = i\sqrt{k}$

   ① $x^2 = 5$ ② $x^2 = 6$

   ③ $x^2 + 4 = 0$ ④ $3 + x^2 = 0$

   ⑤ $(x-1)^2 + 5 = 0$ ⑥ $(1-x)^2 = 5$

   Blank : ① $\pm\sqrt{4}$ ② 2

⑦ $(2-3x)^2 - 16 = 0$

⑧ $9 + (2x+3)^2 = 0$

⑨ $3(x-2)^2 = -12$

⑩ $\dfrac{(x+3)^2}{4} = 8$

⑪ $x^2 + 10x + 25 = 16$

⑫ $x^2 - 14x + 49 = 9$

⑬ $9x^2 - 6x + 1 = -12$

⑭ $x^2 - 2x + 1 = -8$

2. Finding Zeros by Completing the Square

※ We can solve $ax^2 + bx + c = 0$ using three methods
  ① By factoring
  ② By completing the square (☞ in this chapter)
  ③ Using Quadratic Formula

※ How to solve $ax^2 + bx + c = 0$ by completing the square
  i) Change to vertex form
  ii) Solve for x

ex)

$-2x^2 + 4x + 3 = 0$ (factor out -2) $\longrightarrow$ $-2(x-1)^2 + 5 = 0$

$-2(x^2 - 2x \boxed{①} \boxed{②}) + 3 = 0$ (complete) $\qquad (x-1)^2 = \boxed{④}$

$-2(x-1)^2 \boxed{③} + 3 = 0 \qquad\qquad x - 1 = \pm\sqrt{\dfrac{5}{2}}$

(vertex form) $-2(x-1)^2 + 5 = 0 \qquad\qquad x = 1 \pm \dfrac{\sqrt{10}}{2}$

EXAMPLE 2. Solve the equation by completing the square.
  ① $x^2 - 10x - 11 = 0$ ② $x^2 - 12x + 27 = 0$

Blank : ① +1 ② −1 ③ +2 ④ $\dfrac{5}{2}$

③ $x^2 + 3x - 9 = 0$ ④ $x^2 + x + 7 = 0$

⑤ $5x^2 + 20x + 14 = 0$ ⑥ $2x^2 + 8x + 7 = 0$

⑦ $-x^2 + 2x - 3 = 0$ ⑧ $5x^2 - 2x + 1 = 0$

⑨ $4x^2 = 7x - 2$ ⑩ $2x^2 - 3x = 9$

⑪ $x^2 - \dfrac{x}{5} + \dfrac{7}{10} = 0$ ⑫ $x^2 - 2x + \dfrac{7}{6} = 0$

⑬ $0.7x^2 + 0.5x + 0.1 = 0$ ⑭ $0.1x^2 - 0.2x = 0.1$

Mia's Algebra 2

4.8 Quadratic Formula

1. Quadratic Formula

> ※ We can solve $ax^2 + bx + c = 0$ using three methods
> ① By factoring
> ② By completing the square
> ③ Using Quadratic Formula (☞ in this chapter)

If you have an equation of the form "**ax² + bx + c = 0**" (a≠0), we can solve it by completing the square.

$$ax^2 + bx + c = 0$$

$$a\left(x^2 + \frac{b}{a}x\right) + c = 0$$

$$a\left(x^2 + \frac{b}{a}x + \boxed{①} \boxed{②}\right) + c = 0$$

↳ complete

$$a\left(x + \boxed{③}\right)^2 \boxed{④} + c = 0$$

$$a\left(x + \frac{b}{2a}\right)^2 = \boxed{⑤}$$

$$\left(x + \frac{b}{2a}\right)^2 = \boxed{⑥}$$

$$x + \frac{b}{2a} = \boxed{⑦}$$

$$x = \boxed{⑧}$$

Blank : ① $+\dfrac{b^2}{4a^2}$ ② $-\dfrac{b^2}{4a^2}$ ③ $+\dfrac{b}{2a}$ ④ $-\dfrac{b^2}{4a}$ ⑤ $\dfrac{b^2}{4a} - c$ ⑥ $\dfrac{b^2 - 4ac}{4a^2}$ ⑦ $\pm\dfrac{\sqrt{b^2 - 4ac}}{2a}$ ⑧ $-\dfrac{b}{2a} \pm \dfrac{\sqrt{b^2 - 4ac}}{2a}$

※ **Quadratic Formula**

$$ax^2 + bx + c = 0$$

$$x = \frac{-b \pm \sqrt{b^2 - 4ac}}{2a}$$ — Quadratic Formula

EXAMPLE 1. Solve the equation by using the Quadratic formula.

① $x^2 - 8x + 14 = 0$ ② $x^2 + x + 9 = 0$

③ $0.6x^2 + x + 0.3 = 0$ ④ $0.2x^2 + x + 0.1 = 0$

⑤ $-8x^2 - 7x = 2$ ⑥ $-5x^2 = 5x + 2$

⑦ $x^2 - \dfrac{2}{3}x = -\dfrac{5}{6}$

⑧ $\dfrac{1}{3}x^2 - x + \dfrac{1}{3} = 0$

⑨ $x^2 - x\sqrt{3} - 2 = 0$

⑩ $x^2 + x\sqrt{2} - 3 = 0$

⑪ $z^2 + iz + 2 = 0$

⑫ $z^2 - 2iz - 1 = 0$

EXAMPLE 2. Find the x intercept of the quadratic by using the method of your choice. Then graph the function and label the x intercept.

① $y = x^2 - x - 6$

② $y = -5x^2 + 7x - 2$

③ $y = -x^2 - 4x + 7$

④ $y = -x^2 + 5x + 4$

⑤ $y = 2x^2 + 4x + 3$

⑥ $y = 2x^2 - x + 4$

2. Expand Knowledge

EXAMPLE 3. * Solve $z^2 - (2+i)z + (i+1) = 0$

※ Alternative Form of **Quadratic Formula**

$$ax^2 + 2Bx + c = 0 \quad \text{(when even)}$$

$$x = \frac{-B \pm \sqrt{B^2 - ac}}{a}$$

EXAMPLE 4. * Solve the equation by using the Quadratic formula.

① $2x^2 + 8x + 7 = 0$ 　　　　　　　② $x^2 - 12x + 7 = 0$

③ $x^2 - 6x + 11 = 0$ 　　　　　　　④ $3x^2 + 4x + 6 = 0$

Mia's Algebra 2

4.9 Solving Equations in Quadratic Form

1. Equations in Quadratic Form

※ Equations in Quadratic Form

$$x^2 - 2x - 3 = 0 \quad \text{is a quadratic in } x.$$

$$(3x+2)^2 - 2(3x+2) - 3 = 0 \quad \text{is a quadratic in } 3x+2.$$

$$x - 2\sqrt{x} - 3 = 0 \quad \text{is a quadratic in } ①\underline{\quad\quad}.$$

Equation in quadratic form can be written as;

$$a[f(x)]^2 + b[f(x)] + c = 0$$

(function of x)

When solving an equation in quadratic form,
it is helpful to replace f(x) by a single variable z or t.

EXAMPLE 1. Solve the equation.

☺ Tip: $x^2 = 2 \implies$ ②_____ $x^2 = -2 \implies$ ③_____

$\sqrt{x} = 2 \implies$ ④_____ $\sqrt{x} = -2 \implies$ ⑤_____

Blank : ① $\sqrt{x}$ ② $\pm\sqrt{2}$ ③ $\pm\sqrt{2}\,i$ ④ 4   ⑤ ∅ (no solution)

① a) $(x+2)^2 + 7(x+2) - 30 = 0$

② a) $(1-3x)^2 + 6(1-3x) - 16 = 0$

b) $y^4 + 7y^2 - 30 = 0$

b) $\left(\dfrac{1}{x}\right)^2 + 6\left(\dfrac{1}{x}\right) - 16 = 0$

③ a) $3(2y-1)^2 - 8(2y-1) + 5 = 0$

④ a) $2(x+3)^2 + 12 = 11(x+3)$

b) $3x^{-2} - 8x^{-1} + 5 = 0$

b) $2x^{-2} + 12 = 11x^{-1}$

⑤ a) $x^4 + 3x^2 - 4 = 0$

⑥ a) $x^4 + 6x^2 - 7 = 0$

b) $x + 3\sqrt{x} - 4 = 0$

b) $x + 6\sqrt{x} - 7 = 0$

EXAMPLE 2. Solve the equation.

① $x^4 + 24x^2 + 144 = 0$

② $x^{-2} + 6x^{-1} + 5 = 0$

③ $2x - 2\sqrt{x} - 40 = 0$ ④ $x - 32 - 4\sqrt{x} = 0$

⑤ $(x^2 - 3x)^2 - 14(x^2 - 3x) + 40 = 0$ ⑥ $(x^2 - 2x)^2 - 11(x^2 - 2x) + 24 = 0$

⑦ $x^{2/5} - 2x^{1/5} + 1 = 0$ ⑧ $x^{2/3} - 5x^{1/3} + 4 = 0$

⑨ $\dfrac{2}{x} - \dfrac{3}{\sqrt{x}} = 2$

⑩ $\dfrac{4}{y} - \dfrac{4}{\sqrt{y}} + 1 = 0$

⑪ $|x|^2 - 5|x| - 14 = 0$

⑫ $2|x|^2 - 3|x| - 2 = 0$

Mia's Algebra 2

4.10 Quadratic Inequalities using graphs

1. Quadratic Inequality (Graphically)

Inequalities	Meaning
$f(x)>0$	When is the function f(x) ①_____ the x-axis?
$f(x)<0$	When is the function f(x) ②_____ the x-axis?
$f(x)\geq 0$	When is the function f(x) ③_____ and _____ the x-axis?
$f(x)\leq 0$	When is the function f(x) ④_____ and _____ the x-axis?

※ Solving Quadratic Inequalities

Inequalities	Graph	Solutions
$(x-2)(x-5)>0$	zeros at 2, 5	⑤
$(1-x)(x+3)\geq 0$	-3, 1	⑥
$x^2 \leq 1$	-1, 1	⑦

Blank : ① above ② below ③ above and on ④ below and on ⑤ x<2 or x>5 ⑥ -3≤x≤1 ⑦ -1≤x≤1

258　Mia's Algebra 2

EXAMPLE 1. Use the graph of its related function to write the solutions of each inequality.

① $f(x) > 0$

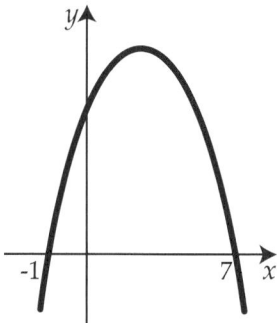

② $f(x) > 0$

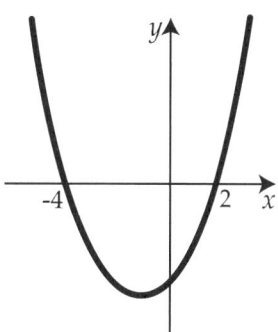

③ $f(x) \geq 0$

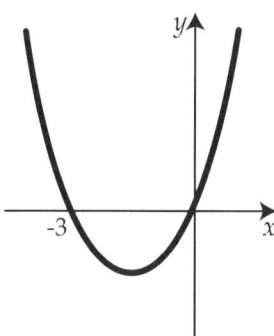

④ $f(x) \geq 0$

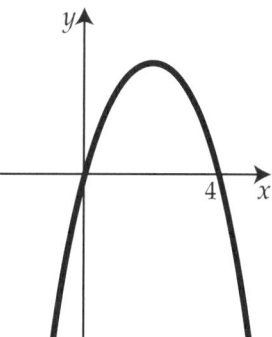

⑤ $f(x) < 0$

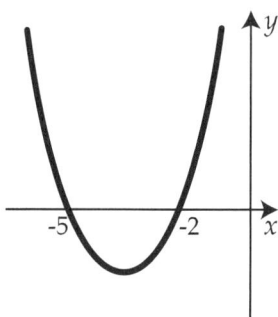

⑥ $f(x) < 0$

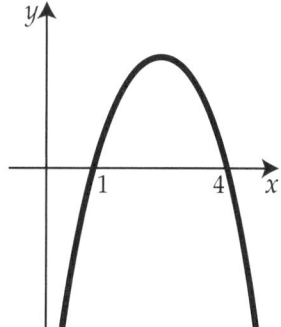

⑦ $f(x) \geq 0$

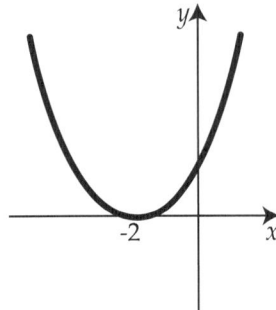

⑧ $f(x) \geq 0$

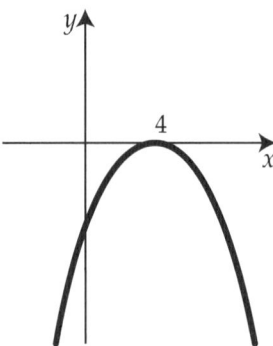

⑨ $f(x) \geq 0$

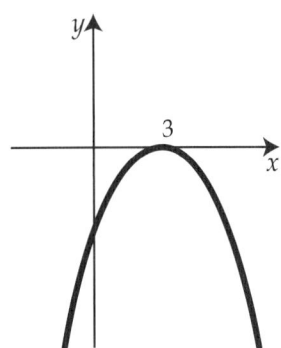

⑩ $f(x) \geq 0$

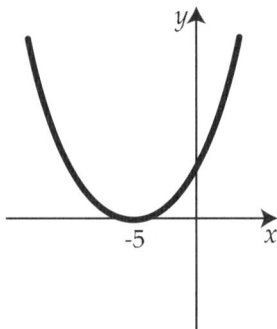

EXAMPLE 2. Solve the inequalities using the graph.

① $x^2 + 7x \geq -12$ ② $x^2 \geq 16$

③ $36 < x^2$

④ $x^2 - 9x + 14 < 0$

⑤ $x^2 + 4x + 2 \leq 0$

⑥ $x^2 > 7 - 2x$

⑦ $132 - x - x^2 > 0$

⑧ $-x^2 - 4x - 3 \geq 0$

⑨ $x^2 - 4x + 4 > 0$

⑩ $x^2 - 6x + 9 \geq 0$

⑪ $x^2 - 2x + 1 \geq 0$

⑫ $-x^2 - 8x - 16 < 0$

⑬ $x^2 - 10x + 25 \leq 0$

⑭ $x^2 + 2x + 1 < 0$

⑮ $-4x^2 + 12x - 9 > 0$

⑯ $9x^2 - 24x + 16 \leq 0$

2. Quadratic Inequality (Numerically)

※ Short cut for Quadratic Inequalities

If you have **less than** (< or ≤), then ①_____ part of the zeros,

if you have **greater than** (> or ≥), then ②_____ part of the zeros

will be the answer.

If you have **equal sign** (≥ or ≤), then include the zeros.

If you **don't have equal sign** (> or <), then don't include the zeros.

ex)

$(x-2)(x-5) < 0$ $(x-2)(x-5) \geq 0$

inside   outside

③ _____   ④ _____

☺ Remember, this works when a is ⑤_____ for $ax^2 + bx + c$.

ex) If $-2(x+2)(x-6) > 0$, then change to ⑥_____.

Blank : ① inside ② outside ③ 2<x<5 ④ x<2 or x>5 ⑤ positive ⑥ 2(x+2)(x-6)<0

EXAMPLE 3. Solve the inequalities using the short cut.

☺ Careful!
$$x^2 < 4 \Rightarrow x < 2 \quad \text{(Wrong!!)}$$
$$x^2 < 4 \Rightarrow x^2 - 4 < 0 \Rightarrow (x+2)(x-2) < 0 \Rightarrow -2 < x < 2 \quad \text{(Correct!!)}$$

① $(x-2)(x+3) \leq 0$ ② $(x+3)(x+7) > 0$

③ $y^2 \geq 1$ ④ $a^2 < 25$

⑤ $m^2 + 3m - 4 > 0$ ⑥ $z^2 + z - 2 < 0$

⑦ $7m^2 < 9m$

⑧ $2x^2 > 2x$

⑨ $2x^2 - 1 < x^2 - 3x$

⑩ $2k^2 > 3k + 3$

⑪ $(x-4)(x+6) \geq 56$

⑫ $(3x+3)(x+10) < 50x + 10$

4.11 Discriminant

Mia's Algebra 2

1. Discriminant

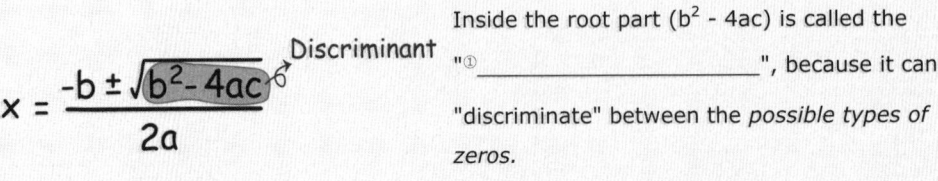

$$x = \frac{-b \pm \sqrt{b^2 - 4ac}}{2a}$$

Inside the root part ($b^2 - 4ac$) is called the "①_____", because it can "discriminate" between the *possible types of zeros*.

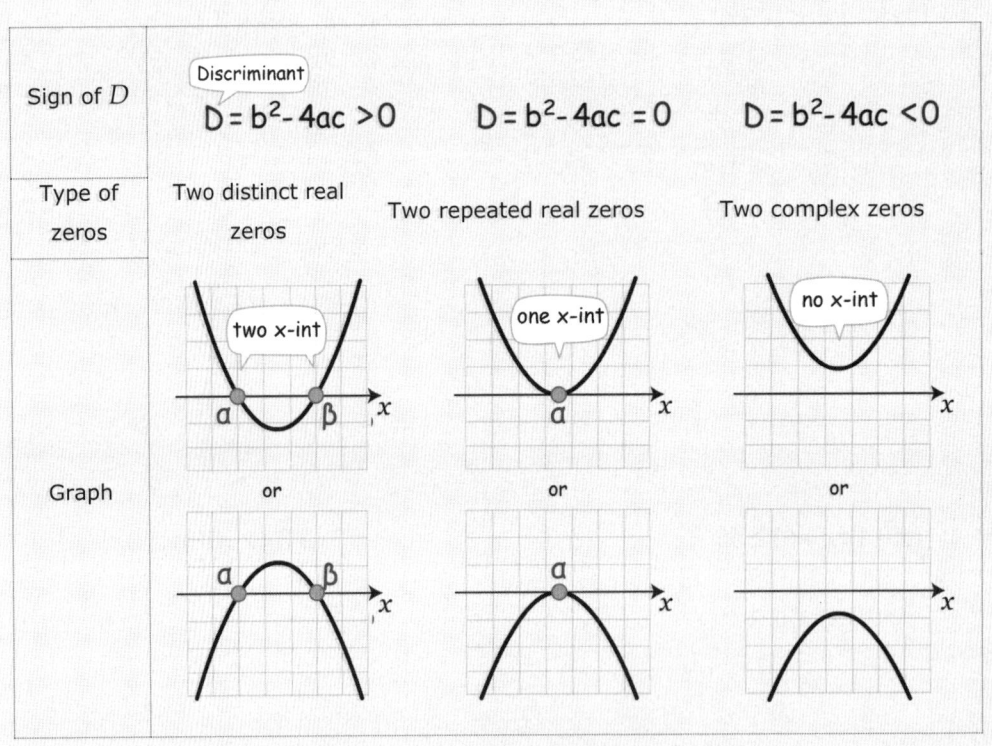

Blank : ① discriminant

EXAMPLE 1. Find the value of the discriminant for the quadratic. Then describe the number and type of roots for the equation.

> ☺ Tip: Try to answer from these four;
>
> ① If $D = b^2 - 4ac > 0$ and is a *perfect square* : Two distinct Rational zeros
>
> ② If $D = b^2 - 4ac > 0$ and is *not perfect square* : Two distinct Irrational zeros
>
> ③ If $D = b^2 - 4ac = 0$: Two repeated real zeros
>
> ④ If $D = b^2 - 4ac < 0$: Two complex zeros

① $x^2 - 8x + 16 = 0$ ② $2x^2 - 7x - 9 = 0$

③ $3x^2 - 2x = 0$ ④ $2x^2 - 7x - 9 = 0$

⑤ $x^2 + 8x + 13 = 0$ ⑥ $2x^2 - 3x = -2$

⑦ $x^2 - x + 1 = 0$ ⑧ $x^2 - 6 = 0$

⑨ $7x^2 = 2 - 6x$ ⑩ $3x^2 = 4x + 7$

EXAMPLE 2. Find the values of k for which:

① $3x^2 - 4x + k = 0$
   has two distinct real roots

② $2x^2 - x + k = 0$
   has equal roots

③ $2x^2 + x - k + 1 = 0$
   has equal roots

④ $2x^2 + 3x + 2k - 1 = 0$
   has no real solutions

⑤ $3kx^2 - x + 1 = 0$
   has real roots ($k \neq 0$)

⑥ $kx^2 - x + k = 0$
   has a repeated zero ($k \neq 0$)

⑦ $0.5x^2 - kx - (k-4) = 0$

has no real solutions

⑧ $x^2 - (k+1)x + 1 = 0$

has real roots

⑨ $y = x^2 + (k+1)x + k$

intersects the x-axis twice

⑩ $y = 4x^2 + (k-3)x + 1$

is tangent to the x-axis

⑪ $y = x^2 - 7kx + 4$

is tangent to the x-axis

⑫ $y = x^2 - kx + (k-1)$

does not touch the x-axis

EXAMPLE 3. Graph of $y = ax^2 + bx + c$ is shown. Find the sign of a and $b^2 - 4ac$ for given graphs.

①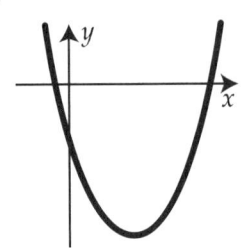

②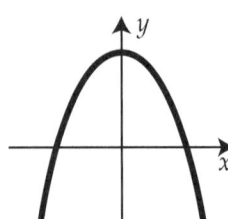

③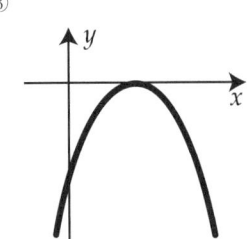

④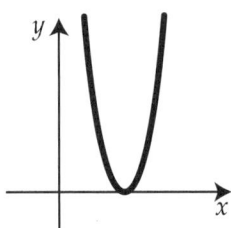

⑤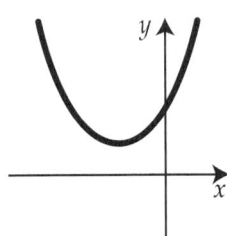

⑥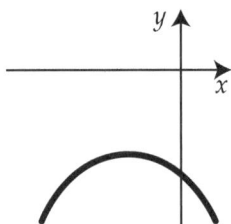

2. Systems of linear and Quadratic

※ Systems of linear and Quadratic

Intersection points of

$f(x) = ax^2 + bx + c$ and $g(x) = mx + n$

is the solutions of the equation ①_____.

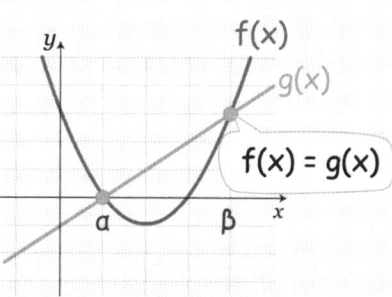

$$(ax^2 + bx + c = mx + n \Rightarrow ax^2 + (b-m)x + c - n = 0)$$

※ Number of intersection of linear and Quadratic

The number of intersection of of $f(x)$ and $g(x)$ can be determined by the

②_____ of $ax^2 + (b-m)x + c - n = 0$.

Sign of D	Discriminant $D = b^2 - 4ac > 0$	$D = b^2 - 4ac = 0$	$D = b^2 - 4ac < 0$
Type of zeros	Two intersections	One intersection (=③_____ to the curve)	no intersections
Graph	cutting	touching	missing

Blank : ① f(x) = g(x)　② discriminant　③ tangent

EXAMPLE 4. Find the coordinates of the points of intersection between the line and the parabola.

① $\begin{cases} y = 6x^2 - 5x \\ 0 = 2x - y + 3 \end{cases}$

② $\begin{cases} y = x^2 - 12x + 36 \\ x + y = 8 \end{cases}$

③ $\begin{cases} y = (x + 5)^2 + 1 \\ 2x - y + 10 = 0 \end{cases}$

EXAMPLE 5. Find the value or inverval of the values of k or m for which;

① the line $y = kx+1$ are tangents to the curve with equation $y = x^2 - 4x + 2$.

② the line $g(x) = 3x + k$ intersects the quadratic function $y = 2x^2 - 5x + 3$ twice

③ the line $y = mx + m$ intersects the curve $y = x^2 + 2x + 2$ twice.

④ the line $y = mx - (m+2)$ is tangent to the curve $y = x^2 + x$.

3. Expand Knowledge*

EXAMPLE 6. * Find the maximum integer of k so that the quadratic $y = x^2 + (1-2k)x + k^2$ intersects the x-axis twice.

EXAMPLE 7. * Find the equation of the line that is tangent to $y = x^2 - 4x + 5$ at the point $(1, 2)$.

EXAMPLE 8. * Find the values of k such that the quadratic expression $kx^2 + 12x + 6$ is always positive.

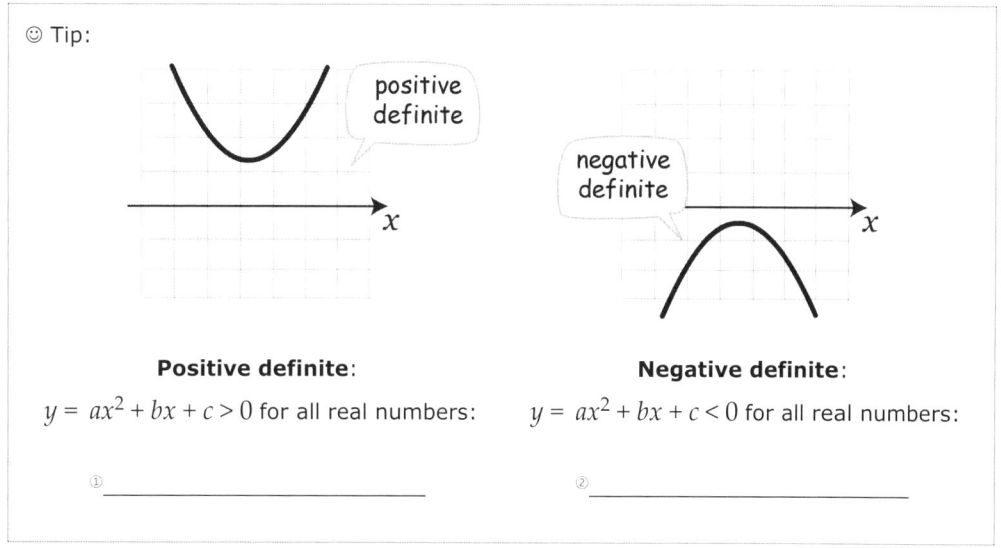

☺ Tip:

Positive definite:
$y = ax^2 + bx + c > 0$ for all real numbers:

① _____

Negative definite:
$y = ax^2 + bx + c < 0$ for all real numbers:

② _____

EXAMPLE 9. * Find the range of value k such that the quadratic graph $y = kx^2 + (k+3)x - 1$ is always negative.

Blank : ① a>0, Discriminant D<0   ② a<0, Discriminant D<0

Mia's Algebra 2

4.12 Sum and product of the roots

1. Quadratic : Sums and Products of Roots

Let's say we have a Quadratic Function ax^2+bx+c which has zeros p, q.

Then the same quadratic function (in factored form) becomes;

$$a(x - p)(x - q)$$

If we expand this, then ;

$$a(x - p)(x - q) = \text{①}\underline{\hspace{3cm}}$$

If we compare each terms;

Quadratic	ax^2	$+ bx$	$+ c$
Expanded Factors:	②	③	④

we can find out that $p + q =$ ⑤ _____ and $pq =$ ⑥ _____

※ **Sum and Product of the roots**

If a Quadratic equation $ax^2 + bx + c = 0$ has roots of p, q ;

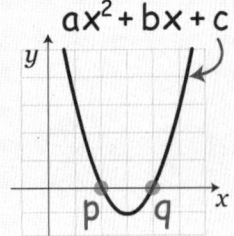

$ax^2 + bx + c = 0$

$$p + q = -\frac{b}{a} \qquad pq = \frac{c}{a}$$

sum of the roots   product of the roots

Blank : ① $ax^2 - a(p+q)x + apq$ ② ax^2 ③ $- a(p+q)x$ ④ $+ apq$ ⑤ $-\dfrac{b}{a}$ ⑥ $\dfrac{c}{a}$

276   Mia's Algebra 2

EXAMPLE 1. Find the sum and the product of the given quadratic equation.

① $x^2 - 8x = 14$　　　　　　　　② $x^2 - 7x + 6 = 0$

③ $5x^2 - 36x + 7 = 0$　　　　　　④ $9x^2 - 6x + 1 = 0$

⑤ $-2x^2 + 5x = 9$　　　　　　　⑥ $3x = 3x^2 + 7$

⑦ $x^2 - 100 = 0$　　　　　　　　⑧ $x^2 = 16$

⑨ $-x^2 + 6x = 0$　　　　　　　　⑩ $-2x^2 = 7x$

Let's say we have a Quadratic Function ax^2+bx+c which has zeros p, q.

Then the same quadratic function (in factored form) becomes;

$$a(x - p)(x - q)$$

If we expand this, then;

$$a(x - p)(x - q) = a[x^2 - (p + q)x + pq] = a[x^2 - (①\underline{\quad})x + ②\underline{\quad}]$$

If we know two roots of a quadratic equation, then the equation will be

$$a[\, x^2 - (\text{Sum of roots})x + (\text{Product of roots})\,] = 0$$

EXAMPLE 2. Write a quadratic equation with integer coefficients that has the given roots.

① 6, –7

② –1, 8

③ $2 \pm \sqrt{7}$

④ $4 \pm \sqrt{3}$

Blank : ① sum ② product

⑤ $\dfrac{2 \pm 2\sqrt{5}}{3}$

⑥ $\dfrac{7 \pm 4\sqrt{2}}{2}$

⑦ $2 \pm 3i$

⑧ $3 \pm 5i$

⑨ $\dfrac{5 \pm i\sqrt{2}}{2}$

⑩ $\dfrac{3 \pm i\sqrt{3}}{5}$

2. Expand Knowledge*

EXAMPLE 3. *If the roots of a quadratic equation $2x^2 + 5x - 4 = 0$ are α and β, what is the value of

a) $\alpha + \beta$

b) $\alpha\beta$

c) $\dfrac{1}{\alpha} + \dfrac{1}{\beta}$

d) $\alpha^2 + \beta^2$

EXAMPLE 4. *If the roots of a quadratic equation $x^2 - 3x + 4 = 0$ are α and β, what is the value of

a) $\alpha + \beta$

b) $\alpha\beta$

c) $\dfrac{1}{\alpha} + \dfrac{1}{\beta}$

d) $\alpha^2 + \beta^2$

EXAMPLE 5. * If the roots of a quadratic equation $3x^2 + x - 2 = 0$ are α and β, what is the product of $\alpha - 1$ and $\beta - 1$?

EXAMPLE 6. *The quadratic equation $x^2 - 4x + 7 = 0$ has roots p and q. Find a quadratic equation with integer coefficients and roots $\dfrac{1}{p}$ and $\dfrac{1}{q}$.

EXAMPLE 7. *The quadratic equation $x^2 - 4x + 9 = 0$ has roots p and q. Find a quadratic equation with integer coefficients and roots $p + 1$ and $q + 1$.

EXAMPLE 8. * The quadratic equation $|x^2 - x - 9| = 3$ has roots p, q, r and s. What is the value of $\dfrac{1}{p} + \dfrac{1}{q} + \dfrac{1}{r} + \dfrac{1}{s}$?

Part 5
Polynomials

5.1 Graphing Polynomials

5.2 Dividing Polynomials

5.3 The Remainder and Factor Theorems

5.4 Theorems about Roots of Polynomial

5.5 Complex Roots of Polynomial function

Mia's Algebra 2

5.1 Graphing Polynomials

1. Shape of Polynomial Functions

Each graph, based on their degree, has a different shape and characteristics.

	when $a > 0$	when $a < 0$
Linear function $y = ax + b$	/	\
Quadratic Function $y = ax^2 + bx + c$	$\cup$	$\cap$
Cubic Function $y = ax^3 + bx^2 + cx + d$	∕ ∿	∖ ⌒∖
Quartic Function $y = ax^4 + bx^3 + cx^2 + dx + e$	U ∪∧∪ W	∩ ∩∨∩ M

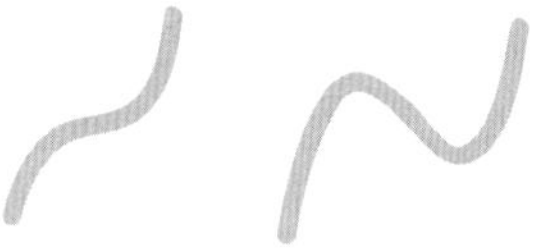

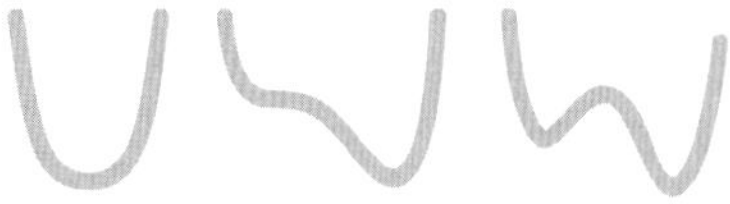

2. Graphing Polynomial

1) End behavior Model

※ **End behavior** (shape of the end of graph)

The end behavior of polynomial $P(x) = a_n x^n + a_{n-1} x^{n-1} + \dots + a_1 x^1 + a_0$ is determined by *the leading term* ① _____.

	Odd degree		**Even** Degree	
Sign of Leading Coefficient	Positive $+x^{odd}$	Negative $-x^{odd}$	Positive $+x^{even}$	Negative $-x^{even}$
End Behavior	↙ ↗	↑ ↓	↑ ↗	↙ ↓

EXAMPLE 1. Determine the end behavior for each graph.

As $x \to \infty$ means when x gets bigger(go to the right),
as $x \to -\infty$ means when x gets smaller (go to the left)

$y \to \infty$ means the graph is going ② _____.

$y \to -\infty$ means the graph is going ③ _____.

Blank : ① $a_n x^n$ ② up ③ down

ex)

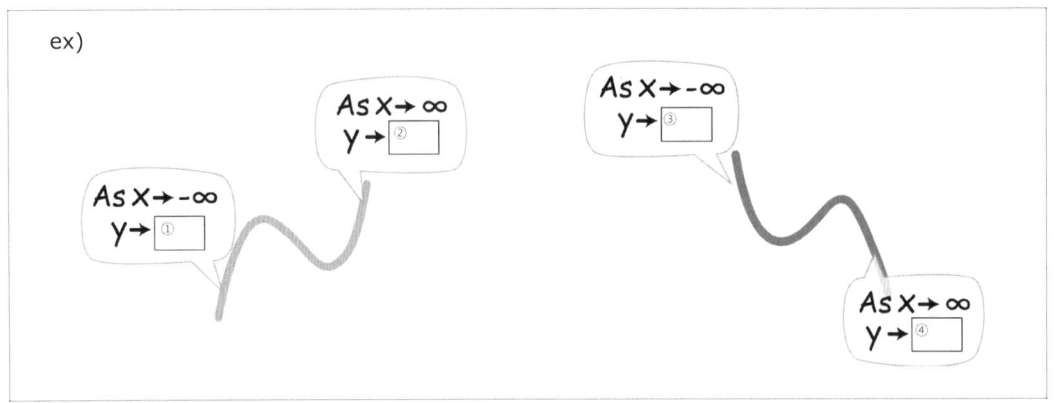

① $f(x) = 4x^3 - 3x^2 + 2x - 5$

② $f(x) = -x^4 + 4x^2 - 5x - 7$

③ $f(x) = -2x^3(x-2)^2$

④ $f(x) = 0.5x(x+4)^3(x-2)^3$

⑤ $f(x) = -2(x-3)^2(x^2+4)^3$

⑥ $f(x) = -(x^2+1)^2(x+4)^3$

⑦ $f(x) = 3x^2(x^3-2)^3(x^2+1)$

⑧ $f(x) = x^4(x^3+1)^2(x^6-1)$

Blank : ① -∞   ② ∞   ③ ∞   ④ -∞

2) Zeros of Polynomial

① When we have a ①_____ form of a polynomial,

then we can find the zeros(=roots = x intercept) using *zero product property*.

$$X \cdot Y = 0 \text{ then } X = 0 \text{ or } Y = 0$$

② Multiplicity: how often a root appears.

ex) $(x-1)^2$: The root(zero) x = 1 appears twice, so the multiplicity is ②____.

Odd multiplicity	**Even** multiplicity
$(x-r)^{odd}$	$(x-r)^{even}$
or	or
③_____ the x axis at r.	④_____ the x axis at r.

ex)

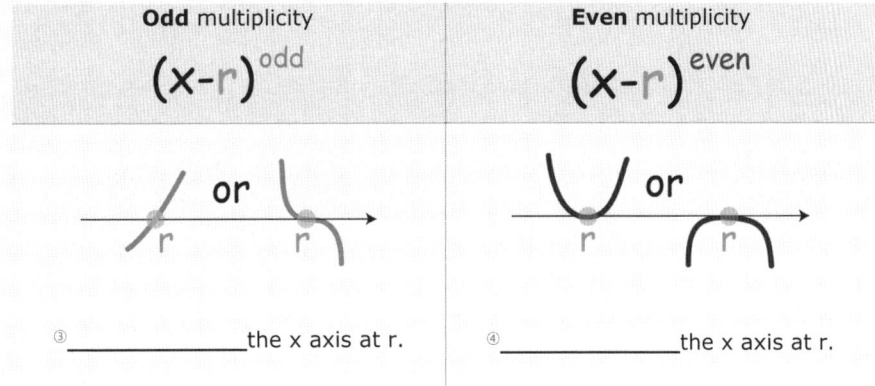

$$P(x) = -2(x-1)^2(x+2)^3$$

multiplicity

P(x) has x-intercept at ⑤_____.

P(x) (⑥crosses/touches) at x = 1, and (⑦crosses/touches) at x = -2.

Blank : ① factored   ② 2   ③ crosses   ④ touches   ⑤ x=1, x=-2   ⑥ touches   ⑦ crosses

EXAMPLE 2. For the polynomial,

a) determine the end behavior,

b) determine whether the graph crosses or touches the x-axis at each x-intercept.

c) Sketch the graph briefly.

① $f(x)=(x-2)(x+3)(2x-1)$ ② $f(x)=(x+1)^2(x-2)$

③ $f(x)=-2x^2(x-2)$ ④ $f(x)=-2x(x-2)^2$

⑤ $f(x)=-2(x+2)^2(x-1)^4$ ⑥ $f(x)=(x-1)^2(x-5)^4$

⑦ $f(x) = -2x^2(x-1)(x+6)^4$

⑧ $f(x) = x(x-\sqrt{3})^2(x-2)^4$

⑨ $f(x) = -2x^2(x+1)^2(x-3)^4$

Mia's Algebra 2

5.2 Dividing Polynomials

1. Dividing Polynomial

When you divide a polynomial P(x) by another polynomial D(x), we get a quotient polynomial ① _____ and a remainder polynomial ② _____ .

$$D(x) \overline{\smash{)}\begin{array}{r} Q(x) \\ P(x) \\ \vdots \\ R(x) \end{array}}$$

We can rewrite this as;

dividend → P(x) = D(x)·Q(x) + R(x)
            ↑   ↑   ↑
       divisor Quotient Remainder

or

dividend → $\dfrac{P(x)}{D(x)} = Q(x) + \dfrac{R(x)}{D(x)}$
divisor ↗

Notice that the **degree of the remainder** is always *less than* the **degree of the divisor**.

Blank : ① Q(x)   ② R(x)

2. Long Division of Polynomial

This is a method similar to division for *Numbers*.

Divide $2x^3 - 7x^2 + 5$ by $x - 3$.

☺ Careful:

Rewrite the polynomial P(x) from highest to lowest exponent.

When you have a missing term, include the missing terms with a coefficient of ① _____.

```
              Quotient
              2x²-x-3

         2x² -x  -3
x-3 ) 2x³-7x²+0x+5
      2x³-6x²
      ─────────
          -x²+0x
          -x²+3x
          ─────────
              -3x+5
              -3x+9
              ─────
                -4
              Remainder
                -4
```

You can write the result as ;

② _____

Blank : ① 0   ② $2x^2 - x - 3 + \dfrac{-4}{x-3}$

Part 5 Polynomials 291

EXAMPLE 1. Use long division to perform the division.

① $\dfrac{x^2 + 8x + 12}{x + 3}$

② $\dfrac{-68 + 17x - x^2}{6 - x}$

③ $\dfrac{x^3 - 9x^2 + 27x - 27}{x^2 - 3}$

④ $\dfrac{6x^3 - 19x^2 + 10}{3x - 5}$

⑤ $\dfrac{4x^3 - 3}{x + 5}$

⑥ $\dfrac{x^3 + 6x + 2}{x^2 - 2x + 2}$

⑦ $\dfrac{x^4 - x^3 + 7x + 5}{x^2 + 2x + 5}$

⑧ $\dfrac{3x^4 - x^3 - 10x - 30}{x^2 + x + 5}$

3. Synthetic Division

Synthetic division is a quick method of dividing polynomials;

it can be used *only* when we divide a polynomial by ① _____.

Divide $2x^3 - 7x^2 + 5$ by $x - 3$ using synthetic division.

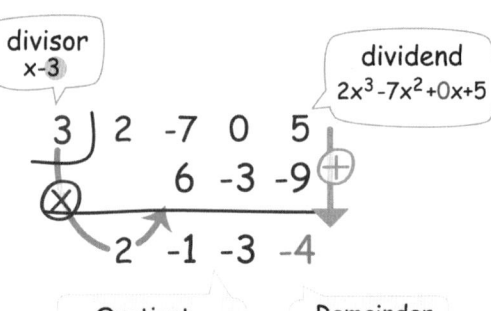

☺ Careful:

When you have a missing term, include the missing terms with ② _____.

EXAMPLE 2. Use synthetic division to perform the division.

① $\dfrac{x^3 - 9x^2 + 27x - 27}{x - 3}$

② $\dfrac{3x^3 + 5x^2 - 4x + 1}{x + 4}$

Blank : ① x – c ② 0

③ $\dfrac{x^3 - 8x + 2}{x + 2}$

④ $\dfrac{5x^3 + 4x^2 - 3}{x + 3}$

⑤ $\dfrac{x^4 - 5x^2 - 10}{x - 4}$

⑥ $\dfrac{2x^4 - 10x^3 + 8}{x - 2}$

⑦ $\dfrac{x^5 - 32}{x - 2}$

⑧ $\dfrac{x^6 - 1}{x - 1}$

⑨ $\dfrac{2x^3+4x^2-2x+3}{2x-1}$ ⑩ $\dfrac{8x^4+10x^3+5x+1}{2x+3}$

4. Expand Knowledge*

EXAMPLE 3. * Use long division to perform the division.

① $\dfrac{2a^3+3b^3+4ab^2+3a^2b}{2a-b}$ ② $\dfrac{x^3+y^3+6x^2y+6xy^2}{x+3y}$

Mia's Algebra 2

5.3 The Remainder and Factor Theorem

1. The Remainder Theorem

※ **Remainder Theorem**

When you divide a polynomial $P(x)$ by $(x-c)$, the remainder R will be $P(c)$.

☺ Proof:

The polynomial $P(x)$ can be expressed as; ① _____

And when we plug in $x=c$, ② _____

EXAMPLE 1. Find the remainder using remainder theorem or synthetic division.

① $\dfrac{2x^3 - 3x^2 + 9x + 1}{x - 2}$ ② $\dfrac{x^3 - x^2 + x + 5}{x + 1}$

③ $\dfrac{2x^4 + 4x^3 - 10x^2 + 3x + 10}{x - 5}$ ④ $\dfrac{x^4 - 8x^3 + 10x^2 - x + 5}{x - 7}$

Blank : ① P(x) = (x −c)Q + R   ② P(c) = R

⑤ $\dfrac{x^{20}+3x^{7}-7x+6}{x-1}$ ⑥ $\dfrac{x^{117}+3x^{10}-3x+1}{x+1}$

EXAMPLE 2. For each polynomial, evaluate $P(c)$.

☺ Tip: Instead of plugging in values,
using synthetic division and finding the remainder might be easier.

① $P(x)=5x^{4}+30x^{3}-40x^{2}-36x+14$
 find $P(-7)$.

② $P(x)=2x^{4}-21x^{3}-30x^{2}+8x-100$
 find $P(12)$.

③ $P(x)=x^{5}-7x^{4}+11x^{3}+10x+12$
 find $P(4)$.

④ $P(x)=x^{4}+8x^{3}-4x^{2}-12x-10$
 find $P(-8)$.

⑤ $P(x) = 3x^3 + 4x^2 - 2x - 1$

find $P\left(\dfrac{2}{3}\right)$.

⑥ $P(x) = 4x^4 + 5x^2 + x - 1$

find $P\left(\dfrac{1}{2}\right)$.

EXAMPLE 3. If the polynomial $f(x) = 2x^3 - kx^2 - 5x + 2$ is divided by $x - 2$, the remainder is 2. What is the value of k?

2. Factor Theorem

When you divide a polynomial $P(x)$ by $(x-c)$, what happen when remainder is 0?

When $P(c) = 0$,

then $(x-c)$ is the **factor** of the polynomial P.

then polynomial P is **divisible by** $(x-c)$.

EXAMPLE 4. Use the Factor Theorem to determine whether the function $f(x) = x^4 + x^3 - 19x^2 + 11x + 30$ has a factor;

① $x-1$ ② $x+1$

③ $x-2$ ④ $x+2$

⑤ $x-4$ ⑥ $x-3$

⑦ $x+5$ ⑧ $x+6$

EXAMPLE 5. If a polynomial P(x) = $x^3 + 4x^2 - kx - 6$ has a factor of $x+3$, then what is the value of constant k?

EXAMPLE 6. If the polynomial $f(x) = 2x^3 - kx^2 - 5x + 2$ is divisible by $x-2$, what is the value of k?

Mia's Algebra 2

5.4 Theorems about Roots of Polynomial

1. The Rational Zeros Theorem

The **possible rational zeros** of the polynomial
$P(x) = a_n x^n + a_{n-1} x^{n-1} + \ldots + a_1 x^1 + a_0$ is

$$\text{Possible Rational Zeroes of } P(x) = \frac{\text{Factors of constant term } (a_0)}{\text{Factors of Leading Coefficient } (a_n)}$$

ex) Find the possible rational zeros of $f(x) = 2x^3 + x^2 - 13x + 6$.

$$\text{possible Rational Zeros of } f(x) = \frac{\text{factor of } \underline{\text{①}}}{\text{factor of } \underline{\text{②}}} = \frac{\text{③}}{\text{④}} = \underline{\text{⑤}}$$

EXAMPLE 1. List the possible rational zeros of the polynomial function.

① $f(x) = 6x^4 + 4x^3 - 3x^2 + 2$

② $f(x) = 2x^4 - 5x^2 + 5x - 8$

③ $f(x) = 5x^4 + 6x^3 - 2x^2 - 8$

④ $f(x) = 4x^3 - 2x^2 + x + 7$

Blank : ① 6 ② 2 ③ ±1, ±2, ±3, ±6 ④ ±1, ±2 ⑤ $\pm 1, \pm 2, \pm 3, \pm 6, \pm\frac{1}{2}, \pm\frac{3}{2}$

2. Descartes' Rule of Signs

Descartes rule of signs determines the number of positive and negative zeros

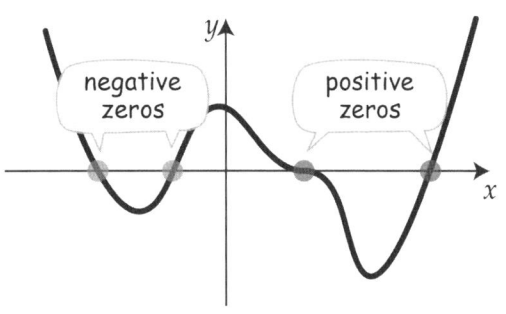

First, rewrite the polynomial P(x) from highest to lowest exponent (ignore any missing terms) Then, count how many times there is a change of sign.

※ **Descartes' Rule of Sign**

Number of positive roots equals the number of sign changes of P(x) , or minus even integers (-2, -4, ..).

Number of negative roots equals the number of sign changes of P(-x) , or minus even integers.

$$P(x) = \oplus 2x^5 \ominus 3x^4 \ominus 3x^3 \oplus 4x^2 \ominus x \ominus 1$$

3 Sign changes : P(x) will have 3 or 1 positive roots

$$P(-x) = \ominus 2x^5 \ominus 3x^4 \oplus 3x^3 \oplus 4x^2 \oplus x \ominus 1$$

2 Sign changes : P(x) will have 2 or 0 negative roots

EXAMPLE 2. Use Descartes' Rule of Signs to determine how many positive and how many negative real zeros the polynomial can have.

① $P(x) = -x^3 - x^2 - x + 2$ ② $P(x) = x^4 - 3x^3 + 2x^2 - x - 3$

③ $P(x) = x^5 + 2x^3 - x^2 + 5x - 1$ ④ $P(x) = 3x^7 - 8x^5 + 4x^4 - 4x^3 - 4x^2 + 2$

3. Fundamental Theorem of Algebra

We have two different roots (=zeros)

① real roots and ② imaginary roots (roots with imaginary number i)

All together we call it **complex roots**.

complex roots
- real roots (no i) = x intercept (2, 0.5, $\sqrt{3}$ ...)
- imaginary roots (with i) ($2i + 3$, $-4i$ ...)

※ **Fundamental Theorem of Algebra**
  ① Every polynomial equation has at least one **complex roots**.
  ② Any polynomial of **degree n** has **n complex roots**.

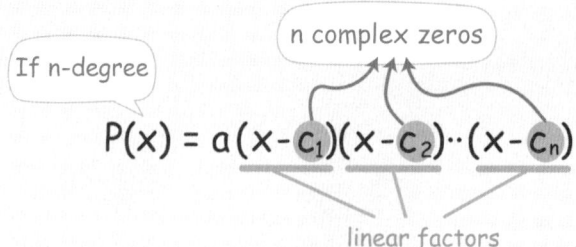

If n-degree, n complex zeros:
$$P(x) = a(x-c_1)(x-c_2)\cdots(x-c_n)$$
linear factors

EXAMPLE 3. Determine the number of distinct real roots and imaginary roots for each function.

> You can see your real roots in the graph (= ①_____)
> but you cannot see your imaginary roots in your graph.

① Degree 2

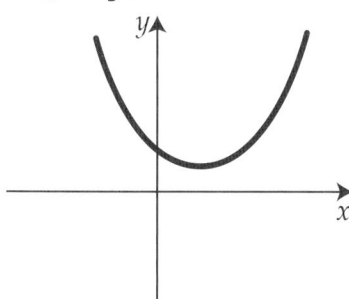

② Degree 2

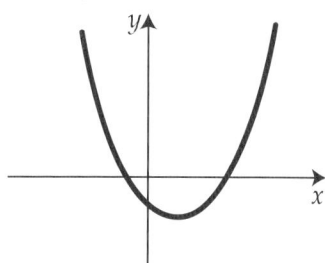

③ Degree 3

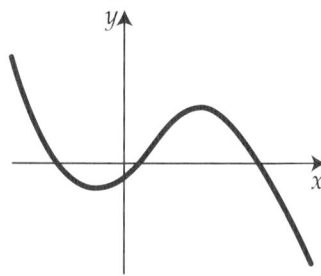

④ Degree 3

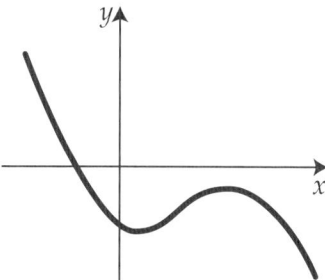

⑤ Degree 3

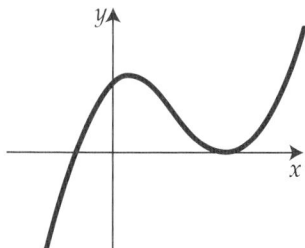

⑥ Degree 4

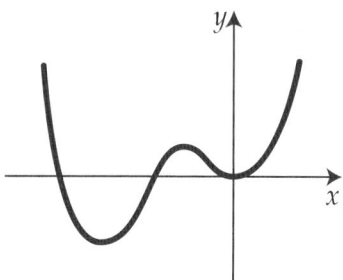

Blank : ① x intercept

⑦ Degree 4

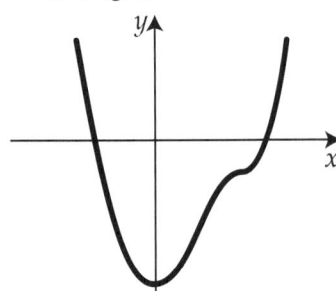

⑧ Degree 6

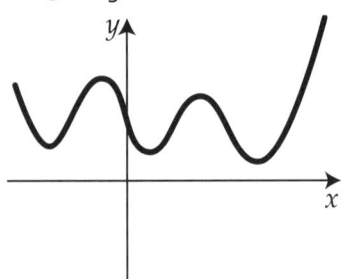

⑨ Degree 5

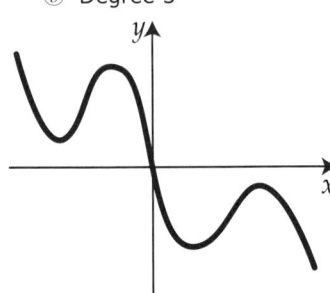

4. Conjugate Zeros Theorem

※ **Conjugate Zeros Theorem**

Complex Roots always come in pairs!

When $a + bi$ is the root, $a - bi$ is also the root.

EXAMPLE 4. Write a polynomial function of least degree with integer coefficients that has the given zeros.

① $1 + 2i$

② $3 + i$

③ $-2, 2 + i$

④ $-1, 1 - i$

⑤ $i, -2i$

⑥ $-1, 1, \sqrt{6}i$

Mia's Algebra 2

5.5 Complex Roots of Polynomial functions

1. Finding Complex Zeros

If we factor the polynomial **completely**, then we will find the *Complex roots*.

EXAMPLE 1. Find all the complex zeros of each polynomial function by factoring.

① $f(x) = x^3 + x$

② $f(x) = x^4 + 4x^2$

③ $f(x) = x^3 - 3x^2 + 2x - 6$

④ $f(x) = x^3 - 4x^2 + x - 4$

⑤ $f(x) = x^4 + 4x^2 - 32$

⑥ $f(x) = x^4 + 9x^2 + 8$

⑦ $f(x) = x^4 - 16$

⑧ $f(x) = x^4 - 1$

⑨ $f(x) = x^5 + 27x^2$

⑩ $f(x) = 27 - 8x^3$

⑪ $f(x) = x^6 - 64$

⑫ $f(x) = x^6 - 1$

※ Factoring Polynomial $x^3 + 3x^2 - 6x - 8$.

$P(1) = (1)^3 + 3(1)^2 - 6(1) - 8 = -10$ (x-1) is NOT factor

$P(-1) = (-1)^3 + 3(-1)^2 - 6(-1) - 8 = 0$ (x+1) IS the factor

i) Find the *first zero* using factor theorem.
(Try P(1), P(-1), P(2), P(-2).. until you get 0)

```
-1 | 1   3   -6   -8
   |    -1   -2    8
   ―――――――――――――――――
     1   2   -8    0
     _____/
     other factor
```

ii) Use synthetic to find the other factors.

$x^3 + 3x^2 - 6x - 8$
$= (x+1)$ ①_____
$=$ ② _____

iii) Find the rest of the zeros.

Blank : ① $x^2 + 2x - 8$ ② $(x+1)(x+4)(x-2)$

EXAMPLE 2. Factor the polynomial and find all the complex zeros of each polynomial function.

① $x^3 + 4x^2 - 7x - 10$

② $x^3 + 15x^2 + 39x - 55$

③ $x^3 - 2x^2 + 4x - 8$

④ $x^3 + x^2 + 9x + 9$

⑤ $x^4 + 3x^3 + 3x^2 - x - 6$

⑥ $x^4 - 5x^3 - 7x^2 + 5x + 6$

⑦ $x^4 - 3x^3 + 6x^2 - 12x + 8$

Part 6
Rational Expressions

6.1 Rational Expressions

6.2 Multiplying and Dividing Rational Expressions

6.3 Sums and Differences of Rational Expressions

6.4 Complex Fractions

6.5 Rational Equations and Word Problems

6.6 Graph of Rational Functions

Mia's Algebra 2

6.1 Rational Expressions

1. Rational Expressions

    ※ **Rational Expression**

    (Rational Function) $R(x) = \dfrac{P(x)}{Q(x)}$ Ratio of two Polynomials

    Rational Function: ①_____ of two polynomials

    (=fraction)

    ※ **Simplifying Rational Expression**

    ① $\dfrac{A \cdot \cancel{B}}{\cancel{B} \cdot C} = \dfrac{A}{C}$: Factor and reduce (=cancel)

    ② $\dfrac{A \pm B}{D} = \dfrac{A}{D} \pm \dfrac{B}{D}$

    ③ $\dfrac{D}{A + B} \neq \dfrac{D}{A} \pm \dfrac{D}{B}$

Blank : ① ratio

☺ Reminder: Factoring Techniques

Number of terms	Factoring Technique	Formula or Examples
any number	GCF	$4a^3b^2 - 8a^2b = 4a^2b(ab - 2)$
two	Difference of squares	$a^2 - b^2 = (a - b)(a + b)$
two	Sum of Cubes	$a^3 + b^3 = (a + b)(a^2 - ab + b^2)$
two	Difference of Cubes	$a^3 - b^3 = (a - b)(a^2 + ab + b^2)$
three	perfect square trinomials	$a^2 + 2ab + b^2 = (a + b)^2$ $a^2 - 2ab + b^2 = (a - b)^2$
three	General trinomials	$acx^2 + (ad + bc)x + bd = (ax + b)(cx + d)$
four or more	grouping	$ax + bx + ay + by = (a + b)(x + y)$ $a^2 + 2ab + b^2 - c^2 = (a+b+c)(a+b-c)$

Part 6 Rational Expressions

EXAMPLE 1. Simplify.

① $\dfrac{5x^3 + 15x^2}{10x}$ 　　　　　② $\dfrac{3y^4 - 9y^3}{6y^2}$

③ $\dfrac{x^2 - y^2}{(y-x)^2}$ 　　　　　④ $\dfrac{(x+a)^2}{x^2 - a^2}$

⑤ $(x-y)(y-x)^{-2}$ 　　　　　⑥ $(a^2 + ab)(a^2 - b^2)^{-1}$

⑦ $\dfrac{x^2 + x - 12}{x^2 + 11x + 28}$ 　　　　　⑧ $\dfrac{6t^2 + 7t - 5}{4t^2 - 1}$

⑨ $\dfrac{9z - z^3}{2z^2 + z - 15}$

⑩ $\dfrac{12y^2 - 5y - 3}{2 + 9y + 9y^2}$

⑪ $\dfrac{x^4 - 1}{x^4 - x^2}$

⑫ $\dfrac{x^4 - a^4}{(x+a)^2(x^2+a^2)}$

⑬ $\dfrac{c^3 + d^3}{c^2 + 2cd + d^2}$

⑭ $\dfrac{x^2 - 4xy + 3y^2}{x^3 - y^3}$

EXAMPLE 2. Simplify.

① $\dfrac{x^3 - x^2 - x + 1}{x^3 + x^2 - x - 1}$ ② $\dfrac{t^4 - 1}{t^3 + t^2 - t - 1}$

③ $\dfrac{a^4 - 3a^2b^2 - 4b^4}{a^4 - b^4}$ ④ $\dfrac{x^4 + 2x^2y^2 + y^4}{x^4 - y^4}$

⑤ $\dfrac{x^2 - y^2 - 4x + 4y}{x^2 - y^2 + 4x - 4y}$ ⑥ $\dfrac{x^2 - y^2 - x + y}{x^2 - y^2 + x - y}$

⑦ $\dfrac{x^2-y^2-4y-4}{x^2+y^2+2xy-4}$ ⑧ $\dfrac{x^2+y^2-2xy-9}{x^2-y^2-6y-9}$

2. Expand Knowledge*

※ Factorial Notation :

$$n! = n \times (n-1) \times \cdots \times 3 \times 2 \times 1$$ (factorial)

It is generally agreed that $0! = $ ①_____ , and $(neg)! = $ ①_____.

EXAMPLE 3. Simplify

① $\dfrac{5!}{6!}$ ② $\dfrac{100!}{98!}$

③ $\dfrac{8!}{6! \times 2!}$ ④ $\dfrac{7! \times 3!}{9!}$

Blank : ① 1   ② does not exist

⑤ $\dfrac{n!}{(n+1)!}$

⑥ $\dfrac{(n+2)!}{n!}$

⑦ $\dfrac{[3(n+1)]!}{(3n)!}$

⑧ $\dfrac{(2n+2)!}{(2n)!}$

⑨ $\dfrac{3^{n+1}}{3^n}$

⑩ $\dfrac{2^{n+2}}{2^n}$

⑪ $\dfrac{n+1}{(n+1)^{n+1}}$

⑫ $\dfrac{n+2}{(n+2)^{n+1}}$

Mia's Algebra 2

6.2 Multiplying and Dividing Rationals

1. Multiplying and Dividing Rational Expressions

  ※ **Multiplying Rational Expression**

  $$\frac{A}{B} \times \frac{C}{D} = \frac{AC}{BD}$$

  ※ **Dividing Rational Expression**

  $$\frac{A}{B} \div \frac{C}{D} = \frac{A}{B} \times \frac{D}{C}$$

  (multiply by reciprocal)

  EXAMPLE 1. Multiply or divide.

  ① $\dfrac{2p}{q} \cdot \dfrac{pq^2}{8q^3}$ ② $\dfrac{5a}{2b^3} \cdot \dfrac{4b^2}{a^4b}$

③ $5xy \div \dfrac{10x^2}{y^2} \div \dfrac{y^3}{x}$

④ $\dfrac{12a^2}{b} \div \dfrac{2}{3ab} \div \dfrac{54a^3}{b}$

⑤ $\dfrac{2t^2-5t-3}{1-4t^2} \div \dfrac{t^2-6t+9}{2t^2+9t-5}$

⑥ $\dfrac{t^2-5t+6}{t+1} \cdot \dfrac{1+2t+t^2}{t^2-2t-3}$

⑦ $\dfrac{x^2-9}{x^2+6x+9} \div \dfrac{x-3}{x^2+x-6} \cdot \dfrac{x+3}{x-2}$

⑧ $\dfrac{x^2}{x+1} \cdot \dfrac{x^2-1}{x+3} \div \dfrac{x^2-1}{x^2+4x+3}$

⑨ $\dfrac{x^4-y^4}{(x+y)^2} \div (x^2+y^2) \cdot (x^3+y^3)$ ⑩ $\dfrac{x^2-y^2}{x-y} \div (x^4-y^4) \cdot (x^3-y^3)$

2. Expand Knowledge*

EXAMPLE 2. * Multiply or divide.
$$(x^2-y^2) \cdot (x^4+x^2y^2+y^4) \div (x^6-y^6)$$
[Hint: When factoring $x^4+x^2y^2+y^4$, add and subtract x^2y^2]

Mia's Algebra 2

6.3 Sums and Differences of Rationals

1. LCM

※ **Least Common Multiple (LCM)** : Least common multiple (LCM) of a polynomial is the smallest monomial that is divisible by all terms.

ex) The LCM of 8 and 12 is ①_____

The LCM of $8xy^3z$ and $12x^2y^2$ is ②_____

(→ All variable factors with the ③_____ power)

EXAMPLE 1. Find the LCM of each set of polynomials.

① $14xy^2, 42yz^3, 21x^2z$

② $8abc^2, 28b^3c, 35b^4c^3$

③ x^2-1, x^2+3x-4

④ $2a+2, a^2+a, a+1$

⑤ $x^2+3x, x^2+6x+9, x^3+x^2$

⑥ $3b^2+10b-8, 9b^2-12b+4$

Blank : ① 24   ② $24x^2y^3z$ ③ highest

2. Adding or Subtracting Rational Function

What is $\dfrac{7}{12}+\dfrac{5}{12}=$ ①_____ $\dfrac{1}{4}+\dfrac{5}{3}=$ ②_____ $\dfrac{7}{12}+\dfrac{5}{18}=$ ③_____

※ Adding or Subtracting Rational Expression

① $\dfrac{A}{D} \pm \dfrac{B}{D} = \dfrac{A \pm B}{D}$

② $\dfrac{A}{B} \pm \dfrac{C}{D} = \dfrac{AD \pm BC}{BD}$ — LCD

Find the ④_____ of the denominator.

EXAMPLE 2. Add or subtract.

① $\dfrac{3}{5xy^2} - \dfrac{2}{x^3 y}$

② $\dfrac{1}{rs^3} - \dfrac{1}{r^3 s}$

③ $\dfrac{c}{ab} + \dfrac{a}{bc} + \dfrac{b}{ca}$

④ $\dfrac{1}{xy} + \dfrac{1}{yz} - \dfrac{1}{zx}$

Blank : ① $\dfrac{12}{12}=1$ ② $\dfrac{3+20}{12}=\dfrac{23}{12}$ ③ $\dfrac{21+10}{36}=\dfrac{31}{36}$ ④ LCD (least common denominator)

⑤ $\dfrac{y-z}{yz} - \dfrac{z-x}{zx} + \dfrac{y+x}{xy}$

⑥ $\dfrac{a+b}{ab} - \dfrac{b+c}{bc} - \dfrac{c+a}{ca}$

⑦ $(x+y)^{-2} - (x-y)^{-2}$

⑧ $(x-y)^{-1} + (x+y)^{-1}$

⑨ $\dfrac{x}{x-1} + \dfrac{4}{x+1}$

⑩ $\dfrac{2}{b-3} + \dfrac{4}{b+3}$

⑪ $\dfrac{1}{x^2-2x} - \dfrac{1}{x^2-4}$

⑫ $\dfrac{1}{x^2-4} + \dfrac{1}{(x-2)^2}$

⑬ $\dfrac{1}{t^2-3t+2} - \dfrac{1}{t^3-2t^2+t}$

⑭ $\dfrac{1}{x^2-2x+1} - \dfrac{1}{x^3-x}$

⑮ $\dfrac{a}{a^2-25} + \dfrac{5}{a+5} - \dfrac{6}{a}$

⑯ $\dfrac{4m}{m-10} + \dfrac{3+m}{m} - \dfrac{2}{m^2-10m}$

⑰ $\dfrac{a+b}{a-b} + \dfrac{a-b}{a+b} - \dfrac{b-a}{a-b} - \dfrac{a-b}{a+b}$

⑱ $\dfrac{a+b}{a-b} + \dfrac{b-a}{a+b} + \dfrac{b^2-a^2}{(a-b)^2} - \dfrac{b^2+a^2}{(a+b)^2}$

⑲ $\dfrac{2}{x^2-y^2+4x+4} - \dfrac{1}{x+y+2}$

⑳ $\dfrac{1}{a^3+a^2+a+1} + \dfrac{1}{a^2-1}$

3. Expand Knowledge*

EXAMPLE 3.* Add and subtract.

$$\frac{x}{(x-y)(x-z)} - \frac{y}{(x-y)(y-z)} + \frac{z}{(x-z)(y-z)}$$

Mia's Algebra 2

6.4 Complex Fractions

1. Complex Fraction

※ **Simplifying Complex Fractions**

$$\cfrac{\frac{A}{B}}{\frac{C}{D}} = \underset{\text{inside}}{\left(\cfrac{\frac{A}{B}}{\frac{C}{D}}\right)}^{\text{outside}} = \frac{AD}{BC} \begin{matrix}\text{← outside}\\ \text{← inside}\end{matrix}$$

$$\frac{\text{multiplying outside}}{\text{multiplying inside}}$$

☺ Tip: You can cancel (=reduce) the factors of complex fractions as;

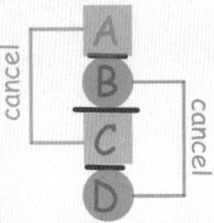

ex) $\dfrac{\frac{ab^3}{c}}{\frac{a^2}{c^4}} = \dfrac{\frac{b^3}{1}}{\boxed{①}} = \dfrac{\boxed{③}}{a}$
$\boxed{②}$

Blank : ① a ② c^3 ③ b^3c^3

330 Mia's Algebra 2

EXAMPLE 1. Simplify.

① $\dfrac{\dfrac{x^3 y^2 z}{ab^2}}{\dfrac{a^3 x^2 y}{b^2}}$

② $\dfrac{\dfrac{a^2 bc^3}{x^2 y^2}}{\dfrac{ab^2}{c^4 x^2 y^3}}$

③ $\dfrac{\dfrac{x^2-1}{2x-1}}{\dfrac{x+1}{2x^2-3x+1}}$

④ $\dfrac{\dfrac{a^2-100}{a^2}}{\dfrac{3a^2-31a+10}{2a}}$

⑤ $\dfrac{\dfrac{a-b}{a^4-b^4}}{\dfrac{a^3+b^3}{a^2+b^2}}$

⑥ $\dfrac{\dfrac{x^4-1}{x^2-2x+1}}{\dfrac{x^3-1}{x^2+x}}$

⑦ $\dfrac{\dfrac{x}{2x+4}}{4x}$

⑧ $\dfrac{\dfrac{x^2-1}{x+1}}{x}$

⑨ $\dfrac{\dfrac{3x^2+5x-2}{x-3}}{3x-1}$

⑩ $\dfrac{\dfrac{2x+4}{5x}}{x+2}$

EXAMPLE 2. Simplify.

① $\dfrac{a-b}{a^{-1}-b^{-1}}$

② $\dfrac{a^{-2}-b^{-2}}{a^{-1}-b^{-1}}$

③ $\dfrac{x^{-2}+x}{x^{-1}+1}$

④ $\dfrac{x^2-x^{-2}}{x-x^{-1}}$

⑤ $\dfrac{\dfrac{1}{x^2}-\dfrac{1}{y^2}}{\dfrac{1}{x^2}-\dfrac{2}{xy}+\dfrac{1}{y^2}}$

⑥ $\dfrac{\dfrac{1}{x^2}-\dfrac{1}{y^2}}{\dfrac{2}{x^2}-\dfrac{1}{xy}-\dfrac{1}{y^2}}$

⑦ $\dfrac{1-\dfrac{1}{x+1}}{1+\dfrac{1}{x-1}}$

⑧ $\dfrac{1-\dfrac{1}{x+1}}{1+\dfrac{1}{x^2-1}}$

⑨ $\dfrac{\dfrac{x+y}{x-y}+\dfrac{x-y}{x+y}}{\dfrac{x+y}{x-y}-\dfrac{x-y}{x+y}}$

⑩ $\dfrac{\dfrac{x}{y}-\dfrac{x-y}{x+y}}{\dfrac{x}{y}+\dfrac{x+y}{x-y}}$

⑪ $\dfrac{1+\dfrac{1}{1+\dfrac{1}{x}}}{\dfrac{1}{x+1}}$

⑫ $\dfrac{1}{1-\dfrac{1}{1-\dfrac{1}{a}}}$

2. Expand Knowledge*

EXAMPLE 3. * Simplify.

① $\dfrac{\dfrac{(n+3)!}{3^{n+1}}}{\dfrac{n!}{3^n}}$

② $\dfrac{\dfrac{n!}{2^n}}{\dfrac{(n+2)!}{2^{n+2}}}$

③ $\dfrac{\dfrac{(n+1)^{n+1}}{(n+1)!}}{\dfrac{n+1}{n!}}$

④ $\dfrac{\dfrac{(n+1)!}{n^n}}{\dfrac{n!}{n^{n+1}}}$

Mia's Algebra 2

6.5 Rational Equations & Word Problems

1. Rational Equations

※ **Rational Equations**

Try to clear the denominators by multiplying each side by ①_____ (least common denominator) of all of the denominators.

$$\frac{x}{2} - \frac{4}{x} = -1$$

$$\frac{x}{2}(2 \cdot x) - \frac{4}{x}(2 \cdot x) = -1(2 \cdot x)$$

multiply LCD

$$x^2 - 8 = -2x$$

clear the denominator

☺ Careful! Check if the solution is okay.

Sometimes it gives an "*extraneous solutions*". (= solution that does not actually work)

So put them into the original equation and ②_____ !

(Especially see if makes the denominator 0)

EXAMPLE 1. Solve the equations.

① $\dfrac{3}{x} + \dfrac{1}{5} = \dfrac{7}{x}$

② $1 + \dfrac{1}{x} = \dfrac{30}{x^2}$

Blank : ① LCD ② check

③ $\dfrac{6}{x+1} = \dfrac{3}{x-2}$

④ $\dfrac{12}{a} = \dfrac{4}{a-4}$

⑤ $\dfrac{1}{x} + \dfrac{1}{x+5} = \dfrac{x+6}{x+5}$

⑥ $\dfrac{2}{x-6} + \dfrac{7}{6-x} = \dfrac{9}{x+3}$

⑦ $\dfrac{6}{y+4} - \dfrac{3}{y-4} = \dfrac{15}{y^2-16}$

⑧ $\dfrac{60}{c^2-36} = \dfrac{5}{c-6} + 1$

⑨ $\dfrac{1}{x+6} + \dfrac{3}{x+4} = -2$

⑩ $\dfrac{x+8}{x^2+7x+12} - \dfrac{8}{x^2+8x+16} = \dfrac{x-8}{x^2+7x+12}$

2. Word Problems

1) Numbers and General

EXAMPLE 2. The reciprocal of half a number decreased by half the reciprocal of the number is $\dfrac{1}{2}$. Find the number.

EXAMPLE 3. Find two numbers that differ by 1 and whose reciprocals differ by $\frac{1}{2}$.

EXAMPLE 4. A car rented by a group of friends for 20$ and the cost is shared equally. If there is one less person in the group then each of the remaining friends will pay 1$ more. How many friends rented the car?

2) Motions

EXAMPLE 5. Tim can run 10 miles in the same amount of time it takes Mike to run 20 miles. If Mike runs 3 mph faster than Tim, how fast does Mike run?

EXAMPLE 6. Jenny hikes 6 miles from A to B at a rate of x mph. For the return trip her rate was 1 mph faster. It took her 5 hours for the entire round trip. What is x?

EXAMPLE 7. During a marathon, Albert jogged 30 miles. When he got tired, he walked 5 miles to finish the line. Albert jogs 5 mph faster than he walks. If it took him 6 hours to finish his marathon, how fast he was jogging?

3) Tail wind and Head wind

With a tail wind: ground speed = aircraft speed + wind speed.

With a head wind: ground speed = aircraft speed − wind speed.

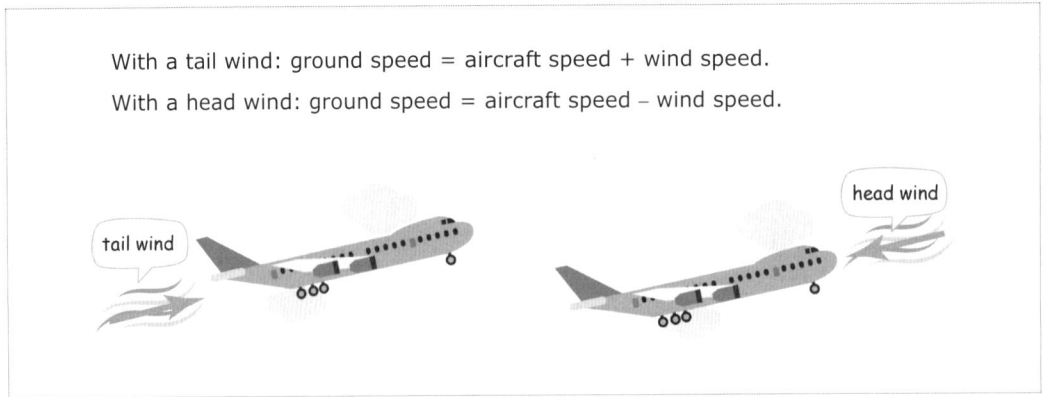

EXAMPLE 8. An airline travels 400 miles against the wind in the same amount of time that it travels 600 miles with the wind. If the speed of the wind is 10 mph, how fast does the airline travel against the wind?

EXAMPLE 9. A boat travels 10km upstream and then back in 8 hours total. If the speed of the boat is 5 km/h in still water, what is the speed of the current?

EXAMPLE 10. Karl is training for swimming. One day he swam for a total 5 hours. He swam 30 miles against the current, and 20 miles with the current. The speed of the current was 4 mph. How fast was Karl swimming with the current?

4) Average Speed

> ☺ Tip:
>
> $$\text{Average Speed} = \frac{\text{Total Distance}}{\text{Total Time}}$$
>
> Careful! Average speed of two speeds NOT equal to their arithmetic mean.

EXAMPLE 11. Esther drove halfway of the trip at 40 mph and rest of the way at x mph. If the average speed during the trip was 50mph, then what is x?

[Hint: If the distance is not given, then let it 1 mile or just pick a number]

EXAMPLE 12. Maria traveled for 90 km/h for the first 30% of the trip, and she averaged 60 km/h for the whole trip. What was her average speed for the last 70% of the trip?

5) Work

☺ Tip: When you have a work problem, remember;

① work = work rate × time
② work rate of A + work rate of B = rate of working together

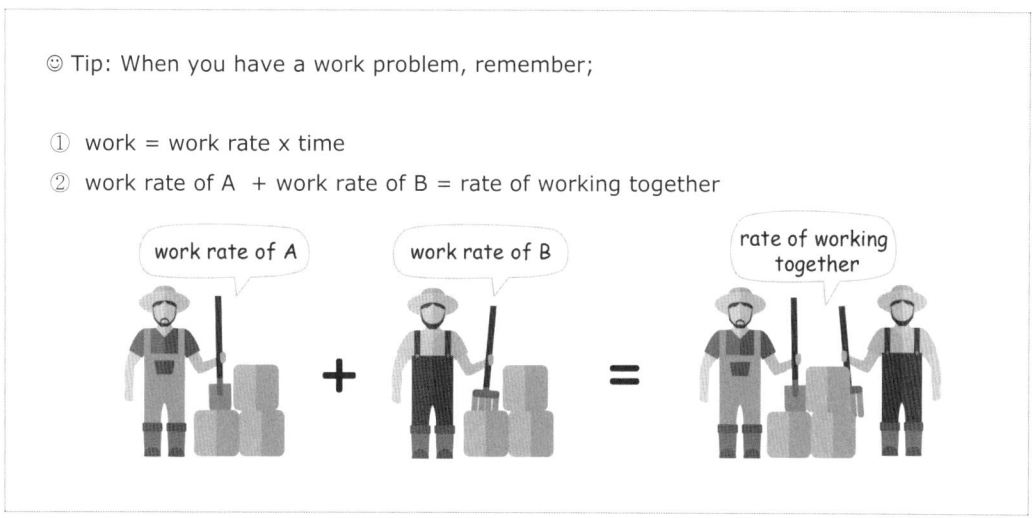

EXAMPLE 13. Noah and John paint houses together. If Noah can paint 2 houses in 6 days and John can paint 4 houses in 6 days, how long would it take the two of them to paint 20 houses together?

EXAMPLE 14. It took Anthony and Britney 6 hours to rake the leaves together last year. The previous year it took Britney 10 hours to do it alone. How long will it take Anthony if he takes them by himself this year?

[Hint: If the work amount is not given, then let it 1]

EXAMPLE 15. A big pipe can empty the swimming pool in 5 less time than a smaller second pipe can. Together they can empty the pool in 6 hours. How much time would it take the big pipe alone to empty it?

EXAMPLE 16. * Pipe A can fill a tank in 5 hours. Pipe B can fill the tank in 2 hours less time than it takes pipe C to *empty it*. With all pipes open it takes 3 hours to fill the tank. How long will it take pipe C to empty the tank?

EXAMPLE 17. * Annie is working on an art project for 10 days and then Cindy joined. Together, they finish the art project in 6 more days. Cindy could have done the entire art project alone in 30 days. How long would it have Annie to do the entire art project alone?

Mia's Algebra 2

6.6 Graph of Rational Functions

1. Asymptotes of Rational expressions

   Asymptotes are invisible lines which are graph *approaches* very closely.

   ☺ Notation: $x \to 2$ means x approaches to (get closer to) 2.

   $x \to \infty$ means x gets bigger and bigger.

   'Vertical' Asymptote :

   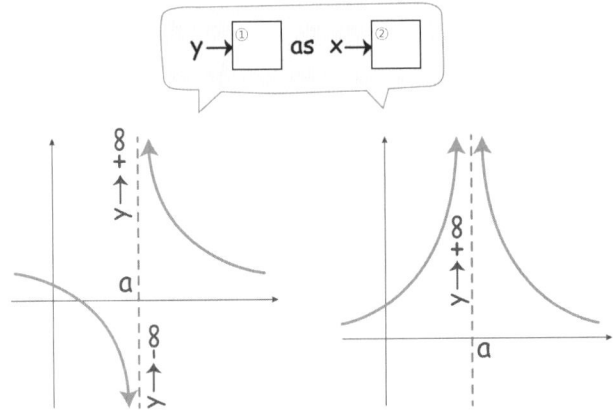

   'Horizontal' Asymptote :

   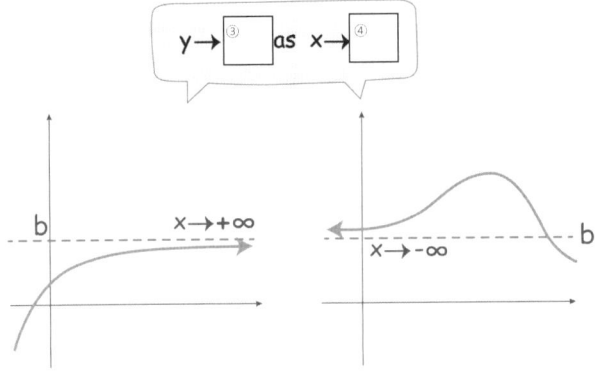

   Blank : ① ± ∞   ② a   ③ b   ④ ± ∞

346   Mia's Algebra 2

※ **Rational Functions**

Rational Function

$$R(x) = \frac{P(x)}{Q(x)}$$

Ratio of two Polynomials

① Domain : ①_____ (②Reduce / Do not reduce)

② Vertical Asymptotes : ③_____ (④Reduce / Do not reduce)

③ Hole: When you **reduce (x-h)** from the top and the bottom, then there will be a hole at ⑤_____.

④ Horizontal Asymptotes

: ⑥_____ the degrees of the top and the bottom

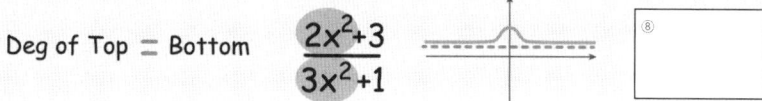

Deg of Top < Bottom $\dfrac{2x+3}{3x^2+1}$ ⑦

Deg of Top = Bottom $\dfrac{2x^2+3}{3x^2+1}$ ⑧

Deg of Top > Bottom $\dfrac{2x^3+3}{3x+1}$ ⑨

Blank : ① Q(x) ≠ 0   ② Do not reduce   ③ Q(x) = 0   ④ Reduce   ⑤ x=h   ⑥ Compare
⑦ y=0   ⑧ y=$\dfrac{2}{3}$ (ratio of leading coefficients)   ⑨ none

EXAMPLE 1. Determine the equations of
① Domain,
② vertical asymptotes,
③ and the values of x for any holes,
④ horizontal asymptotes
in the graph of each rational function.

① $f(x) = \dfrac{4}{x^2 + 3x - 10}$

② $f(x) = \dfrac{3x^2 - 5x - 2}{x + 3}$

③ $f(x) = \dfrac{x^2 - x - 12}{x^2 - 4x}$

④ $f(x) = \dfrac{3x - 1}{3x^2 + 5x - 2}$

⑤ $f(x) = \dfrac{x-1}{x^2 - 6x + 5}$

⑥ $f(x) = \dfrac{x^2 - 6x - 7}{x^2 + 6x - 7}$

⑦ $f(x) = \dfrac{8x^3 + 1}{2x^2 - 9x - 5}$

⑧ $f(x) = \dfrac{x^3 - 1}{3x^2 - x - 2}$

⑨ $f(x) = \dfrac{2x^2 - 9x - 5}{8x^3 + 1}$

⑩ $f(x) = \dfrac{3x^2 - x - 2}{x^3 - 1}$

2. Finding x-intercepts

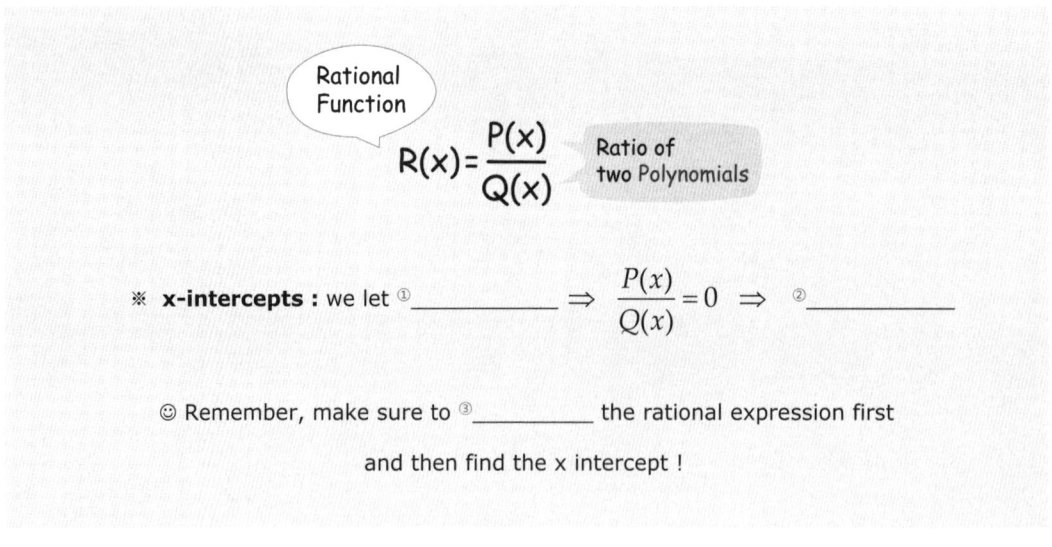

※ **x-intercepts** : we let ① _____ $\Rightarrow \dfrac{P(x)}{Q(x)} = 0 \Rightarrow$ ② _____

☺ Remember, make sure to ③ _____ the rational expression first and then find the x intercept !

Blank : ① y = 0   ② P(x) = 0   ③ reduce

EXAMPLE 2. Find the x intercept.

① $f(x) = \dfrac{x^2 - 4}{x^2 - 4x}$

② $g(x) = \dfrac{x^2 + 5x - 24}{x^2 - 36}$

③ $F(x) = \dfrac{x^2 - x - 2}{2x^2 - 5x + 2}$

④ $h(x) = \dfrac{4x^2 - 11x + 6}{16x^2 - 24x + 9}$

⑤ $R(x) = \dfrac{x^4 - 16}{x^2 - 2x}$

⑥ $R(x) = \dfrac{x^3 - 8}{x^2 - 5x + 6}$

EXAMPLE 3. Match the graph of the rational function with its equation.

A. $f(x) = \dfrac{(x+2)(x-3)}{x+4}$

B. $f(x) = \dfrac{-2}{x^2+1}$

C. $f(x) = \dfrac{x+2}{(x-4)(x-8)}$

D. $f(x) = \dfrac{(x+2)(x-8)}{(x-4)(x-8)}$

①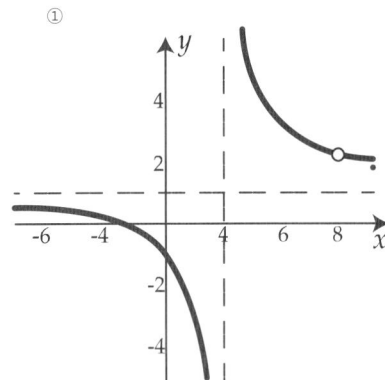

②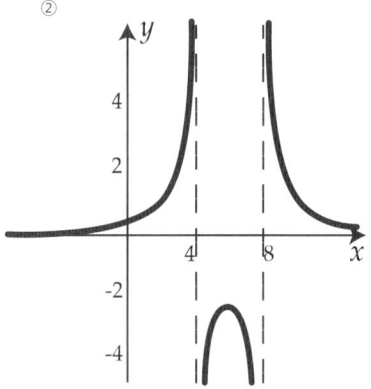

③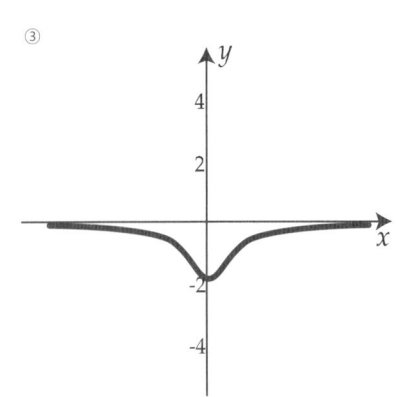

④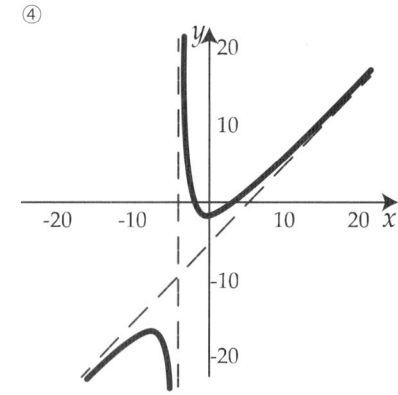

3. Expand Knowledge*

EXAMPLE 4.* What is the difference between $y = \dfrac{x^2-1}{x+1}$ and $y = x-1$?

Part 7
Radicals

7.1 Roots of Real Numbers

7.2 Properties of Radicals

7.3 Operations of Radicals

7.4 Radical Equations

7.5 Graph of Radical Function

7.6 Rational and Real Exponents

Mia's Algebra 2
7.1 Roots of Real Numbers

1. Finding Roots

Squaring means multiplying a number by itself
A **square root** goes the other way!

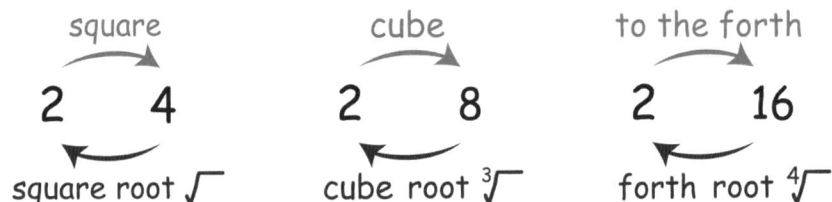

Likewise we have **cube root**, **forth root**, **fifth root**,….

This is the special symbol that means "**nth root**", it is the "①_____" symbol with a little n to mean nth root.

※ **nth root**

$$a^n = b \Longleftrightarrow a = \sqrt[n]{b} = b^{\frac{1}{n}}$$

(nth power) (nth root)

☺ Real / Imaginary?

$\sqrt[\text{even}]{+}$ (②Real/Imaginary) $\sqrt[\text{even}]{-}$ (③Real/Imaginary)

$\sqrt[\text{odd}]{+}$ (④Real/Imaginary) $\sqrt[\text{odd}]{-}$ (⑤Real/Imaginary)

Blank : ① radical   ② real   ③ imaginary   ④ real   ⑤ real

☺ Remember : negative sign can come out from the odd roots.

$$\sqrt[\text{odd}]{-\#} = -\sqrt[\text{odd}]{\#}$$

ex) $\sqrt[3]{-8} = -\sqrt[3]{8} = -2$

☺ Reminder :

$10^2 = $ ____ $11^2 = $ ____ $12^2 = $ ____ $13^2 = $ ____ $14^2 = $ ____

$15^2 = $ ____ $16^2 = $ ____ $17^2 = $ ____ $20^2 = $ ____ $100^2 = $ ____

$2^3 = $ ____ $3^3 = $ ____ $4^3 = $ ____ $5^3 = $ ____ $6^3 = $ ____

$2^4 = $ ____ $3^4 = $ ____ $4^4 = $ ____ $5^4 = $ ____

$2^5 = $ ____ $2^6 = $ ____ $2^7 = $ ____ $2^{10} = $ ____

EXAMPLE 1. Simplify each expression that has a real root. If the expression does not represent a real number, say none.

① a) $\sqrt{9}$ b) $-\sqrt{9}$ c) $\sqrt{-9}$ d) $\sqrt{0.0009}$

② a) $\sqrt{100}$ b) $\sqrt{-100}$ c) $-\sqrt{100}$ d) $\sqrt[4]{10000}$

Blank : $10^2=100$ $11^2=121$ $12^2=144$ $13^2=169$ $14^2=196$
          $15^2=225$ $16^2=256$ $17^2=289$ $20^2=400$ $100^2=10000$
          $2^3=8$ $3^3=27$ $4^3=64$ $5^3=125$ $6^3=216$
          $2^4=16$ $3^4=81$ $4^4=256$ $5^4=625$ $2^5=32$ $2^6=64$ $2^7=128$ $2^{10}=1024$

③ a) $\sqrt{0.81}$ b) $-\sqrt{0.81}$ c) $\sqrt{-0.81}$ d) $\sqrt[4]{0.0081}$

④ a) $\sqrt{0.64}$ b) $\sqrt{-0.64}$ c) $-\sqrt{0.64}$ d) $\sqrt[3]{0.064}$

⑤ a) $\sqrt[3]{27}$ b) $\sqrt[3]{-27}$ c) $-\sqrt[3]{-27}$ d) $\sqrt[3]{-0.027}$

⑥ a) $\sqrt[3]{125}$ b) $-\sqrt[3]{-125}$ c) $-\sqrt[3]{125}$ d) $-\sqrt[3]{-0.125}$

⑦ a) $\sqrt[3]{64}$ b) $\sqrt[3]{-125}$ c) $\sqrt[4]{16}$ d) $\sqrt[4]{81}$

⑧ a) $\sqrt[3]{-216}$ b) $\sqrt[3]{8}$ c) $\sqrt[4]{625}$ d) $\sqrt[4]{256}$

⑨ a) $\sqrt[4]{-16}$ b) $\sqrt[5]{-32}$ c) $\sqrt[6]{64}$ d) $\sqrt[10]{1024}$

⑩ a) $\sqrt[4]{-81}$ b) $\sqrt[6]{-64}$ c) $\sqrt[7]{-128}$ d) $\sqrt[9]{-512}$

⑪ a) $\sqrt{\dfrac{225}{81}}$ b) $\sqrt{\dfrac{16}{81}}$ c) $\sqrt[4]{\dfrac{1}{81}}$ d) $\sqrt[4]{\dfrac{16}{81}}$

⑫ a) $\sqrt{\dfrac{169}{64}}$ b) $\sqrt{\dfrac{256}{64}}$ c) $\sqrt[3]{\dfrac{1}{64}}$ d) $\sqrt[6]{\dfrac{1}{64}}$

⑬ a) $\sqrt{3^2}$ b) $\sqrt{3^4}$ c) $\sqrt{3^{12}}$ d) $\sqrt{3^{24}}$

⑭ a) $\sqrt{4^2}$ b) $\sqrt{4^6}$ c) $\sqrt{4^{10}}$ d) $\sqrt{4^{100}}$

⑮ a) $\sqrt{3^2}$ b) $(\sqrt{3})^2$ c) $\sqrt{-3^2}$ d) $\sqrt{(-3)^2}$

⑯ a) $\sqrt{6^2}$ b) $\sqrt{-6^2}$ c) $(\sqrt{6})^2$ d) $\sqrt{(-6)^2}$

⑰ a) $(-\sqrt{3})^2$ b) $-(-\sqrt{3})^2$ c) $-\sqrt{(-3)^2}$ d) $-\sqrt{(-0.09)^2}$

⑱ a) $(-\sqrt{6})^2$ b) $-(-\sqrt{6})^2$ c) $-\sqrt{(-6)^2}$ d) $-\sqrt{(-0.36)^2}$

⑲ a) $\sqrt{(-8)^2}$ b) $\sqrt[3]{(-8)^3}$ c) $\sqrt[4]{(-8)^4}$ d) $\sqrt[5]{(-8)^5}$

⑳ a) $\sqrt{(-3)^2}$ b) $\sqrt[3]{(-3)^3}$ c) $\sqrt[8]{(-3)^8}$ d) $\sqrt[23]{(-3)^{23}}$

2. Simplify Radicals

Let's compare $\sqrt[3]{x^3}$ vs $\sqrt{x^2}$

$\sqrt[3]{x^3} = \boxed{①}$

ex) $\sqrt[3]{(3)^3} = +3$

ex) $\sqrt[3]{(-3)^3} = -3$

itself!

$\sqrt{x^2} = \boxed{②}$

ex) $\sqrt{(3)^2} = +3$

ex) $\sqrt{(-3)^2} = +3$

always positive

So we can say that

$\sqrt[n]{x^n} \begin{cases} \boxed{③}, & \text{if } n \text{ is odd} \\ \boxed{④}, & \text{if } n \text{ is even} \end{cases}$

※ **Properties of Radicals**

$\sqrt[n]{x^n} \begin{cases} x, & \text{if } n \text{ is odd} \quad \text{(itself!)} \\ |x|, & \text{if } n \text{ is even} \quad \text{(always positive)} \end{cases}$

Blank : ① x ② $|x|$ ③ x ④ $|x|$

☺ Tip: When do we need absolute value?

$$\sqrt[n]{(x^m)^n} = |x^m|$$

(even root, even power, odd power, absolute value)

EXAMPLE 2. Simplify the radical expressions. Variables may be either positive or negative.

☺ Tip: Perfect square is $x^{multiples\ of\ 2}$, perfect cube is $x^{multiples\ of\ 3}$, ...

$$\sqrt{x^8 y^{10}} = \sqrt[2]{x^8 y^{10}} = x^4 |y^5|$$

(½ power, perfect squares, from 8/2, from 10/2)

① $\sqrt{144 p^6 q^{18}}$

② $\sqrt{121 x^6 y^{14}}$

③ $-\sqrt{100 a^2 b^4 c^6}$

④ $-\sqrt{144 a^8 b^{10} c^{12}}$

⑤ $\sqrt{\dfrac{16 a^4 b^8}{25 c^{12}}}$

⑥ $\sqrt{\dfrac{225 a^{14}}{64 c^6 b^2}}$

Blank : ① 4 ② 5

⑦ $\sqrt[3]{-8x^{15}y^{21}z^6}$

⑧ $\sqrt[3]{216m^3n^{12}p^{15}}$

⑨ $\sqrt[4]{16x^{12}y^{16}z^{24}}$

⑩ $\sqrt[4]{81x^4y^{20}z^{28}}$

⑪ $\sqrt{(2x-1)^2}$

⑫ $\sqrt{(x+5)^2}$

⑬ $\sqrt[3]{(5m+4)^6}$

⑭ $\sqrt[3]{(7m-2)^9}$

⑮ $\sqrt{36x^2-12x+1}$

⑯ $\sqrt{x^2-10x+25}$

3. Expand Knowledge*

EXAMPLE 3. * Evaluate.

$$\sqrt{(-2)^2} + \sqrt[3]{(-3)^3} + \sqrt[4]{(-4)^4} + \sqrt[5]{(-5)^5} + \ldots + \sqrt[20]{(-20)^{20}}$$

※ **Radical Property = Absolute Value definition** (learned in Chapter 1.8)

$$\sqrt{x^2} = |x| = \begin{cases} \boxed{①} \,,\ x \geq 0 \\ \boxed{②} \,,\ x < 0 \end{cases}$$

"flip back to positive"

EXAMPLE 4. * Simplify using the radical property.

① $\sqrt{(x-2)^2}$, $x \geq 2$

② $\sqrt{(2-y)^2}$, $y < 2$

Blank : ① x   ② –x

③ $\sqrt{(1-2x)^2}$, $x > \dfrac{1}{2}$

④ $\sqrt{(2-c)^2}$, $c \geq 2$

⑤ $\sqrt{(x-1)^2} + \sqrt{(x-5)^2}$, $1 < x < 5$

⑥ $\sqrt{(2-x)^2} + \sqrt{4(x+2)^2}$, $-2 < x < 2$

⑦ $\sqrt{(-x+1)^2} + \sqrt{(2-x)^2}$, $-1 < x < 2$

⑧ $\sqrt{(x-1)^2} + \sqrt{(5-x)^2}$, $1 < x < 5$

⑨ $\sqrt{(x-y)^2} + \sqrt{x^2} + \sqrt{(y-x)^2}$, $0 \leq x \leq y$ ⑩ $\sqrt{(a-b)^2} + \sqrt{(b-a)^2}$, $a \geq b$

⑪ $\sqrt{(a-1)^2} + \sqrt{a^2} + \sqrt{(1-a)^2}$, $0 < a < 1$

Mia's Algebra 2

7.2 Properties of Radicals

1. Properties of Radicals

   ※ **Product Property**

   $$\sqrt[odd]{ab} = \sqrt[odd]{a} \cdot \sqrt[odd]{b}$$ when a, b are real numbers.

   $$\sqrt[even]{ab} = \sqrt[even]{a} \cdot \sqrt[even]{b}$$ when a, b are ① _____ real numbers.

   ex) $\sqrt{200} = \sqrt{100 \cdot 2} = \sqrt{100} \cdot \sqrt{2} = \boxed{②} \sqrt{2}$

   ※ **Quotient Property**

   $$\sqrt[n]{\frac{a}{b}} = \frac{\sqrt[n]{a}}{\sqrt[n]{b}}$$ when a, b are real numbers, $b \neq 0$

EXAMPLE 1. Simplify.

① a) $\sqrt{8}$ b) $\sqrt{48}$ c) $\sqrt{250}$

② a) $\sqrt{24}$ b) $\sqrt{32}$ c) $\sqrt{128}$

Blank : ① positive   ② 10

③ a) $\sqrt[3]{8}$ b) $\sqrt[3]{16}$ c) $\sqrt[3]{250}$

④ a) $\sqrt[3]{24}$ b) $\sqrt[3]{64}$ c) $\sqrt[3]{192}$

⑤ a) $\sqrt[4]{16}$ b) $\sqrt[4]{32}$ c) $\sqrt[4]{48}$

⑥ a) $\sqrt[4]{81}$ b) $\sqrt[4]{162}$ c) $\sqrt[4]{256}$

⑦ a) $\sqrt[5]{64}$ b) $\sqrt[6]{192}$

EXAMPLE 2. Simplify the radical expressions. <u>Variables may be either positive or negative.</u>

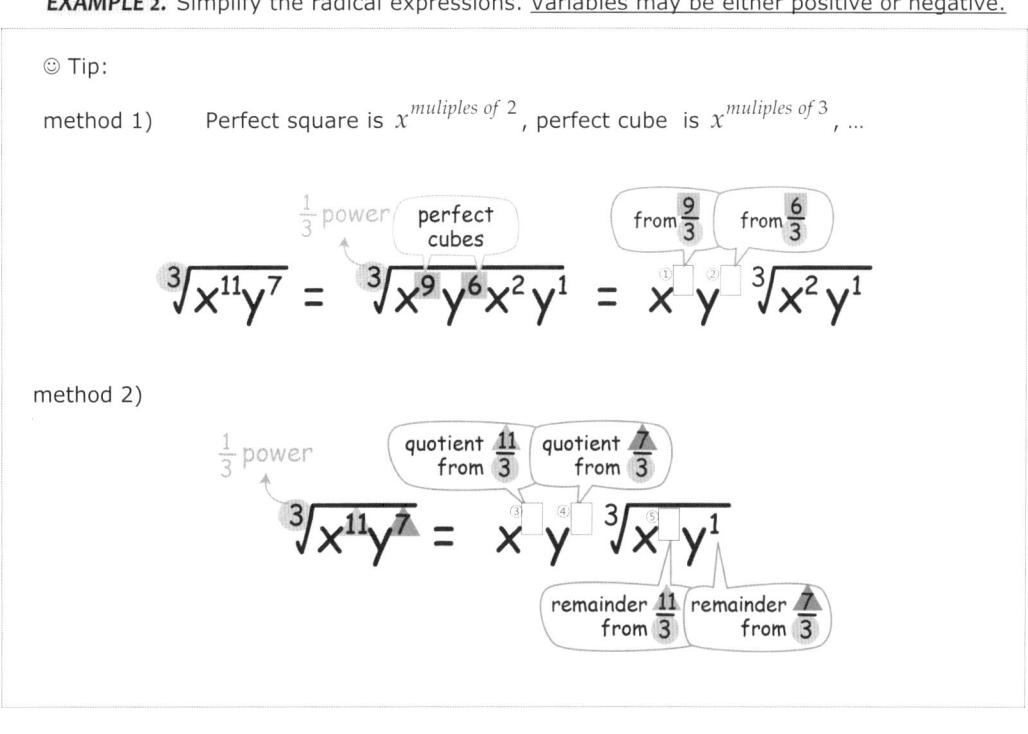

① $\sqrt{75p^7q^6}$

② $\sqrt{45x^5y^3}$

③ $\sqrt{128a^4b^7c^{11}}$

④ $\sqrt{128a^3b^6c^9}$

Blank : ① 3 ② 2 ③ 3 ④ 2 ⑤ 2

⑤ $\sqrt{\dfrac{50a^2b}{c^{14}}}$ 　　　　　　　⑥ $\sqrt{\dfrac{108a^9}{c^2b^8}}$

⑦ $\sqrt[3]{54a^4b^7}$ 　　　　　　　⑧ $\sqrt[3]{64x^{11}y^7}$

⑨ $\sqrt[3]{24x^9y^{20}z^4}$ 　　　　　　　⑩ $\sqrt[3]{81m^6n^5p^8}$

⑪ $\sqrt[3]{\dfrac{125a^7b^8}{c^{12}}}$ 　　　　　　　⑫ $\sqrt[3]{\dfrac{32a^{15}}{c^8b^{11}}}$

⑬ $\sqrt[4]{162x^6y^5z^{13}}$ 　　　　　　　⑭ $\sqrt[4]{32x^9y^{20}z^6}$

⑮ $\sqrt[5]{a^{11}b^{15}c^{22}}$ 　　　　　　　⑯ $\sqrt[6]{x^{10}y^{12}z^7}$

EXAMPLE 3. Simplify the radical expressions.

① $\sqrt{70} \cdot \sqrt{21}$ 　　　　　　　② $\sqrt{125} \cdot \sqrt{10}$

③ $\sqrt[3]{15} \cdot \sqrt[3]{18}$ 　　　　　　　④ $\sqrt[3]{16} \cdot \sqrt[3]{12}$

⑤ $\dfrac{\sqrt{6}}{\sqrt{33}}$ 　　　　　　　⑥ $\dfrac{\sqrt{13}}{\sqrt{8}}$

⑦ $\sqrt{\dfrac{7}{3}}$ 　　　　　　　⑧ $\sqrt{\dfrac{11}{5}}$

⑨ $\dfrac{\sqrt[3]{14}}{\sqrt[3]{6}}$ 　　　　　　　⑩ $\dfrac{\sqrt[3]{40}}{\sqrt[3]{48}}$

⑪ $\sqrt[3]{\dfrac{11}{3}}$ ⑫ $\sqrt[3]{\dfrac{9}{4}}$

⑬ $\dfrac{\sqrt[4]{15}}{\sqrt[4]{6}}$ ⑭ $\dfrac{\sqrt[4]{6}}{\sqrt[4]{8}}$

2. Expand Knowledge*

EXAMPLE 4. *When x > 0 and y > 0, is this true or false?

I. $\sqrt{2} \cdot \sqrt{3} = \sqrt{6}$

II. $\sqrt{-2} \cdot \sqrt{-3} = \sqrt{6}$

III. $\sqrt{x^2 + y^2} = x + y$

IV. $\sqrt{x} + \sqrt{x} = \sqrt{2x}$

V. $(\sqrt{x} + \sqrt{y})(\sqrt{x} - \sqrt{y}) = x - y$

Mia's Algebra 2

7.3 Operations of Radicals

1. Operations with Radical Expressions

   EXAMPLE 1. Simplify.

   ① $\sqrt{27} + \sqrt{12} - \sqrt{48}$

   ② $\sqrt{125} - 2\sqrt{80} + \sqrt{45}$

   ③ $\sqrt[3]{54} - \sqrt[3]{16} - \sqrt[3]{27}$

   ④ $\sqrt[3]{32} + \sqrt[3]{64} + \sqrt[3]{108}$

   ⑤ $\sqrt{\dfrac{50}{3}} - \sqrt{\dfrac{2}{3}}$

   ⑥ $\sqrt{\dfrac{3}{5}} + \sqrt{\dfrac{7}{5}}$

   ⑦ $\sqrt{2}(\sqrt{32} + \sqrt{12})$

   ⑧ $\sqrt{11}(2\sqrt{66} - 3\sqrt{55})$

⑨ $(2+3\sqrt{2})(3-\sqrt{2})$ ⑩ $(6\sqrt{7}+\sqrt{2})(\sqrt{7}-\sqrt{2})$

⑪ $(2+\sqrt{10})(2-\sqrt{10})$ ⑫ $(1-\sqrt{5})(1+\sqrt{5})$

⑬ $(\sqrt{10}-3)(\sqrt{10}+3)$ ⑭ $(2\sqrt{2}+3)(2\sqrt{2}-3)$

⑮ $(3\sqrt{2}-4)(3\sqrt{2}+4)$ ⑯ $(2\sqrt{5}+\sqrt{3})(2\sqrt{5}-\sqrt{3})$

⑰ $(\sqrt{11}+2)^2$ ⑱ $(3-\sqrt{7})^2$

⑲ $(2\sqrt{6}-\sqrt{21})^2$ ⑳ $(\sqrt{5}+2\sqrt{3})^2$

2. Rationalization

$$(\sqrt{a}+\sqrt{b})(\sqrt{a}-\sqrt{b}) = (\sqrt{a})^2 - (\sqrt{b})^2 = \boxed{①}$$

We can notice that the product of a pair of conjugates is a ②_____ number.

※ **Rationalization**

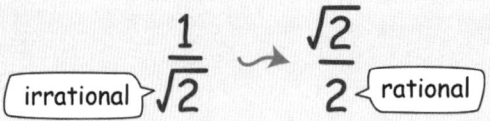

"Rationalizing the denominator" is when we remove a root (square root or cube root) from the denominator of a fraction.

We can remove the roots
by multiplying both top and bottom by a *root* or ③_____.

Blank : ① a − b   ② rational   ③ conjugate

EXAMPLE 2. Rationalize.

① $\dfrac{5\sqrt{48} + \sqrt{75}}{2\sqrt{2}}$

② $\dfrac{4\sqrt{45} - 3\sqrt{3}}{4\sqrt{5}}$

③ $\dfrac{\sqrt{2}}{\sqrt{5} - 2}$

④ $\dfrac{5}{\sqrt{2} - 1}$

⑤ $\dfrac{1 - \sqrt{2}}{1 + \sqrt{2}}$

⑥ $\dfrac{2 + \sqrt{5}}{2 - \sqrt{5}}$

⑦ $\dfrac{5 - \sqrt{3}}{4 - \sqrt{3}}$

⑧ $\dfrac{3 + \sqrt{2}}{2 - \sqrt{2}}$

EXAMPLE 3. Simplify. Assume that each radical represents a positive real number.

① $(\sqrt{5}-\sqrt{x})^2$

② $(\sqrt{x}+2)^2$

③ $(\sqrt{x-1}+1)^2$

④ $(\sqrt{2}+\sqrt{x+1})^2$

⑤ $(\sqrt{x-1}+\sqrt{x})(\sqrt{x-1}-\sqrt{x})$

⑥ $(\sqrt{x+y+1}+\sqrt{x+1})(\sqrt{x+y+1}-\sqrt{x+1})$

⑦ $(x+\sqrt{x})^2 + (x-\sqrt{x})^2$

⑧ $(\sqrt{x}+1)^2 + (\sqrt{x}-1)^2$

⑨ $(\sqrt{x}+\sqrt{y})^2 - (\sqrt{x}-\sqrt{y})^2$

⑩ $(\sqrt{x}-1)^2 - (\sqrt{x}+1)^2$

⑪ $\dfrac{1}{\sqrt{x}+\sqrt{2}}$

⑫ $\dfrac{1}{\sqrt{5}-\sqrt{x}}$

⑬ $\sqrt{x+\sqrt{x}} \cdot \sqrt{x-\sqrt{x}} \cdot \sqrt{x^2+x}$

⑭ $\sqrt{x+y} \cdot \sqrt{\sqrt{x}+\sqrt{y}} \cdot \sqrt{\sqrt{x}-\sqrt{y}}$

⑮ $\dfrac{1}{\sqrt{x+1}-\sqrt{x}}$

⑯ $\dfrac{1}{\sqrt{x+2}+\sqrt{x}}$

⑰ $\dfrac{\sqrt{x+y}+\sqrt{x-y}}{\sqrt{x+y}-\sqrt{x-y}}$

⑱ $\dfrac{\sqrt{x^2-1}+\sqrt{x^2+1}}{\sqrt{x^2-1}-\sqrt{x^2+1}}$

3. Expand Knowledge*

EXAMPLE 4.* Solve the problem.

☺ Tip: Before plugging in, simplify the question first.

① When $x = \sqrt{3} - \sqrt{2}, y = \sqrt{3} + \sqrt{2}$, find $\dfrac{1}{x} + \dfrac{1}{y}$.

② When $x = \sqrt{7} + \sqrt{3}, y = \sqrt{7} - \sqrt{3}$, find $x^2 - y^2$.

③ When $x = 2 + \sqrt{5}, y = 2 - \sqrt{5}$, find $\left(x^2 + \dfrac{1}{y^2}\right) - \left(y^2 + \dfrac{1}{x^2}\right)$.

④ When $x = \sqrt{2} + 1, y = \sqrt{2} - 1$, find $\left(x + \dfrac{1}{y}\right)\left(y + \dfrac{1}{x}\right)$.

EXAMPLE 5. * Solve the problem.

> ☺ Tip: Before plugging in,
> change the question to vertex form by completing the square.

① When $x = 4 + \sqrt{3}$, find $x^2 - 8x + 13$.

② When $x = \dfrac{1}{\sqrt{3} - 2}$, find $x^2 + 4x + 8$.

EXAMPLE 6. * Add.

$$\frac{\sqrt{x} - \sqrt{x+1}}{\sqrt{x} + \sqrt{x+1}} + \frac{\sqrt{x} + \sqrt{x+1}}{\sqrt{x} - \sqrt{x+1}}$$

EXAMPLE 7. * Multiply.
$$(7+5\sqrt{2})(7-5\sqrt{2})(5+2\sqrt{6})(5-2\sqrt{6})(3+2\sqrt{2})(3-2\sqrt{2})$$

EXAMPLE 8. * Add.
$$\frac{1}{1+\sqrt{2}}+\frac{1}{\sqrt{2}+\sqrt{3}}+\frac{1}{\sqrt{3}+\sqrt{4}}+\frac{1}{\sqrt{4}+\sqrt{5}}+\ldots+\frac{1}{\sqrt{8}+3}$$

Mia's Algebra 2

7.4 Radical Equations

1. Radical Equations

※ **How to solve a radical equation?**

i) Isolate the square root on one side of the equation.

ii) Get rid of a square root by ① _____ both sides.

$$\sqrt{x} = 4$$
$$(\sqrt{x})^2 = (4)^2$$
$$x = 16$$

☺ Careful! Check if the solution is okay.

Sometimes it gives an "*extraneous solutions*". (= solution that does not actually work)
So put them into the original equation and ② _____ !

EXAMPLE 1. Solve the equations.

① $2\sqrt{x} - 3 = 5$ ② $3\sqrt{x+2} - 5 = 4$

Blank : ① squaring ② check

③ $10 + 3\sqrt{x+1} = 1$

④ $5\sqrt{2-x} - 7 = 3$

⑤ $\sqrt{2x+15} - x = 6$

⑥ $x = \sqrt{4x-15} + 5$

⑦ $\sqrt{x-2} - \sqrt{3-x} = 1$ ⑧ $\sqrt{4x+1} - 1 = x$

⑨ $\sqrt{3x+1} = 3 + \sqrt{x-4}$ ⑩ $\sqrt{2x+3} - \sqrt{x+1} = 1$

⑪ $\sqrt{x+6}+\sqrt{2-x}=4$

⑫ $\sqrt{x+2}+\sqrt{x+5}=3$

⑬ $\sqrt{4x+5}=\sqrt{x+2}+\sqrt{x+1}$

⑭ $\sqrt{2x+6}=\sqrt{x-2}+\sqrt{x+2}$

2. Expand Knowledge*

EXAMPLE 2. *Solve the equation.

$$\sqrt{x-1}+\sqrt{x-\sqrt{x}}=1$$

EXAMPLE 3. *Solve the equation.

$$\sqrt{x\sqrt{x}+x}+\sqrt{x}=x$$

EXAMPLE 4. *Solve the inequality.

> ☺ Tip: If you have even root in your inequality,
> then you should consider where inside the root is positive or 0!

① $3\sqrt{x-1} + 6 < 15$

② $8 - \sqrt{x+2} \geq 3$

③ $9 - \sqrt{5x+10} \leq 6$

④ $2\sqrt{x-2} - 1 > 5$

⑤ $\sqrt{x-3} + \sqrt{x+4} \leq 7$

Mia's Algebra 2

7.5 Graph of Radical Function

1. Radical Function

   ※ **Graph of a Radical Function**

   Domain : ①_____

   Range : ②_____

   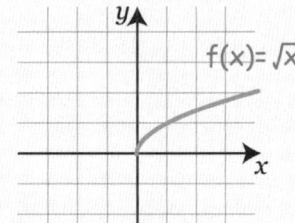

   ☺ Reminder: Transformation

y=f(x)	original function (parent function)
y=f(x) + k	Vertically Shifted ③_____ k units
y=f(x) - k	Vertically Shifted ④_____ k units (k>0)
y=f(x + h)	Horizontal Shift to the ⑤_____ h units
y=f(x - h)	Horizontal Shift to the ⑥_____ h units (h>0)
y=-f(x)	reflected over ⑦_____-axis
y=f(-x)	reflected over ⑧_____-axis
y=2f(x)	vertically ⑨_____ by the factor 2
y=0.5 f(x)	vertically ⑩_____ by the factor 0.5
y=f(2x)	horizontally shrink
y=f(0.5x)	horizontally stretch

   Blank : ① x≥0   ② y≥0   ③ up   ④ down   ⑤ left   ⑥ right   ⑦ x   ⑧ y   ⑨ stretch   ⑩ shrink

388 Mia's Algebra 2

EXAMPLE 1. Graph each function. State the domain and range of the function.

① $y = \sqrt{x-2}$

② $y = \sqrt{x+4} - 2$

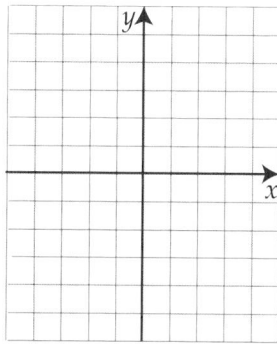

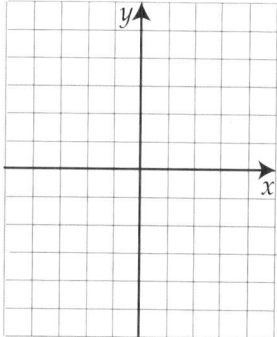

③ $y = -\sqrt{x-1}$

④ $y = -\sqrt{x+2}$

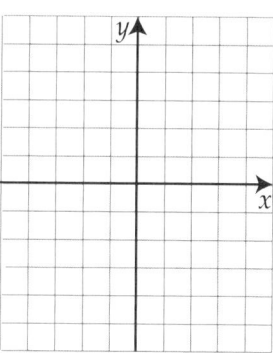

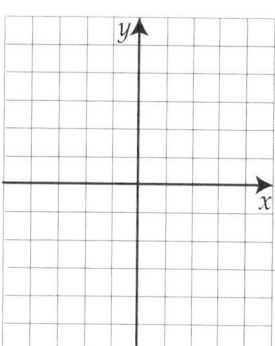

⑤ $y = 2\sqrt{-x}$

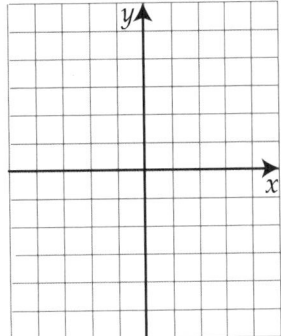

⑥ $y = 0.5\sqrt{-x}$

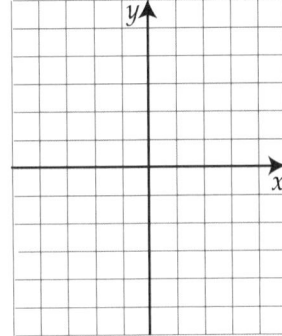

⑦ $y = 2\sqrt{x+2} + 1$

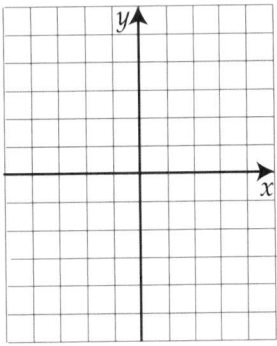

⑧ $y = 1 - \sqrt{x+3}$

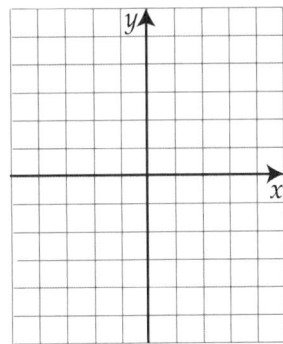

⑨ $y = \sqrt{-x-1}$

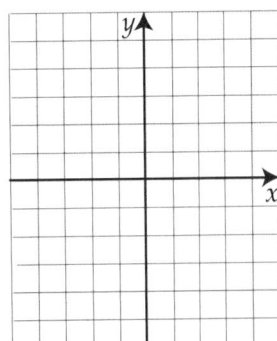

⑩ $y = \sqrt{-x+3}$

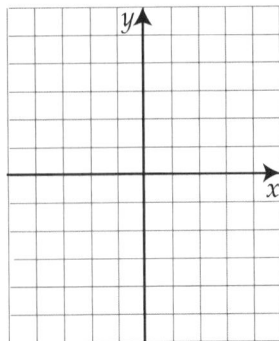

EXAMPLE 2. Find the domain of each function.

① a) $y = \sqrt{4-x}$

② a) $y = \sqrt{x-1}$

b) $y = \sqrt[3]{4-x}$

b) $y = \sqrt[3]{x-1}$

c) $y = \sqrt{4-x^2}$

c) $y = \sqrt{x^2-1}$

d) $y = \sqrt{4+x^2}$

d) $y = \sqrt{x^2+1}$

③ a) $y = \sqrt{x+2} - 1$

④ a) $y = \sqrt{x-3} + 2$

b) $y = \sqrt[3]{x+2} + 7$

b) $y = \sqrt[3]{x-3} + 5$

c) $y = \sqrt{(x+2)(x-1)}$

c) $y = \sqrt{(x-3)(x+4)}$

Mia's Algebra 2

7.6 Rational and Real Exponents

1. Rational Exponents

We know the meaning of exponents. But what if we have a rational exponent?

$b^1 =$ ①☐ $b^0 =$ ②☐ $b^{-2} =$ ③☐ (reciprocal) $b^{\frac{1}{n}} =$ ④☐

※ Rational Exponents

A rational exponent ($1/n$ power) means to take the ⑤_____:

$$b^{\frac{m}{n}} \text{ (nth root)} = \sqrt[n]{b^m} = \left(\sqrt[n]{b}\right)^m$$

ex) $x^{\frac{1}{2}} =$ ⑥____ $x^{\frac{1}{3}} =$ ⑦____ $x^{\frac{4}{3}} =$ ⑧____ $x^{\frac{3}{2}} =$ ⑨____

EXAMPLE 1. Write each expression in radical form.

① $3^{\frac{1}{6}}$ ② $8^{\frac{1}{5}}$

③ $a^{\frac{2}{3}}$ ④ $b^{\frac{4}{7}}$

⑤ $\left(x^2\right)^{\frac{3}{4}}$ ⑥ $\left(n^5\right)^{\frac{2}{7}}$

Blank : ① b ② 1 ③ $\frac{1}{b^2}$ ④ $\sqrt[n]{b}$ ⑤ nth root   ⑥ $\sqrt{x}$ ⑦ $\sqrt[3]{x}$ ⑧ $\sqrt[3]{x^4}$ ⑨ $\sqrt{x^3}$

EXAMPLE 2. Evaluate each expression.

① $32^{\frac{2}{5}}$ ② $81^{\frac{1}{4}}$

③ $27^{-\frac{2}{3}}$ ④ $8^{-\frac{2}{3}}$

⑤ $(16^{\frac{3}{2}})^3$ ⑥ $(243^{\frac{4}{5}})^{-2}$

⑦ $5^{\frac{1}{3}} \cdot 5^{\frac{5}{3}}$ ⑧ $81^{\frac{3}{4}} \cdot 81^{\frac{1}{4}}$

⑨ $\dfrac{64^{\frac{2}{3}}}{125^{\frac{2}{3}}}$ ⑩ $\dfrac{256^{\frac{3}{2}}}{16^{\frac{3}{2}}}$

⑪ $\dfrac{9^{\frac{1}{4}}}{9^{\frac{3}{4}}}$

EXAMPLE 3. Simplify each expression. Write the answers in rational exponent. (Assume that all the variables are positive.)

① $\sqrt{a} \cdot \sqrt[3]{a}$

② $\sqrt[3]{a} \cdot \sqrt[4]{a}$

③ $\sqrt[5]{c^4} \cdot c^{\frac{3}{5}}$

④ $\sqrt[5]{a^7} \cdot \sqrt[3]{a^5}$

⑤ $(\sqrt{q})^3 \cdot \sqrt[3]{q}$

⑥ $(\sqrt[4]{p})^6 \cdot \sqrt[8]{p}$

⑦ $(\sqrt[9]{a^6} \cdot \sqrt[4]{a^2})^3$

⑧ $(\sqrt[5]{b^3} \cdot \sqrt{b^5})^2$

⑨ $\sqrt{a^2b^3} \cdot \sqrt[6]{a^5b^2}$

⑩ $\sqrt[3]{m^4n^6} \cdot \sqrt[6]{m^2n^3}$

⑪ $\dfrac{\sqrt[3]{a}}{\sqrt[4]{a}}$

⑫ $\dfrac{\sqrt[7]{a}}{\sqrt[5]{a}}$

⑬ $\dfrac{\sqrt[3]{x^2}}{\sqrt[4]{x}}$

⑭ $\dfrac{\sqrt[3]{x}}{\sqrt[5]{x^3}}$

⑮ $\dfrac{(\sqrt{xy^3})^3}{\sqrt[3]{x\sqrt{y}}}$

⑯ $\dfrac{\sqrt[5]{m^6n^2}}{\sqrt{m\sqrt{n}}}$

EXAMPLE 4. Simplify each expression. Write the answers in rational exponent. (Assume that all the variables are positive.)

① $\sqrt{\sqrt[3]{a}}$

② $\sqrt[3]{\sqrt{a}}$

③ $\sqrt{\sqrt{a^3}}$

④ $\sqrt[3]{\sqrt{a^3}}$

⑤ $\sqrt[5]{\sqrt{\sqrt[3]{a}}}$

⑥ $\sqrt{\sqrt{\sqrt{a}}}$

⑦ $\sqrt{a \cdot \sqrt[3]{a}}$

⑧ $\sqrt{a^3 \cdot \sqrt{a}}$

⑨ $a\sqrt{a\sqrt{a}}$

⑩ $a \cdot \sqrt{a^2 \cdot \sqrt{a}}$

EXAMPLE 5. Solve the equations.

① $(3x-6)^{\frac{1}{2}} = 3$

② $(d+2)^{\frac{1}{3}} = 2$

③ $6 + (m-4)^{\frac{1}{3}} = 9$

④ $(x-7)^{\frac{1}{5}} + 3 = 1$

⑤ $(y-9)^{\frac{1}{4}} - 4 = 0$

⑥ $(7x-2)^{\frac{1}{4}} + 4 = 7$

2. Real Number Exponents

EXAMPLE 6. Simplify each expression. (Assume that all the variables are positive.)

① $a^{\sqrt{3}} \cdot a^{\sqrt{3}}$

② $x^{1+\sqrt{5}} \cdot x^{1-\sqrt{5}}$

③ $(b^{2+\sqrt{3}})^{2-\sqrt{3}}$

④ $(t^{\sqrt{2}})^{\sqrt{2}}$

⑤ $\dfrac{x^{\sqrt{3}+3}}{(x^{\sqrt{3}})^{\sqrt{3}}}$

⑥ $\dfrac{x^{\sqrt{5}-2}}{x^{\sqrt{5}+2}}$

⑦ $\left((\sqrt{2})^{\sqrt{2}}\right)^{\sqrt{2}}$

⑧ $(\sqrt{2})^{\sqrt{2}} \cdot (\sqrt{2})^{\sqrt{2}}$

⑨ $\dfrac{a^{\frac{1}{\sqrt{2}}} \cdot a^{\frac{\sqrt{2}}{2}}}{a^{\sqrt{2}}}$

⑩ $(a^{\frac{1}{\sqrt{6}}} \cdot a^{\sqrt{\frac{2}{3}}})^{\sqrt{3}}$

⑪ $\sqrt[4]{\dfrac{a^{\frac{1}{\sqrt{5}}}}{a^{\sqrt{5}}}}$

⑫ $\sqrt{\dfrac{a^{\sqrt{2}}}{a^{\frac{1}{\sqrt{2}}}}}$

3. Expand Knowledge*

EXAMPLE 7.   * Expand. (Assume that all the variables are positive.)

① $(\sqrt[3]{x} + \sqrt[3]{x^2})^2$

② $(\sqrt{x} + \sqrt[3]{x})^2$

③ $\left(\sqrt[4]{x} - \dfrac{1}{\sqrt[4]{x}}\right)^2$

④ $\left(\sqrt{x} - \dfrac{1}{\sqrt{x}}\right)^2$

⑤ $(\sqrt[3]{x^2} + \sqrt[4]{y^3})(\sqrt[3]{x^2} - \sqrt[4]{y^3})$

⑥ $(\sqrt[4]{x^3} + \sqrt[6]{y^5})(\sqrt[4]{x^3} - \sqrt[6]{y^5})$

⑦ $\left(x - \dfrac{1}{x}\right)\left(x + \dfrac{1}{x}\right)$ ⑧ $\left(\dfrac{1}{\sqrt{x}} - \sqrt{x}\right)\left(\dfrac{1}{\sqrt{x}} + \sqrt{x}\right)\left(\dfrac{1}{x} + x\right)$

⑨ $\left(\sqrt[4]{x} - \dfrac{1}{\sqrt[4]{x}}\right)\left(\sqrt[4]{x} + \dfrac{1}{\sqrt[4]{x}}\right)\left(\sqrt{x} + \dfrac{1}{\sqrt{x}}\right)\left(x + \dfrac{1}{x}\right)$

EXAMPLE 8. * Write the value in increasing order. (Do not use calculator)

$$A = \sqrt[3]{4}, \quad B = \sqrt[4]{6}, \quad C = \sqrt[6]{15}$$

EXAMPLE 9. * Which one is different from the other?

$$A = \sqrt{\left(\sqrt{2^{\sqrt{2}}}\right)^{\sqrt{2}}}, \quad B = \left[\sqrt{(\sqrt{2})^{\sqrt{2}}}\right]^{\frac{1}{\sqrt{2}}}, \quad C = \sqrt{\sqrt{2} \cdot \sqrt{(\sqrt{2})^{\sqrt{2}}}}$$

Part 8
Exponential and Logarithm

8.1 Composite Function

8.2 Inverse Function

8.3 Exponential Function

8.4 Definition of Logarithms

8.5 Laws of Logarithms

8.6 Log and Exp Equations

8.7 The Natural Logarithm Function

8.8 Exponential Growth and Modeling

Mia's Algebra 2

8.1 Composite Function

1. Composite Functions

※ **Composite Functions**

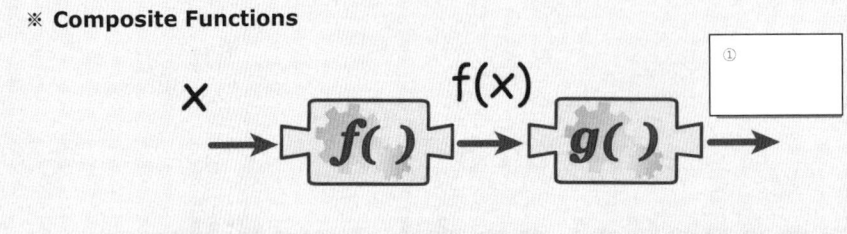

The result of *f* is sent through another function *g*.

Composition of g and f : $(g \circ f)(x) = g(f(x))$

- outer function: g
- inner function: $f(x)$
- composed with: $\circ$

We read it 'g composed with f'.

EXAMPLE 1. For $x \geq 0$, $f(x) = 2x+3$, $g(x) = \sqrt{x}$ and $h(x) = x^2 + 1$, then what is

① $(f \circ g)(x)$ ② $(g \circ f)(x)$

Blank : ① (g ∘ f)(x)

③ $(h \circ g)(x^2)$

④ $(g \circ h)(x^2)$

⑤ $(g \circ g)(x)$

⑥ $(f \circ f)(x)$

⑦ $(g \circ f)(3)$

⑧ $(f \circ h)(1)$

⑨ $(h \circ f \circ g)(x)$

⑩ $(g \circ h \circ h)(x)$

⑪ $(f \circ h \circ g)(x)$

EXAMPLE 2. Use the table to find;

x	1	2	4	10	12
$f(x)$	-4	6	11	3	13

x	-5	-4	3	10	11
$g(x)$	4	10	6	2	12

① $(f \circ g)(-5)$ ② $(g \circ f)(1)$

③ $(g \circ f)(10)$ ④ $(f \circ g)(10)$

⑤ $(f \circ g \circ f)(4)$ ⑥ $(f \circ g \circ g)(-4)$

2. Expand Knowledge*

EXAMPLE 3. * For the function f shown in the figure, what is

$$(f \circ f \circ f \circ f)(1)?$$

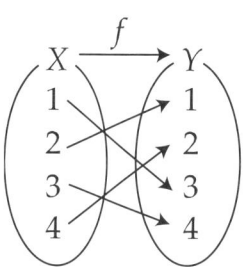

EXAMPLE 4. * When $g(x) = 2\sqrt{x} - 3$ and $(g \circ h)(x) = 2x + 5$, then what is the function $h(x)$?

Mia's Algebra 2
8.2 Inverse Function

1. Inverse Function

※ Inverse function

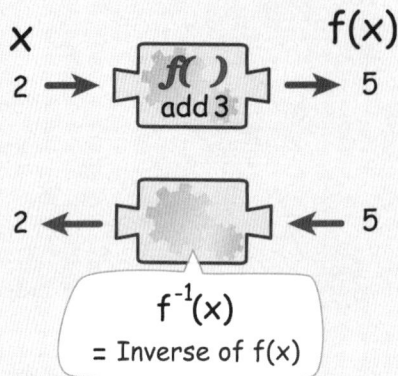

When we **switch input(x)** and **output(y)** of a function $f(x)$,

we will have ① _____ which is the "② _____ Function of $f(x)$"

If $f(a) = b$, then ③ _____ .   ex) $f(2) = 5 \Leftrightarrow 2 = f^{-1}(5)$

☺ Careful: $f^{-1}(x) \neq \dfrac{1}{f(x)}$ (-1 is not a power, it is a 'inverse' notation)

$f^{-1}(x)$?? We **switch x and y**.

Blank : ① $f^{-1}(x)$ ② inverse   ③ $a = f^{-1}(b)$

EXAMPLE 1. Find the inverse of each relation and determine whether the inverse is also a function.

① $f = \{(6, 0), (-1, 1), (-3, 2), (-5, 3)\}$ ② $f = \{(-2, 0), (0, 0), (4, 0), (7, 0)\}$

③ $f = \{(-7, 5), (-5, 7), (6, 5), (-6, 9)\}$ ④ $f = \{(1, 2), (2, 3), (3, 4), (4, 5)\}$

EXAMPLE 2. Use the table to find;

x	1	2	4	10	6
$f(x)$	2	6	11	4	13

x	-5	-4	3	10	11
$g(x)$	4	10	11	2	-5

① $f(2)$ ② $g(-5)$

③ $f^{-1}(4)$ ④ $g^{-1}(11)$

⑤ $g^{-1}(10)$ ⑥ $f^{-1}(2)$

⑦ $(f \circ g^{-1})(2)$ ⑧ $(g^{-1} \circ f^{-1})(6)$

⑨ $(f \circ f^{-1})(11)$ ⑩ $(g^{-1} \circ g)(4)$

Part 8 Exponential and Logarithm

2. Finding the Inverse Algebraically

EXAMPLE 3. Find the inverse of a function.

> ※ How to find the inverse function
> i) Write $y = f(x)$.
> ii) Switch x and y.
> ii) Solve for y.

① $f(x) = 6x + 7$

② $f(x) = \dfrac{4}{x}$

③ $f(x) = \dfrac{1}{2}(2x-3)^3 + 2$

④ $f(x) = 2\sqrt[3]{x+1}$

⑤ $f(x) = x^2 + 1, \quad x \geq 0$

⑥ $f(x) = x^2 - 5, \quad x \geq 0$

⑦ $f(x) = (x-2)^2 + 3, \ x < 2$ ⑧ $f(x) = 2(3-x)^2, \ x > 3$

⑨ $f(x) = \dfrac{2x+6}{-7x-3}$ ⑩ $f(x) = \dfrac{-3x+4}{x-2}$

⑪ $f(x) = \dfrac{2x}{3+x}$ ⑫ $f(x) = \dfrac{-3x}{x+2}$

3. Facts about Inverse Function

1. If $f(a) = b$, then ①_____.

2. The domain of f is the ②_____ of f^{-1}
   and the range of f is the ③_____ of f^{-1}.

3. If the point (a, b) lies on graph of f,
   then the point ④_____ must lie on the graph of f^{-1}.

4. $(f \circ f^{-1})(x) = $ ⑤_____ and $(f^{-1} \circ f)(x) = $ ⑥_____.

5. f^{-1} is a reflection of the graph of f in the line ⑦_____.

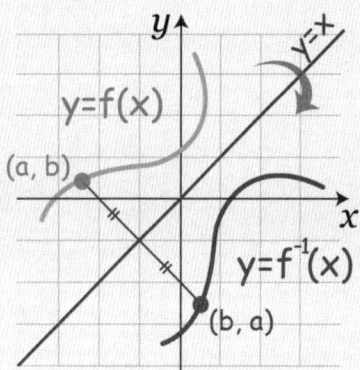

Blank : ① $a = f^{-1}(b)$ ② range ③ domain ④ (b, a) ⑤ x ⑥ x ⑦ $y=x$

EXAMPLE 4. Determine whether each pair of functions are inverse functions.

> ☺ Tip: Since $(f \circ f^{-1})(x) = (f^{-1} \circ f)(x) = $ ① ____ ,
>
> if $(f \circ g)(x) = (g \circ f)(x) = $ ② ____ then f and g are inverse.

① $f(x) = x+4$, $g(x) = x-4$

② $f(x) = -2x+1$, $g(x) = \dfrac{1}{2}(1-x)$

③ $f(x) = 3x-3$, $g(x) = \dfrac{1}{3}x-1$

④ $f(x) = \dfrac{3}{4}x$, $g(x) = \dfrac{4}{3}x$

⑤ $f(x) = 2x$, $g(x) = -2x$

Blank : ① x ② x

EXAMPLE 5. Draw the graph of the inverse function $f^{-1}(x)$.

①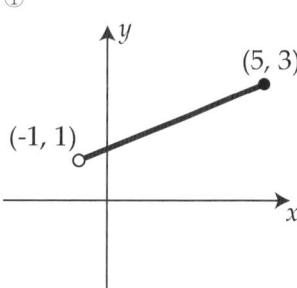

②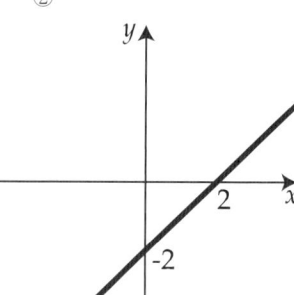

③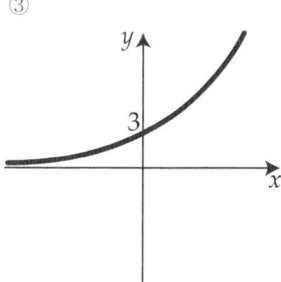

④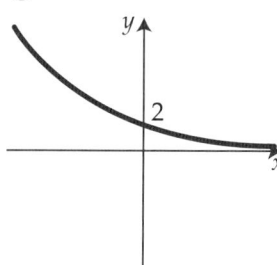

⑤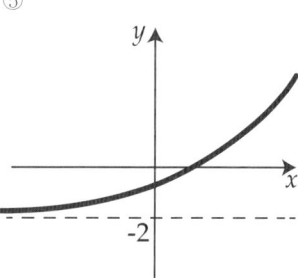

⑥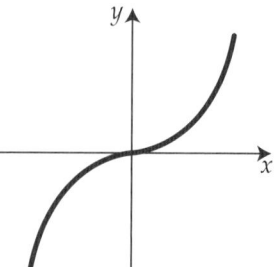

⑦ 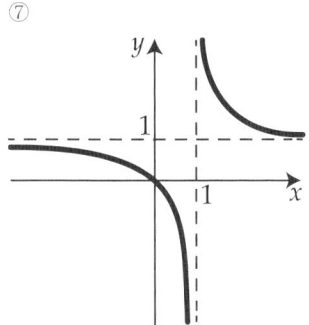   ⑧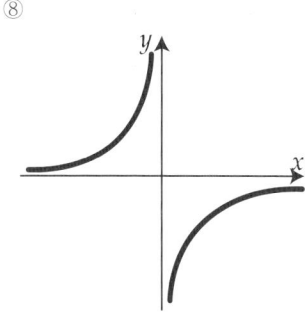

4. Expand Knowledge*

※ Horizontal line Test for Inverse function

A function has an inverse function if and only if
every horizontal line intersects the graph of the function at most one point.

(If the horizontal line crosses the graph only one time, then it HAS an inverse.)

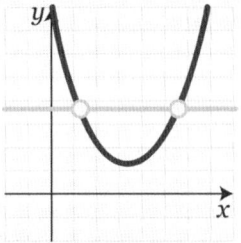 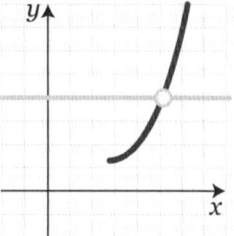

Does NOT have　　　　　has
Inverse Function　　Inverse Function

If a function does not pass the 'Horizontal line Test',
then you can restrict the domain (cut the function) and make it happen.

EXAMPLE 6. * Does the function have an inverse function? If not, then restrict its domain and graph the inverse of the function with the restricted domain.

①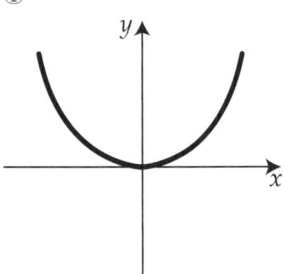

②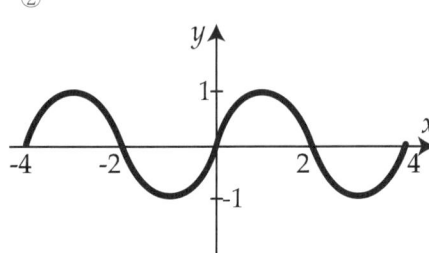

EXAMPLE 7. * Does the function have an inverse function? Set a restricted domain so that we can have an inverse function. Answers may vary.

① $y = (x+2)^2 - 1$ ② $y = (x-1)^2 + 2$

③ $y = |x+1|$

④ $y = |x-2| - 3$

⑤ $y = x^2 + 2x + 2$

Mia's Algebra 2

8.3 Exponential Function

1. Exponential Function

※ **Exponential Functions**

The **exponential function with base b**
is defined for all real numbers x
where $b \neq 1$ and $b > 0$.

$$f(x) = b^x$$

(variable: x; constant: b)

ex) Exponential function: $y = 2^x, y = \left(\dfrac{1}{3}\right)^x$ ...

NOT exponential function: $y = (1)^x, y = (-2)^x$ ...

※ **Graph of Exponential Functions**

When $0 < b < 1$ and when $b > 1$

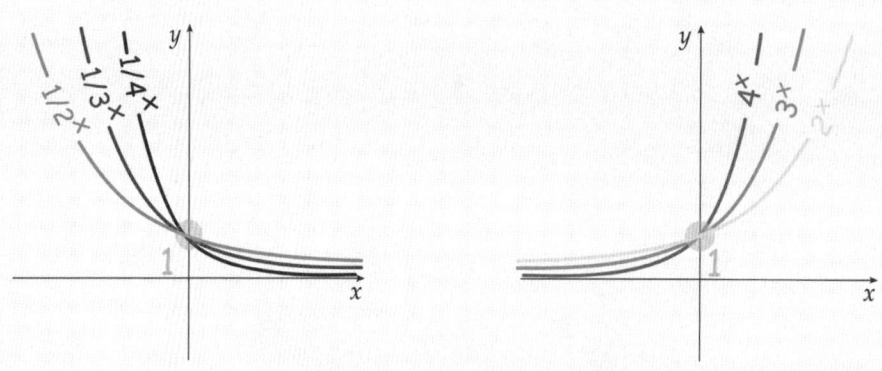

Domain: ①_____,
range: ②_____,
Horizontal asymptote: ③_____.
y intercept : ④_____

Blank : ① All real numbers ($\mathbb{R}$)   ② $y > 0$ ③ $y = 0$ ④ $(0, 1)$

EXAMPLE 1. Graph and label one point on the graph. State the asymptotes.

① $f(x) = 2^x$

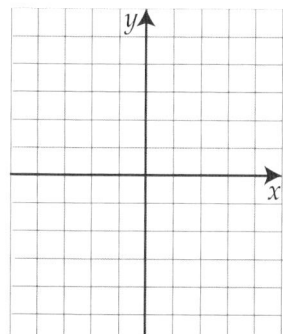

② $f(x) = 3^{x+1}$

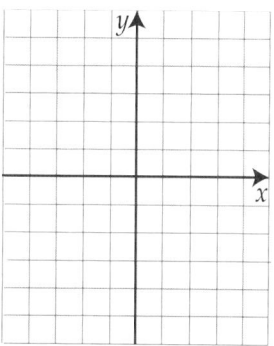

③ $f(x) = 4^{x-2} + 3$

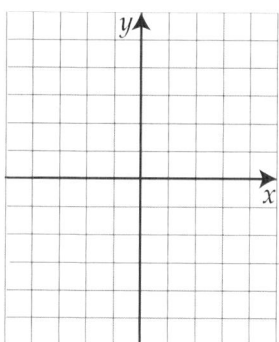

④ $f(x) = 2 + 3^{x+1}$

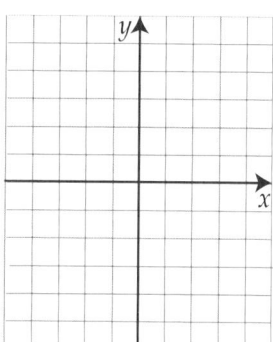

⑤ $f(x) = -2^{-x} + 1$

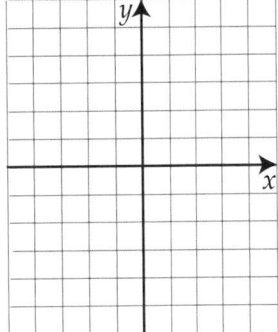

⑥ $f(x) = 1 + 3^{-x}$

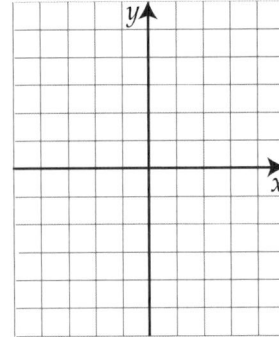

⑦ $f(x) = 2 \cdot 3^x$

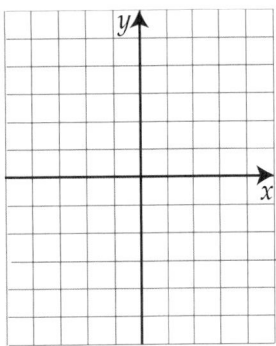

⑧ $f(x) = 3 \cdot 2^x$

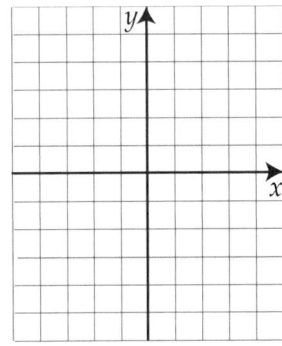

⑨ $f(x) = 0.5^x$

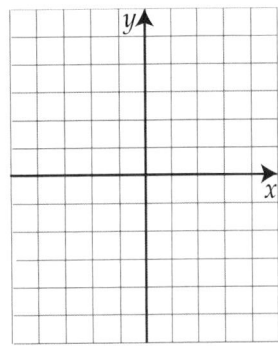

⑩ $f(x) = \left(\dfrac{1}{3}\right)^{x-3} + 1$

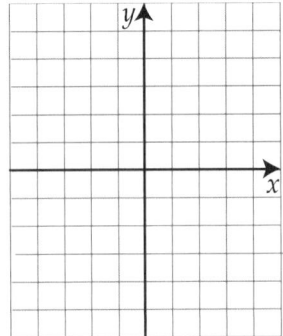

⑪ $f(x) = 1 + \left(\dfrac{3}{4}\right)^{-x}$

⑫ $f(x) = -0.3^{x-1}$

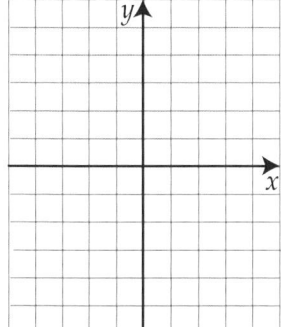
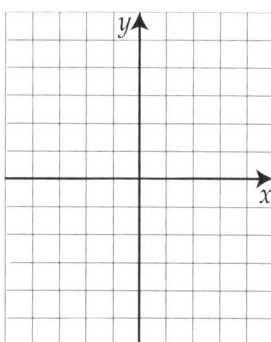

2. Exponential vs. Linear Function

Linear Function When a quantity grows by the same amount during each unit of time.	Exponential Function When a quantity grows by the same relative amount (by the same percentage) during each unit of time.
$\begin{array}{c\|c\|c\|c\|c} x & -1 & 0 & 1 & 2 \\ \hline y & 2 & 5 & 8 & 11 \end{array}$ +3 ① ②	$\begin{array}{c\|c\|c\|c\|c} x & -1 & 0 & 1 & 2 \\ \hline y & 2 & 4 & 8 & 16 \end{array}$ ×2 ③ ④
ex) increase 10 $ every year grows 3cm each week	ex) increase 4 percent every year. grows 3% each week doubling every month.

Blank : ① +3   ② +3   ③ ×2 (multiply 2)   ④ ×2

EXAMPLE 2. Determine a function for the given table.

☺ Tip: If it is exponential, write in $y = a \cdot b^x$ form where b is the multiplier as x increase by 1, a is the y intercept (x = 0).

①

x	f(x)
-2	5/9
-1	5/3
0	5
1	15
2	45

②

x	f(x)
-2	6
-1	2
0	-2
1	-6
2	-10

③

x	f(x)
-4	1
-2	4
0	7
2	10
4	13

④

x	f(x)
0	10
1	20
2	40
3	80
4	160

⑤

x	f(x)
-3	1
0	8
3	64
6	512
9	4096

⑥

x	f(x)
-4	1/27
-2	1/3
0	3
2	27
4	261

⑦
x	f(x)
0	64
2	16
4	4
6	1
8	1/4

⑧
x	f(x)
-2	135
0	45
2	15
4	5
6	5/3

EXAMPLE 3. Is this example linear or exponential?

① The number of students increased by 750 in each of the past six years

② Corn grows at the rate of 3 inches per week.

③ The number of students increased by 7% in each of the past six years

④ Price of gasoline rises by 3% per year.

⑤ Sam opens a bank account that earns 4% interest of the current money each year

⑥ Tom expands the store by 5% of the original square footage each year.

⑦ Sam opens a bank account that earns 4% interest of the original money each year

⑧ Tom increases the square footage by 0.75% each year.

⑨ Population doubles every 4 months

⑩ The mass of the material becomes half everyday.

Mia's Algebra 2

8.4 Definition of Logarithms

1. Logarithm

A **logarithm** is another way of writing an ①_____.

A logarithm gives you the power (exponent) a base must be raised to produce a given number.

※ **Logarithmic function with base** b **is defined by**

$$b^x = a \quad \Leftrightarrow \quad \log_b a = x$$

(base, exponent, value on the left; ③, ②, ④ on the right)

Remember, $b \neq 1$, $b > 0$, and a **has to be** ⑤_____.

We can read it as : 'log base b of a is equal to x'

※ **Special Logarithm :** ⑥_____ log

$$\log_{10} x = \log x$$

(Common Log)

Blank : ① exponent   ② base   ③ value   ④ exponent   ⑤ positive   ⑥ common

EXAMPLE 1. Find x using the definition of log.

> **What power** (exponent) a base must be raised to produce a given value?

① $\log_{10} 100{,}000 = x$

② $\log_2 32 = x$

③ $\log_{10} 0.01 = x$

④ $x = \log_5 \dfrac{1}{25}$

⑤ $\log_2 \dfrac{1}{4} = x$

⑥ $x = \log_{1/2} 2$

⑦ $\log_{16} 4 = x$

⑧ $\log_2 \sqrt{2} = x$

⑨ $4 = \log_x 625$

⑩ $\log_x 4 = -1$

⑪ $\log_5 x = 3$

⑫ $-2 = \log_{1/2} x$

⑬ $\log_{(x-1)} 5 = 1$

2. Basic Properties of Logarithms

※ Basic Properties of Logarithm

$$\log_b 1 = 0$$

$$\log_b b = 1$$

$$\log_b b^x = x \qquad \text{ex) } \log_2 2^x = \text{①}\underline{\quad} , \log 10^2 = \text{②}\underline{\quad}$$

$$b^{\log_b x} = x \qquad \text{ex) } 2^{\log_2 3} = \text{③}\underline{\quad} , 10^{\log x} = \text{④}\underline{\quad}$$

EXAMPLE 2. Evaluate the logarithm using basic log <u>properties</u>.

① $\log_7 1$ ② $\log 1000$

③ $\log_5 25$ ④ $\log 1$

⑤ $\log_4 \dfrac{1}{64}$ ⑥ $\log_5 \dfrac{1}{625}$

⑦ $\log_7 7^x$ ⑧ $\log_4 4^y$

⑨ $\log 0.01$ ⑩ $\log 0.0001$

Blank : ① x ② 2 ③ 3 ④ x

⑪ $\log_2 \sqrt{2}$

⑫ $\log_5 \sqrt[4]{5}$

⑬ $\log_2 \sqrt[3]{4}$

⑭ $\log_4 \sqrt[5]{64}$

⑮ $3^{\log_3 8}$

⑯ $2^{\log_2 5}$

⑰ $10^{\log \sqrt{x}}$

⑱ $10^{\log x^2}$

⑲ $6^{\log_6 \frac{1}{8}}$

⑳ $\left(\dfrac{1}{3}\right)^{\log_{1/3} 27}$

EXAMPLE 3. Fill in the blanks.

① $\log_2 100$ lies between the consecutive integers _____ and _____.

② $\log 200$ lies between the consecutive integers _____ and _____.

③ $\log_3 30$ lies between the consecutive integers _____ and _____.

④ $\log_2 1000$ lies between the consecutive integers _____ and _____.

⑤ $\log 3000$ lies between the consecutive integers _____ and _____.

EXAMPLE 4. Change into an equivalent expression.

To get rid of the LOG, you need ① _____

To get rid of the BASE, you need ② _____

$\log_2 8 = 3 \rightarrow \boxed{③}\log_2 8 = {}_2 3 \rightarrow \boxed{④}$

$2^3 = 8 \rightarrow \boxed{⑤} 2^3 = \log_2 8 \rightarrow \boxed{⑥}$

	Exponential Form	Logarithmic Form
①		$\log 1000 = 3$
②		$\log \dfrac{1}{8} = x$
③	$5^x = 4000$	
④	$6^{1/2} = x$	
⑤		$\log_3 27 = 3$
⑥		$a = \log x^2$
⑦	$10^x = 2$	
⑧	$10^{2z} = a$	
⑨	$2^{x^2 - x} = 3$	
⑩	$5^{4x^2} = 7$	
⑪		$\log x^y = 2$

Blank : ① Base ② Log ③ 2 ④ $8 = 2^3$ ⑤ $\log_2$ ⑥ $3 = \log_2 8$

EXAMPLE 5. Find the inverse.

① $y = \log_2 x$ 　　　　　　　　② $y = \log x$

③ $y = 3\log(x+1) - 5$ 　　　　　　④ $y = 2\log_4 x + 4$

⑤ $y = 3^x$ 　　　　　　　　⑥ $y = 8^{x-1}$

⑦ $y = 5^{x-1} + 2$ 　　　　　　⑧ $y = 1 + 10^{x+2}$

3. Graph of Log

Logarithm and exponential function are ①_____,
so we can draw the log graph
by taking the exponential function and reflecting across the ②_____.

$y = \log_b x$ When $0 < b < 1$ $y = \log_b x$ and when $b > 1$

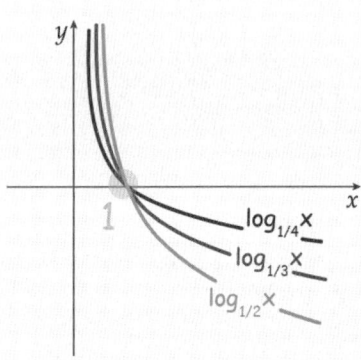
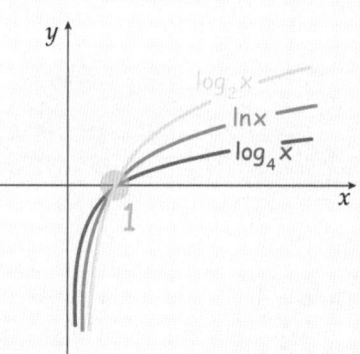

Domain: ③_____,

range: ④_____,

Vertical asymptote: ⑤_____.

x intercept : ⑥_____

Blank : ① inverse   ② y=x   ③ x>0   ④ All real numbers ($\mathbb{R}$)   ⑤ x=0   ⑥ (1, 0)

EXAMPLE 6. Graph and label one point on the graph. State the asymptotes.

① $f(x) = \log x + 1$

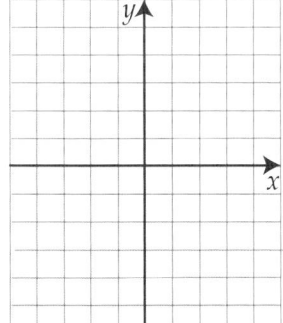

② $f(x) = \log_4(x+1)$

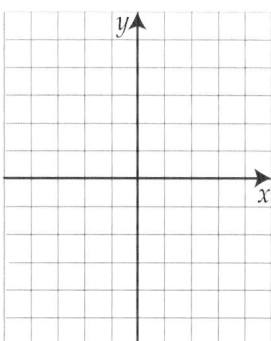

③ $f(x) = -\log_{\frac{3}{2}}(x+1)$

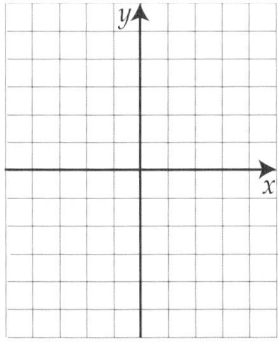

④ $f(x) = -\log x - 1$

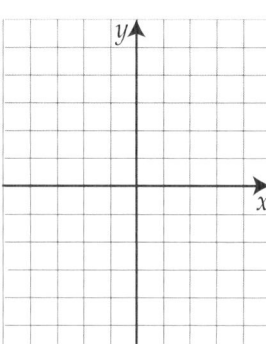

⑤ $f(x) = \log_{0.5}(x-1) - 1$

⑥ $f(x) = \log_{2/3}(x+2) + 2$

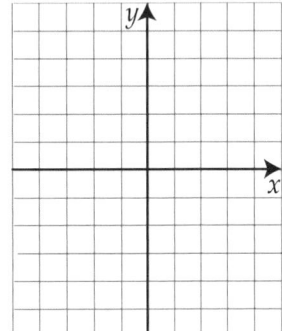

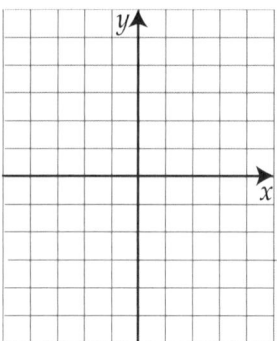

4. Expand Knowledge*

EXAMPLE 7. * Simplify the following.

$$4\log_3 3^{\log 100}$$

EXAMPLE 8. * Simplify the following.

$$10^{\log 10^{\log 2^{10}}}$$

Mia's Algebra 2

8.5 Laws of Logarithms

1. Properties of Logarithms

   ※ **Properties of Log** ($x, y > 0, b > 0, b \neq 1$)

   $$\log_b xy = \log_b x + \log_b y \qquad \text{Product Property}$$

   $$\log_b \frac{x}{y} = \log_b x - \log_b y \qquad \text{Quotient Property}$$

   $$\log_b x^n = n \log_b x \qquad \text{Power Property}$$

   $$\log_{b^n} x = \frac{1}{n} \log_b x$$

   $$\log_b x = \frac{\log_c x}{\log_c b} \qquad \text{Change of Base}$$

   ☺ Careful:

   $(\log x)(\log y) \neq \log x + \log y$

   $\dfrac{\log x}{\log y} \neq \log x - \log y$

   $(\log x)^n \neq n \log x$

☺ proof

Let $m = \log_b x \rightarrow x = b^m$, $n = \log_b y \rightarrow y = b^n$

Muliply x and y : $xy = (b^m)(b^n) = b^{m+n}$

Take $\log_b$ on both sides : $\log_b(xy) = \log_b(b^{m+n})$

$$\log_b(xy) = m+n$$

Replace : $\log_b(xy) = \log_b x + \log_b y$

EXAMPLE 1. Use the properties of logarithms to simplify into single logarithm.

① $\log_{30} 3 + \log_{30} 10$
② $\log_3 24 - \log_3 8$

③ $\log_2 96 - \log_2 3$
④ $\log 25 + \log 4$

⑤ $3\log 2 + \log 6 - 2\log 3$
⑥ $\log 32 - 2\log 4 - \dfrac{1}{3}\log 8$

⑦ $2\log xy - 3\log y - 4\log xz$
⑧ $2\log xy - 4\log xz + 3\log xz$

⑨ $3\log_3 x + 2(\log_3 x - \log_3 y)$

⑩ $2(\log_5 x + 2\log_5 y - 3\log_5 z)$

⑪ $\dfrac{1}{2}(\log x + \log y) - \dfrac{2}{3}\log z$

⑫ $\dfrac{3}{4}\log x - \dfrac{1}{2}(\log y + \log z)$

⑬ $2\log_6(x-1) - \log_6(x^2-1)$

⑭ $\log(x^2 - 2x - 3) - 3\log(x+1)$

⑮ $\log_4 5 \cdot \log_5 6$

⑯ $\log_2 3 \cdot \log_3 4 \cdot \log_4 5$

⑰ $5^{2\log_5 5}$

⑱ $10^{3\log x}$

⑲ $10^{2(\log 30 - \log 5)}$

⑳ $5^{2\log_5 4 - 3\log_5 2}$

㉑ $2 + 5\log x$

㉒ $1 - 3\log_2 x$

EXAMPLE 2. Use the properties of logarithms to expand the logarithm.

① $\log xy^3$

② $\log(xy)^3$

③ $\log \sqrt[3]{xy}$

④ $\log x\sqrt{y}$

⑤ $\log \sqrt[4]{x^2yz^3}$

⑥ $\log 100\sqrt{x^3y}$

⑦ $\log \left(\dfrac{10y^2}{\sqrt{z}} \right)$

⑧ $\log \dfrac{\sqrt[3]{x^2}}{y^3z}$

⑨ $\log \sqrt{x\sqrt{y}}$

⑩ $\log \dfrac{1}{x\sqrt{y}}$

EXAMPLE 3. Use following to express the given log in terms of a, b.

$$\log 3 = a \text{ and } \log 4 = b$$

① $\log 12$

② $\log 9$

③ $\log \dfrac{3}{4}$

④ $\log \dfrac{4}{3}$

⑤ $\log 144$

⑥ $\log 36$

⑦ $\log \sqrt[3]{3}$

⑧ $\log \sqrt[4]{4}$

⑨ $\log 0.25$

⑩ $\log \dfrac{1}{27}$

⑪ $\log\dfrac{27}{16}$ ⑫ $\log\dfrac{9}{16}$

⑬ $\log_4 9$ ⑭ $\log_3 64$

⑮ $\log_{100} 3$ ⑯ $\log_{\sqrt{10}} 4$

2. Expand Knowledge*

EXAMPLE 4. * True or false?

I. $\log(x+y) = \log x + \log y$

II. $\log x \cdot \log y = \log(x+y)$

III. $\log x + \log y = \log xy$

IV. $\dfrac{\log x}{\log y} = \log x - \log y$

V. $\log x - \log y = \log \dfrac{x}{y}$

VI. $\log(x-y) = \log \dfrac{x}{y}$

VII. $(\log x)^2 = 2\log x$

VIII. $\log \dfrac{1}{x} = -\log x$

EXAMPLE 5. * Which one is different from others?

$$\log_3 14 \quad \log_3 2 + \log_3 7 \quad \frac{\log 14}{\log 3} \quad \log_3 2 \cdot \log_3 7 \quad \frac{1}{2}\log_3 196$$

EXAMPLE 6. * Write $\log(x^2 - y^2)$ in expanded form.

EXAMPLE 7. * What is $\log_2 3 \times \log_3 4 \times \log_4 5 \times \ldots \times \log_{63} 64$?

EXAMPLE 8. * What is $2^{\log_2 1 + \log_2 2 + \log_2 3 + \ldots + \log_2 10}$? (Hint: $n! = 1 \cdot 2 \cdot 3 \cdots n$)

Mia's Algebra 2

8.6 Log and Exp Equations

1. Logarithmic Equations

※ For logarithmic Equations,
you must plug in the solution back to the equation
and CHECK whether it is log(positive).

EXAMPLE 1. Solve the equation.

> Type1. If you want to get rid of the log,
> raise both sides to be power of that base!

① $\log_5(x+1) = 2$

② $2\log(x-2) = 6$

③ $\log\left(\log_2(\log_3 x)\right) = 1$

④ $\log_4\left(\log\dfrac{1}{x}\right) = \dfrac{1}{2}$

Part 8 Exponential and Logarithm 443

⑤ $\log_3 x + \log_3(x-24) = 4$

⑥ $\log_2 x + \log_2(x-2) = 3$

⑦ $\log(x^2+9) = 1 + 2\log x$

⑧ $2\log(x-2) - \log x = 0$

⑨ $\log_3 x + \log_9 x = 2$

⑩ $\log_{16} x - \log_4 x = 0.5$

> Type2. Use the one to one property.
>
> If $\log_b x = \log_b y$, then $x = y$

⑪ $\log_8 2 + \log_8 x = \log_8 7$

⑫ $\log_2(x+5) = \log_2 x + \log_2 5$

⑬ $\log_4(x-2) + \log_4(2x-3) = 2\log_4 x$

⑭ $\log_3 x + \log_3(x+3) = \log_3 4$

⑮ $\log x - \log(x+2) = \log(x+6)$

⑯ $\log(4+x) - \log(x-4) = \log 5$

⑰ $\log(3x^2 - 4) + \log(x^2 + 1) = \log(2 + 6x^2)$

⑱ $\log(5x^2 + 4) = \log 9x^4 - \log(2x^2 - 1)$

2. Solving Exponential Equation

EXAMPLE 2. Solve the equation using log.

> Type1. Make the base same if possible.

① $3(2^x) = 24$

② $5\left(\dfrac{1}{2}\right)^x = 20$

③ $32^{x-1} = 4^{x+2}$

④ $\left(\dfrac{5}{4}\right)^{4x} = \left(\dfrac{16}{25}\right)^{9-x}$

⑤ $\left(\dfrac{9}{16}\right)^{3x-2} = \left(\dfrac{4}{3}\right)^{x-4}$

⑥ $49^{\frac{x}{3}} = 7^{x-4}$

Type2. If you want to bring exponent x down, take 'log' on both sides!

⑦ $2^x = 3$ ⑧ $3^{x+1} = 8$

⑨ $3(5^{2x}) = 18$ ⑩ $2(7^{3x-1}) = 16$

⑪ $5^{x-2} = 3^{3x+1}$ ⑫ $11^{x-1} = 7^{2x+1}$

⑬ $7^{1-2x} = 2^x$ ⑭ $4^{x-3} = 6^{2x}$

3. Expand Knowledge*

EXAMPLE 3.* Solve the equation.

Make a Substitution!

① $(\log x)^2 = \log x^4 - 3$ ② $2(\log x)^2 = \log x^3 + 5$

EXAMPLE 4.* Solve the equation.

> Make a Substitution!

① $3^{2x+1} - 11 \times 3^x = 4$

② $4^{2x} - 4^{x+1} - 5 = 0$

③ $5^{2x} - 5^{x+1} + 4 = 0$

Mia's Algebra 2

8.7 The Natural Logarithm Function

1. Euler Number

The number e is a famous (①rational/irrational) number, and is one of the most important numbers in mathematics.

※ **Euler Number**

n	$\left(1+\dfrac{1}{n}\right)^n$
1	2.00000
2	2.00000
5	2.48832
10	2.59374
100	2.59374
1000	2.71692
10000	2.71815

When n becomes larger and larger, then $\left(1+\dfrac{1}{n}\right)^n$ approaches to 2.718281.., and we call that number 'e (Euler number)'

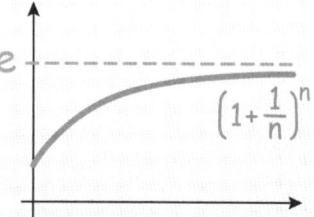

$$e = 2.71828182845...$$

Blank : ① irrational

Euler number e is found in many interesting areas (compound interest, exponential growth...), so it is worth learning about.

2. Natural Logarithm

※ **Natural Logarithm** : logarithm with base e is called ①_____ log

$$\log_e x = \ln x$$ (Natural Log)

('$\ln$' means 'natural log')

※ **Basic Properties of Natural Logarithm**
(same with 'Basic Properties of Logarithm' from chapter 8.4)

$\ln 1 = $ ②☐

$\ln e = $ ③☐

$\ln e^x = $ ④☐   ex) $\ln e^2 = $ ⑤____ , $\ln e^{x^2} = $ ⑥____

$e^{\ln x} = $ ⑦☐   ex) $e^{\ln 8} = $ ⑧____ , $e^{\ln x^2} = $ ⑨____

Blank : ① natural ② 0 ③ 1 ④ x ⑤ 2 ⑥ x^2 ⑦ x ⑧ 8 ⑨ x^2

EXAMPLE 1. Evaluate.

① $\ln 1$

② $\ln e^7$

③ $\ln \dfrac{1}{e}$

④ $\ln \dfrac{1}{\sqrt{e}}$

⑤ $\ln \sqrt[5]{e^2}$

⑥ $\ln \sqrt[3]{e^8}$

⑦ $e^{\ln 3x}$

⑧ $e^{\ln 12}$

⑨ $e^{2\ln x}$

⑩ $e^{3\ln \sqrt{x}}$

EXAMPLE 2. Change into an equivalent expression.

	Exponential Form	Logarithmic Form
①		$\ln 20 = x$
②		$\ln \dfrac{1}{8} = x$
③	$e^x = 4$	
④	$e^{1/2} = x$	
⑤		$\ln x^2 = y$
⑥	$e^{x+2} = y - 8$	

Part 8 Exponential and Logarithm

3. Graph of y = e^x and y = ln x

※ **Graph of** $y = e^x, y = \ln x$

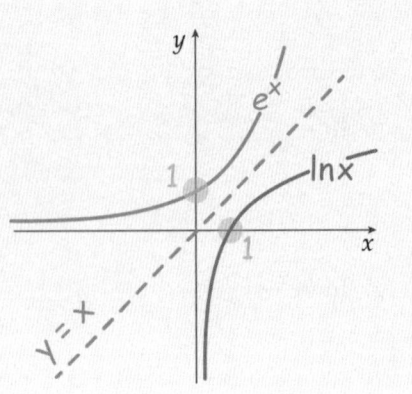

$y = e^x$ and $y = \ln x$ are inverse.

EXAMPLE 3. Use transformation to graph the function. Determine the asymptote of the function.

① $f(x) = e^{-x}$ 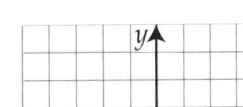② $f(x) = 1 - e^{2+x}$

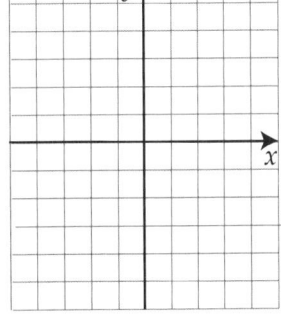
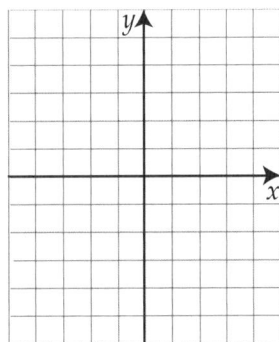

③ $f(x) = -e^{x+2} - 1$ ④ $f(x) = e^{-x} - 3$

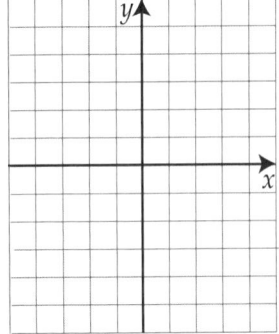
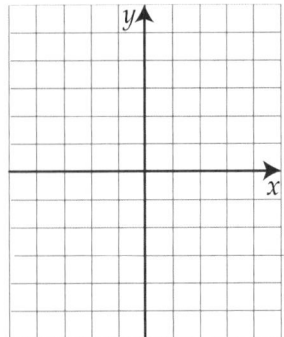

⑤ $f(x) = \ln x + 2$

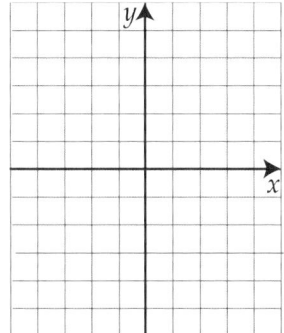

⑥ $f(x) = \ln x - 3$

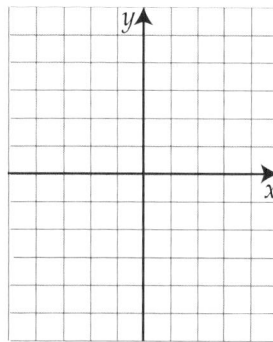

⑦ $f(x) = -\ln(x+2)$

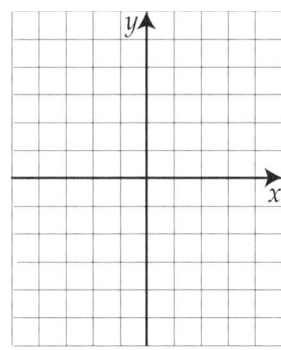

⑧ $f(x) = 1 + \ln(x-3)$

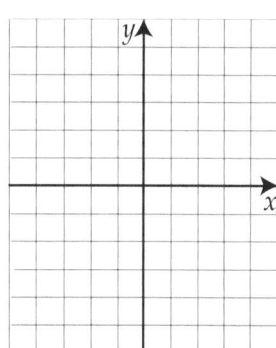

EXAMPLE 4. Solve the equation.

① $e^{x-1} = 10$

② $e^{4x-1} - 2 = 7$

③ $2e^{0.5x} + 1 = 9$ ④ $4 + 10e^x = 9$

⑤ $\ln(3x+2) = 7$ ⑥ $\ln(3x-5) = 4$

⑦ $\ln(\ln x) = 1$ ⑧ $\ln(\ln(\ln x)) = 0$

⑨ $|\ln x| = 2$ ⑩ $1 + |\ln x + 1| = 2$

⑪ $\ln x + \ln(x-1) = \ln 4x$ ⑫ $\ln(x+4) + \ln(x-4) = \ln 9$

⑬ $\ln(x+1) + \ln(x-1) = 2\ln(x-2)$ ⑭ $2\ln x = \ln 2 + \ln(3x-4)$

4. Expand Knowledge*

EXAMPLE 5. * Evaluate each expression.

① $\ln\left[\ln\left(e^{e^{e^7}}\right)\right]$

② $10^{\log e^{\ln x^2}}$

③ $e^{\log_3 3^{\ln 3}}$

EXAMPLE 6. * Solve the equation.

> Make a Substitution!

① $2e^{2x} - e^x = 6$

② $e^{2x} - 15e^x = -56$

③ $e^x + 5e^{-x} = 6$

④ $e^x - 6e^{-x} = 1$

Mia's Algebra 2

8.8 Exponential Growth and Modeling

1. Exponential Growth and Decay Model (Halving or doubling)

A single cell amoeba *doubles* every 4 days. If there were 5 cells initially what is the population of the amoeba after t days?

0 days → after 4 days → after 8 days ... after t days?
  5   5·(2)   ①   ②

after t days, we will get : ③ _____

※ **Exponential Growth Model** (Doubling or Halving)

Doubling every n days   Halving every n days:
(or other time units)   = Half life is n days
                                 (or other time units)

$$\text{New} = P(2)^{\frac{t}{n}} \quad \text{Doubling time} \qquad \text{New} = P\left(\frac{1}{2}\right)^{\frac{t}{n}} \quad \text{Halving time}$$

where P is the initial value, t is the time (with same time units with n).

Blank : ① $5(2)^2$ ② $5(2)^{t/4}$ ③ $5(2)^{t/4}$

EXAMPLE 1. Find the exponential function that satisfies the given conditions.

① Initial population = 1078, doubling every 8 hours

② Initial mass = 420 g, half life is 26 years

③ Initial mass = 416 g, half life is 23 days

④ Initial population = 1081, doubling every hour

EXAMPLE 2. Under ideal conditions a certain bacteria population doubles every three hours. Initially there are 1000 bacteria.

(a) Find a model for the bacteria population after t hours.

(b) How many bacteria are in the colony after 15 hours?

(c) When will the bacteria count reach 200,000?

EXAMPLE 3. A single cell amoeba doubles every 9 days. About how long will it take one amoeba to produce a population of 400?

EXAMPLE 4. The half-life of a certain radioactive substances is 20 days. There are 45g present initially.

(a) Express the amount of substance remaining as a function of time t.

(b) Find the amount of substance remaining after 26 days.

(c) When will there be 10% remaining?

EXAMPLE 5. The half-life of a certain radioactive substances is 7 days. When will there be 20% remaining?

EXAMPLE 6. A certain radioactive isotope has a half-life of approximately 1900 years. How many years to the nearest year would be required for a given amount of this isotope to decay to 30% of that amount?

2. Exponential Growth/decay

In our world, a lot of things grow (or decay) exponentially.

So we have a generally useful formula:

※ **Exponential Growth/decay Model** (Relative Growth Rate)

A population that experiences exponential growth increases according to the model

$$\text{New} = Pe^{rt}$$

where P is the initial value, t is the time, r is the relative growth rate.

(If $r > 0$, then it is ① _____

If $r < 0$, then it is ② _____)

EXAMPLE 7. The initial bacterium count in a culture is 600. A biologist later makes a sample count of bacteria in the culture and finds that the relative rate of growth is 30% per hour.

(a) Find a function that models the number of bacteria after t hours.

(b) What is the estimated count after 10 hours?

(c) When will the bacteria count reach 80,000?

Blank : ① exponential growth ② exponential decay

EXAMPLE 8. The population of rabbits is increasing according to the law of exponential growth. If the relative growth rate is 10% per day, how long will it take for the population of rabbits to double?

EXAMPLE 9. In a research experiment, the population of a city is growing according to exponential model. If the growth rate per year is 4% of the current population, how long will it take for the population to triple?

Part 9
Sequence and Series

9.1 Sequence and Series

9.2 Arithmetic Sequence and Series

9.3 Geometric Sequence and Series

9.4 Infinite Geometric Series

Mia's Algebra 2

9.1 Sequence and Series

1. Sequence

※ **Sequence:** list of numbers which follows a certain rule

$$5, 10, 15, 20, 25, \ldots, \boxed{①}, \ldots$$

1st term: a_1, 2nd term: a_2, 3rd term: a_3, nth term: a_n

※ **The notation for sequences**

a_n represents the ② _____ of the sequence a.

sequence name: a_n (nth term)

ex) $a_n = 5n$

EXAMPLE 1. Find the missing terms using the pattern.

① 2, 7, 12, 17, ____, ____

② $1, \dfrac{1}{2}, \dfrac{1}{4}, \dfrac{1}{8}, $ ____, ____

③ 1, 4, 9, 16, ____, ____

④ 4, 1, −2, −5, ____, ____

Blank : ① $5n$ ② n th term

⑤ $\dfrac{1}{100}, \dfrac{1}{10}, \underline{\hphantom{xxx}}, 10, 100, \underline{\hphantom{xxx}}$

⑥ $\dfrac{1}{3}, \underline{\hphantom{xxx}}, 3, 9, 27, \underline{\hphantom{xxx}}$

⑦ $2^{\frac{1}{4}}, 2^{\frac{1}{2}}, 2^{\frac{3}{4}}, \underline{\hphantom{xxx}}, \underline{\hphantom{xxx}}, 2^{\frac{3}{2}}$

⑧ $2^{-3}, 2^{-1}, \underline{\hphantom{xxx}}, 2^{3}, 2^{5}, \underline{\hphantom{xxx}}$

EXAMPLE 2. Find the first 4 terms of the sequence.

① $a_n = 3^n + 2$

② $a_n = (-1)^{n+1}(n-2)$

③ $a_n = \dfrac{(-1)^n}{2^{n-1}}$

④ $a_n = \dfrac{n+1}{n}$

⑤ $a_n = \log(n+1)$

⑥ $b_n = \log 2^n$

Part 9 Sequence and Series 467

EXAMPLE 3. Write a general term a_n for the sequence.

① $\dfrac{2}{1}, \dfrac{3}{2}, \dfrac{4}{3}, \dfrac{5}{4}, \ldots$

② $\dfrac{1}{6}, \dfrac{2}{7}, \dfrac{3}{8}, \dfrac{4}{9}, \ldots$

③ $-1, 1, -1, 1, \ldots$

④ $1, -1, 1, -1, \ldots$

⑤ $7, -14, 21, -28, 35, \ldots$

⑥ $-2, 4, -6, 8, \ldots$

⑦ $1 \cdot 1, 2 \cdot 3, 3 \cdot 5, 4 \cdot 7, \ldots$

⑧ $2 \cdot 1, 4 \cdot 3, 6 \cdot 5, 8 \cdot 7, \ldots$

⑨ $1, \frac{1}{4}, \frac{1}{9}, \frac{1}{16}, \ldots$

⑩ $1, \frac{1}{\sqrt{2}}, \frac{1}{\sqrt{3}}, \frac{1}{2}, \ldots$

⑪ $2^{\frac{1}{4}}, 2^{\frac{1}{2}}, 2^{\frac{3}{4}}, 2, \ldots$

☞ Usually when you have

$1, -1, 1, -1, 1, \ldots =$ ① even numbers = ③ _____

$-1, 1, -1, 1, -1 \ldots =$ ② odd numbers = ④ _____

Blank : ① $(-1)^{n+1}$ ② $(-1)^n$ ③ $2n$ ④ $2n+1$ or $2n-1$

2. Series or Sigma Notation

※ The notation for series

① S_n denotes the sum of the first n terms of the sequence.

$$S_n = a_1 + a_2 + \cdots + a_n$$

② $\sum\limits_{k=m}^{n} a_k$ denotes the sum of the m th term to the n th term, so $S_n = \sum\limits_{k=1}^{n} a_k$.

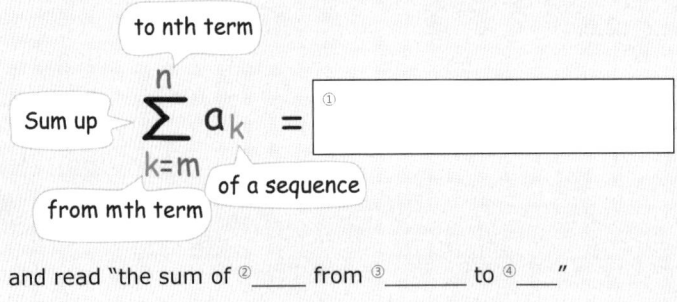

and read "the sum of ②_____ from ③_____ to ④____"

ex) $\sum\limits_{k=2}^{5} a_k =$ ⑤ _____

EXAMPLE 4. Write out the sum.(Do not evaluate.)

① $\sum\limits_{k=1}^{5} 3k$ ② $\sum\limits_{k=5}^{8} k^2$

Blank : ① $a_m + \ldots + a_n$ ② a_k ③ k=m   ④ k=n   ⑤ $a_2 + a_3 + a_4 + a_5$

③ $\sum_{k=4}^{7} 5$

④ $\sum_{k=2}^{4} \pi$

⑤ $\sum_{k=0}^{5} (k+2)^2$

⑥ $\sum_{k=4}^{9} k(k+1)$

⑦ $\sum_{k=1}^{3} \frac{(-1)^k}{6^{k+1}}$

⑧ $\sum_{k=0}^{4} \left(\frac{5}{4}\right) 2^k$

⑨ $\sum_{k=1}^{5} x^{k+1}$

⑩ $\sum_{k=1}^{\infty} \frac{a^{k+1}}{k}$

EXAMPLE 5. Write the sum using sigma notation, assuming the suggested pattern continues.

① $4+5+6+7$

② $8+10+12+14+16$

③ $1-3+5-7+9-11$

④ $\sin\pi - \sin 2\pi + \sin 3\pi - \sin 4\pi$

⑤ $64+81+100+121+144$

⑥ $3^3+4^3+5^3+\ldots+10^3$

⑦ $1+\dfrac{1}{2\sqrt{2}}+\dfrac{1}{3\sqrt{3}}+\dfrac{1}{8}+\ldots$

⑧ $1+\dfrac{1}{4}+\dfrac{1}{9}+\dfrac{1}{16}+\ldots$

⑨ $\sqrt{a}+\sqrt[3]{a}+\sqrt[4]{a}+\sqrt[5]{a}+\ldots$

⑩ $x+x^2+x^3+x^4+\ldots$

3. Expand Knowledge*

EXAMPLE 6. * Tell whether each pair of series is the same.

① $\sum_{k=0}^{10} \frac{1}{k+2}$, $\sum_{k=2}^{12} \frac{1}{k}$

② $\sum_{k=1}^{\infty} \frac{2^k}{k+1}$, $\sum_{k=2}^{\infty} \frac{2^{k+1}}{k}$

③ $\sum_{n=1}^{5} (-1)^n n^2$, $\sum_{n=2}^{6} (-1)^n (n-1)^2$

④ $\sum_{m=1}^{\infty} (-1)^m \frac{m}{m+1}$, $\sum_{n=2}^{\infty} (-1)^{m+1} \frac{m-1}{m}$

EXAMPLE 7. * What is a when;

$$\sum_{k=1}^{5} k \log x = \log x^a$$

EXAMPLE 8. * Evaluate.

$$\sum_{k=5}^{7}\left(\sum_{n=1}^{3}\left(\sum_{m=1}^{n} 3\right)\right)$$

Mia's Algebra 2

9.2 Arithmetic Sequence and Series

1. Arithmetic Sequences

※ **Arithmetic Sequence**

An arithmetic sequence has a constant difference, d, between two consecutive terms.

$$a,\ a+d,\ a+2d,\ a+\boxed{①}d,\ \cdots,\ \boxed{②}$$

(1st term, 2nd term, 3rd term, 4th term, ..., nth term)

where a is the ③_____ term, and d is a ④_____ _____.

General term (nth term): $a_n = a + (n-1)d$ (linear form)

[1st term: a; Common difference: d]

Blank : ① 3 ② a+(n−1)d ③ first ④ common difference

EXAMPLE 1. Find the common difference d and the general term (nth term) of given sequence.

① 2, 5, 8, 11, ...

② 7, 1, -5, -11, ...

③ $2, \dfrac{5}{2}, 3, \dfrac{7}{2}, ...$

④ $8, 8\dfrac{1}{4}, 8\dfrac{1}{2}, 8\dfrac{3}{4}, 9, ...$

⑤ $x-1, x-3, x-5, ...$

⑥ $2t+1, 2t+7, 2t+13, ...$

⑦ $14\sqrt{3}, 19\sqrt{3}, 24\sqrt{3}, ...$

EXAMPLE 2. Find the general term (nth term) of given sequence.
  ① 6th term is 17, 12th term is 29.   ② 3rd term is 13, 8th term is 38.

EXAMPLE 3. Find the number of terms in the sequence.
  ① 3, 5, 7, . . ., 37   ② 7, 3, -1, . . . , -81

2. Arithmetic Series

To find the arithmetic series;

$$\underbrace{(a)+(a+d)+(a+2d)+\cdots+(a+(n-1)d)}_{\text{first n terms}} = S_n \quad \text{(Sum of the first n terms)}$$

$$a \;+\; a+d \;+\cdots+\; a+(n-2)d + a+(n-1)d = S_n$$

$$\underset{③}{+)} \quad \boxed{①} + a+(n-2)d +\cdots+ a+d \;+\; \boxed{②} = S_n$$

※ **Arithmetic Series**

Sum of first n terms: $S_n = \dfrac{n}{2}(2a+(n-1)d) = \dfrac{n}{2}(a+a_n)$

- $\dfrac{n}{2}(2\underset{\text{1st term}}{a}+(n-1)\underset{\text{Common diff}}{d})$
- $\dfrac{n}{2}(\underset{\text{1st term}}{a}+\underset{\text{last term}}{a_n})$

Blank : ① $a+(n-1)d$ ② a ③ $+$

EXAMPLE 4. Evaluate the sum.

① $8+6+4+2+\ldots$ (10 terms)

② $1+4+7+10+\ldots$ (20 terms)

③ $3+5+7+9+\ldots+21$

④ $4+8+12+\ldots+400$

⑤ $4+\dfrac{13}{2}+9+\dfrac{23}{2}+\ldots+29$

⑥ $0.5+0.9+1.3+1.7+\ldots+4.1$

⑦ $\sum_{n=1}^{5}(n-4)$

⑧ $\sum_{n=1}^{10}(4n-2)$

⑨ $\sum_{n=4}^{15}(-2n+3)$

⑩ $\sum_{n=10}^{21}(4n-6)$

⑪ $\sum_{n=0}^{5}(4+4n)$

3. Expand Knowledge*

EXAMPLE 5. *Find the sum of all integers between 1 and 100 which are not multiples of 3.

EXAMPLE 6. *Find the general term (nth term) of given sequence.

$$\log 3, \log 6, \log 12, \log 24, \ldots$$

Mia's Algebra 2

9.3 Geometric Sequence and Series

1. Geometric Sequences

※ Geometric Sequence

An geometric sequence has a constant ratio, r, between two consecutive terms:

$$a,\ ar,\ ar^2,\ ar^{①\_\_},\ \ldots,\ ②\underline{}$$

(×r, ×r, ×r between consecutive terms; 1st term, 2nd term, 3rd term, 4th term)

where a is the ③_____ term, and r is a ④_____ _____.

General term (nth term): $a_n = a\,r^{n-1}$ (exponential form)

(Common ratio; 1st term)

Blank : ① 3   ② ar^{n-1} ③ first   ④ common ratio

EXAMPLE 1. Find the common ratio r and the general term (nth term) of given sequence.

① $2, -1, \dfrac{1}{2}, -\dfrac{1}{4}, \ldots$

② $-\dfrac{1}{4}, \dfrac{1}{2}, -1, \ldots$

③ $\sqrt{2}, 2, 2\sqrt{2}, 4, \ldots$

④ $5, -5, 5, -5, \ldots$

⑤ $x-3, -3x+9, 9x-27, \ldots$

⑥ $2x, 10x, 50x, \ldots$

⑦ $x^{a+2}, x^{a+5}, x^{a+8}, \ldots$

⑧ $x^{1/3}, x^{2/3}, x, x^{4/3}, \ldots$

EXAMPLE 2. Find the general term (nth term) of given sequence. (r > 0)

① 3rd term is $\dfrac{1}{81}$, 9th term is $\dfrac{1}{3}$.

② 7th term is 4, 12th term is 128.

EXAMPLE 3. Find the number of terms in the sequence.

① $\dfrac{3}{4}, \dfrac{3}{2}, 3, 6, \ldots, 192$

② -6, -12, -24, . . . , -384

2. Geometric Series

To find the geometric series;

$$\underbrace{(a)+(ar)+(ar^2)+\ldots+(ar^{n-1})}_{\text{first n terms}} = S_n \quad \text{Sum of the first n terms}$$

$$S_n = (a)+(ar)+(ar^2)+\cdots+(ar^{n-1})$$

$$\underset{\text{③}}{)}\; rS_n = \boxed{①} +(ar^2)+\cdots+(ar^{n-1})+\boxed{②}$$

※ **Geometric Series**

Sum of first n terms: $\quad S_n = \dfrac{\overset{\text{1st term}}{a}(1-\overset{\text{Common ratio}}{r}{}^n)}{1-r}$

Blank : ① ar ② ar^n ③ $-$

EXAMPLE 4. Find the sum of the first n terms of the sequence.

① $4, -16, 64, -256, \ldots$ (6 term)   ② $7, -21, 63, \ldots$ (5 term)

③ $\sum_{k=1}^{3} \left(\frac{3}{4}\right) 4^k$ ④ $\sum_{k=0}^{3} \left(\frac{2}{3}\right)^{k+1}$

⑤ $\sum_{k=0}^{5} 10 \left(\frac{1}{5}\right)^k$ ⑥ $\sum_{k=1}^{4} (0.1)^k$

3. Expand Knowledge*

EXAMPLE 5. * Find the general term (nth term) of given sequence.

$$\ln 2, \ln 2^3, \ln 2^9, \ln 2^{27}, \ldots$$

EXAMPLE 6. * Find the general term (nth term) of given sequence.

$$\sqrt{3}, \sqrt[3]{3}, \sqrt[6]{3}, 1, \cdots$$

Mia's Algebra 2

9.4 Infinite Geometric Series

1. Infinite Geometric Series

A geometric series that does not end is called an **infinite geometric series**.

If the common ratio $|r| \geq 1$ (① _____), then the sum (② diverges/converges).

ex) $1 + 2 + 4 + 8 + 16 + \cdots$

If the common ratio $|r| < 1$ (③ _____), then the sum (④ diverges/converges).

ex) $1 + \dfrac{1}{2} + \dfrac{1}{4} + \dfrac{1}{8} + \dfrac{1}{16} + \cdots$

☺ Vocabulary

Converge: getting closer to a certain value

Diverge: Not getting closer to a certain value (Not converge)

※ **Infinite Geometric Series**

For infinite geometric series, if the common ratio $|r|<1$, then the sum converges to $\dfrac{a}{1-r}$.

Sum of infinite terms

$$S_\infty = \sum_{k=1}^{\infty} ar^{n-1} = \dfrac{a}{1-r}$$

when $-1 < r < 1$

Blank : ① $r \leq -1$ or $r \geq 1$ ② diverges   ③ $-1 < r < 1$ ④ converges

EXAMPLE 1. Determine whether the infinite series is convergent or divergent. If it is convergent, find its sum.

① $1 + \dfrac{1}{2} + \dfrac{1}{4} + \dfrac{1}{8} + \ldots$

② $1 + \dfrac{4}{3} + \left(\dfrac{4}{3}\right)^2 + \left(\dfrac{4}{3}\right)^3 + \ldots$

③ $\dfrac{2}{3} - 2 + 6 - \ldots$

④ $0.5 + 0.25 + 0.125 + \ldots$

⑤ $1 + 1.1 + 1.21 + 1.331 + \ldots$

⑥ $\dfrac{1}{\sqrt{2}} + \dfrac{1}{2} + \dfrac{1}{2\sqrt{2}} + \dfrac{1}{4} + \ldots$

⑦ $\sum\limits_{k=1}^{\infty} 3(0.75)^{k-1}$

⑧ $\sum\limits_{k=2}^{\infty} \left(\dfrac{2}{3}\right)^{k-1}$

⑨ $\sum_{k=0}^{\infty} 2(-0.1)^k$

⑩ $\sum_{k=1}^{\infty} (1.01)^k$

⑪ $\sum_{k=0}^{\infty} \left(-\frac{4}{5}\right)^k$

⑫ $\sum_{k=1}^{\infty} 2\left(\frac{2}{3}\right)^k$

⑬ $\sum_{k=1}^{\infty} \left(\frac{\pi}{2}\right)^k$

EXAMPLE 2. Express the rational number as a fraction of integers.

① 0.66666....

② 0.030303...

③ 0.234234234...

④ 0.2535353...

⑤ 0.1252525...

2. Expand Knowledge*

EXAMPLE 3. * A ball is dropped from a height of 3 m. Each time it hits the ground it bounces up to 90% of its previous height.

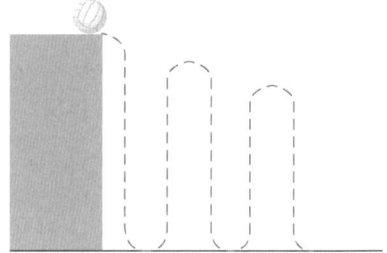

(a) How high will it bounce after it strikes the ground for the 5th time?

(b) What total distance does the ball travel before it stops bouncing?

EXAMPLE 4. *The sides of a square are 16 inches in length. A new square is formed by connecting the midpoints of the sides of the original square, and two of the resulting triangles are shaded (see figure). If this process is repeated infinitely, determine the total area of the shaded region.

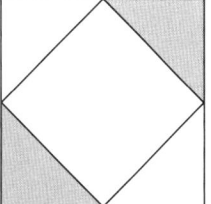 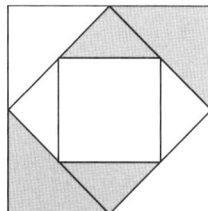 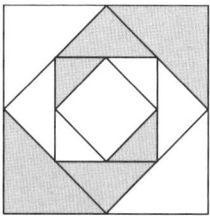 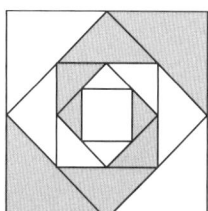

EXAMPLE 5. * What fraction of the square is eventually shaded if the indicated shading process continues infinitely?

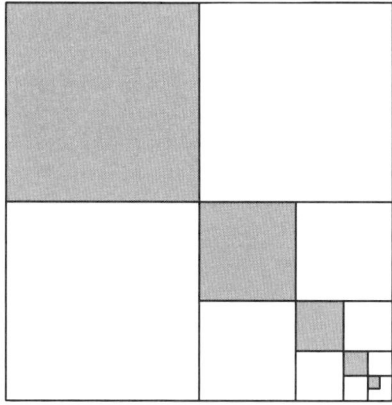

Part 10
Coordinate Geometry

10.1 Distance and midpoint Formulas

10.2 Equation of Circle

10.3 Basics of Conic Sections

Mia's Algebra 2

10.1 Distance and midpoint Formulas

1. Midpoint Formula

   ※ **Midpoint Formula**

   The **midpoint** between any two points (x_1, y_1) and (x_2, y_2) is;

   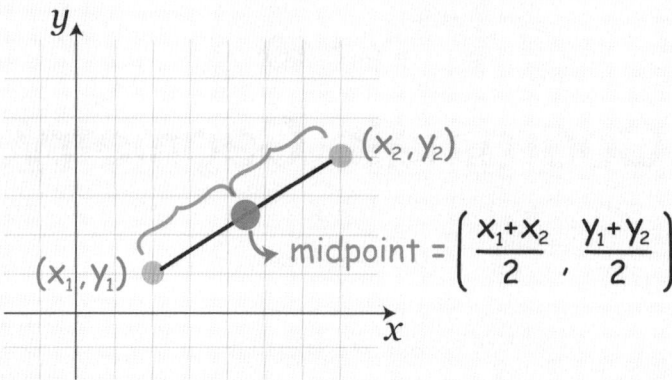

   $$\text{midpoint} = \left(\frac{x_1+x_2}{2}, \frac{y_1+y_2}{2}\right)$$

   EXAMPLE 1. Find the midpoint.

   ① $(5,2), (2,4)$ ② $(-2,-4), (4,4)$

   ③ $(\sqrt{3}, 3), (-\sqrt{3}, -3)$ ④ $(0, \sqrt{5})(1, 2\sqrt{5})$

⑤ $(2+\sqrt{3}, 1+\sqrt{7}), (-2+\sqrt{3}, 1-\sqrt{7})$ ⑥ $(1-4\sqrt{2}, -\sqrt{5}), (1-6\sqrt{2}, 5\sqrt{5})$

⑦ $(a, \sqrt{ab}), (b, -\sqrt{ab})$ ⑧ $(a+b, a-b), (a-b, a+b)$

EXAMPLE 2. The diameter of a circle connects two points (2, -3) and (6, 4) on the circle. Find the coordinates of the center of the circle.

2. Distance Formula

Let's say we have two points (x_1, y_1) and (x_2, y_2).

Vertical distance between two points; ① _____

Horizontal distance between two points; ② _____

Then according to Pythagorean Theorem the distance between two points is ;

③ _____

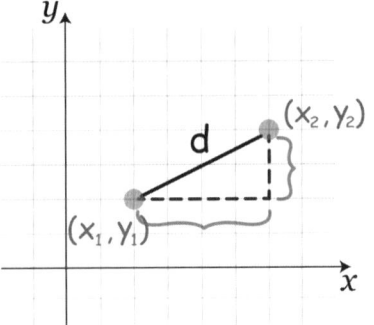

※ Distance Formula

The **distance d** between any two points (x_1, y_1) and (x_2, y_2) is;

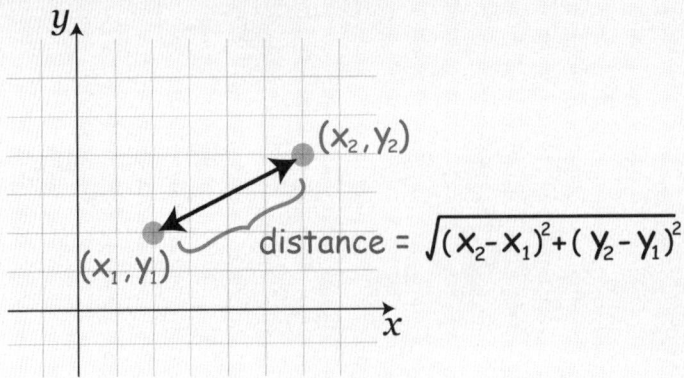

$$\text{distance} = \sqrt{(x_2-x_1)^2 + (y_2-y_1)^2}$$

Blank : ① $y_2 - y_1$ ② $x_2 - x_1$ ③ $\sqrt{(x_2-x_1)^2 + (y_2-y_1)^2} = r$

EXAMPLE 3. Find the distance.

① $(5,2),(2,4)$

② $(-2,-4),(4,4)$

③ $(\sqrt{3},3),(-\sqrt{3},-3)$

④ $(0,\sqrt{5})(1,2\sqrt{5})$

⑤ $(2+\sqrt{3},1+\sqrt{7}),(-2+\sqrt{3},1-\sqrt{7})$

⑥ $(1-4\sqrt{2},-\sqrt{5}),(1-6\sqrt{2},5\sqrt{5})$

⑦ $(a,\sqrt{ab}),(b,-\sqrt{ab})$

⑧ $(a+b,a-b),(a-b,a+b)$

EXAMPLE 4. The diameter of a circle connects two points (2, -3) and (6, 4) on the circle. Find the radius of the circle.

3. Expand Knowledge*

EXAMPLE 5. * Show that the points $A\,(3, -4)$, $B\,(-2, 5)$ and $C\,(7, 10)$ are the vertices of an isosceles right-angled triangle.

Mia's Algebra 2

10.2 Equation of Circle

1. Equation of a circle

A **circle** is a set of all points on a plane that are a ①_____ distance from a center.

The circle is **all the points** ②_____ that are "③_____" away from the center ④_____.

It means the distance btwn (x, y) and (a, b) is r;

⑤ _____

※ **Equation of a Circle**

$$(x-a)^2 + (y-b)^2 = r^2$$

center (a, b)   radius r

A circle with center (a,b) and radius r.

Blank : ① same ② (x, y) ③ r ④ (a, b) ⑤ $\sqrt{(x-a)^2 + (y-b)^2} = r$

EXAMPLE 1. Find the center and radius of the circle with the given equation. Then graph the circle.

① $(x-1)^2 + (x+3)^2 = 9$

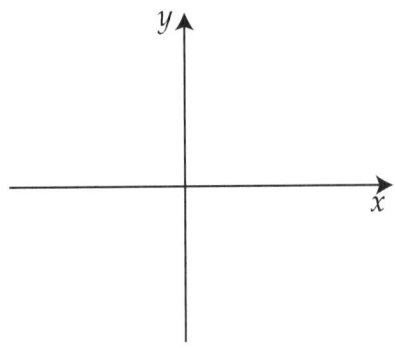

② $(x+2)^2 + (y-4)^2 = 4$

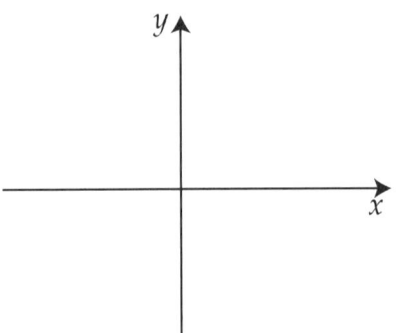

③ $(x+2)^2 + y^2 = 16$

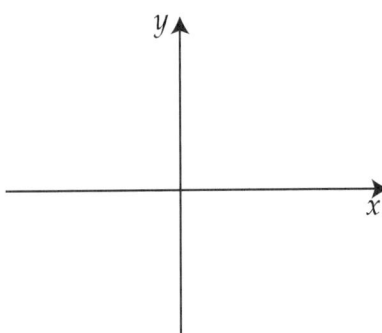

④ $x^2 + (y-4)^2 = 16$

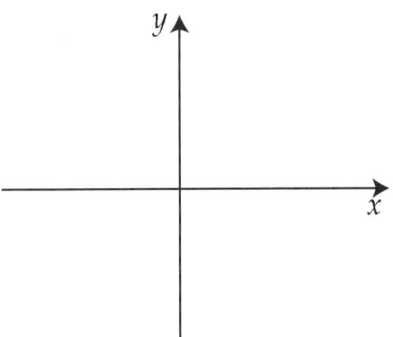

⑤ $x^2 + y^2 = 27$

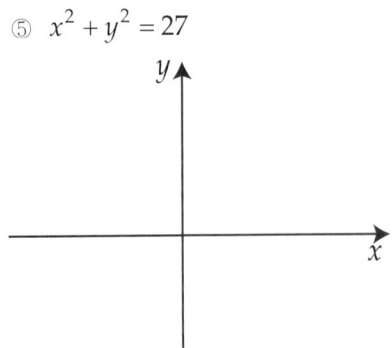

⑥ $x^2 + (y+1)^2 = 12$

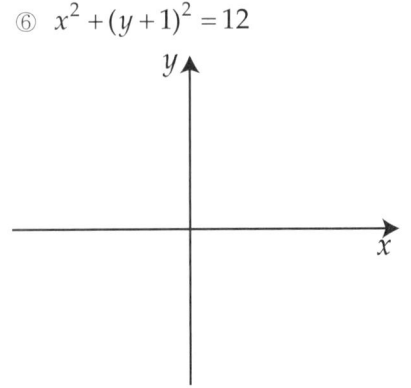

EXAMPLE 2. Write an equation for the circle that satisfies each set of conditions.

① center (3, -7) and radius 5

② center (0, 2) and radius 3

③ center (0, 0) and radius $\sqrt{5}$

④ center (-1, 7) and radius $\sqrt{2}$

⑤ center (0, -3) and diameter $\sqrt{8}$

⑥ center (-2, 0) and diameter 8

⑦ center (-2, 3) and passes through origin

⑧ center (-5, 2) and passes through (-9, 4)

⑨ endpoints of a diameter at (0, 6) and (-8, -2)

⑩ endpoints of a diameter at (-4, -2) and (8, 6)

⑪ center (-8, -5) and tangent to x-axis

⑫ center (5, -4) and tangent to y-axis

⑬ center (-7, 3) and tangent to $x = 2$

⑭ center (-3, -2) and tangent to $y = 3$

⑮ Tangent to the lines $x=2, x=6$ and $y=0$ (Two answers)

⑯ Tangent to both axes and the line $x=-4$ (Two answers)

⑰ Center on line $x+y=2$, tangent to both axes

⑱ Center on line $y=x+2$, tangent to both axes

2. General Form of the Equation of a Circle

More *neat* way to show it?

※ **General Form of the Equation of a Circle**
$$x^2 + y^2 + Ax + By + C = 0$$

EXAMPLE 3. Find the center and radius of the circle with the given equation.

☺ Tip: Try to complete the square!

① $x^2 + y^2 - 10x + 8y + 16 = 0$ ② $x^2 + y^2 + 2x + 6y + 2 = 0$

③ $x^2 - 6x + y^2 = 12$ ④ $x^2 + y^2 + 10y + 14 = 0$

⑤ $2x^2 + 2y^2 + 4x + 20y + 6 = 0$ ⑥ $3x^2 + 3y^2 - 6x - 24y + 24 = 0$

3. Expand Knowledge*

EXAMPLE 4. * Graph the inequalities.

☺ Tip: If $x^2 + y^2 \leq 0$ (or <0), then shade the ①_____ of circle.

If $x^2 + y^2 \geq 0$ (or >0), then shade the ②_____ of circle.

① $x^2 + y^2 < 10$ ② $x^2 + y^2 \geq 9$

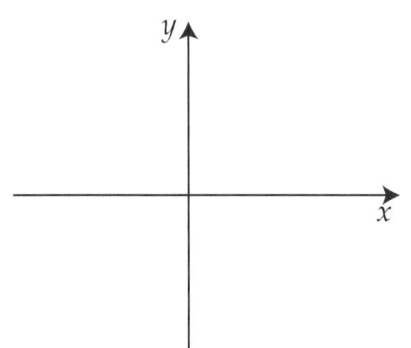   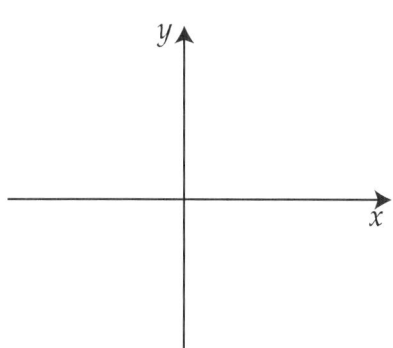

③ $x^2 + y^2 - 6y \geq 0$ ④ $x^2 + y^2 + 4x < 0$

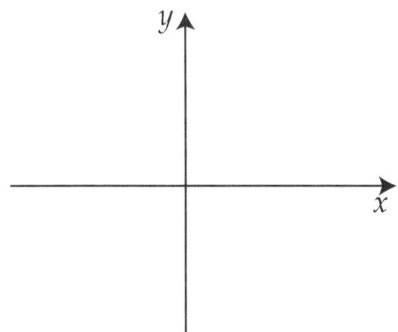   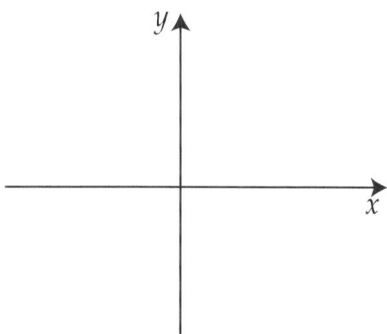

Blank : ① inside   ② outside

⑤ $x^2 + y^2 + 10x - 6y + 9 \leq 0$

⑥ $x^2 + y^2 - 8x - 2y + 1 \leq 0$

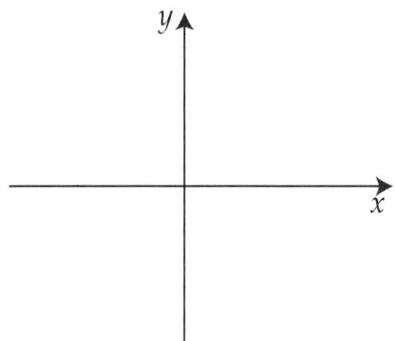

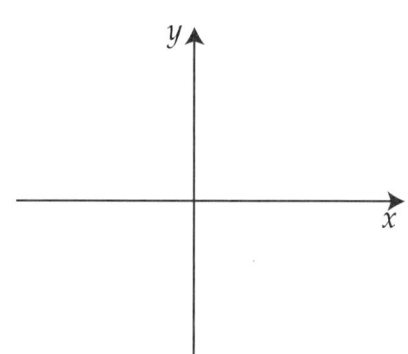

EXAMPLE 5. * Graph the semicircle.

☺ Tip: $x^2 + y^2 = r^2 \Rightarrow y = \pm\sqrt{r^2 - x^2}$

$y = +\sqrt{r^2 - x^2}$ is the upper semicircle.

$y = -\sqrt{r^2 - x^2}$ is the lower semicircle.

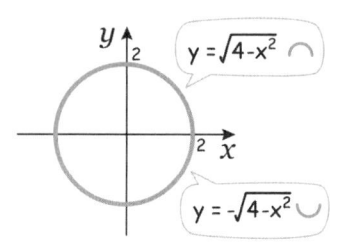

① $y = \sqrt{9 - x^2}$

② $y = -\sqrt{25 - x^2}$

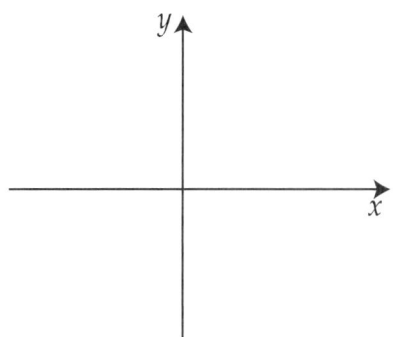

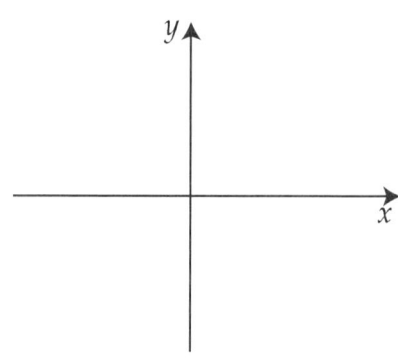

③ $y = -\sqrt{9-x^2}$

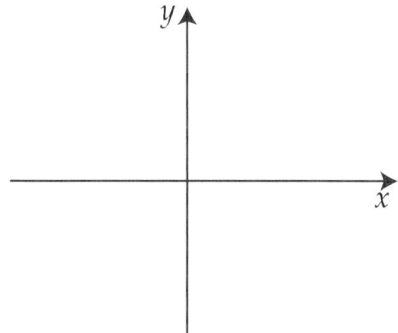

④ $y = \sqrt{25-x^2}$

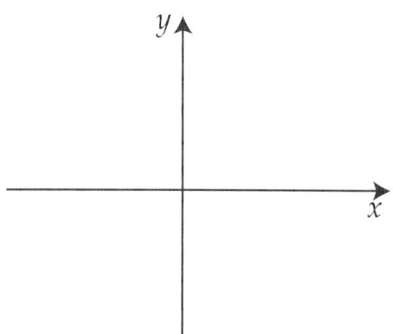

⑤ $y = \sqrt{4x-x^2}$

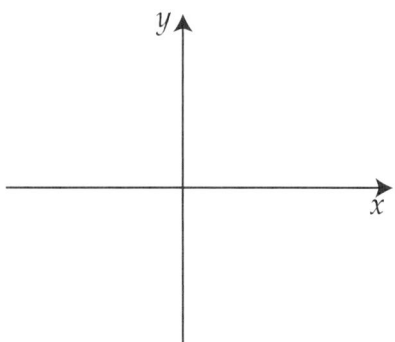

⑥ $y = \sqrt{6x-x^2}$

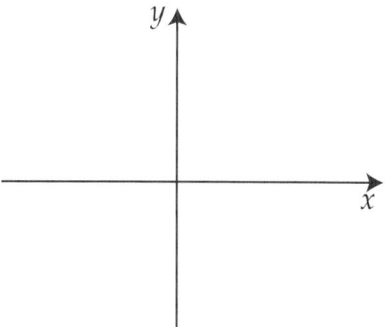

Mia's Algebra 2
10.3 Basics of Conic Sections

1. Conic Section

What shape do we have if we cut a cone ..

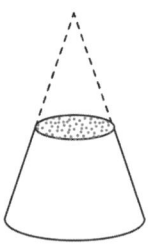 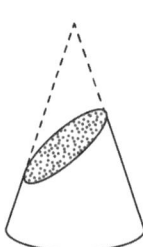 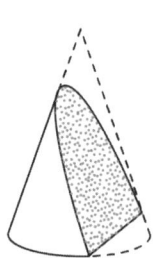 

straight through   slight angle   parallel to edge of cone   steep angle

: ①_____   : ②_____   : ③_____   : ④_____

These curves are related!

2. Parabola

A ⑤_____ is a curve where any point is at an **equal distance** from

a straight line(⑥_____)

and *a fixed point*(⑦_____).

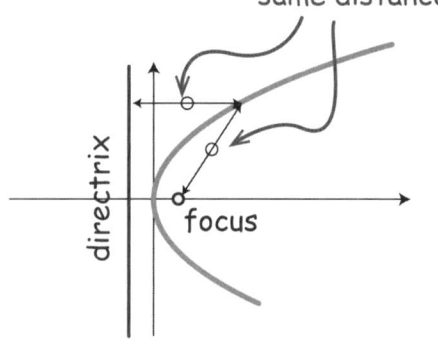

Blank : ① circle   ② ellipse   ③ parabola   ④ hyperbola   ⑤ parabola   ⑥ directrix   ⑦ focus

A **parabola** is the set of all points in a plane that are equidistant from a fixed line, the directrix, and a fixed point, the focus.

※ **Standard form of Parabola**

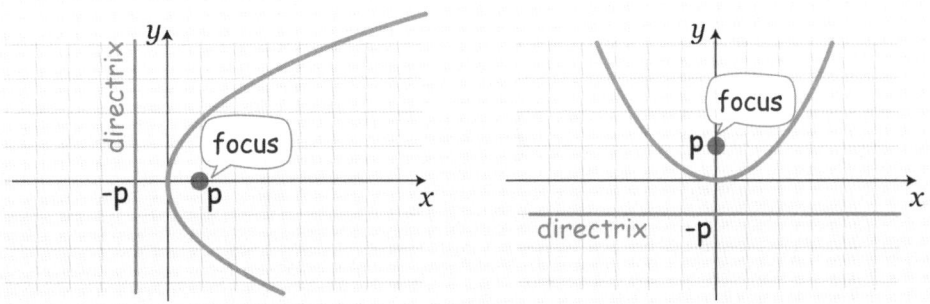

	Formula	
$4px = y^2$ (focus x)		$4py = x^2$ (focus y)
① to the right	..it opens..	up
② (p, 0)	Focus	(0, p)
③ x = -p	Directrix	y = -p
④ (0, 0)	Vertex	(0, 0)
⑤ x axis	Axis of Symmetry	y-axis

p gives you the location of the focus and directrix.

Blank : ① to the right   ② (p, 0)   ③ x = -p   ④ (0, 0)   ⑤ x axis

EXAMPLE 1. Graph the parabola. Label the focus, directrix.

① $y = \dfrac{1}{4}x^2$

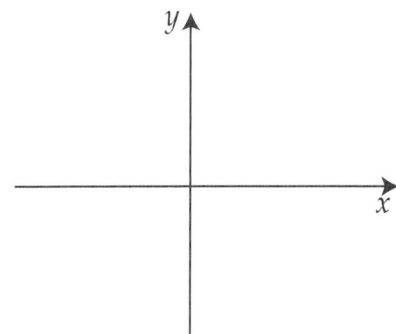

Focus:
directrix:

② $16y = x^2$

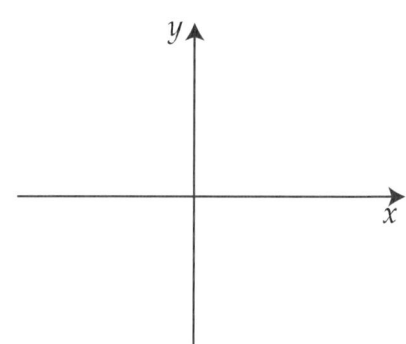

Focus:
directrix:

③ $x = 8y^2$

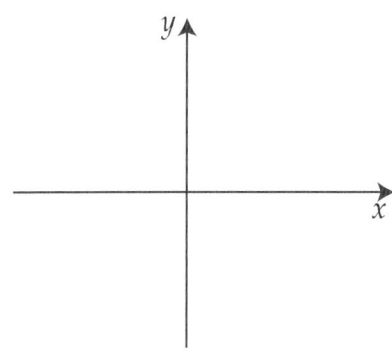

Focus:
directrix:

④ $8x = y^2$

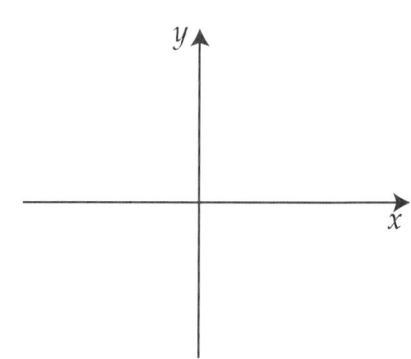

Focus:
directrix:

⑤ $y^2 + 6x = 0$

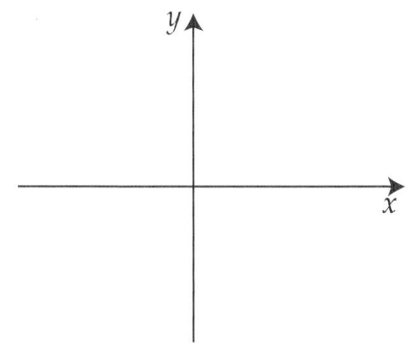

Focus:
directrix:

⑥ $0 = x^2 + 16y$

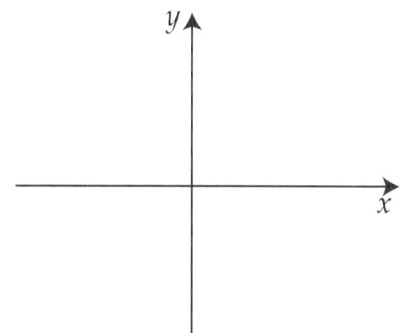

Focus:
directrix:

3. Ellipse

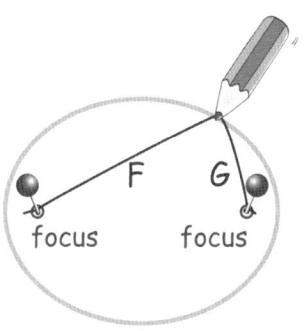

We can draw an ellipse using a string whose ends are attached to two nails. The pencil is moved all the way around while always keeping the string tight.

(The length of the sting F + G always be the① _____)

Blank : ① same

An **ellipse** is the set of all points (x, y) in a plane, the sum of whose distances from two distinct fixed point (foci) is constant.

※ **Standard form of ellipse**

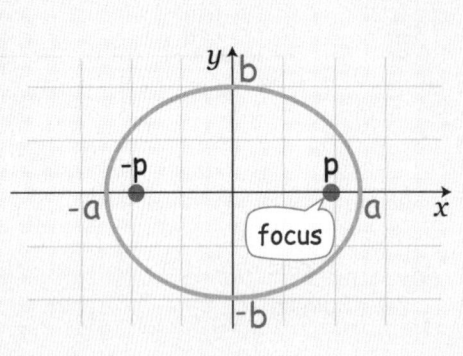
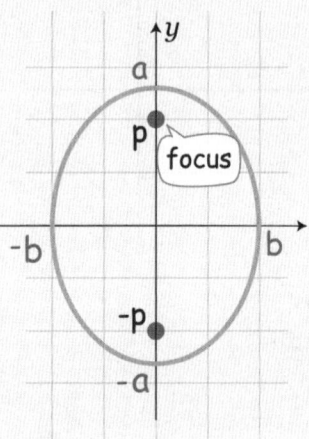

	Standard Equation	
$\dfrac{x^2}{a^2} + \dfrac{y^2}{b^2} = 1$ (vertex)	Standard Equation	$\dfrac{y^2}{a^2} + \dfrac{x^2}{b^2} = 1$ (vertex)
①	center	(0, 0)
②	Foci	(0, ±p)
③	Vertices	(0, ±a)
④	Pythagorean Relation	$p = \sqrt{a^2 - b^2}$

Blank : ① (0, 0)   ② (±p, 0)   ③ (±a, 0)   ④ $p = \sqrt{a^2 - b^2}$

EXAMPLE 2. Graph the ellipse. Label the Foci, vertices.

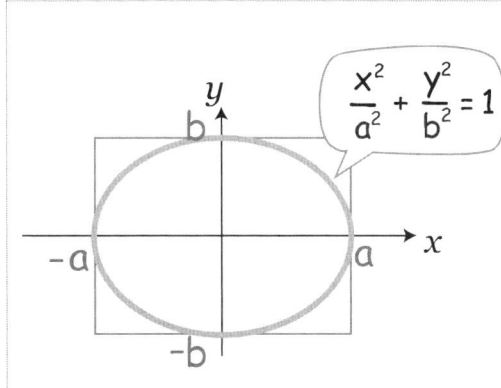

$$\frac{x^2}{a^2} + \frac{y^2}{b^2} = 1$$

i) Mark points a units along x directions from the center and points b units along y directions from the center.

ii) Draw an ellipse through these points

① $\dfrac{x^2}{16} + \dfrac{y^2}{25} = 1$

② $\dfrac{x^2}{49} + \dfrac{y^2}{3} = 1$

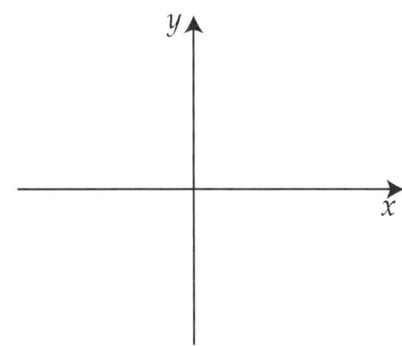

Foci:
Vertices:

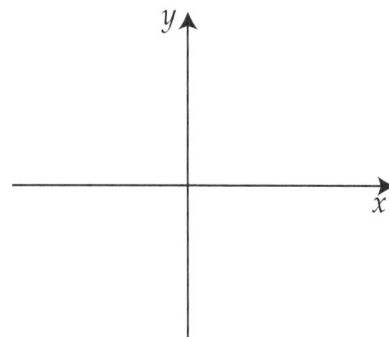

Foci:
Vertices:

Part 10 Coordinate Geometry 515

③ $4x^2 + 16y^2 = 64$

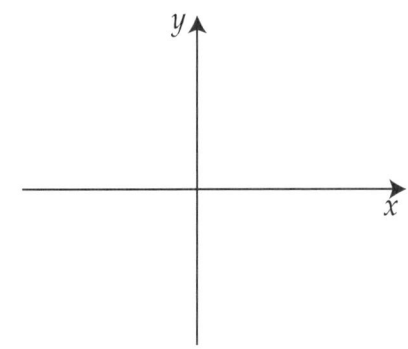

Foci:

Vertices:

④ $16x^2 + 9y^2 = 144$

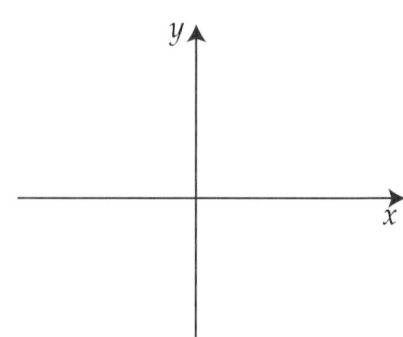

Foci:

Vertices:

⑤ $16x^2 + 4y^2 = 1$

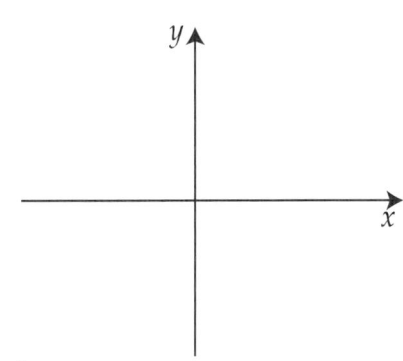

Foci:

Vertices:

⑥ $x^2 + 9y^2 = 1$

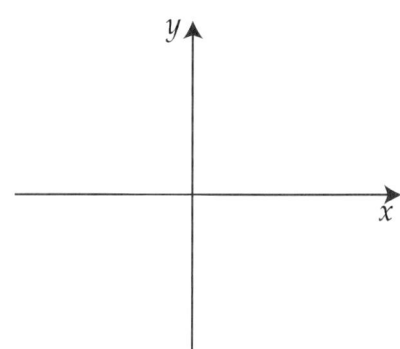

Foci:

Vertices:

4. Hyperbola

A **hyperbola** is the set of points in a plane, the difference of whose distances from two distinct foci is constant.

※ **Standard form of hyperbola**

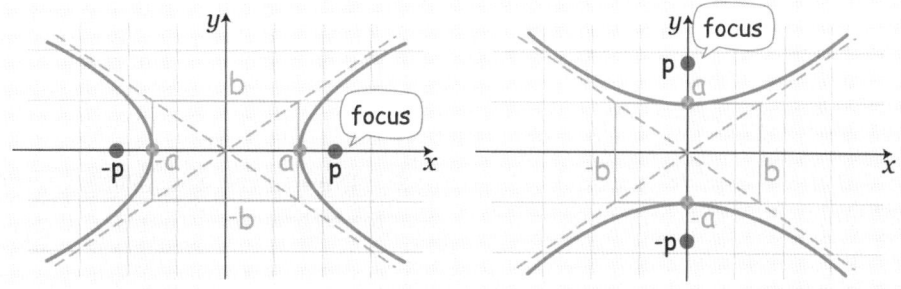

	Standard Equation	
$\dfrac{x^2}{a^2} - \dfrac{y^2}{b^2} = 1$ (vertex)		$\dfrac{y^2}{a^2} - \dfrac{x^2}{b^2} = 1$ (vertex)
①	center	(0, 0)
②	Foci	(0, ±p)
③	Vertices	(0, ±a)
④	Pythagorean Relation	$p = \sqrt{a^2 + b^2}$
⑤	Asymptotes	$y = \pm \dfrac{a}{b} x$

Blank : ① (0, 0)　② (±p, 0)　③ (±a, 0)　④ $p = \sqrt{a^2 + b^2}$　⑤ $y = \pm \dfrac{b}{a} x$

EXAMPLE 3. Graph the hyperbola. Label the Foci, vertices, and asymptotes.

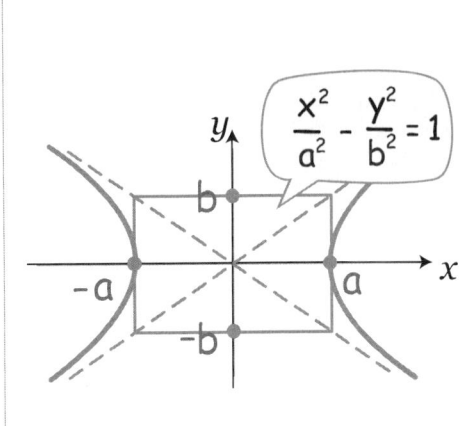

i) Mark points a units along x directions from the center and points b units along y directions from the center.

ii) draw a rectangle and asymptotes as shown

ii) Draw a hyperbola. (shape depends on the first term)

① $\dfrac{x^2}{25} - \dfrac{y^2}{36} = 1$

② $\dfrac{x^2}{16} - \dfrac{y^2}{4} = 1$

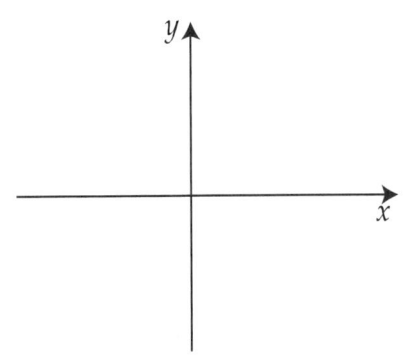

Foci:
Vertices:
Asymptotes:

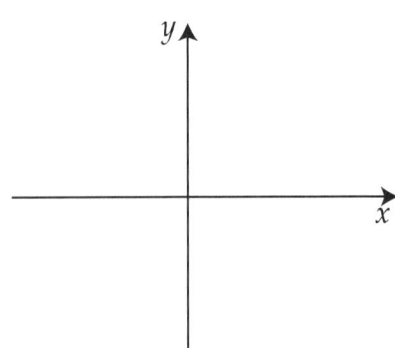

Foci:
Vertices:
Asymptotes:

③ $16y^2 - x^2 = 1$

Foci:
Vertices:
Asymptotes:

④ $y^2 - 9x^2 = 1$

Foci:
Vertices:
Asymptotes:

Part 11
Basic Statistics

11.1 Measuring Center of Data

11.2 Measuring Spread of Data

11.3 Probability

11.4 Independent and dependent Event

Mia's Algebra 2
11.1 Measuring Center of Data

1. Displaying Data

These are 20 scores from a 50-point quiz given to a high school statistics class ;

| 40 | 32 | 48 | 18 | 30 | 07 | 22 | 25 | 34 | 22 |
| 27 | 34 | 15 | 25 | 05 | 25 | 30 | 49 | 25 | 18 |

1) Dotplot

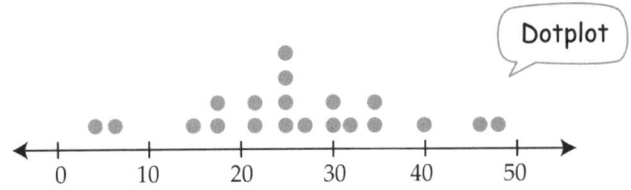

2) Stemplot (Stem and Leaf Plot)

```
0 | 57
1 | 588
2 | 2255557
3 | 00244
4 | 089
```

Stem and leaf

1 | 5 means 15

3) Histogram

Histograms take values and place them in "bins".

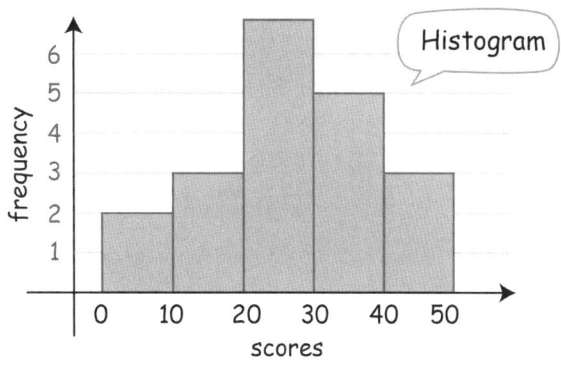

Using dotplots, stemplots, histograms we can see the ①_____ of the data.

2. Measuring the Center of Data

We want to be more specific describing data. We use three different values to find the center;

① mean   ② median   ③ Mode

1) Mean

※ **Mean** (= Arithmetic mean = Average): Add up the numbers and divide by how many numbers.

$$\text{Mean } \bar{x} = \frac{\sum_{}^{n} x}{n}$$
(Sum of data / How many)

$$\sum_{}^{n} x = \boxed{②}$$
(Sum of data)

Blank : ① distribution   ② $\bar{x} \cdot n$

※ **Facts about mean**

The mean is (①sensitive / NOT sensitive) to the extreme data.

: The mean will get pulled up towards to very high data.
The mean will get pulled down towards to very low data.

$$8 \quad 9 \quad 9.5 \quad 10 \quad 10.6 \quad 12.7 \quad 13 \quad \text{Mean is } 10.4$$
$$8 \quad 9 \quad 9.5 \quad 10 \quad 10.6 \quad 12.7 \quad 50 \quad \text{Mean is } 15.69$$

2) Median

※ **Median:** ②_____ number

odd numbers of value: single middle value.

ex) median of 1, 2, 3, 4, 8 is ③____.

even numbers of value: the average of the two middle values.

ex) median of 1, 2, 3, 4 is ④____.

To find the median, arrange the data in order and use the formula to find the LOCATION of the median.

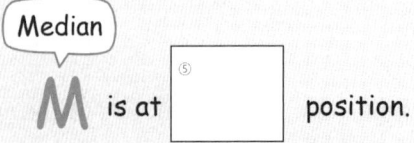

where n is the number of data.

ex) If we have 100 data, then the median will located at ⑥_____.

※ **Facts about the median**

The median is (⑦sensitive / NOT sensitive) to the extreme data.

: If large values are to the far right or far left the median doesn't care because he is in the middle!

$$8 \quad 9 \quad 9.5 \quad 10 \quad 10.6 \quad 12.7 \quad 13 \quad \text{Median is } 10$$
$$8 \quad 9 \quad 9.5 \quad 10 \quad 10.6 \quad 12.7 \quad 50 \quad \text{Median is } 10$$

Blank : ① sensitive ② middle ③ 3 ④ 2.5 ⑤ $\frac{n+1}{2}$ ⑥ $\frac{101}{2} = 50.5$ th data (average of 50th and 51st data) ⑦ not sensitive

3) Mode

※ **Mode** is the value that appears ①_____ frequent.

EXAMPLE 1. Find the mean, median, and mode of the data set. You may use calculator for only simple calculations.

① 12, 16, 19, 20, 20

② 2, 8, 12, 17, 17, 19, 22, 23

mean:
median:
mode:

mean:
median:
mode:

③ 4, 4, 18, 21, 22, 22

④ 24, 25, 26, 30, 30, 33, 37

mean:
median:
mode:

mean:
median:
mode:

⑤
```
1 | 2
2 | 0 0 4
3 | 1 2
4 | 0
```

⑥
```
2 | 1 2
3 | 1 2 3 8
5 | 0 0
```

mean:
median:
mode:

mean:
median:
mode:

Blank : ① most

⑦

data	Frequency
1	1
2	3
3	4
4	5
5	2

mean:
median:
mode:

⑧

data	Frequency
2	2
4	4
5	5
6	1
9	3

mean:
median:
mode:

⑨

Shoes Size	Frequency
230	2
235	4
240	5
245	1

mean:
median:
mode:

⑩

weight	Frequency
40	3
45	2
50	3
55	2

mean:
median:
mode:

☺ Tip: finding mean with frequency table

$$\bar{x} = \frac{\sum_{n} x \cdot f}{\sum_{n} f}$$

Mean = (Sum of data·frequency) / (Sum of frequency)

EXAMPLE 2. The mean of 24 test scores is 82. When the 25th class member takes the test, the mean goes down by 2 points. What was that 25th score?

EXAMPLE 3. In a class, 18 students had an average midterm exam grade of 85 and the 12 remaining students had an average midterm exam grade of 90. What is the average midterm exam grade of the entire class?

3. Shape of the distribution

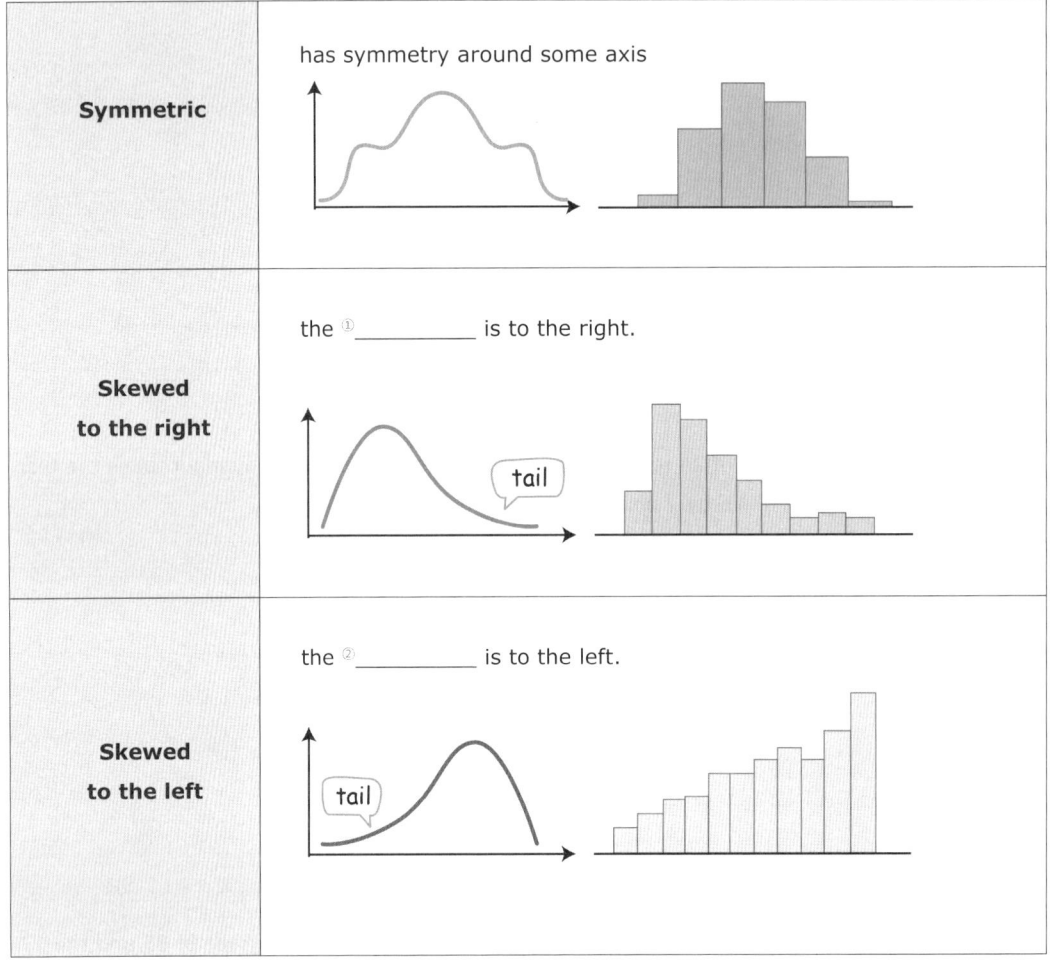

Blank : ① tail ② tail

※ **Comparing the Mean and Median**

When data has a roughly symmetric distribution the mean and median are almost the same.

But when data is skewed either way, the MEAN will go out towards the ①_____.

(because mean has to adjust for those few high or low values. Whereas the median stays in the middle.)

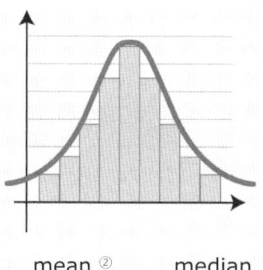 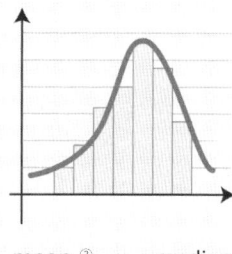 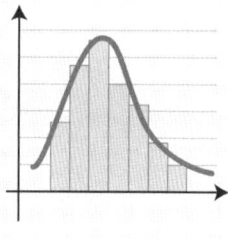

mean ②____ median   mean ③____ median   mean ④____ median

EXAMPLE 4. What is the shape of the distribution? Compare the mean and Median.

①
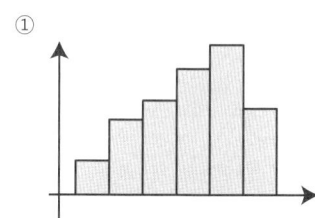

②
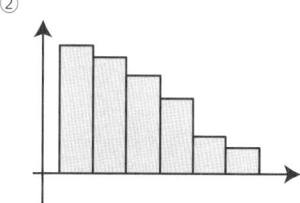

③

1	2 2 5
2	0 0 4 5 5 6 8
3	1 2 3 3 3
4	0 1
5	2
6	0

④

1	2 2
2	0 1
3	1 2 4
4	0 0 4 5 5 7
5	1 2 2 5 8 9 9
6	0 0 1 2 5

Blank : ① tail   ② =   ③ <   ④ >

⑤

1	0 1
2	0 1 1 2
3	2 4 5 5 7 8 9
4	4 5 7 7 8 9
5	2 4 5 7 6
6	4 5

⑥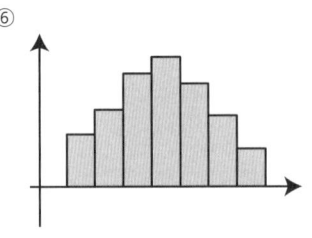

⑦

age	Frequency
15	6
16	5
17	4
18	3
19	1
20	1

⑧

shoes size	Frequency
230	1
235	1
240	2
245	4
250	6
255	9

4. Expand Knowledge*

EXAMPLE 5.* The average of four different positive integers is 25. If the numbers are not less than 10, then what is the greatest possible value of one of these numbers?

Mia's Algebra 2

11.2 Measuring Spread of Data

1. Measuring the Spread

We want to be more specific describing data. We use three different values to find the spread;

① range ② IQR ③ standard deviation

1) Range and IQR

※ **Range**

$$\text{Range} = \text{highest value} - \text{lowest value}$$

Only issue is; with extreme values the range can easily be misinterpreted.

ex) 1 2 5 7 10 1000
     1 200 400 500 700 1000

※ **Inter Quartile Range (IQR)** = Upper quartile − lower quartile

Quartiles are the values that divide a list of numbers into quarters.

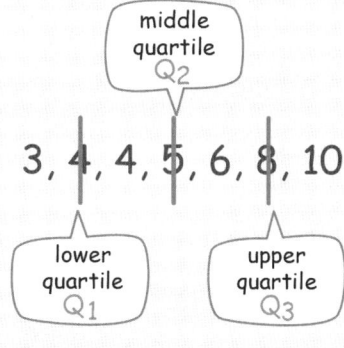

IQR = ①_____

IQR is the range of the middle half of the data.

Blank : ① $Q_3 - Q_1$

Part 11 Basic Statistics 531

※ **Box Plot** shows the 5 important values such as;

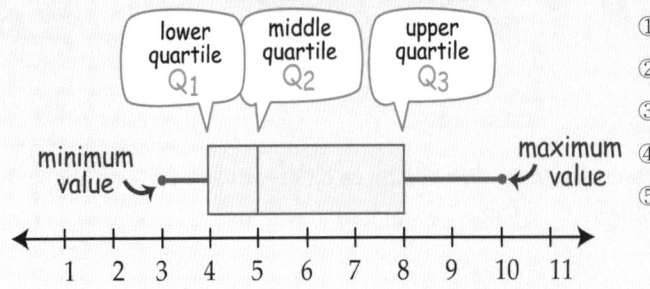

① minimum value
② lower quartile (Q1)
③ median (Q2)
④ upper quartile (Q3)
⑤ maximum value

· Small section means (①less data/ less spread out).

· Each section has ② _____ of the data.

EXAMPLE 1. Find the 5-number summary for the data and construct a boxplot. Also find the range and IQR.

① 5, 5, 6, 7, 8, 9, 11, 13, 17

② 2, 8, 12, 17, 17, 19, 22, 23

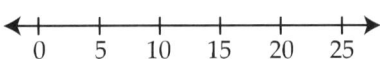

range: IQR:

range: IQR:

Blank : ① less spread out   ② 25%

③ 2, 3, 4, 10, 10, 12, 13, 17, 19, 21

④ 24, 25, 26, 30, 30, 33, 37

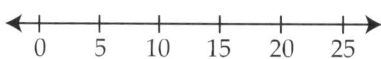

range: IQR:

range: IQR:

⑤
```
1 | 2 4 5
2 | 0 0 4
3 | 1 2
4 | 0
```

⑥
```
2 | 0 1
3 | 2 3 7
4 | 1 3 3 9
5 | 0 0 5
```

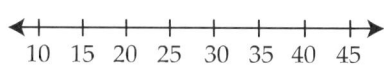

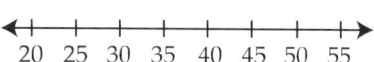

range: IQR:

range: IQR:

EXAMPLE 2. After the final examination, scores of two classes studying the same subject is shown as a boxplot.

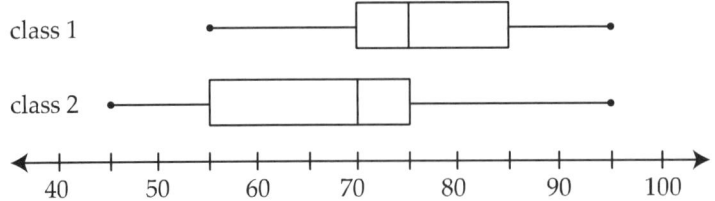

(a) Find the range and IQR of class 1.

(b) If the student who scored at least 75 received an achievement award, what percentage of students received as award in
   (i) class 1   (ii) class 2

(c) True/False?

I. For class 2, half of the class scored a mark greater than or equal to 70.

II. For class 1, the top 25% of the class scored at least 75 marks for the test.

III. For class 2, the middle half of the class had scores between 55 and 75 for this test.

IV. The students in class 1 generally scored higher.

V. The marks in class 1 are more varied.

VI. At least 50% of the data in class 1 are greater than 50% of the data in class 2.

EXAMPLE 3. The given parallel boxplots represent the 100-meter sprint times for the members of three athletics team.

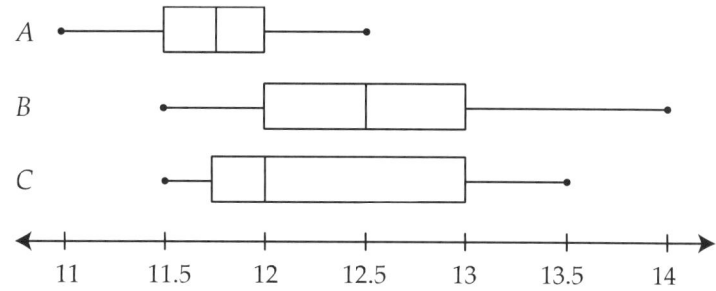

(a) Find the range and IQR of team B.

(b) If the members who have a record at most 12 sec will go to the final ground, what percentage of students will go to the final ground?
    (i) Team A   (ii) Team B   (ii) Team C

(c) True/False?

    I. For team B and C, 25% of the members have a record more than 13 sec.

    II. Team A generally ran faster.

    III. Team B is more varied than team A.

    IV. At least 75% of the data in A ran faster than 75% of the data in B.

    V. At least 50% of the data in B ran faster than 25% of the data in C.

4) Standard Deviation

※ **Standard Deviation** (SD)

Standard Deviation measures how far the typical data is from the ①_____.

Small SD : most data is (②far/close) to/from the mean.

Large SD: most data is (③far/close) to/from the mean.

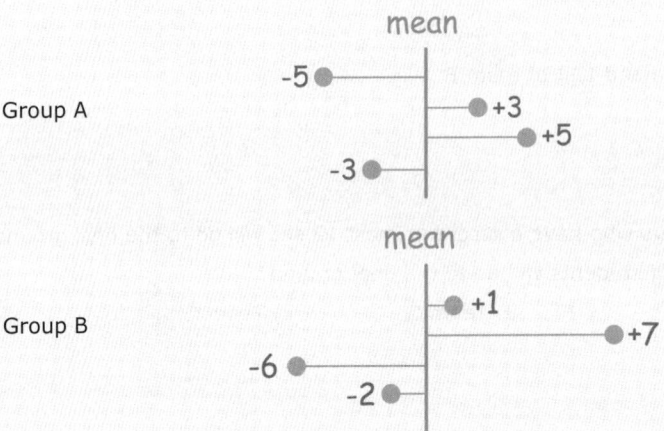

※ **Formula of Variance and Standard Deviation**

The **variance (σ^2)** shows you the

"④_____ of the 'squared' ⑤_____ from the mean"

The *square root* of that value is the **standard deviation (σ)**.

Blank : ① mean ② close ③ far ④ average ⑤ difference

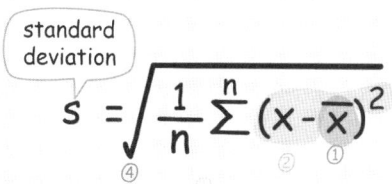
standard deviation
$$s = \sqrt{\frac{1}{n}\sum_{i=1}^{n}(x-\bar{x})^2}$$

① Work out the **mean**.
② Find the **difference** btwn the data and the mean and **Square** it.
③ find the **Average** of them.
④ Take the square root.

Why do we *square* the difference?

Squaring always gives a ①_____ value and emphasizes larger differences

※ **Facts about IQR and Standard Deviation** (SD)

Standard deviation is (②sensitive / NOT sensitive) to extreme values.

IQR is (③sensitive / NOT sensitive) to extreme values.

EXAMPLE 4. Find the variance and standard deviation of each data. You may use calculator for only simple calculations.

① 5, 5, 7, 9, 14   (mean = 8)   ② 3, 5, 8, 11, 13   (mean = 8)

EXAMPLE 5. Pair of histograms is given as shown. Both histograms has same unit of axes. Compare the standard deviation of A and B.

① A. 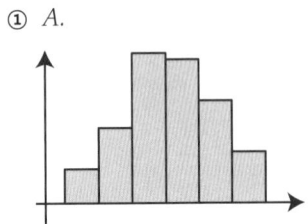   B.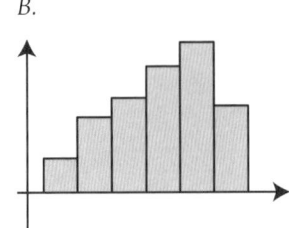

② A. 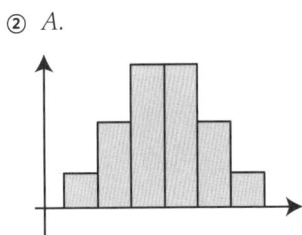   B.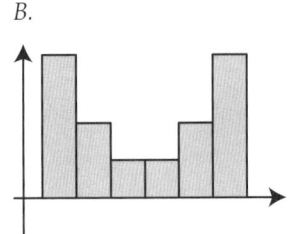

③ A. 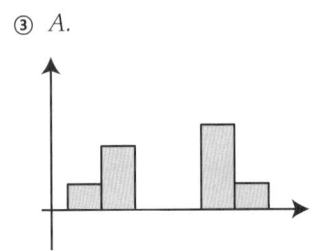   B.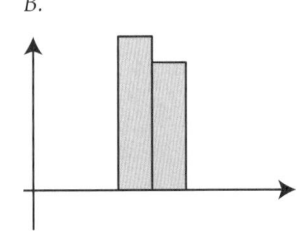

④ A. 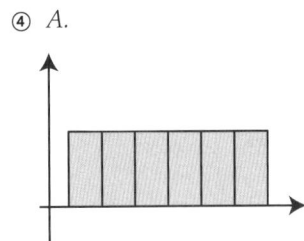   B.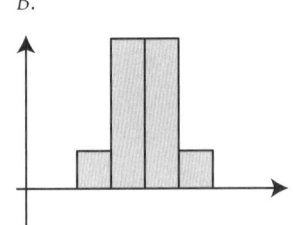

EXAMPLE 6. Rank the mean, median, range and standard deviation of three distributions.

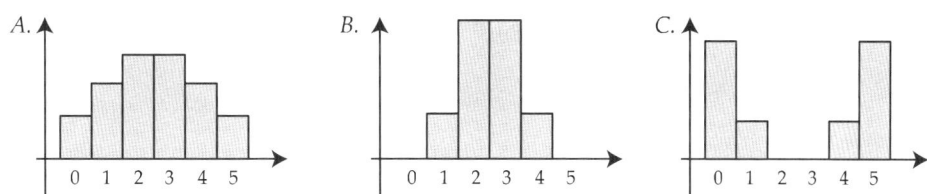

2. Expand Knowledge*

※ Constant Changes to data

If every data item is increased by the value a,

new center = old center ①_____

new spread = old spread ②_____

If every data item is multiplied by the value a,

new center = old center ③_____

new spread = old spread ④_____

(center: mean, median, mode   spread: range, IQR, SD)

Blank : ① +a (increased by a)   ② none (spread does not change)   ③ x a (multiplied by a)   ④ x a (multiplied by a)

EXAMPLE 7. * If the mean of a set of test scores is 78 and standard deviation is 5.

① Each test score is increased by 6. What are the new mean and the standard deviation?

② Each test score is decreased by 3. What are the new mean and the standard deviation?

③ Each test score is decreased by 10%. What are the new mean and the standard deviation?

④ Each test score is increased by 10%. What are the new mean and the standard deviation?

⑤ Each test score is doubled. What are the new mean and the standard deviation?

Mia's Algebra 2

11.3 Probability

1. Probability

Probability: How **likely** something is to happen.

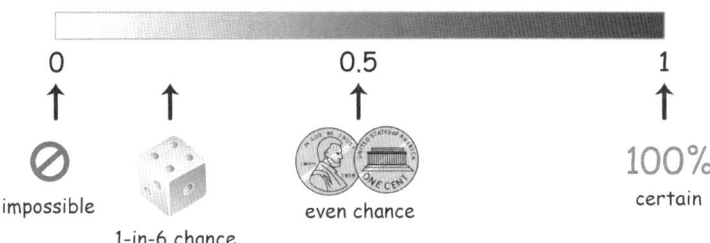

※ **Probability**

$$\text{Probability of an event A} = \frac{\text{Number of ways it can happen}}{\text{Total number of outcomes}}$$

$$P(A) = \frac{n(A)}{n(U)}$$

(Probability of event A)

☺ Vocabulary

- **Sample Space** U: collection of the possible outcomes of an experiment

  (= ① _____ set)

- **Event** A: a certain result of an experiment

Blank : ① universal

※ **Facts about Probability**

- Notation: probability of event A = ① _____

- Probability is ② _____.

- Complement event: Probability that the event A would NOT occur is ③ _____.

$$P(A) + P(A^c) = 1$$

- P(at least one A) = 1 − P(none of A)

EXAMPLE 1. Two coins are tossed. Find the probability of;

① one head

② both come up tails

③ at least one coin is tail

④ at least one coin is head

⑤ the coins match

⑥ the coins does not match

EXAMPLE 2. Three coins are tossed. Find the probability of;

① exactly two are tails

② exactly two are heads

Blank : ① P(A)   ② 0≤P(A)≤1   ③ P(A^C)   ④ A^C (Complement of A)

③ at least one coin is tail ④ at least one coin is head

⑤ all coins does not match ⑥ all coins match

EXAMPLE 3. Two dice are rolled. Find the probability of;
① sum of the numbers is 4 ② sum of the numbers is 10

③ sum of the numbers is less than 4 ④ sum of the numbers is less than 10

⑤ sum of the numbers is at least 4 ⑥ sum of the numbers is at most 10

⑦ product of the numbers at most 29 ⑧ product of the numbers is at least 4

⑨ Rolling 5 as the larger value ⑩ Rolling 3 as the larger value

2. Properties of Combined Events

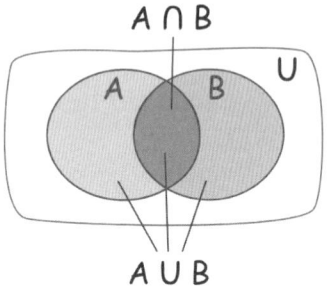

Things you have in EITHER sets : "**Union**"

and we write as A ①_____ B. (in words A ②_____ B)

Things you have in BOTH sets : "**Intersection**"

and we write as A ③_____ B. (in words A ④_____ B)

※ **Finding Probability of A or B**

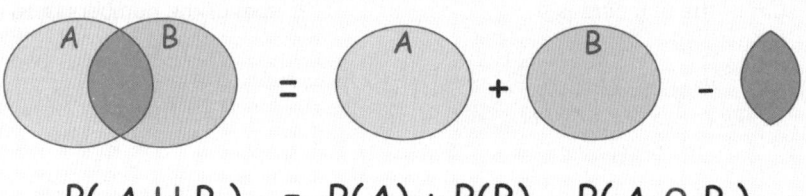

$$P(A \cup B) = P(A) + P(B) - P(A \cap B)$$

※ **Mutually Exclusive**

When two events (call them "A" and "B") are

⑤_____, it

is impossible for them to happen together.

ex) rolling 1 die: even and odd

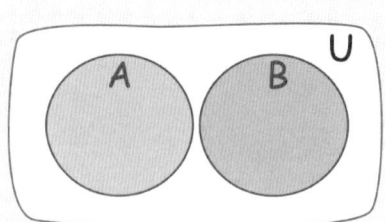

When A and B are mutually exclusive;

$$P(A \cap B) = \boxed{}$$

$$P(A \cup B) = P(A) + P(B)$$

Blank : ① ∪   ② or   ③ ∩   ④ and   ⑤ mutually exclusive   ⑥ 0

EXAMPLE 4. Use the Venn diagram.
Find the elements for;

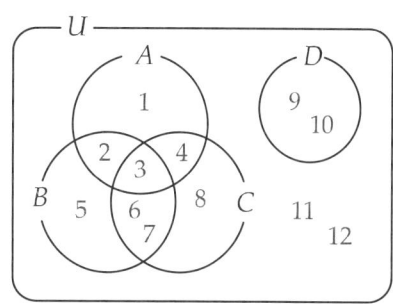

① A ∪ B ② B ∪ D

③ B ∩ C ④ A ∩ C

⑤ (B ∪ C) ∩ A ⑥ (B ∩ C) ∪ A

Find the probability of;
⑦ P(A ∪ D) ⑧ P(A ∪ C)

⑨ P(A ∩ B) ⑩ P(B ∩ D)

⑪ P(B^c) ⑫ P(D^c)

Tell whether the events are mutually exclusive
⑬ A and B ⑭ B and D

⑮ A and D ⑯ B and C

EXAMPLE 5. Solve the problem.
① Suppose $P(A) = 0.2$, $P(B) = 0.7$, and $P(A \cup B) = 0.8$. Find $P(A \cap B)$.

② Suppose $P(A) = 0.3$, $P(B) = 0.9$, and $P(A \cap B) = 0.5$. Find $P[(A \cup B)^c]$.

EXAMPLE 6. Solve the problem.

① Suppose $P(A) = 0.3$, $P(B^c) = 0.4$, and $P(A \cap B) = 0.8$. Find $P[(A \cup B)^c]$.

② Suppose $P(A^c) = 0.7$, $P(B) = 0.6$, and $P(A \cap B) = 0.5$. Find $P(A \cup B)$.

EXAMPLE 7. Suppose E and F are mutually exclusive events ;

① such that $P(E) = 0.3$ and $P(F) = 0.1$. Find $P((E \cup F)^c)$.

② such that $P(E) = 0.3$ and $P(F^c) = 0.7$. Find $P(E \cup F)$.

3. Two way tables, Venn diagram and Probability

Shade the appropriate region.

$P(A)$	$P(B)$	$P(A^c)$
$P(B^c)$	$P(A \text{ and } B)$	$P(A \text{ or } B)$

EXAMPLE 8. What is your favorite sport to watch on television?

	Soccer	Basketball	Baseball	Total
Males	40	22	15	77
Females	35	24	14	73
Total	75	46	29	150

Find the probability of ;

① $P(\text{Male})$

② $P(\text{Basketball})$

③ $P(\text{Female and Baseball})$

④ $P(\text{Soccer and Male})$

⑤ $P(\text{Male or Basketball})$

⑥ $P(\text{Female or Soccer})$

⑦ $P(\text{Female and Not Baseball})$

⑧ $P(\text{Male or Not Soccer})$

Mia's Algebra 2

11.4 Independent and dependent Event

1. Conditional Probability

EXAMPLE 1. Fifty students were asked which flavor of ice cream they prefer. The results are shown in the table below. Find the probability that

	Chocolate	Vanilla	Strawberry	Total
Male	15	7	4	26
Female	13	5	6	24
Total	28	12	10	50

(a) a randomly selected student prefers vanilla ice cream.

(b) a randomly selected student is a male student *or* prefers vanilla ice cream.

(c) a randomly selected student is a male student *and* prefers vanilla ice cream.

(d) a randomly selected student is a male student given that the student prefers vanilla ice cream.

(e) a randomly selected student prefers vanilla ice cream given that the student is a male student.

※ Conditional Probability

$$P(B|A) = \frac{P(A \cap B)}{P(A)}$$

(B given that A has occurred)

☺ Words: P(B|A) = Probability of B given that A
= Of A, probability of B
= Among A, probability of B
= If A, probability of B
= Probability of A will be B.

EXAMPLE 2. Use the Venn diagram.
Find the probability of;

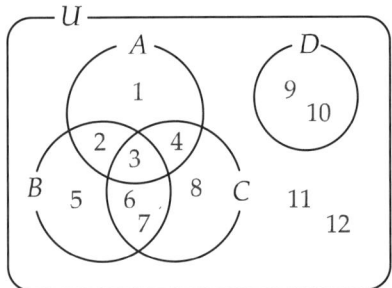

① P(A | B) ② P(A | C)

③ P(B | C) ④ P(C | B)

⑤ P(B^c | A) ⑥ P(A^c | C)

⑦ P(A | B^c) ⑧ P(D | C^c)

2. Two way tables, Venn diagram and Conditional Probability

Shade the appropriate region. (total: ▨, event: ▨)

P(A|B)

P(B|A)

P(A^c | B)

P(A^c | B^c)

EXAMPLE 3. What is your favorite sport to watch on television?

	Soccer	Basketball	Baseball	Total
Males	40	22	15	77
Females	35	24	14	73
Total	75	46	29	150

Find the probability of ;

① $P(\text{Male} \mid \text{Basketball})$

② $P(\text{Female} \mid \text{Soccer})$

③ $P(\text{Basketball} \mid \text{Male})$

④ $P(\text{Soccer} \mid \text{Female})$

⑤ $P(\text{Female} \mid \text{Baseball})$

⑥ $P(\text{Not Soccer} \mid \text{Male})$

⑦ $P(\text{Female} \mid \text{Not Baseball})$

⑧ $P(\text{Male} \mid \text{Not Soccer})$

EXAMPLE 4. Jay sorted his 50 toys as shown;

	Plastic	Non Plastic	Total
Red	17	4	21
Black	6	9	15
Yellow	1	13	14
Total	24	26	50

① Find the probability that it is a red and plastic toy.

② Find the probability that it is yellow and not plastic toy.

③ Of the yellow toys, find the probability that it is plastic.

④ Given that it is a plastic toy, find the probability that it is not red.

⑤ If it is not a plastic toy, find the probability that it is red.

⑥ Find the probability that it is plastic among the non-black toys.

⑦ Find the probability that a randomly selected red toy will be a plastic.

⑧ Find the probability that a randomly selected plastic toy will not be yellow.

EXAMPLE 5. The survey asks customers in three cities whether they would recommend a new shampoo to a friend. The result is given in two way table.

	Seoul	Hong Kong	Tokyo	Total
Yes	13	15	20	48
No	23	16	13	52
Total	36	31	33	100

① Among the customer who lives is Seoul, what is the probability he/she would recommend the shampoo?

② Of a customer who will not recommend the shampoo, find the probability that he/she lives is Hong Kong.

③ What is the probability that a customer who lives in Tokyo will recommend the new shampoo?

④ What is the probability that a customer who lives in Hong Kong will not recommend the new shampoo?

⑤ What is the probability that a customer who will not recommend the new shampoo is living in Seoul?

3. Properties of Consecutive Events

: repeated trials.

※ Independent Event

If we have independent event, an event ① _____ the next event.

ex) Taking two balls from a bag with replacement.
　　Tossing a coin twice.

If the event A **does not affect** the next event B,
the probability of the next event B will be simply just P(B).

If A and B are **independent events** then

$$P(A \cap B) = P(A) \times P(B)$$

(P(A and B))

Or

$$P(B|A) = P(B) \quad\quad P(A|B) = P(A)$$

※ Dependent Event

If we have dependent event, an event *can* ② _____ the next event.

ex) Taking two balls from a bag without replacement..

If A and B are **dependent events** then

$$P(A \cap B) = P(A) \times P(B|A)$$

(P(A and B))　　　　　　　　(B given that A has occurred)

Blank : ① does not affect　② affect

EXAMPLE 6. A bag contains 3 yellow balls and 5 red balls. Two balls are taken from the bag, *with replacement*. Determine the probability that:

① both balls are red   ② both balls are the same color

③ the balls are different colors   ④ at least one ball is red

⑤ at least one ball is yellow

EXAMPLE 7. A bag contains 3 yellow balls and 5 red balls. Two balls are taken from the bag, *without replacement*. Determine the probability that:

① both balls are red   ② both balls are the same color

③ the balls are different colors   ④ at least one ball is red

⑤ at least one ball is yellow

EXAMPLE 8. Use the information to tell whether A and B are independent or not.

① $P(A) = \dfrac{1}{4}$, $P(B) = \dfrac{1}{9}$, $P(A \cap B) = \dfrac{1}{36}$

② $P(A) = \dfrac{1}{5}$, $P(B) = \dfrac{1}{4}$, $P(A \cap B) = \dfrac{1}{2}$

③ $P(A) = \dfrac{1}{2}$, $P(B) = \dfrac{1}{9}$, $P(A \cap B) = \dfrac{1}{9}$

④ $P(A) = \dfrac{1}{5}$, $P(B) = \dfrac{1}{4}$, $P(A \cap B) = \dfrac{1}{20}$

⑤ $P(A) = \dfrac{1}{4}$, $P(B) = \dfrac{1}{9}$, $P(A \mid B) = \dfrac{1}{4}$

⑥ $P(A) = \dfrac{1}{5}$, $P(B) = \dfrac{1}{4}$, $P(B \mid A) = \dfrac{1}{4}$

⑦ $P(A) = \dfrac{1}{4}$, $P(B) = \dfrac{1}{9}$, $P(B \mid A) = \dfrac{1}{4}$

4. Expand Knowledge*

EXAMPLE 9. * The probability of event A is $P(A) = 0.2$ and the probability of event B is $P(B) = 0.3$. What is $P(A \text{ or } B) = ?$

a) if mutually exclusive?

b) If independent?

Answers

Answers

1. Functions and Linear

1.1 Function and Relations

Ex1.	①	Function
	②	Not a function
	③	Function
	④	Not a function
	⑤	Not a function
	⑥	Function
	⑦	Not a function
	⑧	Not a function
	⑨	Not a function
	⑩	Function
	⑪	Function
	⑫	Not a function
Ex2.	$\mathbb{R}$	means 'All real numbers'
	①	$\mathbb{R}, x \neq 0, 5$
	②	$\mathbb{R}, x \neq 1, -1$
	③	$\mathbb{R}$
	④	$\mathbb{R}, x \geq -6$
	⑤	$\mathbb{R}, x \geq -\dfrac{2}{3}$
	⑥	$\mathbb{R}, x \neq \pm 2$
	⑦	$\mathbb{R}$
	⑧	$\mathbb{R}$
	⑨	$\mathbb{R}$
Ex3.	① 1	② 11
	③ 3	④ $\dfrac{5}{2}$
	⑤ $-2m-1$	⑥ $\dfrac{5}{a}$
	⑦ $\dfrac{5}{9}$	⑧ -3
	⑨ $\dfrac{66}{25}$	⑩ 3
	⑪ -2	⑫ -2
Ex4.	$\dfrac{2}{3}$	
Ex5.	30	
Ex6.	III, IV	
Ex7.	III, IV	
Ex8.	IV	

1.2 Transformation

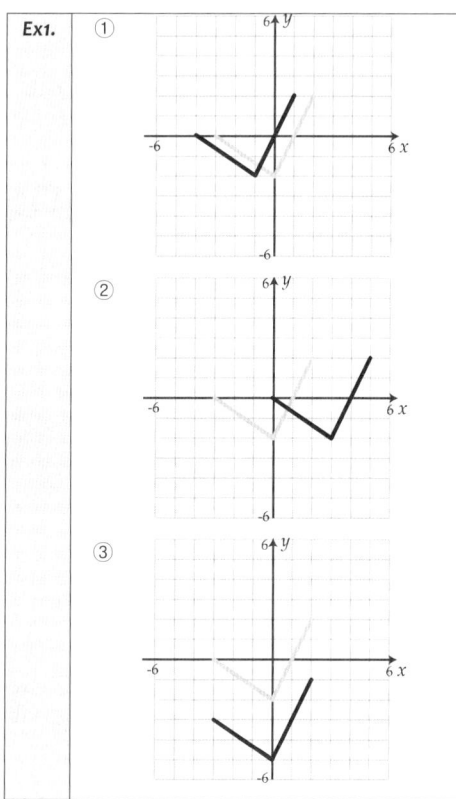

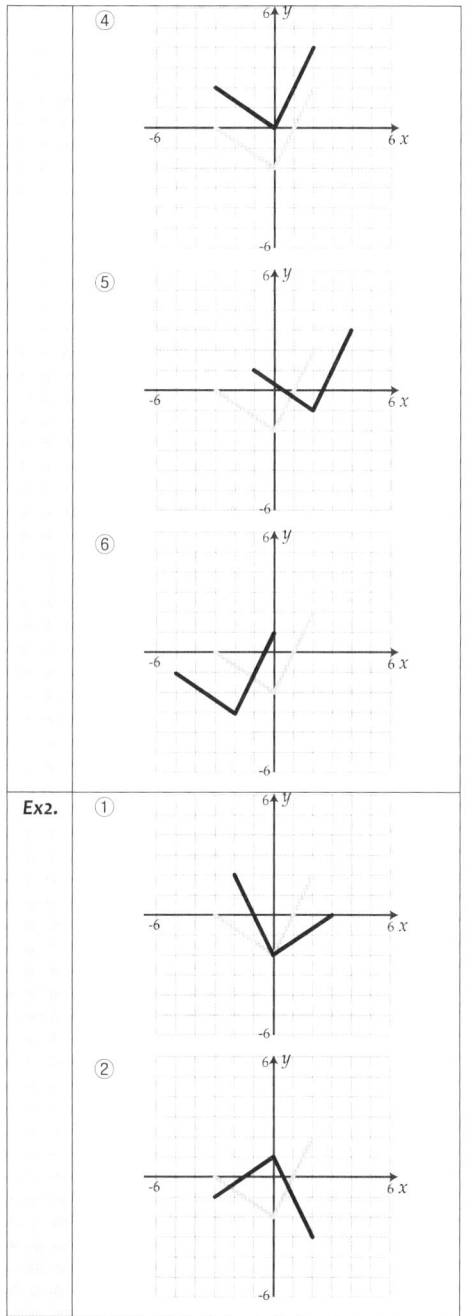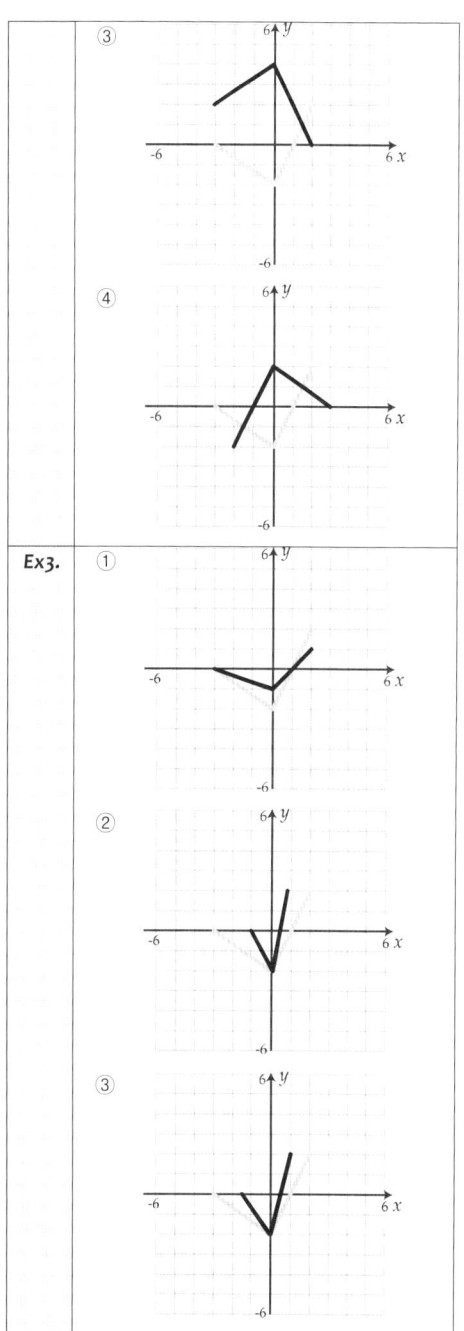

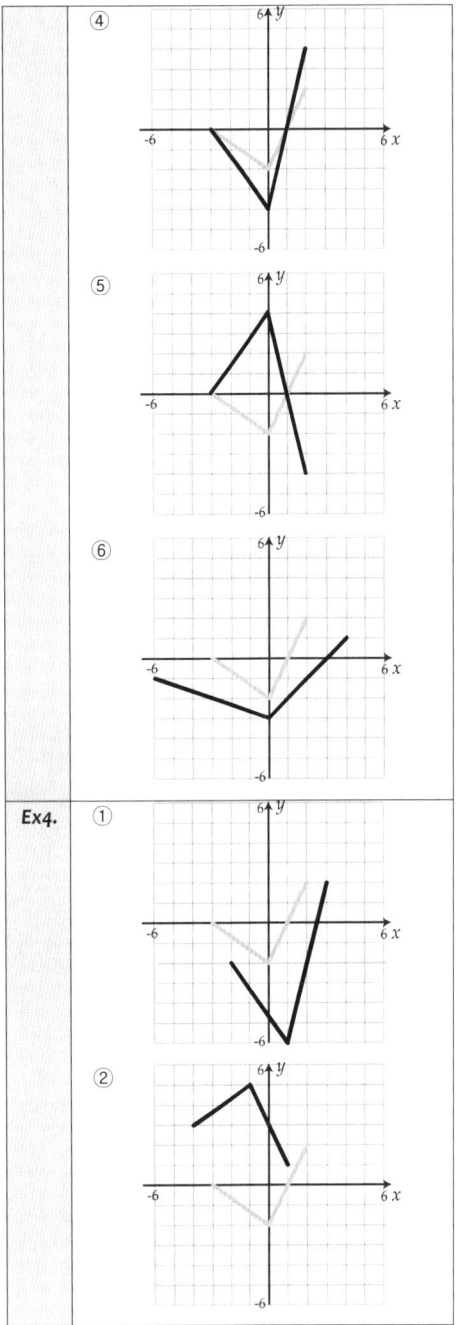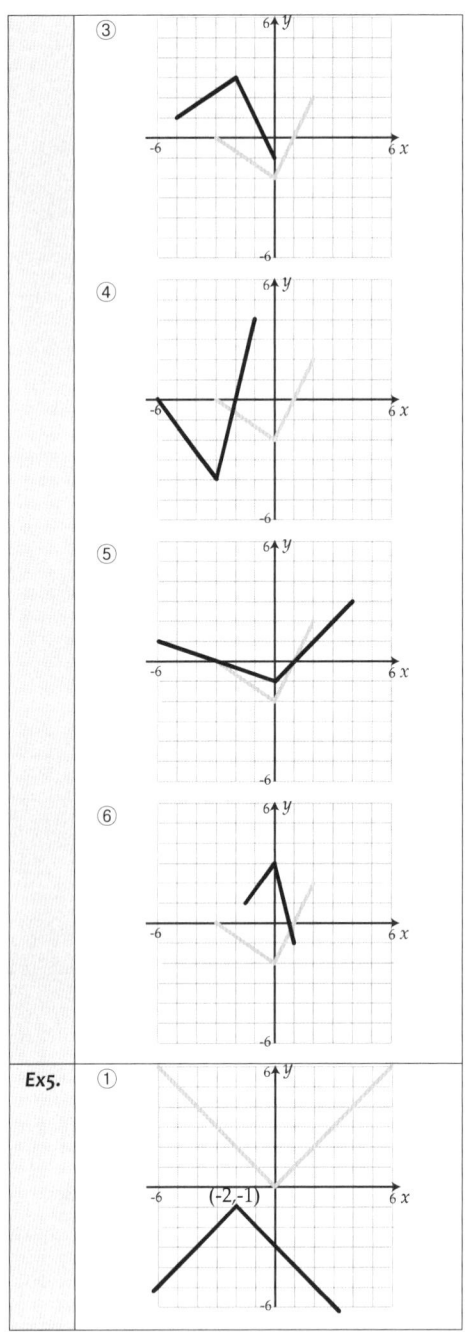

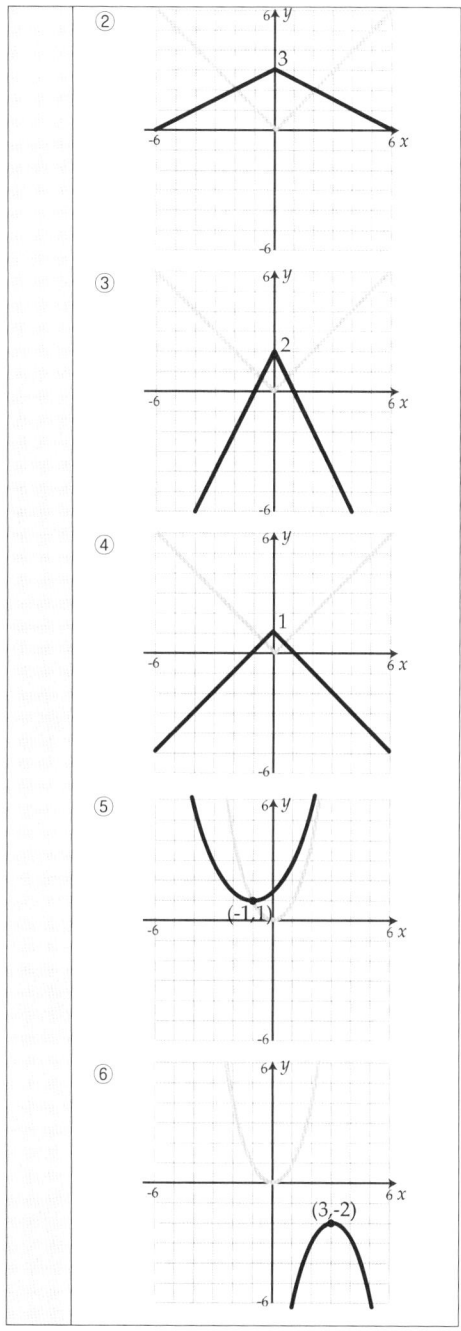
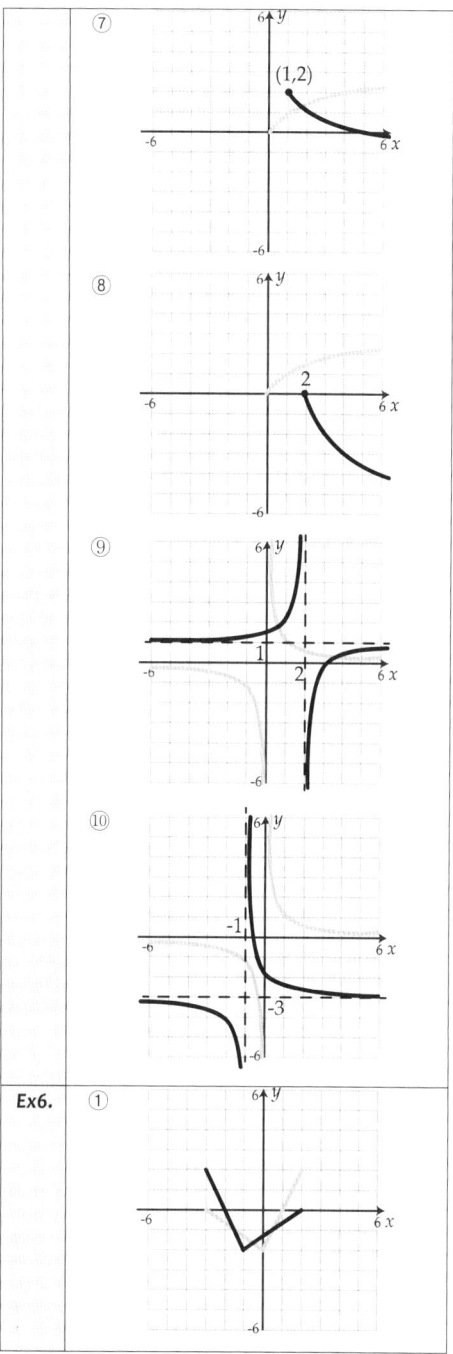

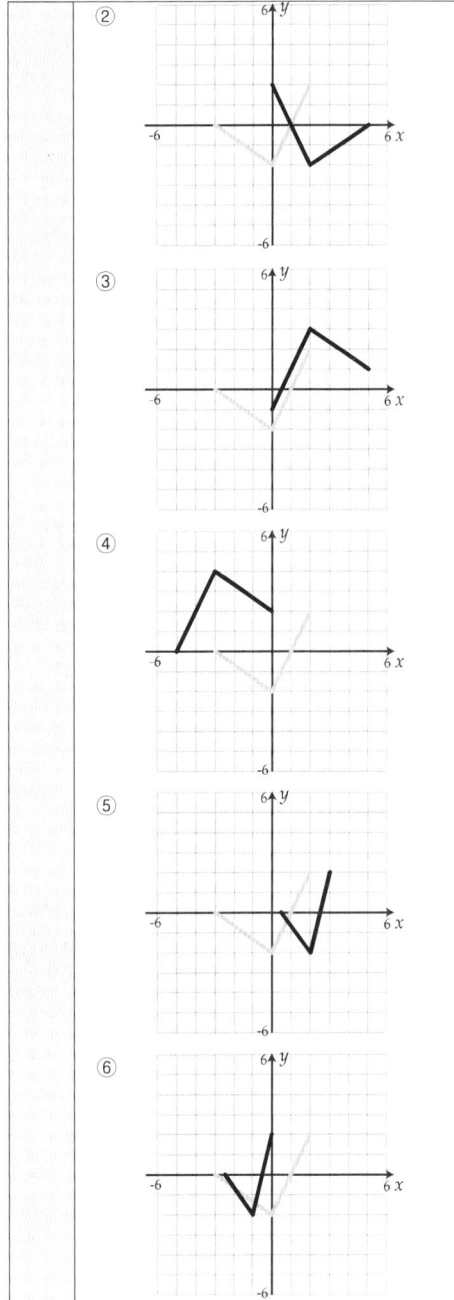
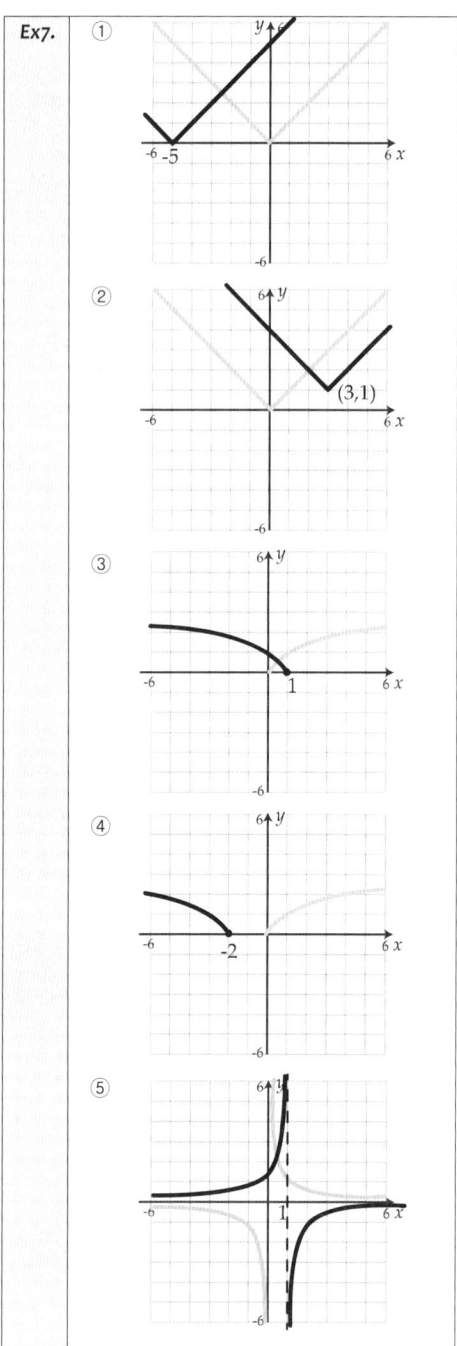

⑥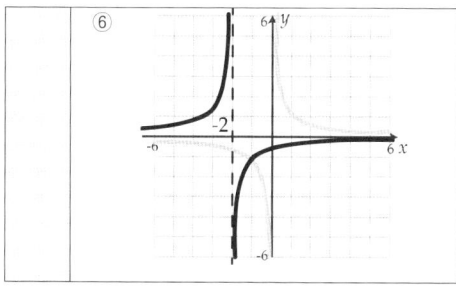

1.3 The Slope of a Line

Ex1.	① $\frac{5}{3}$	② $-\frac{2}{3}$
	③ $-\frac{2}{7}$	④ $\frac{1}{5}$
	⑤ Undefined	⑥ 0
	⑦ 0	
Ex2.	① 4	② 3
	③ $-\frac{2}{3}$	④ $-\frac{3}{4}$
	⑤ $\frac{12}{7}$	⑥ 2
	⑦ 0	⑧ Undefined
Ex3.	① 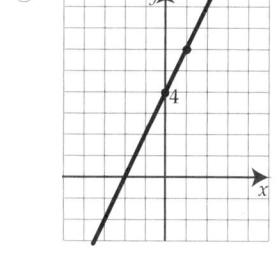	
	② 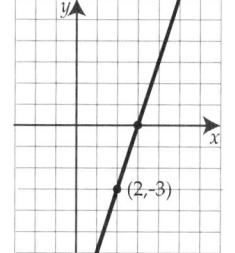	

③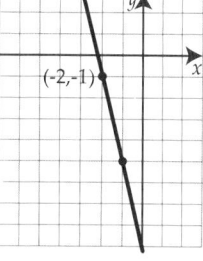

④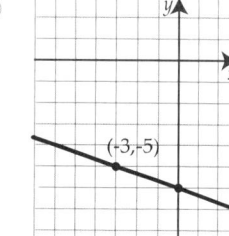

⑤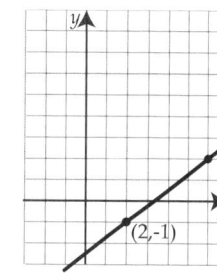

⑥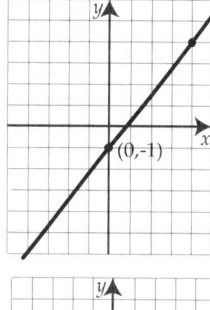

⑦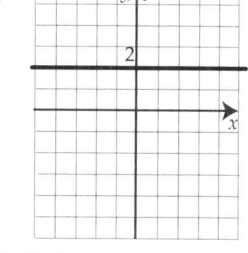

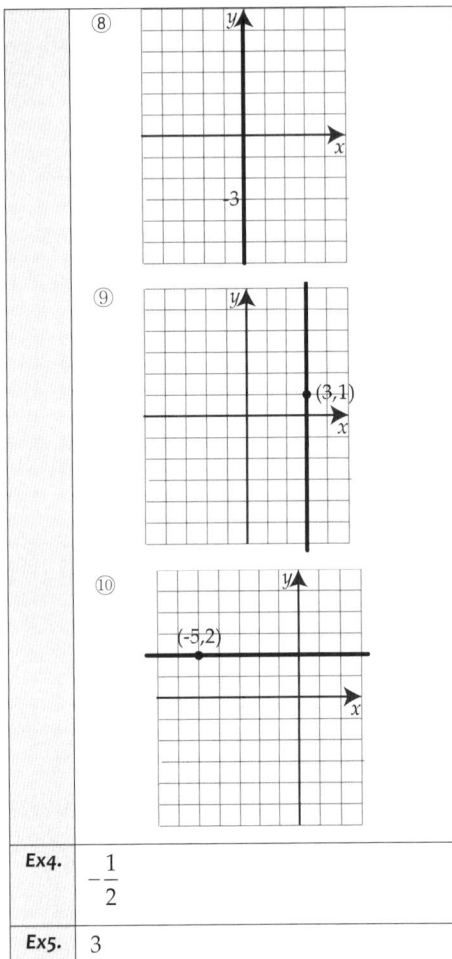

Ex4.	$-\dfrac{1}{2}$
Ex5.	$\dfrac{3}{2}$

1.4 Graphs of Linear Functions

Ex1.	①	Linear
	②	Linear
	③	Not Linear
	④	Not Linear
	⑤	Not Linear
	⑥	Linear
	⑦	Linear
	⑧	Not Linear

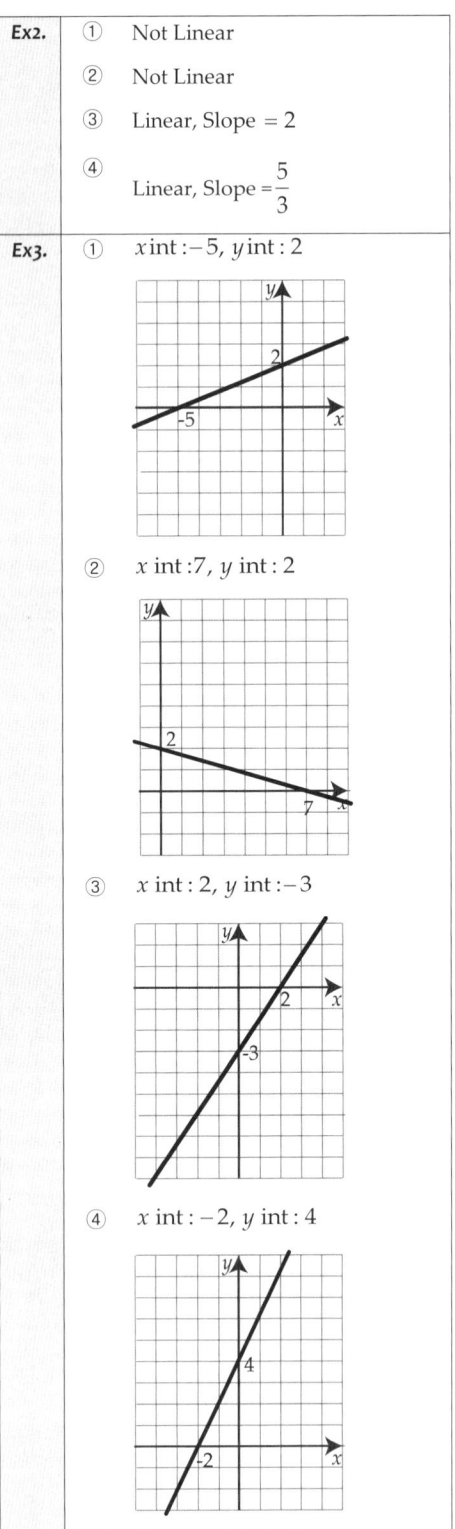

⑤ x int: -9, y int: 8

⑥ x int: 5, y int: 6

⑦ x int: 0, y int: 0

⑧ x int: 0, y int: 0

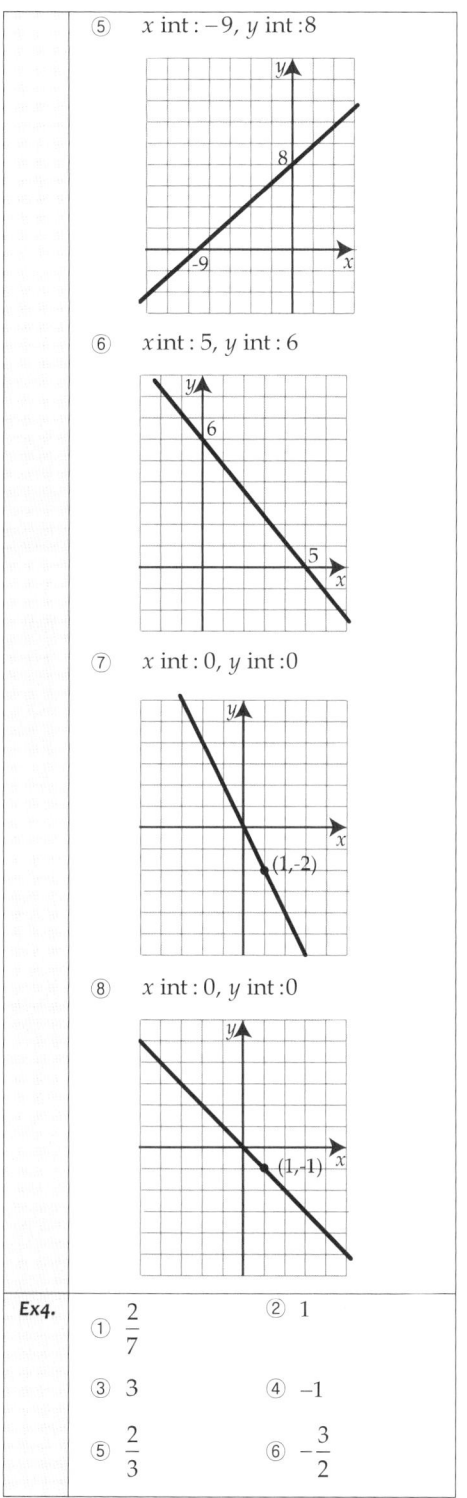

Ex4.	① $\dfrac{2}{7}$	② 1
	③ 3	④ -1
	⑤ $\dfrac{2}{3}$	⑥ $-\dfrac{3}{2}$

Ex5. ① ② ③ ④

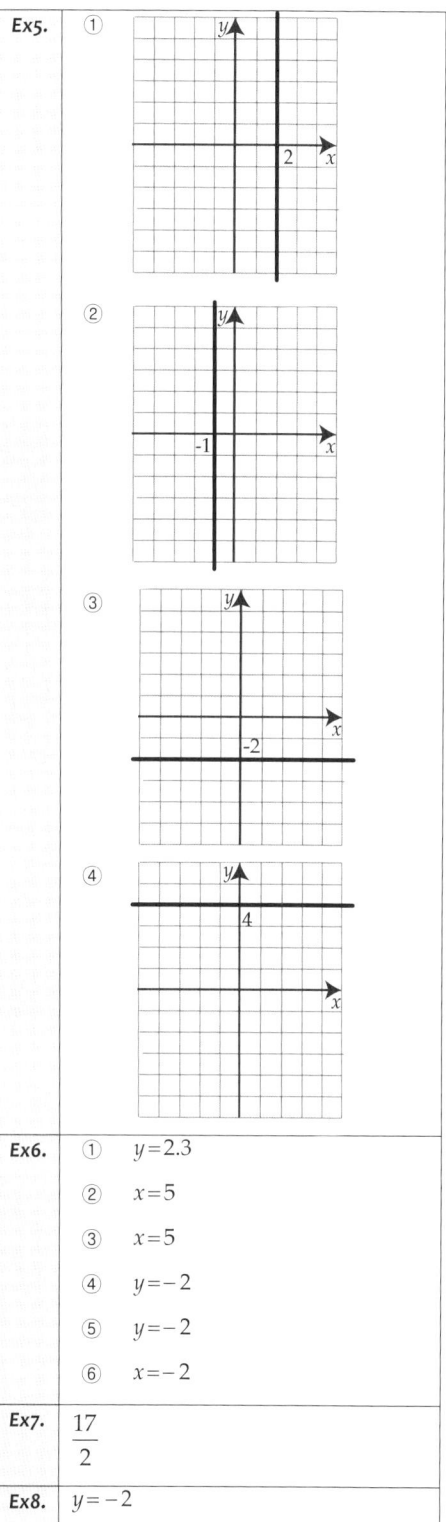

Ex6.	① $y = 2.3$
	② $x = 5$
	③ $x = 5$
	④ $y = -2$
	⑤ $y = -2$
	⑥ $x = -2$
Ex7.	$\dfrac{17}{2}$
Ex8.	$y = -2$

1.5 Finding Equation of the Line

Ex1.		
	①	$m=3$, y int $=-5$
	②	$m=-\dfrac{3}{5}$, y int $=2$
	③	$m=-\dfrac{2}{3}$, y int $=0$
	④	$m=0$, y int $=-\dfrac{5}{3}$
	⑤	$m=\dfrac{4}{5}$, y int $=-\dfrac{7}{5}$
	⑥	$m=\dfrac{3}{2}$, y int $=3$
	⑦	$m=2$, y int $=1$
	⑧	$m=-\dfrac{5}{2}$, y int $=3$
Ex2.	①	$y=\dfrac{2}{3}x-4$
	②	$y=-\dfrac{5}{3}x+2$
	③	$y=-1$
	④	$y=\dfrac{7}{4}x-3$
	⑤	$y=-\dfrac{2}{3}x-1$
	⑥	$y=4$
Ex3.	①	$y=2x+2$
	②	$y=-x-1$
	③	$y=-2x-5$
	④	$y=2x+1$
	⑤	$y=-\dfrac{3}{4}x+\dfrac{1}{2}$
	⑥	$y=\dfrac{5}{4}x-1$
Ex4.	①	$y=-7x+11$
	②	$y=-\dfrac{1}{2}x+4$
	③	$y=-\dfrac{3}{4}x-\dfrac{11}{4}$
	④	$y=\dfrac{4}{3}x-\dfrac{4}{3}$
	⑤	$y=\dfrac{4}{3}x-4$
	⑥	$y=-\dfrac{6}{5}x+3$
Ex5.		$\dfrac{36}{25}$
Ex6.		$\dfrac{144}{25}$
Ex7.		$k=-6$
Ex8.		$-\dfrac{3}{2}<k<-1$
Ex9.		III, V

1.6 Two Linear Graphs

Ex1.	①	$y=-2x+9$		
	②	$y=\dfrac{1}{4}x-7$		
	③	$y=-\dfrac{5}{2}x+\dfrac{15}{2}$		
	④	$y=\dfrac{2}{3}x-\dfrac{5}{3}$		
	⑤	$y=\dfrac{5}{2}x$		
	⑥	$y=2x+7$		
Ex2.	① $x=7$		② $x=-5$	
	③ $y=3$		④ $x=2$	
	⑤ $x=2$		⑥ $y=3$	
	⑦ $y=4$		⑧ $y=-1$	
Ex3.	$a=3$, $b=-2$			
Ex4.	$y=2x+8$			

Ex5.	$-\dfrac{11}{2}$
Ex6.	$y = -\dfrac{5}{4}x + 7$

1.7 Piecewise Function

Ex1.	① D : All Real R : $y < 0, y = 3$ 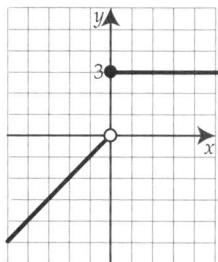 ② D : $\mathbb{R}$ R : $y = -4$ or $y \geq -2$ 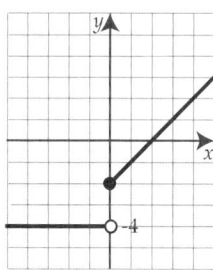 ③ D : $\mathbb{R}$ R : $y < 3$ 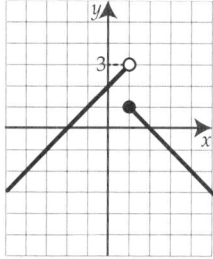

	④ D : $\mathbb{R}$ R : $y \geq -2$ 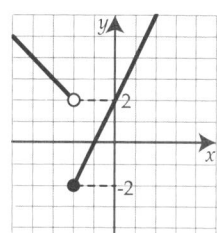 ⑤ D : $\mathbb{R}$ R : $y \leq 1$ 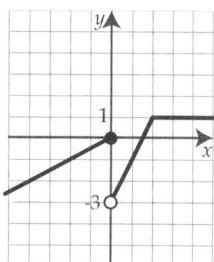
Ex2.	① $\begin{cases} -2x-3, & x \leq 0 \\ 2, & x > 0 \end{cases}$ ② $\begin{cases} 1, & x < -2 \\ -x+2, & x \geq -2 \end{cases}$ ③ $\begin{cases} \dfrac{1}{2}x-2, & x < 1 \\ 1, & x = 1 \\ \dfrac{1}{2}x-2, & x > 1 \end{cases}$ (or $\begin{cases} 1, & x = 1 \\ \dfrac{1}{2}x-2, & x \neq 1 \end{cases}$) ④ $\begin{cases} -3, & x = 0 \\ x^2, & x \neq 0 \end{cases}$
Ex3.	① $f(0) = 2, f(1) = 2, f(3) = 3$ ② $g(9) = 3, g(-2) = -\dfrac{1}{2}, g(0) = 0$ ③ $f(-4) = 9, f(1) = 2, f(2) = 4$

1.8 Absolute Value Function

Ex1.	①	a) 5.1, b) 5
	②	a) 3.2, b) −4
	③	a) 0.5, b) −1
	④	a) 0.5, b) 0
	⑤	a) 7, b) 7
	⑥	a) 5, b) 5
	⑦	a) 3, b) −3
	⑧	a) 2, b) −2
Ex2.	①	x
	②	$-y$
	③	$x-1$
	④	$-u-2$
	⑤	$c-2$
	⑥	$-1+2x$
	⑦	$2a-2b$
	⑧	0
	⑨	$2-a$
	⑩	$-3x+4$
	⑪	2
	⑫	5
	⑬	$-2x$
	⑭	$-2x-9$
Ex3.	①	$\begin{cases} 2x, & x \geq 0 \\ -2x, & x < 0 \end{cases}$

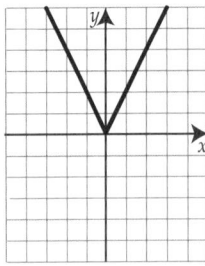

② $\begin{cases} x+2, & x \geq 0 \\ -x+2, & x < 0 \end{cases}$

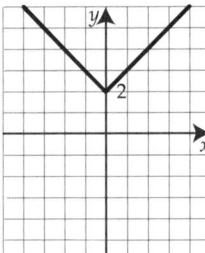

③ $\begin{cases} x+3, & x \geq -3 \\ -x-3, & x < -3 \end{cases}$

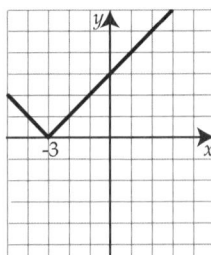

④ $\begin{cases} x-2, & x \geq 2 \\ -x-2, & x < 2 \end{cases}$

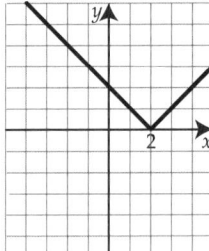

⑤ $\begin{cases} 2x-1, & x \geq \frac{1}{2} \\ -2x+1, & x < \frac{1}{2} \end{cases}$

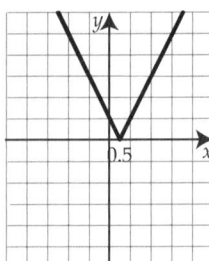

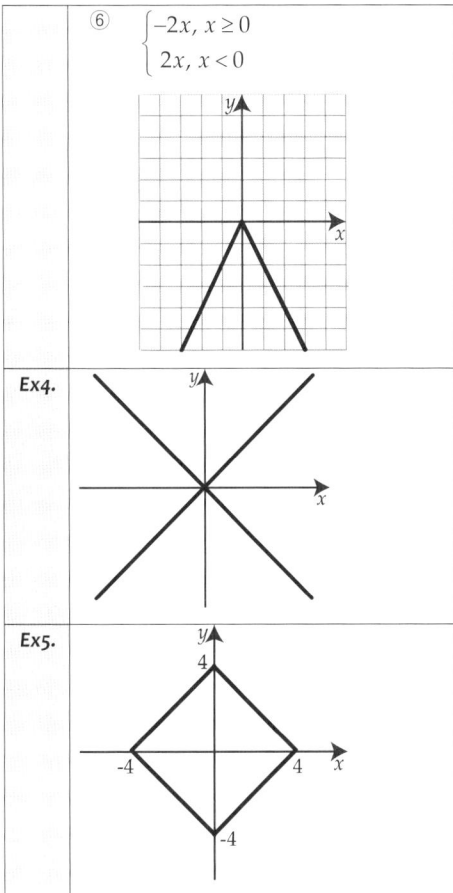

	⑥	$\begin{cases} -2x, x \geq 0 \\ 2x, x < 0 \end{cases}$
Ex4.		
Ex5.		

1.9 Abs Value Equation and Inequalities

Ex1.	①	$n = 12$ or -8
	②	$x = 15$ or 11
	③	$c = -6$ or 8
	④	$a = \dfrac{3}{4}$ or $\dfrac{1}{4}$
	⑤	$y = 3$ or 9
	⑥	$d = \dfrac{3}{2}$ or 1
	⑦	$x = \dfrac{13}{2}$ or $-\dfrac{11}{2}$
	⑧	$y = \dfrac{7}{2}$ or $\dfrac{3}{2}$
	⑨	$\varnothing$
	⑩	$\varnothing$
	⑪	$\varnothing$
	⑫	$\varnothing$
	⑬	$x = -4$
	⑭	$p = 12$
	⑮	$x = \dfrac{4}{3}$ or $-\dfrac{2}{5}$
	⑯	$r = \dfrac{3}{2}$ or $-\dfrac{1}{8}$
Ex2.	①	$-7 \leq y \leq -3$
	②	$x \leq 0$ or $x \geq 16$
	③	$h \leq -5$ or $h \geq 3$
	④	$-\dfrac{3}{2} \leq z \leq \dfrac{5}{2}$
	⑤	$2 \leq x \leq 8$
	⑥	$x < \dfrac{2}{3}$ or $x > \dfrac{8}{3}$
	⑦	$x < -2$ or $x > 1$
	⑧	$-\dfrac{2}{3} \leq x \leq 0$
	⑨	$\varnothing$
	⑩	$x = -\dfrac{2}{3}$
	⑪	$\mathbb{R}$
	⑫	$\varnothing$
	⑬	$\mathbb{R}$
	⑭	$\mathbb{R}$
	⑮	$k = 5$
	⑯	$\mathbb{R}$

Ex3.	$\mathbb{R}, x \neq 0, -2$
	(All real number except 0, -2)
Ex4.	$x = \pm 6$
Ex5.	$\dfrac{5}{2}, \dfrac{5}{4}$
Ex6.	four
Ex7.	$k = -3$

Answers
2. Systems and Matrices

2.1 System of Linear Equation

Ex1.	①	$n = 12, m = 8$
	②	$x = 3, y = -2$
	③	$x = 3, y = 2$
	④	$w = 7, z = -10$
	⑤	$\varnothing$
	⑥	$\varnothing$
Ex2.	①	$x = 2, y = -1$
	②	$p = 1, q = -1$
	③	$x = 1, y = 1$
	④	$m = 3, n = 1$
	⑤	$a = -1, b = 4$
	⑥	$x = -3, y = -5$
	⑦	$a = 3, b = \dfrac{5}{3}$
	⑧	$x = 2, y = 1$
	⑨	$\mathbb{R}$
	⑩	$\varnothing$

	⑪	$\varnothing$
	⑫	$\mathbb{R}$
Ex3.	①	$x = -\dfrac{3}{2}, y = -\dfrac{1}{2}$
	②	$x = -9, y = 7$
Ex4.	①	No Solution
		, Inconsistent
	②	Infinite Solution
		, Consistent and dependent
	③	One Solution
		, Consistent and independent
	④	No Solution
		, Inconsistent
	⑤	Infinite Solution
		, Consistent and dependent
	⑥	One Solution
		, Consistent and independent
	⑦	No Solution
		, Inconsistent
	⑧	Infinite Solution
		, Consistent and dependent
Ex5.	$a = 16$
Ex6.	$m = 12, n = -16$
Ex7.	$x = \dfrac{1}{2}$
Ex8.	$x = 0, y = 1$
Ex9.	2
Ex10.	-1

2.2 Word Problems about System

Ex1.	83
Ex2.	x : tens digit, y : ones digit $$\begin{cases} y = 2x \\ 10x + y + 27 = 10y + x \end{cases}$$ $x = 3, y = 6$ Answer: 36
Ex3.	14
Ex4.	x : ticket number for single, y : ticket number for couple $$\begin{cases} x + y = 110 \\ 25x + 40y = 3800 \end{cases}$$ $x = 40, y = 70$ Answer: Single 40, Couple 70
Ex5.	2
Ex6.	75 years old
Ex7.	f : father's age this year, s : Sally's age this year $$\begin{cases} f - 5 = 3(s - 5) \\ f + 2 = 7 + 2(s + 2) \end{cases}$$ $f = 47, s = 19$ Answer: father is 47 years old, Sally is 19 years old
Ex8.	7500\$ for 8%, 2500\$ for 10%
Ex9.	x : money invested at 12% interest rate, y : money invested at 10% interest rate $$\begin{cases} y = x + 2000 \\ 0.12x + 0.1y = 1300 \end{cases}$$ $x = 5000, y = 7000$ Answer: 5000\$ for 12%, 7000\$ for 10%
Ex10.	$48 ml$
Ex11.	x : gallons of 30% fruit juice, y : gallons of 80% fruit juice $$\begin{cases} x + y = 50 \\ 0.3x + 0.8y = 0.4(50) \end{cases}$$ $x = 40, y = 10$ Answer: 40 gallons
Ex12.	$8hr$
Ex13.			d	=	r	$\cdot$	t
---	---	---	---	---
Sam	$5x$	5	x
Ray	$9y$	9	y	$$\begin{cases} 5x = 9y \\ x = y + 8 \end{cases}$$ $x = 18, y = 10$ Answer: $10hr$
Ex14.	at 4:00pm
Ex15.			d =	r $\cdot$	t
---	---	---	---
traveling 60mph	$60x$	60	x
traveling 20mph	$20y$	20	y	$$\begin{cases} 60x + 20y = 260 \\ x + y = 7 \end{cases}$$ $x = 3, y = 4$ Answer: 4hr x 20mi/hr = 80mi
Ex16.	24km/h, 18km/h
Ex17.	60mi/h
Ex18.	$5 ft$
Ex19.	270mi/h
Ex20.	$\dfrac{13}{12}$ mi/hr
Ex21.	p: aircraft speed, w: wind speed		d =	r $\cdot$	t
---	---	---	---
with wind	420	$p + w$	1.5
against wind	420	$p - w$	2	$$\begin{cases} 420 = 1.5(p + w) \\ 420 = 2(p - w) \end{cases}$$

	$p = 245, w = 35$
	Answer:
	aircraft speed 245mph, wind 35mph
Ex22.	0.3 km/min, 0.2 km/min
Ex23.	70 candies
Ex24.	24 students
Ex25.	220$

2.3 System of Inequalities

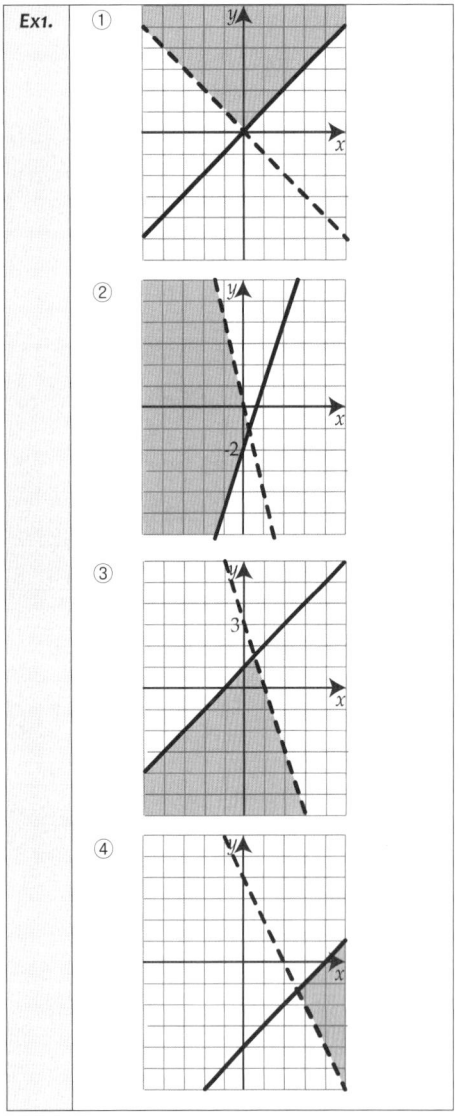

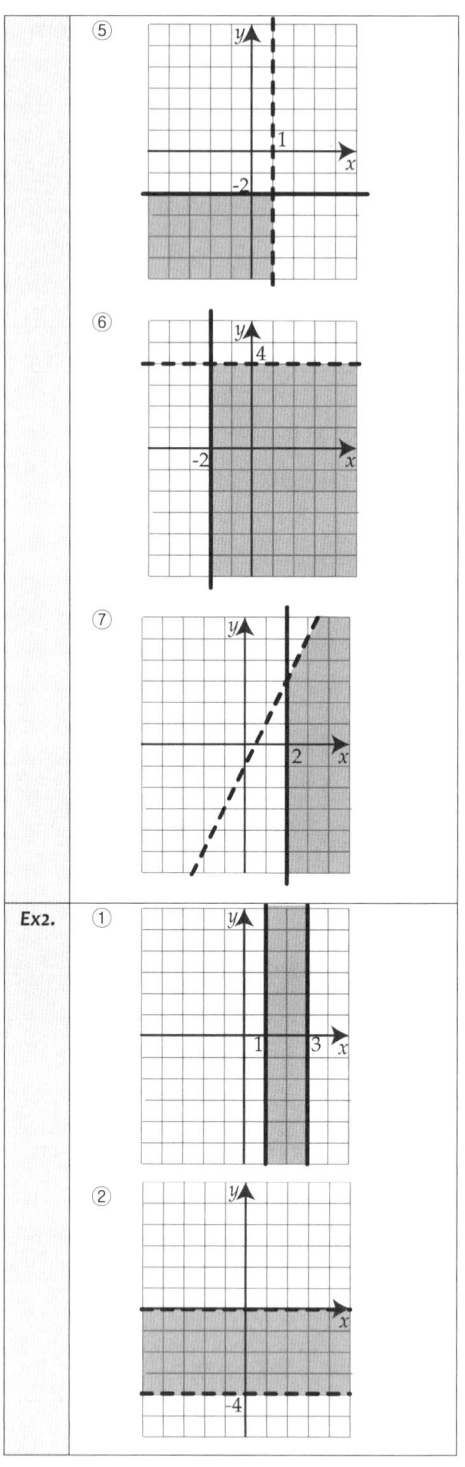

	③ 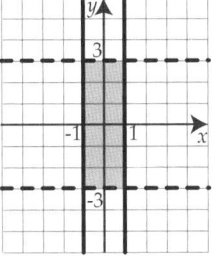	
	④ 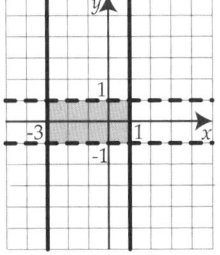	
Ex3.	① $\begin{cases} y > \dfrac{1}{2}x + 6 \\ y \leq -\dfrac{3}{2}x + 2 \end{cases}$ ② $\begin{cases} y > \dfrac{1}{4}x + 6 \\ y \geq \dfrac{1}{4}x + 3 \end{cases}$ ③ $\begin{cases} y \geq 0 \\ y \leq \dfrac{1}{2}x \\ y \leq -2x + 12 \end{cases}$ ④ $\begin{cases} x \geq 1 \\ y \geq x - 3 \\ y \leq -2x + 6 \end{cases}$	
Ex4.	II	
Ex5.	$\dfrac{1}{2}$	
Ex6.	2	

2.4 Linear Programming

Ex1. ①

(x, y)	$P = x - 2y$
(1, 6)	-11
(1, 1)	-1
(6, 6)	-6

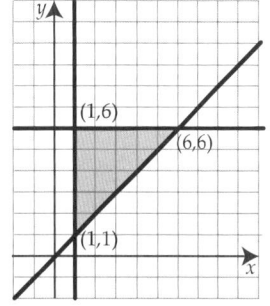

Max -1, Min -11

②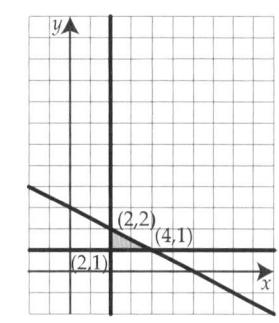

(x, y)	$C = 3x + 4y$
(2, 2)	14
(2, 1)	10
(4, 1)	16

Max 16, Min 10

③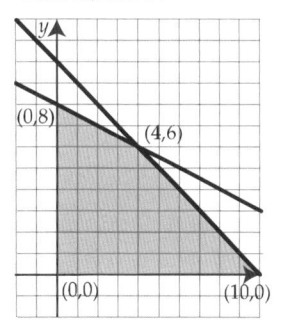

(x, y)	$P = x + 3y$
(0, 0)	0
(0, 8)	24
(10, 0)	10
(4, 6)	22

Max 24, Min 0

④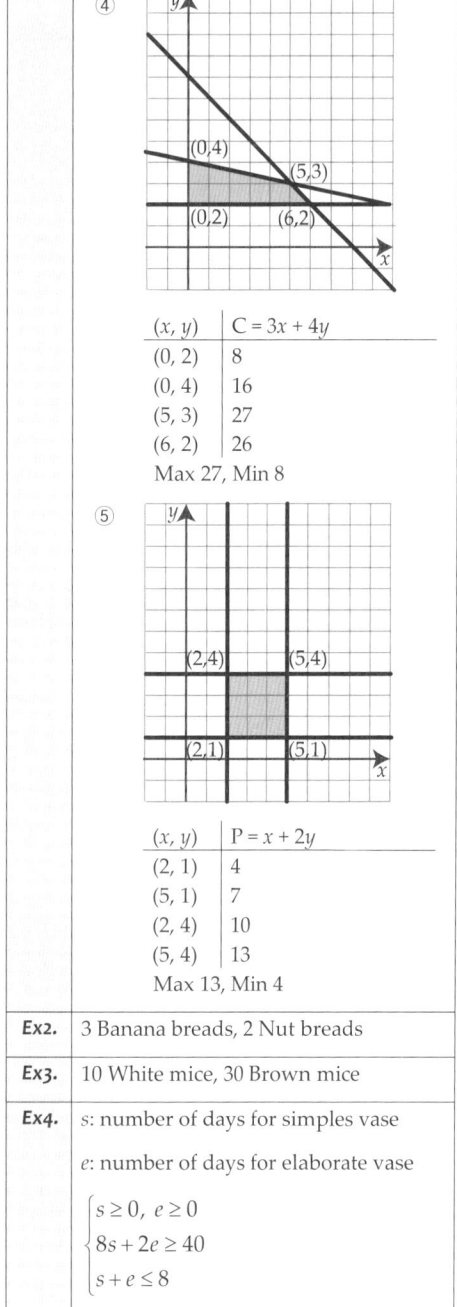

(x, y)	$C = 3x + 4y$
(0, 2)	8
(0, 4)	16
(5, 3)	27
(6, 2)	26

Max 27, Min 8

⑤

(x, y)	$P = x + 2y$
(2, 1)	4
(5, 1)	7
(2, 4)	10
(5, 4)	13

Max 13, Min 4

Ex2.	3 Banana breads, 2 Nut breads
Ex3.	10 White mice, 30 Brown mice
Ex4.	s: number of days for simples vase
	e: number of days for elaborate vase
	$\begin{cases} s \geq 0, \ e \geq 0 \\ 8s + 2e \geq 40 \\ s + e \leq 8 \end{cases}$

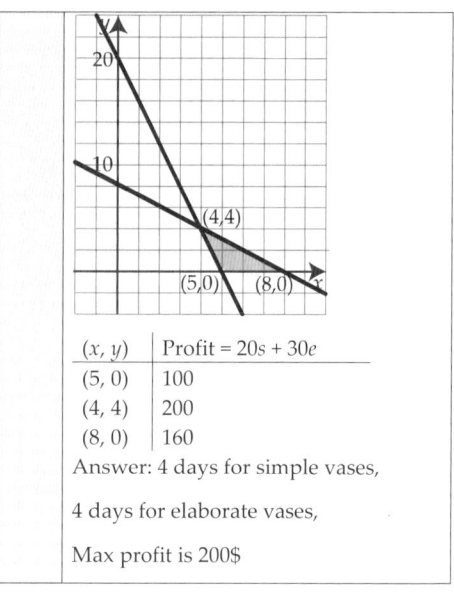

(x, y)	Profit = $20s + 30e$
(5, 0)	100
(4, 4)	200
(8, 0)	160

Answer: 4 days for simple vases,

4 days for elaborate vases,

Max profit is 200$

2.5 Algebra of Matrices

Ex1.	①	$\begin{bmatrix} 3 & 21 \\ -6 & 14 \end{bmatrix}$
	②	$\begin{bmatrix} -13 & 7 & -1 \\ 0 & -8 & -3 \end{bmatrix}$
	③	$\begin{bmatrix} -2 & -21 \\ -16 & 7 \\ -17 & -19 \end{bmatrix}$
	④	Impossible
	⑤	Impossible
Ex2.	①	$\begin{bmatrix} 2 & 1 \\ -3 & 8 \end{bmatrix}$
	②	$\begin{bmatrix} -2 & 14 & 3 \\ -4 & 1 & -11 \end{bmatrix}$
Ex3.	①	$\begin{bmatrix} -2 & -8 \\ -12 & 20 \end{bmatrix}$
	②	$\begin{bmatrix} -1 & 9 \\ -8 & 6 \end{bmatrix}$

	③	$\begin{bmatrix} 7 & 19 \end{bmatrix}$
	④	$\begin{bmatrix} 1 & -4 \\ 5 & 9 \end{bmatrix}$
	⑤	$\begin{bmatrix} 28 & 14 & -14 \\ -4 & 8 & -2 \end{bmatrix}$
	⑥	$\begin{bmatrix} -51 \end{bmatrix}$
	⑦	Impossible
	⑧	Impossible
Ex4.	①	Impossible
	②	2 x 2
	③	2 x 2
	④	2 x 3
	⑤	2 x 2
	⑥	2 x 2
	⑦	2 x 3
Ex5.	B, D	
Ex6.	$A^2 + AB + BA + B^2$	
Ex7.	$A^2 - AB + BA - B^2$	
Ex8.	①	$\begin{bmatrix} -1 & 0 \\ 2 & 4 \end{bmatrix}$
	②	$\begin{bmatrix} 1 & 0 & 2 \\ 0 & 2 & -4 \\ 3 & -5 & 4 \end{bmatrix}$

Ex3.	①	$\begin{bmatrix} 2 & -3 \\ -3 & 5 \end{bmatrix}$
	②	$\begin{bmatrix} 0 & -1 \\ 1 & 10 \end{bmatrix}$
	③	$\begin{bmatrix} 0 & \frac{1}{6} \\ -1 & -\frac{5}{6} \end{bmatrix}$
	④	$\begin{bmatrix} \frac{1}{2} & \frac{1}{2} \\ \frac{1}{2} & \frac{1}{4} \end{bmatrix}$
	⑤	Inverse does not exist
	⑥	Inverse does not exist
Ex4.	$A^{-1}B$	
Ex5.	BA^{-1}	
Ex6.	①	$\begin{bmatrix} -5 \\ 1 \end{bmatrix}$
	②	$\begin{bmatrix} 1 \\ -3 \end{bmatrix}$
Ex7.	①	$x = -2, y = 1$
	②	$x = 2, y = 6$

2.6 Inverse and Matrix Equation

Ex1.	① −1	② 7
	③ 9	④ 8
	⑤ 0	⑥ 0
Ex2.	① 32	② 27
	③ 0	④ −24

Answers

3. Factoring and Expanding Polynomial

3.1 Law of Exponents

Ex1.	① a^5	② c^7
	③ a^6	④ c^{12}
	⑤ $-x^{10}$	⑥ a^{12}
	⑦ x^{10}	⑧ $-a^{12}$
	⑨ $16m^4n^8$	⑩ $16x^4y^6$
	⑪ $-27r^9s^6$	⑫ $-32r^{10}s^{15}$
	⑬ $-12m^4n^7$	⑭ $p^{10}q^4$
	⑮ a^9	⑯ m^{11}
	⑰ $-8x^{15}y^{15}$	⑱ $-16m^{12}n^{36}$
	⑲ x^2	⑳ t^4
	㉑ $\dfrac{5}{a^5}$	㉒ $\dfrac{1}{4a^6}$
	㉓ $\dfrac{3ab^3}{7c^2}$	㉔ $\dfrac{1}{3uv^2w^2}$
	㉕ $\dfrac{x^5z^9}{y^6}$	㉖ $-\dfrac{r^8}{p^3q^2}$
Ex2.	① a^{2n}	② c^{2t+1}
	③ a^{n^2+n}	④ c^{m^2-2m}
	⑤ r^{3m+3}	⑥ p^{7k-3}
	⑦ $p^{n+m+1}+p^m$	⑧ $r-r^{2m+n}$
	⑨ x^{-3}	⑩ y^{2n+1}
	⑪ $\dfrac{a^{5m}}{b^m}$	⑫ $p^{2n+1}q^{2n-3}$
	⑬ x^{m-2}	⑭ t^{3n-1}
Ex3.	① 1	② -1
	③ -1	④ -1
	⑤ $\dfrac{b^2}{ac^2}$	⑥ $\dfrac{u^2}{vw^3}$
	⑦ $\dfrac{x}{y^4}$	⑧ $\dfrac{-3a^4}{b}$
	⑨ $\dfrac{x^8}{y^4}$	⑩ $\dfrac{q^2}{3p^3}$
	⑪ $\dfrac{z^3}{y^4}$	⑫ $\dfrac{x^5}{9y^3}$
	⑬ $\dfrac{a}{2^4}$	⑭ $\dfrac{9}{a}$
	⑮ $\dfrac{y^4}{x^2}$	⑯ c^9d^7
Ex4.	① 8	② 9
	③ $\dfrac{1}{b}$	④ $\dfrac{1}{b^2}$
	⑤ m	⑥ x
	⑦ b^n	⑧ b^{2n}
	⑨ 2^m	⑩ $\left(\dfrac{8}{2^2}\right)^a = 2^a$
Ex5.	a) $a=4$	b) $a=16$
	c) $a=1$	d) $a=12$
Ex6.	31	

3.2 Polynomials

Ex1.	① Polynomial, degree 4
	② Polynomial, degree 4
	③ Not Polynomial
	④ Polynomial, degree 5
	⑤ Not Polynomial
	⑥ Not Polynomial
	⑦ Polynomial, degree 6
	⑧ Not Polynomial
	⑨ Polynomial, degree 5
	⑩ Polynomial, degree 3

Ex2.	①	$2mn^2 + 3n - 6m$
	②	$6w + 4s - 23w^2s + 2$
	③	$-7mp + 5m^2 + 3m - 7p$
	④	$5t^2 - 12ts + 7s^2 - 6$
	⑤	$2b - ab + 4a$
	⑥	$-5mp + 5p^2 - 3m^2$
	⑦	$6x^2y + x + 1$
	⑧	$-uv - 14 + 2u^2$

3.3 Multiplying Polynomials

Ex1.	①	$-5a^5b^2 + 5a^3b^5$
	②	$c^5d^7 - 3c^7d^5 + 7c^3d^4$
	③	$2x^5 + 2x^4y - 4x^3y^2$
	④	$10a^5b^2c^2 - 4a^4bc^3$
	⑤	$x^2 - 4x - 12$
	⑥	$y^2 - 16y + 60$
	⑦	$3a^2 + 2a - 8$
	⑧	$5z^2 - 19z - 4$
	⑨	$2r^2 + 3rs - 2s^2$
	⑩	$4x^2 - 15xy + 9y^2$
	⑪	$6m^2 + 5mn - 6n^2$
	⑫	$6b^2 + 13ba + 6a^2$
	⑬	$a^3 + 6a^2 + 8a - 3$
	⑭	$t^3 + t^2 - 2t - 8$
	⑮	$z^6 + 5z^4 + 5z^2 - 3$
	⑯	$6 - 5y^2 - y^4 + y^6$
Ex2.	①	$x^2 + 4x + 4$
	②	$t^2 - 2t + 1$
	③	$y^2 - 10y + 25$
	④	$n^2 + 12n + 36$
	⑤	$4a^2 - 12a + 9$
	⑥	$16z^2 - 40z + 25$

	⑦	$9h^2 + 24h + 16$
	⑧	$49m^2 + 70m + 25$
	⑨	$2x^2 - 6\sqrt{2}x + 9$
	⑩	$3x^2 - 8\sqrt{3}x + 16$
	⑪	$a^2 - 4$
	⑫	$z^2 - 16$
	⑬	$25s^2 - 16r^2$
	⑭	$16x^2 - 9y^2$
	⑮	$1 - 64t^2$
	⑯	$-4x^2 + 16xy - 16y^2$
	⑰	$-9t^2 + 30t - 25$
Ex3.	①	$x^4 + 2x^2 - 8$
	②	$x^6 - 4x^3 - 21$
	③	$x^4 - 10x^2 + 25$
	④	$25t^6 - 10t^3 + 1$
	⑤	$s^6 - 2s^3t^3 + t^6$
	⑥	$4p^2 - 12pq^2 + 9q^4$
	⑦	$x^2 + 2 + \dfrac{1}{x^2}$
	⑧	$x^2 - 2 + \dfrac{1}{x^2}$
	⑨	$\dfrac{4}{a^2} - 4 + a^2$
	⑩	$\dfrac{25}{z^2} + 10 + z^2$
	⑪	$m^8 + 8m^5 + 16m^2$
	⑫	$4n^4 - 12n^3 - 7n^2$
	⑬	$x^{6n} + 2x^{3n} + 1$
	⑭	$p^{2m} - 2p^m q^{2n} + q^{4n}$
	⑮	$p^{2n} - q^{2n}$
	⑯	$x^{2m} - 1$
	⑰	$64y^8 - x^4$
	⑱	$49b^{10} - 4a^6$

	⑲	$y^4 - 1$
	⑳	$a^8 - b^8$
	㉑	$x^{16n} - 1$
Ex4.	①	$x^3 + 6x^2 + 12x + 8$
	②	$x^3 + 9x^2 + 27x + 27$
	③	$y^3 - 12y^2 + 48y - 64$
	④	$125 - 75t + 15t^2 - t^3$
	⑤	$8m^3 - 36m^2n + 54mn^2 - 27n^3$
	⑥	$64p^3 + 48p^2q + 12pq^2 + q^3$
Ex5.	14	
Ex6.	31	
Ex7.	①	$x^4 + 2x^3 + 2x^2 + x - 2$
	②	$y^4 - 3y^3 + 4y^2 - 3y + 1$
	③	$z^4 - 4z^3 + 7z^2 - 8z + 4$
	④	$a^4 - 2a^3 + 3a^2 - 2a$
	⑤	$x^2 + 4xy + 4y^2 - 9$
	⑥	$9a^4 + b^2 + 6a^2b - 16$
	⑦	$x^2 + 2xz + z^2 - y^2$
	⑧	$x^2 + 2xy + y^2 - z^2$
Ex8.	① xy ② $5x$ ③ $-30x^2y$ ④ $-25x^3$	
Ex9.	10	

3.4 Factoring using GCF

Ex1.	①	GCF $3xy$ LCM $60x^2y^2$
	②	GCF $7q^2$ LCM $392pq^3$
	③	GCF $12mn^2$ LCM $336m^4n^3$
	④	GCF $14y$ LCM $210xyz$
	⑤	GCF $60a^2b$ LCM $240a^3b^3cd$
	⑥	GCF $36pq$ LCM $432p^2q^3r^2$
	⑦	GCF $2rs$ LCM $420r^2s^4t^2$
	⑧	GCF $11y$ LCM $132xy^2z^2$
	⑨	GCF 8 LCM $96xyz$
	⑩	GCF $7ac$ LCM $28a^3b^2c^3d$
Ex2.	①	$4y^2(4y+1)$
	②	$4x(1-7x)$
	③	$3x^2(x^2-2x+4)$
	④	$2x^2(3-4x^2-5x^3)$
	⑤	$4a^2b(2a-3b+4a^2)$
	⑥	$11ab(a^2-2ab+5b^2)$
Ex3.	①	$1 - \dfrac{10}{3}x^2 + \dfrac{4}{3}x^3$
	②	$1 - 2x^2 + \dfrac{11}{4}x^7$
	③	$x^2 - 8x + \dfrac{2}{3}$
	④	$x^2 + 9x - 4$
	⑤	$1 + 5x^2 - 8x^4$
	⑥	$6x^2 - 3 - \dfrac{5}{4}x^3$

3.5 Factoring Quadratics

Ex1.
1. $(x+4)(x+3)$
2. $(z+2)(z+3)$
3. $(k-6)(k-1)$
4. $(a-3)(a-8)$
5. $(s+11)(s-2)$
6. Prime
7. $(a-15)(a+4)$
8. $(b-7)(b+2)$
9. Prime
10. $(x-8)(x+9)$
11. $(2r+3)(3r+4)$
12. $(3a+7)(a+8)$
13. $(2y+1)(y-5)$
14. $(7x-8)(x-4)$
15. Prime
16. Prime
17. $(3t-2)(3t-4)$
18. $(5g-4)(3g+4)$
19. $(5x+2y)(5x-8y)$
20. $(5m+2n)(2m-3n)$
21. $(2mn+5)(5mn+8)$
22. $2(xy+5)(xy-7)$
23. $2k(k-8)(k+7)$
24. $5z(z-2)(z-3)$
25. $3x^2(9x-2)(x+2)$
26. $12x^2(3x+2)(x+1)$

Ex2.
1. $(x+5)^2$
2. $(z-8)^2$
3. $(2k-3)^2$
4. $(2a+7)^2$
5. $(5x+2y)^2$
6. $(3p-q)^2$
7. $3(x+2)^2$
8. $5a(a+3b)^2$
9. $(x+7)(x-7)$
10. $(u+10)(u-10)$
11. $(2y+5)(2y-5)$
12. $(3x+8)(3x-8)$
13. $y^2(x+1)(x-1)$
14. $x(x+10)(x-10)$
15. $r(9p-7q)(9p+7q)$
16. $4y(x+3)(x-3)$
17. Prime
18. Prime

Ex3.
1. $(m^2n-7)^2$
2. $(x^2-3y)^2$
3. $(x+1)(x-1)(x+3)(x-3)$
4. $(x+2)(x-2)(x+3)(x-3)$
5. $(a-b)(a+b)(a^2+b^2)$
6. $(4k^2+1)(2k+1)(2k-1)$
7. $(x+3)(x-3)(x^2+9)$
8. $(m^2n^2+1)(mn+1)(mn-1)$

	⑨	$(8x+y)(2x-3y)$
	⑩	$(a+b-2)(a-b)$
	⑪	$(2x-1)(x+3)(x+9)$
	⑫	$-8x(x+2)(x-2)$
Ex4.	①	$(x^n+1)(x^n-1)$
	②	$(x^n+1)^2$
	③	$(x^n+2y^n)^2$
	④	$(x^n-7y^n)(x^n+y^n)$
	⑤	$x^{2n}(x^n+y^n)(x^n-y^n)$
	⑥	$(x^{2n}+y^n)^2$
	⑦	$(x^{4n}+y^{4n})(x^{2n}+y^{2n})(x^n+y^n)(x^n-y^n)$
Ex5.		$(x^2+1+x)(x^2+1-x)$

3.6 Factoring Polynomials

Ex1.	①	$(x+1)(x^2-x+1)$
	②	$(t+5)(t^2-5t+25)$
	③	$(4-y)(16+4y+y^2)$
	④	$(10+r)(100-10r+r^2)$
	⑤	$5y^2(y+3)(y^2-3y+9)$
	⑥	$16m^2(r-5)(r^2+5r+25)$
	⑦	$3x^2(2x+y)(4x^2-2xy+y^2)$
	⑧	$2x^2(3x-4y)(9x^2+12xy+16y^2)$
	⑨	$(x^2+y)(x^4-x^2y+y^2)$
	⑩	$(z+2)(z-2)(z^4+4z+16)$

	⑪	$(2x+y)(2x-y)(16x^4+4x^2y^2+y^4)$
		$(=(2x+y)(4x^2-2xy+y^2)(2x-y)$
		$(4x^2+2xy+y^2))$
	⑫	$2(2p-q)(2p+q)(16p^4+4p^2q^2+q^4)$
		$(=2(2p+q)(4p^2-2pq+q^2)(2p-q)$
		$(4p^2+2pq+q^2))$
Ex2.	①	$(b+2)(a-3)$
	②	$(n+1)(m-1)$
	③	$(q-2)(p+1)$
	④	$(b-1)(a-1)$
	⑤	$(2x-1)(2x-3)$
	⑥	$(x-7)(x-6)$
	⑦	$(a+b-2c)(a+b-c)$
	⑧	$(x-y-2z)(x-y+z)$
	⑨	$(x-2y+1)^2$
	⑩	$2(x+y+4)(x+y-3)$
Ex3.	①	$(x+1)^2(x-1)$
	②	$c(c+1)^2(c-1)$
	③	$(4x-1)(5x^2+2)$
	④	$(a+1)(10a^2+3)$
	⑤	$(ab-8)(a+1)(a-1)$
	⑥	$(5y-7)(x^2+1)$
	⑦	$(u+v)(u-v-2)$
	⑧	$(a+b)(a-b+1)$
	⑨	$(x+y)(x^2+y^2)$
	⑩	$(x-y)(x^2+y^2)$
	⑪	$(x-4+4y)(x-4-4y)$

	⑫	$(z+5+w)(z+5-w)$
	⑬	$(x+y+3)(x-y-3)$
	⑭	$(a+b-4)(a-b+4)$
	⑮	$(x-1)(x-2)(y+z)(y^2-yz+z^2)$
	⑯	$(t+3)^3(s+p)(s^2-sp+p^2)$
Ex4.	①	$(x^n-y^n)(x^{2n}+x^n y^n+y^{2n})$
	②	$(x^n+y^n)(x^n-y^n)(x^{2n}-x^n y^n+y^{2n})(x^{2n}+x^n y^n+y^{2n})$
	③	$2y(3x^2+y^2)$
	④	$2a(a^2+3b^2)$
	⑤	$8xy(x^2+y^2)$
	⑥	$4xy(x^2+3y^2)(3x^2+y^2)$

3.7 Solving Polynomial Equations

Ex1.	①	$x=2,-3$
	②	$x=-4, 9$
	③	$x=\dfrac{5}{2},-\dfrac{1}{3}$
	④	$x=-\dfrac{7}{4},\dfrac{9}{2}$
	⑤	$x=0, 5, -\dfrac{7}{5}$
	⑥	$x=0, -1, \dfrac{3}{2}$
	⑦	$x=2(double), -4$
	⑧	$x=2(double), -2$
	⑨	$x=-9, 3$
	⑩	$x=7, -2$
	⑪	$x=\dfrac{1}{2}, -\dfrac{1}{3}$

	⑫	$x=\dfrac{1}{3}, -7$
	⑬	$x=0, 4$
	⑭	$x=0, 9$
	⑮	$x=-2, 2$
	⑯	$x=\pm 3$
	⑰	$x=5(double)$
	⑱	$x=\dfrac{1}{2}(double)$
	⑲	$x=0(double), \dfrac{1}{4}$
	⑳	$x=0, \ 9, 2$
	㉑	$x=1, 4$
	㉒	$x=6, -2$
Ex2.	①	$x=\pm 2, \pm 3$
	②	$x=2(double), -2(double)$
	③	$t=0(double), \pm 1, \pm 4$
	④	$x=0(double), \pm 1, \pm 5$
	⑤	$x=2(double), 3$
	⑥	$x=3(double), 4$
	⑦	$x=1, 2, 3$
	⑧	$x=2, 3, 4$
	⑨	$x=10(double), -10(double)$
	⑩	$x=9(double), -1(double)$
	⑪	$x=2(double), -2(double)$
	⑫	$x=\pm 2, \pm 3$

3.8 Word Problems about Poly Equation

Ex1.	$-4, -2$
Ex2.	three numbers: $x-2$, x, $x+2$ $(x-2)^2 + x^2 + (x+2)^2 = 371$ $x = 11 \text{ or } -11$ Answer: 9, 11, 13
Ex3.	8
Ex4.	Katy: 6 years old, Sam: 9 years old
Ex5.	J: Joey's current age $(5+J)(J) = 114 + (3+J)(J-2)$ $J = 27$ Joey: 27 years old, Tim: 32 years old
Ex6.	12m and 16m
Ex7.	width 7m, length 12m
Ex8.	22cm^2
Ex9.	$2x + 2y = 46, x^2 + y^2 = 17^2$ Since $(x+y)^2 = x^2 + 2xy + y^2$, we can say $23^2 = 17^2 + 2xy$. $xy = 120$ Answer: 120ft^2
Ex10.	$20 ft$
Ex11.	x: one side of original square. $(x+6)^2 = 16x^2$ $x = -6/5, 2$ Answer: 2
Ex12.	$\dfrac{5}{2} m$
Ex13.	$\dfrac{1}{2} m$
Ex14.	x: width of the walk $(20+2x)(12+2x) = 560$ $x = 4 \text{ or } -20$ Answer: 4m
Ex15.	width 10 in, length 10 in
Ex16.	x: length of the side of the square cardboard $5(x-10)^2 = 500$ $x = 20 \text{ or } 0$ Answer: 20cm
Ex17.	$\dfrac{1}{4} in$
Ex18.	1cm

3.9 Solving Polynomial Inequalities

Ex1.	①	$x \leq -1 \text{ or } x \geq 5$
	②	$-7 \leq x \leq 1$
	③	$-2 < b < 2$
	④	$0 < t < 3$
	⑤	$x < -1 \text{ or } x > \dfrac{7}{3}$
	⑥	$x \leq -1 \text{ or } x \geq \dfrac{9}{2}$
	⑦	$x = 5$
	⑧	$x = \dfrac{3}{2}$
	⑨	$x < -\dfrac{4}{3} \text{ or } x > -\dfrac{4}{3}$
	⑩	$\mathbb{R}$
	⑪	$t < -3 \text{ or } 0 < t < 2$
	⑫	$-2 \leq y \leq 0 \text{ or } y \geq 2$
	⑬	$-3 < t < 0$
	⑭	$y = -2 \text{ or } 0 \text{ or } y \geq 2$
	⑮	$x \leq -3 \text{ or } x = 0 \text{ or } x \geq 3$
	⑯	$x < 0 \text{ or } 0 < x < 16$

⑰ $t > \dfrac{1}{5}$

⑱ $-\dfrac{1}{2} < x < 0$ or $0 < x < \dfrac{1}{2}$

⑲ $-1 < x < 0$

⑳ $x \leq -1$ or $x \geq 0$

㉑ $x = 0$ or $x = 1$

㉒ $x = 0$ or $x = 5$

Answers

4. Quadratic Function

4.1 Imaginary Numbers

Ex1.	① $6i$	② $11i$
	③ $2\sqrt{3}i$	④ $2\sqrt{5}i$
	⑤ $9\sqrt{2}i$	⑥ $15\sqrt{3}i$
	⑦ $6\sqrt{2}i$	⑧ $7\sqrt{2}i$
	⑨ $-5\sqrt{2}$	⑩ $-3\sqrt{5}$
	⑪ -10	⑫ 15
	⑬ -9	⑭ -16
	⑮ -5	⑯ -12
	⑰ 12	⑱ -90
	⑲ $\dfrac{3}{2}i$	⑳ $-\dfrac{7}{3}i$
Ex2.	① a) $9i$ b) -20	
	② a) $3\sqrt{2}i$ b) -4	
	③ a) $11\sqrt{2}i$ b) -36	
	④ a) $-\sqrt{2}i$ b) -40	
Ex3.	① -1	② 1
	③ i	④ -1
	⑤ $-i$	⑥ $-i$
	⑦ 1	⑧ 1
	⑨ 0	⑩ 0
Ex4.	i	
Ex5.	$50-50i$	
Ex6.	0	

4.2 Complex Numbers

Ex1.	a)	$-22, \dfrac{0}{3}, \dfrac{1}{2}, 0.\bar{3}, 0.3$
	b)	$\sqrt{21}, \pi$
	c)	$-22, \dfrac{0}{3}, \dfrac{1}{2}, \sqrt{21}, 0.\bar{3}, 0.3, \pi$
	d)	All
Ex2.	①	$m=7, n=-7$
	②	$m=6, n=9$
	③	$m=4, n=6$
	④	$m=1, n=-4$
Ex3.	①	$-5+i$
	②	$10i-17$
	③	$5i-14$
	④	$3+43i$
	⑤	$2i+5$
	⑥	$-6-8i$
	⑦	$1+8i$
	⑧	$11-13i$
	⑨	5
	⑩	10
	⑪	-53
	⑫	-52
	⑬	$-21+20i$
	⑭	$-7+24i$
	⑮	$-2-2\sqrt{3}i$
	⑯	$35+12i$
	⑰	4
	⑱	81
	⑲	256
	⑳	2500
Ex4.	①	$\dfrac{3-i}{2}$

	②	$\dfrac{12+3i}{17}$
	③	$\dfrac{8+i}{5}$
	④	$\dfrac{1+12i}{5}$
	⑤	$\dfrac{5-12i}{13}$
	⑥	$\dfrac{3-4i}{5}$
	⑦	$\dfrac{2-3\sqrt{5}i}{7}$
	⑧	$\dfrac{7+4\sqrt{2}i}{9}$
Ex5.	①	$\dfrac{-\sqrt{2}-3i}{11}$
	②	$\dfrac{-\sqrt{5}+\sqrt{3}i}{8}$
Ex6.	0	
Ex7.	0	

4.3 Graphing Quadratic Functions

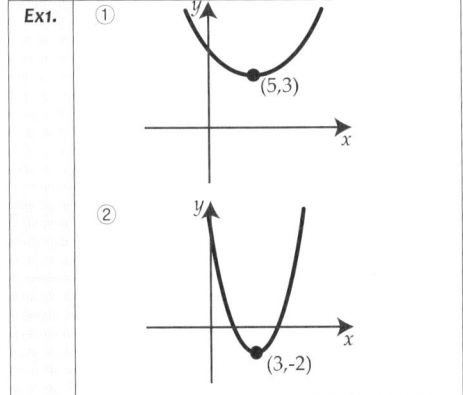

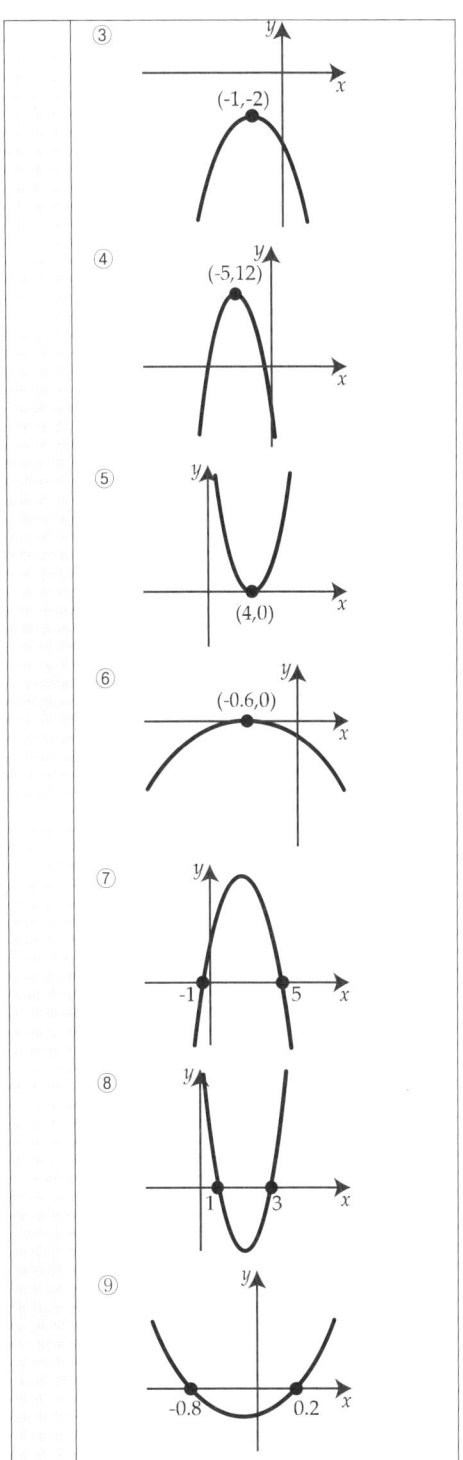

	⑩	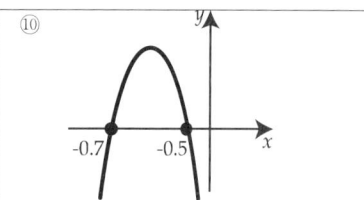 −0.7, −0.5
Ex2.	①	$x=-3, (-3,-1)$
		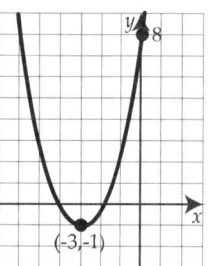
	②	$x=-1, (-1, 3)$
		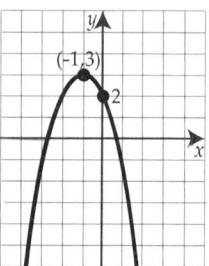
	③	$x=1, (1,0)$
		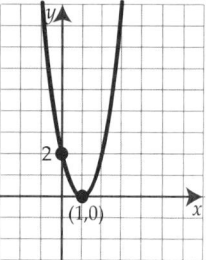
	④	$x=2, (2,0)$
		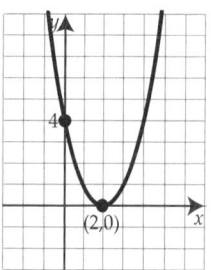

Ex3.	①	min −11
	②	max 5
	③	max 19
	④	max 18
	⑤	max 0
	⑥	min 3
	⑦	max $\dfrac{9}{2}$
	⑧	min $-\dfrac{49}{4}$
Ex4.	① II ② V ③ I ④ IV ⑤ III ⑥ VI	
Ex5.	$0 < a < \dfrac{5}{8}$	
Ex6.	$y = -3x - 4$	
Ex7.	$h = 4, k = -4$	

4.4 Vertex of Quadratic Graphs

Ex1.	①	$c = 25, (x+5)^2$
	②	$c = 36, (x-6)^2$
	③	$c = 121, (x-11)^2$
	④	$c = 81, (x+9)^2$
	⑤	$c = \dfrac{9}{4}, \left(x+\dfrac{3}{2}\right)^2$
	⑥	$c = \dfrac{1}{4}, \left(x-\dfrac{1}{2}\right)^2$
	⑦	$c = 0.16, (x-0.4)^2$
	⑧	$c = 1.21, (x+1.1)^2$

	⑨ $c = \dfrac{9}{100}, \left(x + \dfrac{3}{10}\right)^2$	
	⑩ $c = \dfrac{1}{16}, \left(x - \dfrac{1}{4}\right)^2$	

Ex2.

① $y = (x-5)^2 - 3, (5, -3)$

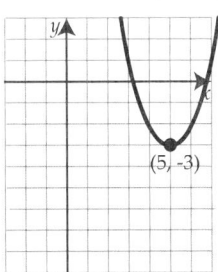

② $y = (x+4)^2 - 9, (-4, -9)$

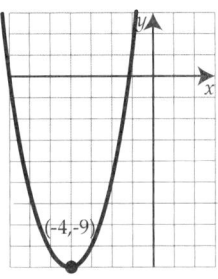

③ $y = (x+3)^2 - 9, (-3, -9)$

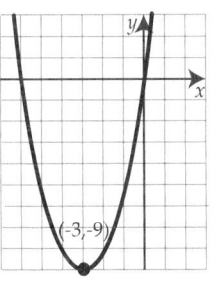

④ $y = (x-5)^2 - 25, (5, -25)$

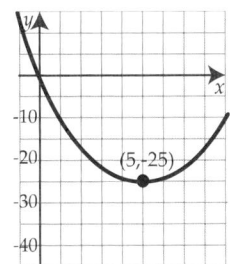

⑤ $y = \left(x + \dfrac{1}{2}\right)^2 + \dfrac{15}{4}, \left(-\dfrac{1}{2}, \dfrac{15}{4}\right)$

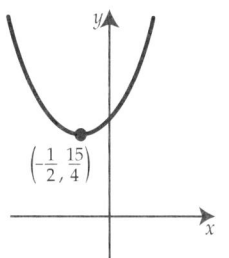

⑥ $y = \left(x - \dfrac{5}{2}\right)^2 - \dfrac{5}{4}, \left(\dfrac{5}{2}, -\dfrac{5}{4}\right)$

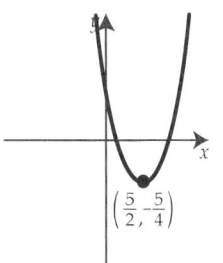

Ex3.

① $y = -(x-3)^2 + 4, (3, 4)$

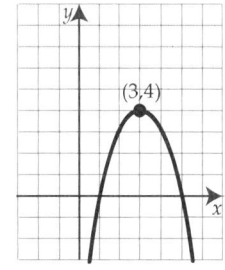

② $y = 3(x-2)^2 - 5, (2, -5)$

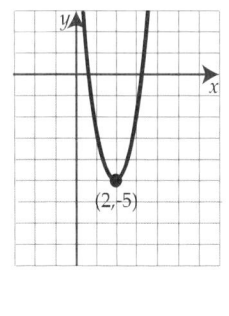

③ $y = -4(x-2)^2 + 3, (2, 3)$

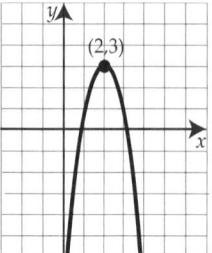

④ $y = -5(x+1)^2 + 12, (-1, 12)$

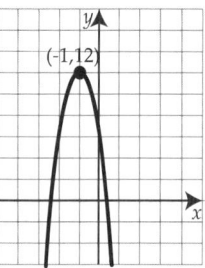

⑤ $y = 4(x+1)^2 - 4, (-1, -4)$

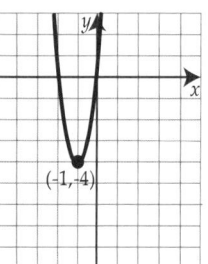

⑥ $y = -4(x-2)^2 + 16, (2, 16)$

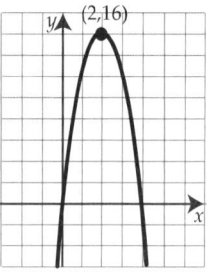

⑦ $y = 3\left(x - \frac{1}{2}\right)^2 + \frac{1}{4}, \left(\frac{1}{2}, \frac{1}{4}\right)$

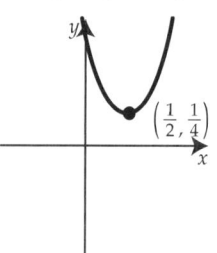

⑧ $y = 4\left(x + \frac{1}{8}\right)^2 + \frac{47}{16}, \left(-\frac{1}{8}, \frac{47}{16}\right)$

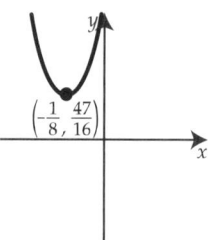

⑨ $y = 2\left(x - \frac{1}{4}\right)^2 + \frac{79}{8}, \left(\frac{1}{4}, \frac{79}{8}\right)$

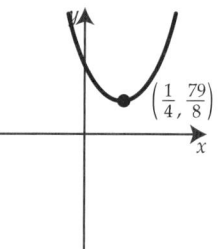

⑩ $y = -\left(x - \frac{5}{2}\right)^2 + \frac{33}{4}, \left(\frac{5}{2}, \frac{33}{4}\right)$

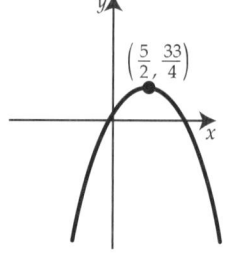

Ex4.	① min 5
	② min -18
	③ max $\frac{1}{3}$
	④ max 3
	⑤ min $\frac{11}{8}$
Ex5.	① $y = -\frac{1}{3}(x-2)^2 + 5$
	② $y = \frac{1}{8}(x+3)^2 + 2$
	③ $y = -\frac{2}{3}(x-3)^2 + 1$
	④ $y = \frac{1}{2}(x-2)^2 - 4$
	⑤ $y = -3(x+1)^2 + 7$
	⑥ $y = -\frac{5}{4}(x-4)^2 + 5$
Ex6.	① III ② VI
	③ I ④ IV
	⑤ II ⑥ V
Ex7.	III
Ex8.	$a < 0$
	$b > 0$
	$c > 0$
Ex9.	$y = -2(x-4)^2 - 1$
Ex10.	$p = 18$
Ex11.	$k = 4$, $p = -7$
Ex12.	$\frac{1}{10^4}$

4.5 Word Problems about Optimization

Ex1.	a) $\frac{5}{2}$ sec
	b) 103 m
Ex2.	6 sec
Ex3.	area 25 in², 5 in by 5 in
	(width is 5 in, length is 5 in)
Ex4.	y: length of the garden
	$16-2y$: width of the garden
	$Area = y(16-2y) = -2(y-4)^2 + 32$
	Answer: 32m²
Ex5.	$\frac{25}{2}$ ft by 25 ft
Ex6.	x: width of the garden
	$-\frac{2}{3}x + 200$: length of the garden
	$Area = x\left(-\frac{2}{3}x + 200\right)$
	$= -\frac{2}{3}(x-150)^2 + 15000$
	Answer: 150 yd by 100 yd
Ex7.	$\frac{20}{\pi}$ mi
Ex8.	a) $Area = x(-2x+4)$
	b) largest area = 2, 1 by 2
Ex9.	162
Ex10.	x: x coordinate of the right upper corner of the rectangle
	$Perimeter = 4x + 2(-x^2 + 5)$
	$= -2(x-1)^2 + 12$
	Answer: 12
Ex11.	20
Ex12.	$\frac{7}{8}$

Ex13.	vertical distance $= (x^2+3)-(x)$
	$\qquad = \left(x-\dfrac{1}{2}\right)^2 + \dfrac{11}{4}$
	Answer: $\dfrac{11}{4}$
Ex14.	a) Revenue $=(60+5x)(600-10x)$
	b) 180 $
	c) 64800 $
Ex15.	x : the number of price increase
	income $=(100-10x)(8+2x)$
	$\qquad = -20(x-3)^2 + 980$
	Answer: $8+2(3)=14$ $

4.6 Finding Zeros by Factoring

Ex1.	① x^2+x-12
	② $x^2+10x+16$
	③ x^2-7x+6
	④ $x^2-15x+50$
	⑤ $x^2+8x+16$
	⑥ x^2-4x+4
	⑦ $3x^2-5x-2$
	⑧ $5x^2-19x+12$
	⑨ $21x^2+x-2$
	⑩ $12x^2+25x+12$

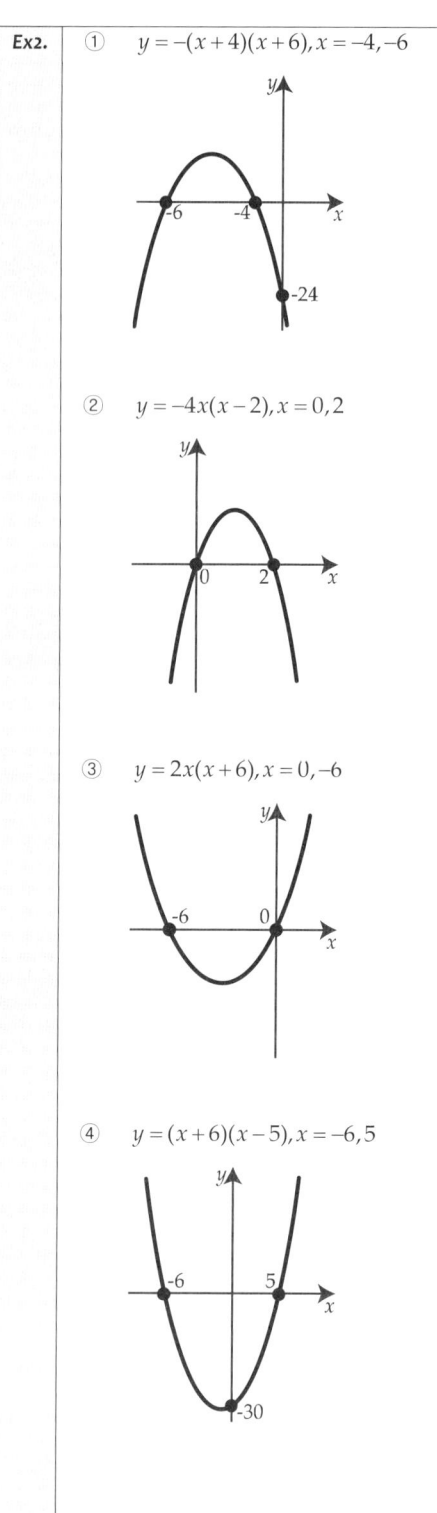

Ex2.
① $y=-(x+4)(x+6), x=-4,-6$

② $y=-4x(x-2), x=0,2$

③ $y=2x(x+6), x=0,-6$

④ $y=(x+6)(x-5), x=-6,5$

⑤ $y=(2x-9)(x+1), x=\dfrac{9}{2},-1$

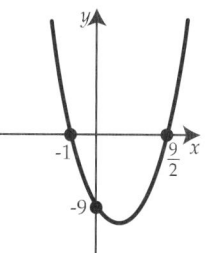

⑥ $y=(3x-7)(x+1), x=\dfrac{7}{3},-1$

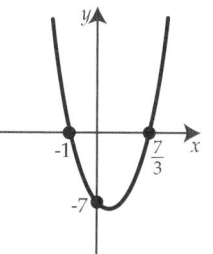

⑦ $y=-(x+12)^2, x=-12$

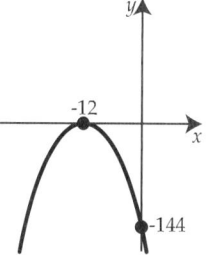

⑧ $y=-(x-3)^2, x=3$

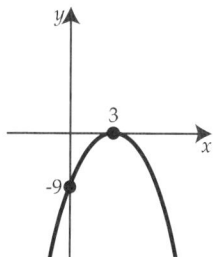

Ex3.	①	$y=-2(x+2)(x-8)$
	②	$y=\dfrac{1}{2}(x+6)(x-1)$
	③	$y=x(x+4)$
	④	$y=-x(x-5)$
Ex4.	80	
Ex5.	$a+2$	

4.7 Finding Zeros by Completing Squares

Ex1.	①	$x=\pm\sqrt{5}$
	②	$x=\pm\sqrt{6}$
	③	$x=\pm 2i$
	④	$x=\pm\sqrt{3}i$
	⑤	$x=1\pm\sqrt{5}i$
	⑥	$x=1\pm\sqrt{5}$
	⑦	$x=-\dfrac{2}{3}$ or 2
	⑧	$x=\dfrac{-3\pm 3i}{2}$
	⑨	$x=2\pm 2i$
	⑩	$x=-3\pm 4\sqrt{2}$
	⑪	$x=-1$ or -9
	⑫	$x=4$ or 10
	⑬	$x=\dfrac{1\pm 2\sqrt{3}i}{3}$
	⑭	$x=1\pm 2\sqrt{2}i$

4.8 Quadratic Formula

Ex1.
① $x = 4 \pm \sqrt{2}$
② $x = \dfrac{-1 \pm \sqrt{35}i}{2}$
③ $x = \dfrac{-5 \pm \sqrt{7}}{6}$
④ $x = \dfrac{-5 \pm \sqrt{23}}{2}$
⑤ $x = \dfrac{-7 \pm \sqrt{15}i}{16}$
⑥ $x = \dfrac{-5 \pm \sqrt{15}i}{10}$
⑦ $x = \dfrac{2 \pm \sqrt{26}i}{6}$
⑧ $x = \dfrac{3 \pm \sqrt{5}}{2}$
⑨ $x = \dfrac{\sqrt{3} \pm \sqrt{11}}{2}$
⑩ $x = \dfrac{-\sqrt{2} \pm \sqrt{14}}{2}$
⑪ $x = i \text{ or } -2i$
⑫ $x = i$

Ex2.
① $x = 3, -2$

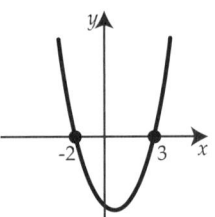

② $x = 1, \dfrac{2}{5}$

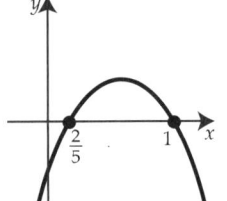

Ex2.
① $x = -1 \text{ or } 11$
② $x = 3 \text{ or } 9$
③ $x = -\dfrac{3}{2} \pm \dfrac{3\sqrt{5}}{2}$
④ $x = -\dfrac{1}{2} \pm \dfrac{3\sqrt{3}}{2}i$
⑤ $x = -2 \pm \dfrac{\sqrt{30}}{5}$
⑥ $x = -2 \pm \dfrac{\sqrt{2}}{2}$
⑦ $x = 1 \pm \sqrt{2}i$
⑧ $x = \dfrac{1}{5} \pm \dfrac{2}{5}i$
⑨ $x = \dfrac{7}{8} \pm \dfrac{\sqrt{17}}{8}$
⑩ $x = 3 \text{ or } -\dfrac{3}{2}$
⑪ $x = \dfrac{1}{10} \pm \dfrac{\sqrt{69}}{10}i$
⑫ $x = 1 \pm \dfrac{\sqrt{6}}{6}i$
⑬ $x = -\dfrac{5}{14} \pm \dfrac{\sqrt{3}}{14}i$
⑭ $x = 1 \pm \sqrt{2}$

	③	$x = -2 \pm \sqrt{11}$ 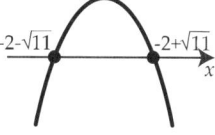
	④	$x = \dfrac{5 \pm \sqrt{41}}{2}$ 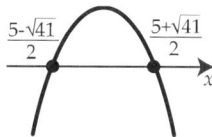
	⑤	$x = \dfrac{-2 \pm \sqrt{2}i}{2}$ 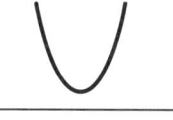
	⑥	$x = \dfrac{1 \pm \sqrt{31}i}{4}$ 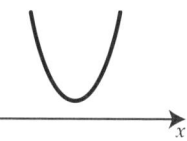
Ex3.	$z = 1,\ 1+i$	
Ex4.	①	$x = \dfrac{-4 \pm \sqrt{2}}{2}$
	②	$x = 6 \pm \sqrt{29}$
	③	$x = 3 \pm \sqrt{2}i$
	④	$x = \dfrac{-2 \pm \sqrt{14}i}{3}$

4.9 Solving Equations in Quadratic Form

Ex1.	①	a) $x = -12,\ 1$
		b) $y = \pm\sqrt{10}i,\ \pm\sqrt{3}$
	②	a) $x = 3,\ -\dfrac{1}{3}$
		b) $x = -\dfrac{1}{8},\ \dfrac{1}{2}$
	③	a) $y = \dfrac{4}{3},\ 1$
		b) $x = 1,\ \dfrac{3}{5}$
	④	a) $x = 1,\ -\dfrac{3}{2}$
		b) $x = \dfrac{2}{3},\ \dfrac{1}{4}$
	⑤	a) $\pm 1,\ \pm 2i$
		b) $x = 1$
	⑥	a) $\pm 1,\ \pm\sqrt{7}i$
		b) $x = 1$
Ex2.	①	$x = \pm 2\sqrt{3}i$
	②	$x = -1,\ -\dfrac{1}{5}$
	③	$x = 25$
	④	$x = 64$
	⑤	$x = 4, -1,\ x = 5, -2$
	⑥	$x = 4, -2,\ x = -1, 3$
	⑦	$x = 1$
	⑧	$x = 1,\ x = 64$
	⑨	$x = \dfrac{1}{4}$
	⑩	$y = 4$
	⑪	$x = \pm 7$
	⑫	$x = \pm 2$

4.10 Quadratic Inequalities using Graphs

Ex1.	①	$-1 < x < 7$
	②	$x < -4$ or $x > 2$
	③	$x \leq -3$ or $x \geq 0$
	④	$0 \leq x \leq 4$
	⑤	$-5 < x < -2$
	⑥	$x < 1$ or $x > 4$
	⑦	$\mathbb{R}$
	⑧	$x = 4$
	⑨	$x = 3$
	⑩	$\mathbb{R}$
Ex2.	①	$x \leq -4$ or $x \geq -3$
	②	$x \leq -4$ or $x \geq 4$
	③	$x < -6$ or $x > 6$
	④	$2 < x < 7$
	⑤	$-2 - \sqrt{2} \leq x \leq -2 + \sqrt{2}$
	⑥	$x < -1 - 2\sqrt{2}$ or $x > -1 + 2\sqrt{2}$
	⑦	$-12 < x < 11$
	⑧	$-3 \leq x \leq -1$
	⑨	$\mathbb{R}, x \neq 2$
	⑩	$\mathbb{R}$
	⑪	$\mathbb{R}$
	⑫	$\mathbb{R}, x \neq -4$
	⑬	$x = 5$
	⑭	$\emptyset$
	⑮	$\emptyset$
	⑯	$x = \dfrac{4}{3}$
Ex3.	①	$-3 \leq x \leq 2$
	②	$x < -7$ or $x > -3$
	③	$y \leq -1$ or $y \geq 1$
	④	$-5 < a < 5$
	⑤	$m < -4$ or $m > 1$

	⑥	$-2 < z < 1$
	⑦	$0 < m < \dfrac{9}{7}$
	⑧	$x < 0$ or $x > 1$
	⑨	$\dfrac{-3 - \sqrt{13}}{2} < x < \dfrac{-3 + \sqrt{13}}{2}$
	⑩	$x < \dfrac{3 - \sqrt{33}}{4}$ or $x > \dfrac{3 + \sqrt{33}}{4}$
	⑪	$x \leq -10$ or $x \geq 8$
	⑫	$\dfrac{5}{3} < x < 4$

4.11 Discriminants

Ex1.	①	$D = 0$
		Two repeated real zeros(roots)
	②	$D = 121$
		Two distinct rational zeros
	③	$D = 4$
		Two distinct rational zeros
	④	$D = 0$
		Two repeated real zeros
	⑤	$D = 12$
		Two distinct irrational zeros
	⑥	$D = -7$
		Two complex zeros
	⑦	$D = -3$
		Two complex zeros
	⑧	$D = 24$
		Two distinct irrational zeros
	⑨	$D = 92$
		Two distinct irrational zeros
	⑩	$D = 100$
		Two distinct rational zeros

Ex2.	①	$k < \dfrac{4}{3}$
	②	$k = \dfrac{1}{8}$
	③	$k = \dfrac{7}{8}$
	④	$k > \dfrac{17}{16}$
	⑤	$k \leq \dfrac{1}{12}$
	⑥	$k = \pm \dfrac{1}{2}$
	⑦	$-4 < k < 2$
	⑧	$k \leq -3$ or $k \geq 1$
	⑨	$\mathbb{R}, k \neq 1$
	⑩	$k = 7$ or -1
	⑪	$k = \pm \dfrac{4}{7}$
	⑫	$\varnothing$
Ex3.	①	$a > 0$ $b^2 - 4ac > 0$
	②	$a < 0$ $b^2 - 4ac > 0$
	③	$a < 0$ $b^2 - 4ac = 0$
	④	$a > 0$ $b^2 - 4ac = 0$
	⑤	$a > 0$ $b^2 - 4ac < 0$
	⑥	$a < 0$ $b^2 - 4ac < 0$
Ex4.	①	$\left(\dfrac{3}{2}, 6\right), \left(-\dfrac{1}{3}, \dfrac{7}{3}\right)$
	②	$(4, 4), (7, 1)$
	③	$(-4, 2)$

Ex5.	①	$k = -2, -6$
	②	$k > -5$
	③	$m < -2$ or $m > 2$
	④	$m = 7$ or -1
Ex6.	$k = 0$	
Ex7.	$y = -2x + 4$	
Ex8.	$k > 6$	
Ex9.	$-9 < k < -1$	

4.12 Sum and Product of the roots

Ex1.	①	sum = 8, product = –14
	②	sum = 7, product = 6
	③	sum = $\dfrac{36}{5}$, product = $\dfrac{7}{5}$
	④	sum = $\dfrac{2}{3}$, product = $\dfrac{1}{9}$
	⑤	sum = $\dfrac{5}{2}$, product = $\dfrac{9}{2}$
	⑥	sum = 1, product = $\dfrac{7}{3}$
	⑦	sum = 0, product = –100
	⑧	sum = 0, product = –16
	⑨	sum = 6, product = 0
	⑩	sum = $-\dfrac{7}{2}$, product = 0
Ex2.	①	$x^2 + x - 42$
	②	$x^2 - 7x - 8$
	③	$x^2 - 4x - 3$
	④	$x^2 - 8x + 13$
	⑤	$9x^2 - 12x - 16$
	⑥	$4x^2 - 28x + 17$

Answers

5. Polynomials

5.1 Graphing Polynomials

Ex1.		
	①	As $x \to -\infty$, $y \to -\infty$ As $x \to \infty$, $y \to \infty$
	②	As $x \to -\infty$, $y \to -\infty$ As $x \to \infty$, $y \to -\infty$
	③	As $x \to -\infty$, $y \to \infty$ As $x \to \infty$, $y \to -\infty$
	④	As $x \to -\infty$, $y \to -\infty$ As $x \to \infty$, $y \to \infty$
	⑤	As $x \to -\infty$, $y \to -\infty$ As $x \to \infty$, $y \to -\infty$
	⑥	As $x \to -\infty$, $y \to \infty$ As $x \to \infty$, $y \to -\infty$
	⑦	As $x \to -\infty$, $y \to -\infty$ As $x \to \infty$, $y \to \infty$
	⑧	As $x \to -\infty$, $y \to \infty$ As $x \to \infty$, $y \to \infty$

	⑦	$x^2 - 4x + 13$
	⑧	$x^2 - 6x + 34$
	⑨	$4x^2 - 20x + 27$
	⑩	$25x^2 - 30x + 12$
Ex3.	a)	$-\dfrac{5}{2}$
	b)	-2
	c)	$\dfrac{5}{4}$
	d)	$\dfrac{41}{4}$
Ex4.	a)	3
	b)	4
	c)	$\dfrac{3}{4}$
	d)	1
Ex5.	$\dfrac{2}{3}$	
Ex6.	$7x^2 - 4x + 1$	
Ex7.	$x^2 - 6x + 14$	
Ex8.	$-\dfrac{1}{4}$	

Ex2. ① (graph with x-intercepts at -3, $\tfrac{1}{2}$, 2)

② (graph with x-intercepts at -1, 2)

③ (graph through 0 and 2)

598 Mia's Algebra 2

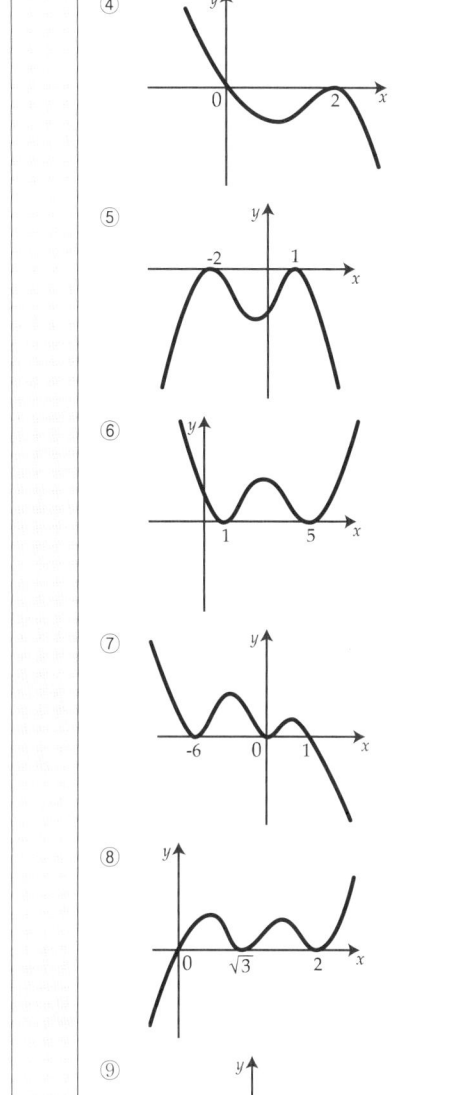

5.2 Dividing Polynomials

Ex1.	①	$x+5-\dfrac{3}{x+3}$
	②	$x-11-\dfrac{2}{6-x}$
	③	$x-9+\dfrac{30x-54}{x^2-3}$
	④	$2x^2-3x-5-\dfrac{15}{3x-5}$
	⑤	$4x^2-20x+100-\dfrac{503}{x+5}$
	⑥	$x+2+\dfrac{8x-2}{x^2-2x+2}$
	⑦	$x^2-3x+1+\dfrac{20x}{x^2+2x+5}$
	⑧	$3x^2-4x-11+\dfrac{21x+25}{x^2+x+5}$
Ex2.	①	x^2-6x+9
	②	$3x^2-7x+24-\dfrac{95}{x+4}$
	③	$x^2-2x-4+\dfrac{10}{x+2}$
	④	$5x^2-11x+33-\dfrac{102}{x+3}$
	⑤	$x^3+4x^2+11x+44+\dfrac{166}{x-4}$
	⑥	$2x^3-6x^2-12x-24-\dfrac{40}{x-2}$
	⑦	$x^4+2x^3+4x^2+8x+16$
	⑧	$x^5+x^4+x^3+x^2+x+1$
	⑨	$x^2+\dfrac{5}{2}x+\dfrac{1}{4}+\dfrac{\frac{13}{4}}{2x-1}$
	⑩	$4x^3-x^2+\dfrac{3}{2}x+\dfrac{1}{4}+\dfrac{\frac{1}{4}}{2x+3}$

Ex3.	① $a^2 + 2ba + 3b^2 + \dfrac{6b^3}{2a-b}$
	② $x^2 + 3xy - 3y^2 + \dfrac{10y^3}{x+3y}$

5.3 The Remainder & Factor Theorem

Ex1.	① 23	② 2
	③ 1525	④ 145
	⑤ 3	⑥ 6
Ex2.	① 21	② 860
	③ −12	④ −170
	⑤ $\dfrac{1}{3}$	⑥ 1
Ex3.	$k = \dfrac{3}{2}$	
Ex4.	① Not factor	
	② Factor	
	③ Factor	
	④ Not factor	
	⑤ Not factor	
	⑥ Factor	
	⑦ Factor	
	⑧ Not factor	
Ex5.	$k = -1$	
Ex6.	$k = 2$	

5.4 Theorems about Roots of Polynomial

Ex1.	①	$\pm 1, \pm 2, \pm \dfrac{1}{2}, \pm \dfrac{1}{3}, \pm \dfrac{2}{3}, \pm \dfrac{1}{6}$
	②	$\pm 1, \pm 2, \pm 4, \pm 8, \pm \dfrac{1}{2}$
	③	$\pm 1, \pm 2, \pm 4, \pm 8, \pm \dfrac{1}{5}, \pm \dfrac{2}{5}, \pm \dfrac{4}{5}, \pm \dfrac{8}{5}$
	④	$\pm 1, \pm 7, \pm \dfrac{1}{2}, \pm \dfrac{7}{2}, \pm \dfrac{1}{4}, \pm \dfrac{7}{4}$
Ex2.	①	positive: 1 negative: 2 or 0
	②	positive: 3 or 1 negative: 1
	③	positive: 3 or 1 negative: 0
	④	positive: 4 or 2 or 0
		negative: 3 or 1
Ex3.	①	real 0, imaginary 2
	②	real 2, imaginary 0
	③	real 3, imaginary 0
	④	real 1, imaginary 2
	⑤	real 3 (one distinct root, one double root), imaginary 0
	⑥	real 4 (two distinct roots, one double root), imaginary 0
	⑦	real 2, imaginary 2
	⑧	real 0, imaginary 6
	⑨	real 1, imaginary 4
Ex4.	①	$x^2 - 2x + 5$
	②	$x^2 - 6x + 10$
	③	$x^3 - 2x^2 - 3x + 10$
	④	$x^3 - x^2 + 2$
	⑤	$x^4 + 5x^2 + 4$
	⑥	$x^4 + 5x^2 - 6$

5.5 Complex Roots of Polynomial function

Ex1.	①	$x = 0, \pm i$
	②	$x = 0 \text{(double)}, \pm 2i$
	③	$x = 3, \pm \sqrt{2}i$
	④	$x = 4, \pm i$
	⑤	$x = \pm 2, \pm 2\sqrt{2}i$
	⑥	$x = \pm i, \pm 2\sqrt{2}i$
	⑦	$x = \pm 2, \pm 2i$
	⑧	$x = \pm 1, \pm i$
	⑨	$x = 0 \text{(double)}, -3, \dfrac{3 \pm 3\sqrt{3}i}{2}$
	⑩	$x = \dfrac{3}{2}, \dfrac{-3 - 3\sqrt{3}i}{4}$
	⑪	$x = \pm 2, 1 \pm \sqrt{3}i, -1 \pm \sqrt{3}i$
	⑫	$x = \pm 1, \dfrac{1 \pm \sqrt{3}i}{2}, \dfrac{-1 \pm \sqrt{3}i}{2}$
Ex2.	①	$x = -1, -5, 2$
	②	$x = 1, -5, -11$
	③	$x = 2, \pm 2i$
	④	$x = -1, \pm 3i$
	⑤	$x = 1, -2, -1 \pm \sqrt{2}i$
	⑥	$x = -1 \text{(double)}, 1, 6$
	⑦	$x = 1, 2, \pm 2i$

Answers
6. Rational Expressions

6.1 Rational Expressions

Ex1.	①	$\dfrac{x^2}{2} + \dfrac{3x}{2}$
	②	$\dfrac{y^2}{2} - \dfrac{3y}{2}$
	③	$-\dfrac{x+y}{y-x} \left(= \dfrac{x+y}{x-y} \right)$
	④	$\dfrac{x+a}{x-a}$
	⑤	$-\dfrac{1}{y-x} \left(= \dfrac{1}{x-y} \right)$
	⑥	$\dfrac{a}{a-b}$
	⑦	$\dfrac{x-3}{x+7}$
	⑧	$\dfrac{3t+5}{2t+1}$
	⑨	$\dfrac{z(3-z)}{2z-5}$
	⑩	$\dfrac{4y-3}{3y+2}$
	⑪	$\dfrac{x^2+1}{x^2}$
	⑫	$\dfrac{x-a}{x+a}$
	⑬	$\dfrac{c^2 - cd + d^2}{c+d}$
	⑭	$\dfrac{x-3y}{x^2 + xy + y^2}$

Ex2.	①	$\dfrac{x-1}{x+1}$
	②	$\dfrac{t^2+1}{t+1}$
	③	$\dfrac{(a-2b)(a+2b)}{(a+b)(a-b)}$
	④	$\dfrac{x^2+y^2}{(x+y)(x-y)}$
	⑤	$\dfrac{x+y-4}{x+y+4}$
	⑥	$\dfrac{x+y-1}{x+y+1}$
	⑦	$\dfrac{x-y-2}{x+y-2}$
	⑧	$\dfrac{x-y+3}{x+y+3}$
Ex3.	①	$\dfrac{1}{6}$
	②	9900
	③	28
	④	$\dfrac{1}{12}$
	⑤	$\dfrac{1}{n+1}$
	⑥	$(n+2)(n+1)$
	⑦	$(3n+3)(3n+2)(3n+1)$
	⑧	$(2n+2)(2n+1)$
	⑨	3
	⑩	4
	⑪	$\dfrac{1}{(n+1)^n}$
	⑫	$\dfrac{1}{(n+2)^n}$

6.2 Multiplying and Dividing Rational Expressions

Ex1.	①	$\dfrac{p^2}{4q^2}$
	②	$\dfrac{10}{a^3b^2}$
	③	$\dfrac{1}{2}$
	④	$\dfrac{b}{3}$
	⑤	$-\dfrac{(t+5)}{(t-3)}$
	⑥	$t-2$
	⑦	$x+3$
	⑧	x^2
	⑨	$(x-y)(x^2-xy+y^2)$
	⑩	$\dfrac{x^2+xy+y^2}{x^2+y^2}$
Ex2.		1

6.3 Sum and Difference of Rational Expressions

Ex1.	①	$42x^2y^2z^3$
	②	$280ab^4c^3$
	③	$(x+1)(x-1)(x+4)$
	④	$2a(a+1)$
	⑤	$x^2(x+3)^2(x+1)$
	⑥	$(3b-2)^2(b+4)$

Ex2.	①	$\dfrac{3x^2-10y}{5x^3y^2}$
	②	$\dfrac{(r+s)(r-s)}{r^3s^3}$
	③	$\dfrac{c^2+a^2+b^2}{abc}$
	④	$\dfrac{z+x-y}{xyz}$
	⑤	$\dfrac{2}{z}$
	⑥	$-\dfrac{2}{c}$
	⑦	$\dfrac{-4xy}{(x+y)^2(x-y)^2}$
	⑧	$\dfrac{2x}{(x+y)(x-y)}$
	⑨	$\dfrac{x^2+5x-4}{(x+1)(x-1)}$
	⑩	$\dfrac{6(b-1)}{(b+3)(b-3)}$
	⑪	$\dfrac{2}{x(x+2)(x-2)}$
	⑫	$\dfrac{2x}{(x-2)^2(x+2)}$
	⑬	$\dfrac{t^2-2t+2}{t(t-1)^2(t-2)}$
	⑭	$\dfrac{x^2+1}{x(x+1)(x-1)^2}$
	⑮	$\dfrac{-25a+150}{a(a+5)(a-5)}$
	⑯	$\dfrac{5m^2-7m-32}{m(m-10)}$
	⑰	$\dfrac{2a}{a-b}$
	⑱	$\dfrac{-2a^2}{(a+b)^2}$
	⑲	$\dfrac{-x+y}{(x+y+2)(x-y+2)}$
	⑳	$\dfrac{a}{(a-1)(a^2+1)}$
Ex3.	0	

6.4 Complex Fractions

Ex1.	①	$\dfrac{xyz}{a^4}$
	②	$\dfrac{ayc^7}{b}$
	③	$(x-1)^2$
	④	$\dfrac{2(a+10)}{a(3a-1)}$
	⑤	$\dfrac{1}{(a+b)^2(a^2-ab+b^2)}$
	⑥	$\dfrac{x(x+1)^2(x^2+1)}{(x-1)^2(x^2+x+1)}$
	⑦	$\dfrac{2x^2}{x+2}$
	⑧	$x(x-1)$
	⑨	$\dfrac{x+2}{x-3}$
	⑩	$\dfrac{2}{5x}$
Ex2.	①	$-ab$
	②	$\dfrac{b+a}{ab}$

	③	$\dfrac{1-x+x^2}{x}$
	④	$\dfrac{x^2+1}{x}$
	⑤	$\dfrac{y+x}{y-x}$
	⑥	$\dfrac{y+x}{2y+x}$
	⑦	$\dfrac{x-1}{x+1}$
	⑧	$\dfrac{x-1}{x}$
	⑨	$\dfrac{x^2+y^2}{2xy}$
	⑩	$\dfrac{x-y}{x+y}$
	⑪	$2x+1$
	⑫	$1-a$
Ex3.	①	$\dfrac{(n+3)(n+2)(n+1)}{3}$
	②	$\dfrac{4}{(n+2)(n+1)}$
	③	$(n+1)^{n-1}$
	④	$n(n+1)$

6.5 Rational Equations and Word Problems

Ex1.	①	$x=20$
	②	$x=5,-6$
	③	$x=5$
	④	$a=6$
	⑤	$x=1$
	⑥	$x=\dfrac{39}{14}$
	⑦	$y=17$
	⑧	$c=-11$
	⑨	$x=-5,-7$
	⑩	$x=-5$
Ex2.	$x=3$	
Ex3.	two numbers: $x, x+1$ $\dfrac{1}{x}-\dfrac{1}{x+1}=\dfrac{1}{2} \Rightarrow x=1\ or\ -2$ $1, 2\ or\ -2, -1$	
Ex4.	5 friends	
Ex5.	6 mph	
Ex6.	2 mph	
Ex7.	x : speed when albert walk	

	d =	r ·	t
jog	30	$x+5$	$\dfrac{30}{x+5}$
walk	5	x	$\dfrac{5}{x}$

$\dfrac{30}{x+5}+\dfrac{5}{x}=6 \Rightarrow x=\dfrac{5}{2}\ or\ -\dfrac{5}{3}$

Answer: $\dfrac{5}{2}+5=\dfrac{15}{2}$ mph

Ex8.	40 mph
Ex9.	$\dfrac{5\sqrt{2}}{2}$ km/h

Ex10.	k : speed when Karl swimming in still water

	$d =$	$r \cdot$	t
against current	30	$k-4$	$\dfrac{30}{k-4}$
with current	20	$k+4$	$\dfrac{20}{k+4}$

$\dfrac{30}{k-4} + \dfrac{20}{k+4} = 5 \Rightarrow k = 12 \text{ or } -2$

Answer: 12+4 = 16 mph

Ex11.	$\dfrac{200}{3}$ mph

Ex12.	x : speed of last 70% of trip

	$d =$	$r \cdot$	t
first 30% of trip	30	90	$\dfrac{30}{90}$
last 70% of trip	70	x	$\dfrac{70}{x}$

$60 = \dfrac{100}{\dfrac{30}{90} + \dfrac{70}{x}} \Rightarrow x = \dfrac{105}{2}$

Answer: $\dfrac{105}{2}$ km/h

Ex13.	20 days

Ex14.	x : time for Anthony to work alone

	$d =$	$r \cdot$	t
Anthony	1	$\dfrac{1}{x}$	x
Britney	1	$\dfrac{1}{10}$	10
together	1	$\dfrac{1}{6}$	6

$\dfrac{1}{x} + \dfrac{1}{10} = \dfrac{1}{6} \Rightarrow x = 15$

Answer: 15 hrs

Ex15.	10 hrs

Ex16.	x : time for pipe C to work alone

	$d =$	$r \cdot$	t
pipe A	1	$\dfrac{1}{5}$	5
pipe B	1	$\dfrac{1}{x-2}$	$x-2$
pipe C	1	$\dfrac{1}{x}$	x
together	1	$\dfrac{1}{3}$	3

$\dfrac{1}{5} + \dfrac{1}{x-2} - \dfrac{1}{x} = \dfrac{1}{3} \Rightarrow x = 5 \text{ or} -3$

Answer: 5 hrs

Ex17.	20 days

6.6 Graph of Rational Functions

Ex1.	①	D : $x \neq 5, 2$
		V·A : $x = -5$ and $x = 2$
		hole : none
		H·A : $y = 0$
	②	D : $x \neq -3$
		V·A : $x = -3$
		hole : none
		H·A : none
	③	D : $x \neq 0, 4$
		V·A : $x = 0$
		hole : at $x = 4$
		H·A : $y = 1$
	④	D : $x \neq \dfrac{1}{3}, -2$
		V·A : $x = -2$
		hole : at $x = \dfrac{1}{3}$
		H·A : $y = 0$

	⑤	D: $x \neq 1, 5$
		V·A: $x = 5$
		hole: at $x = 1$
		H·A: $y = 0$
	⑥	D: $x \neq -7, 1$
		V·A: $x = -7, 1$
		hole: none
		H·A: $y = 1$
	⑦	D: $x \neq -\dfrac{1}{2}, 5$
		V·A: $x = 5$
		hole: at $x = -\dfrac{1}{2}$
		H·A: none
	⑧	D: $x \neq 1, -\dfrac{2}{3}$
		V·A: $x = -\dfrac{2}{3}$
		hole: at $x = 1$
		H·A: none
	⑨	D: $x \neq -\dfrac{1}{2}$
		V·A: none
		hole: at $x = -\dfrac{1}{2}$
		H·A: $y = 0$
	⑩	D: $x \neq 1$
		V·A: none
		hole: at $x = 1$
		H·A: $y = 0$
Ex2.	①	$(2, 0)(-2, 0)$
	②	$(-8, 0)(3, 0)$
	③	$(-1, 0)$
	④	$(2, 0)$

	⑤	$(-2, 0)$
	⑥	none
Ex3.	① D	② C
	③ B	④ A
Ex4.	Both have same shape, but $y = \dfrac{x^2 - 1}{x + 1}$ has a hole at $x = -1$.	

Answers

7. Radicals

7.1 Roots of Real Numbers

Ex1.
① a) 3 b) –3
c) none d) 0.03
② a) 10 b) none
c) –10 d) 10
③ a) 0.9 b) –0.9
c) none d) 0.3
④ a) 0.8 b) none
c) –0.8 d) 0.4
⑤ a) 3 b) –3
c) 3 d) –0.3
⑥ a) 5 b) 5
c) –5 d) 0.5
⑦ a) 4 b) –5
c) 2 d) 3
⑧ a) –6 b) 2
c) 5 d) 4
⑨ a) none b) –2
c) 2 d) 2
⑩ a) none b) none
c) –2 d) –2
⑪ a) $\dfrac{5}{3}$ b) $\dfrac{4}{9}$
c) $\dfrac{1}{3}$ d) $\dfrac{2}{3}$
⑫ a) $\dfrac{13}{8}$ b) 2
c) $\dfrac{1}{4}$ d) $\dfrac{1}{2}$
⑬ a) 3 b) 3^2
c) 3^6 d) 3^{12}
⑭ a) 4 b) 4^3
c) 4^5 d) 4^{50}
⑮ a) 3 b) 3
c) none d) 3
⑯ a) 6 b) none
c) 6 d) 6
⑰ a) 3 b) –3
c) –3 d) –0.09
⑱ a) 6 b) –6
c) –6 d) –0.36
⑲ a) 8 b) –8
c) 8 d) –8
⑳ a) 3 b) –3
c) 3 d) –3

Ex2.
① $12|p^3||q^9|$
② $11|x^3||y^7|$
③ $-10|a|b^2|c^3|$
④ $-12a^4|b^5|c^6$
⑤ $\dfrac{4a^2b^4}{5c^6}$
⑥ $\dfrac{15|a^7|}{8|c^3||b|}$
⑦ $-2x^5y^7z^2$
⑧ $6mn^4p^5$
⑨ $2|x^3|y^4z^6$
⑩ $3|x||y^5||z^7|$
⑪ $|2x-1|$
⑫ $|x+5|$
⑬ $(5m+4)^2$

	⑭	$(7m-2)^3$
	⑮	$\|6x-1\|$
	⑯	$\|x-5\|$
Ex3.	11	
Ex4.	① $x-2$	② $2-y$
	③ $2x-1$	④ $c-2$
	⑤ 4	⑥ $x+6$
	⑦ $-2x+3$	⑧ 4
	⑨ $2y-x$	⑩ $2a-2b$
	⑪ $2-a$	

7.2 Properties of Radicals

Ex1.	①	a) $2\sqrt{2}$	b) $4\sqrt{3}$
		c) $5\sqrt{10}$	
	②	a) $2\sqrt{6}$	b) $4\sqrt{2}$
		c) $8\sqrt{2}$	
	③	a) 2	b) $2\sqrt[3]{2}$
		c) $5\sqrt[3]{2}$	
	④	a) $2\sqrt[3]{3}$	b) 4
		c) $4\sqrt[3]{3}$	
	⑤	a) 2	b) $2\sqrt[4]{2}$
		c) $2\sqrt[4]{3}$	
	⑥	a) 3	b) $3\sqrt[4]{2}$
		c) 4	
	⑦	a) $2\sqrt[5]{2}$	b) $2\sqrt[6]{3}$
Ex2.	①	$5p^3\|q^3\|\sqrt{3p}$	
	②	$3x^2y\sqrt{5xy}$	
	③	$8a^2b^3c^5\sqrt{2bc}$	
	④	$8a\|b^3\|c^4\sqrt{2ac}$	
	⑤	$\dfrac{5\|a\|}{\|c^7\|}\sqrt{2b}$	
	⑥	$\dfrac{6a^4}{\|c\|b^4}\sqrt{3a}$	
	⑦	$3ab^2\sqrt[3]{2ab}$	
	⑧	$4x^3y^2\sqrt[3]{x^2y}$	
	⑨	$2x^3y^6z\sqrt[3]{3y^2z}$	
	⑩	$3m^2np^2\sqrt[3]{3n^2p^2}$	
	⑪	$\dfrac{5a^2b^2}{c^4}\sqrt[3]{ab^2}$	
	⑫	$\dfrac{2a^5}{c^2b^3}\sqrt[3]{\dfrac{4}{c^2b^2}}$	
	⑬	$3\|x\|yz^3\sqrt[4]{2x^2yz}$	
	⑭	$2x^2\|y^5z\|\sqrt[4]{2xz^2}$	
	⑮	$a^2b^3c^4\sqrt[5]{ac^2}$	
	⑯	$\|x\|y^2z\sqrt[6]{x^4z}$	
Ex3.	① $7\sqrt{30}$	② $25\sqrt{2}$
	③ $3\sqrt[3]{10}$	④ $4\sqrt[3]{3}$
	⑤ $\dfrac{\sqrt{22}}{11}$	⑥ $\dfrac{\sqrt{26}}{4}$
	⑦ $\dfrac{\sqrt{21}}{3}$	⑧ $\dfrac{\sqrt{55}}{5}$
	⑨ $\dfrac{\sqrt[3]{63}}{3}$	⑩ $\dfrac{\sqrt[3]{180}}{6}$
	⑪ $\dfrac{\sqrt[3]{99}}{3}$	⑫ $\dfrac{\sqrt[3]{18}}{2}$
	⑬ $\dfrac{\sqrt[4]{40}}{2}$	⑭ $\dfrac{\sqrt[4]{12}}{2}$
Ex4.	I. T II. F III. F IV. F V. T	

7.3 Operation of Radicals

Ex1.
1. $\sqrt{3}$
2. 0
3. $\sqrt[3]{2} - 3$
4. $5\sqrt[3]{4} + 4$
5. $\dfrac{4\sqrt{6}}{3}$
6. $\dfrac{\sqrt{15} + \sqrt{35}}{5}$
7. $8 + 2\sqrt{6}$
8. $22\sqrt{6} - 33\sqrt{5}$
9. $7\sqrt{2}$
10. $40 - 5\sqrt{14}$
11. -6
12. -4
13. 1
14. -1
15. 2
16. 17
17. $15 + 4\sqrt{11}$
18. $16 - 6\sqrt{7}$
19. $45 - 12\sqrt{14}$
20. $17 + 4\sqrt{15}$

Ex2.
1. $\dfrac{25\sqrt{6}}{4}$
2. $\dfrac{60 - 3\sqrt{15}}{20}$
3. $\sqrt{10} + 2\sqrt{2}$
4. $5(\sqrt{2} + 1)$
5. $2\sqrt{2} - 3$
6. $-9 - 4\sqrt{5}$
7. $\dfrac{17 + \sqrt{3}}{13}$
8. $\dfrac{8 + 5\sqrt{2}}{2}$

Ex3.
1. $5 + x - 2\sqrt{5x}$
2. $x + 4 + 4\sqrt{x}$
3. $x + 2\sqrt{x - 1}$
4. $x + 3 + 2\sqrt{2x + 2}$
5. -1
6. y
7. $2x^2 + 2x$
8. $2x + 2$
9. $4\sqrt{xy}$
10. $-4\sqrt{x}$
11. $\dfrac{\sqrt{x} - \sqrt{2}}{x - 2}$
12. $\dfrac{\sqrt{5} + \sqrt{x}}{5 - x}$
13. $\sqrt{x^4 - x^2}\ (= |x|\sqrt{x^2 - 1})$
14. $\sqrt{x^2 - y^2}$
15. $\sqrt{x + 1} + \sqrt{x}$
16. $\dfrac{\sqrt{x + 2} - \sqrt{x}}{2}$
17. $\dfrac{x + \sqrt{x^2 - y^2}}{y}$
18. $-x^2 - \sqrt{x^4 - 1}$

Ex4.
1. $2\sqrt{3}$
2. $4\sqrt{21}$
3. $16\sqrt{5}$
4. 4

Ex5.
1. 0
2. 7

Ex6. $-4x - 2$

Ex7. -1

Ex8. 2

7.4 Radical Equations

Ex1.	① $x = 16$	② $x = 7$
	③ $\varnothing$	④ $x = -2$
	⑤ $x = -3$	⑥ $x = 10$
	⑦ $x = 3$	⑧ $x = 0, 2$
	⑨ $x = 5, 8$	⑩ $x = 3, -1$
	⑪ $x = -2$	⑫ $x = -1$
	⑬ $x = -1$	⑭ $x = \sqrt{13}$
Ex2.	$x = \dfrac{4}{3}$	
Ex3.	$x = 0, 9$	
Ex4.	① $1 \leq x < 10$	
	② $-2 \leq x \leq 23$	
	③ $x \geq -\dfrac{1}{5}$	
	④ $x > 11$	
	⑤ $3 \leq x \leq 12$	

7.5 Graph of Radical Functions

Ex1. ① D: $x \geq 0$,   R: $y \geq 0$

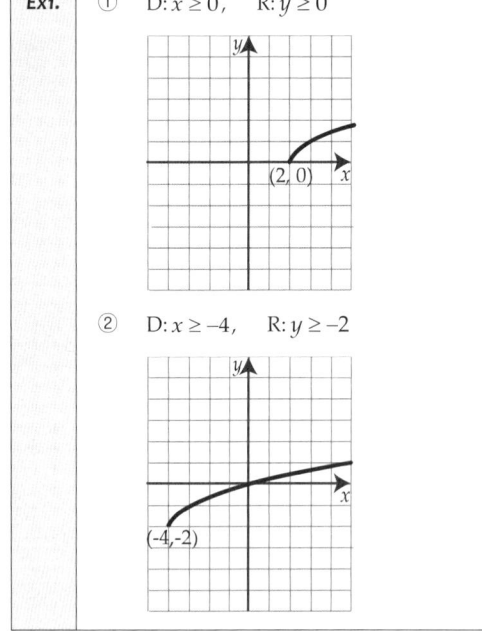

② D: $x \geq -4$,   R: $y \geq -2$

③ D: $x \geq 1$,   R: $y \leq 0$

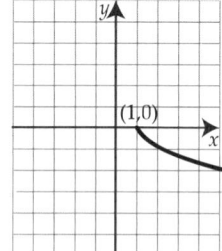

④ D: $x \geq -2$,   R: $y \leq 0$

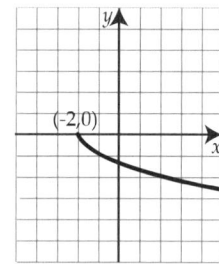

⑤ D: $x \leq 0$,   R: $y \geq 0$

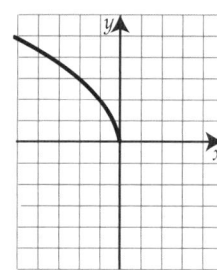

⑥ D: $x \leq 0$,   R: $y \geq 0$

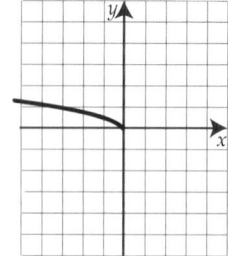

⑦ D: $x \geq -2$, R: $y \geq 1$

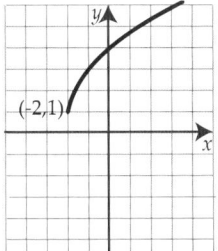

⑧ D: $x \geq -3$, R: $y \leq 1$

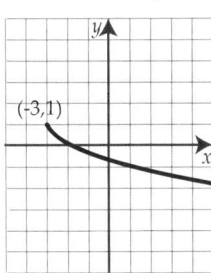

⑨ D: $x \leq -1$, R: $y \geq 0$

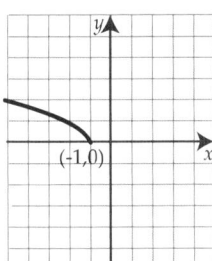

⑩ D: $x \leq 3$, R: $y \geq 0$

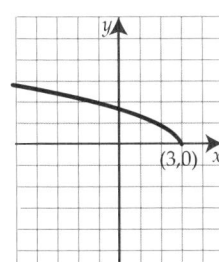

Ex2.	① a) $\mathbb{R}$, $x \leq 4$	b) $\mathbb{R}$
	c) $\mathbb{R}$, $-2 \leq x \leq 2$	d) $\mathbb{R}$
	② a) $\mathbb{R}$, $x \geq 1$	b) $\mathbb{R}$
	c) $\mathbb{R}$, $x \leq -1$ or $x \geq 1$	
	d) $\mathbb{R}$	

	③ a) $\mathbb{R}$, $x \geq -2$	b) $\mathbb{R}$
	c) $\mathbb{R}$, $x \leq -2$ or $x \geq 1$	
	④ a) $\mathbb{R}$, $x \geq 3$	b) $\mathbb{R}$
	c) $\mathbb{R}$, $x \leq -4$ or $x \geq 3$	

7.6 Rational and Real Exponents

Ex1.	① $\sqrt[6]{3}$	② $\sqrt[5]{8}$
	③ $\sqrt[3]{a^2}$	④ $\sqrt[7]{b^4}$
	⑤ $\sqrt[4]{x^6}$	⑥ $\sqrt[7]{n^{10}}$

Ex2.	① 4	② 3
	③ $\dfrac{1}{9}$	④ $\dfrac{1}{4}$
	⑤ 2^{18}	⑥ $\dfrac{1}{3^8}$
	⑦ 25	⑧ 81
	⑨ $\dfrac{16}{25}$	⑩ 64
	⑪ $\dfrac{1}{3}$	

Ex3.	① $a^{\frac{5}{6}}$	② $a^{\frac{7}{12}}$
	③ $c^{\frac{7}{5}}$	④ $a^{\frac{46}{15}}$
	⑤ $q^{\frac{11}{6}}$	⑥ $p^{\frac{13}{8}}$
	⑦ $a^{\frac{7}{2}}$	⑧ $b^{\frac{31}{5}}$
	⑨ $a^{\frac{11}{6}} b^{\frac{11}{6}}$	⑩ $m^{\frac{5}{3}} n^{\frac{5}{2}}$
	⑪ $a^{\frac{1}{12}}$	⑫ $\dfrac{1}{a^{\frac{2}{35}}}$
	⑬ $x^{\frac{5}{12}}$	⑭ $\dfrac{1}{x^{\frac{4}{15}}}$
	⑮ $x^{\frac{7}{6}} y^{\frac{13}{3}}$	⑯ $m^{\frac{7}{10}} n^{\frac{3}{20}}$

Ex4.	① $a^{\frac{1}{6}}$	② $a^{\frac{1}{6}}$
	③ $a^{\frac{3}{4}}$	④ $a^{\frac{1}{2}}$
	⑤ $a^{\frac{1}{30}}$	⑥ $a^{\frac{1}{8}}$
	⑦ $a^{\frac{2}{3}}$	⑧ $a^{\frac{7}{4}}$
	⑨ $a^{\frac{7}{4}}$	⑩ $a^{\frac{9}{4}}$
Ex5.	① $x=5$	② $d=6$
	③ $m=31$	④ $x=-25$
	⑤ $y=265$	⑥ $x=\frac{83}{7}$
Ex6.	① $a^{2\sqrt{3}}$	② x^2
	③ b	④ t^2
	⑤ $x^{\sqrt{3}}$	⑥ $\frac{1}{x^4}$
	⑦ 2	⑧ $\sqrt{2}^{2\sqrt{2}}\ (=2^{\sqrt{2}})$
	⑨ 1	⑩ $a^{\frac{3\sqrt{2}}{2}}$
	⑪ $\frac{1}{a^{\frac{\sqrt{5}}{5}}}$	⑫ $a^{\frac{\sqrt{2}}{4}}$
Ex7.	① $\sqrt[3]{x^2}+2x+\sqrt[3]{x^4}$	
	② $x+2\sqrt[6]{x^5}+\sqrt[3]{x^2}$	
	③ $\sqrt{x}-2+\frac{1}{\sqrt{x}}$	
	④ $x-2+\frac{1}{x}$	
	⑤ $\sqrt[3]{x^4}-\sqrt{y^3}$	
	⑥ $\sqrt{x^3}-\sqrt[3]{y^5}$	
	⑦ $x^2-\frac{1}{x^2}$	
	⑧ $\frac{1}{x^2}-x^2$	
	⑨ $x^2-\frac{1}{x^2}$	

Ex8.	$B<C<A$
Ex9.	B

Answers

8. Exponential and Logarithm

8.1 Composite Function

Ex1.	① $2\sqrt{x}+3$	② $\sqrt{2x+3}$
	③ x^2+1	④ $\sqrt{x^4+1}$
	⑤ $\sqrt[4]{x}$	⑥ $4x+9$
	⑦ 3	⑧ 7
	⑨ $4x+12\sqrt{x}+10$	⑩ $\sqrt{x^4+2x^2+2}$
	⑪ $2x+5$	
Ex2.	① 11	② 10
	③ 6	④ 6
	⑤ 13	⑥ 6
Ex3.	1	
Ex4.	$h(x)=(x+4)^2$	

8.2 Inverse Function

Ex1.	① $f^{-1}\{(0,6),(1,-1),(2,-3),(3,-5)\}$
	Function
	② $f^{-1}\{(0,-2),(0,0),(0,4),(0,7)\}$
	Not function
	③ $f^{-1}\{(5,-7),(7,-5),(5,6),(9,-6)\}$
	Not function

	④ $f^{-1}\{(2,1),(3,2),(4,3),(5,4)\}$ Function	
Ex2.	① 6	② 4
	③ 10	④ 3
	⑤ −4	⑥ 1
	⑦ 4	⑧ 10
	⑨ 11	⑩ 4
Ex3.	① $f^{-1}(x) = \dfrac{x-7}{6}$	
	② $f^{-1}(x) = \dfrac{4}{x}$	
	③ $f^{-1}(x) = \dfrac{1}{2}\left(\sqrt[3]{2x-4}+3\right)$	
	④ $f^{-1}(x) = \left(\dfrac{x}{2}\right)^3 - 1$	
	⑤ $f^{-1}(x) = \sqrt{x-1}$	
	⑥ $f^{-1}(x) = \sqrt{x+5}$	
	⑦ $f^{-1}(x) = 2 - \sqrt{x-3}$	
	⑧ $f^{-1}(x) = 3 + \sqrt{\dfrac{x}{2}}$	
	⑨ $f^{-1}(x) = \dfrac{-3x-6}{7x+2}$	
	⑩ $f^{-1}(x) = \dfrac{2x+4}{x+3}$	
	⑪ $f^{-1}(x) = \dfrac{3x}{2-x}$	
	⑫ $f^{-1}(x) = \dfrac{-2x}{x+3}$	
Ex4.	① Inverse	
	② Inverse	
	③ Not Inverse	
	④ Inverse	
	⑤ Not Inverse	

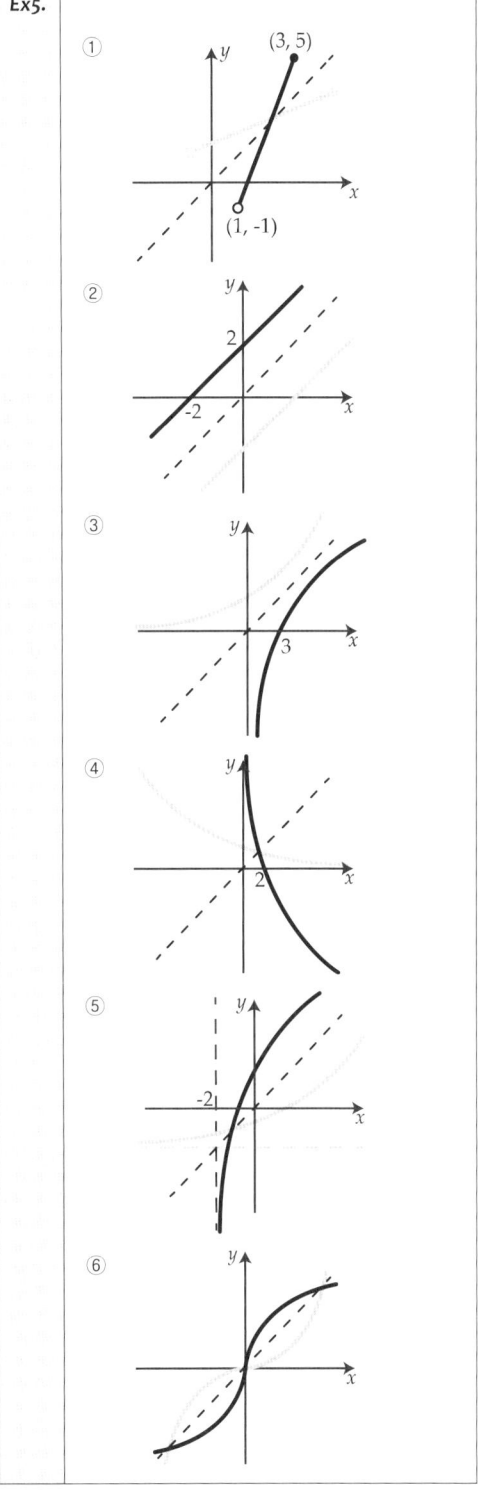

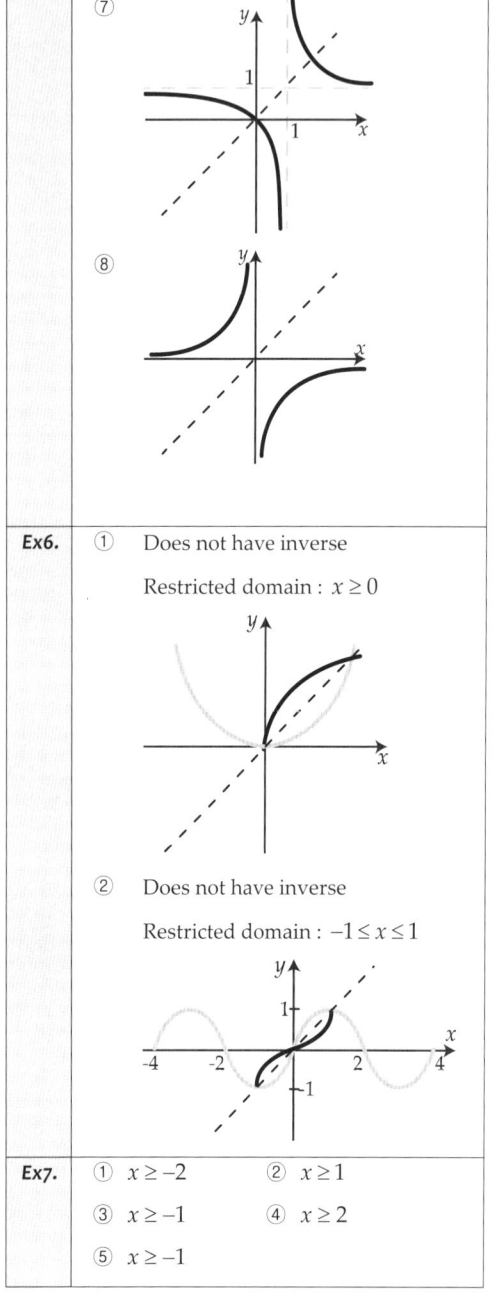

Ex6.	①	Does not have inverse Restricted domain: $x \geq 0$
	②	Does not have inverse Restricted domain: $-1 \leq x \leq 1$
Ex7.	① $x \geq -2$ ② $x \geq 1$ ③ $x \geq -1$ ④ $x \geq 2$ ⑤ $x \geq -1$	

8.3 Exponential Function

Ex1. ① Asymptote: $y = 0$

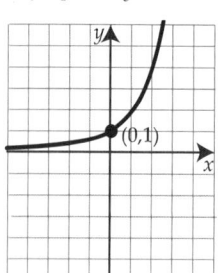

② Asymptote: $y = 0$

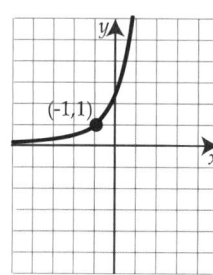

③ Asymptote: $y = 3$

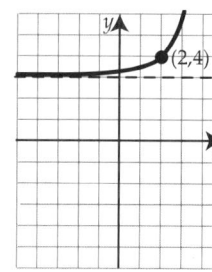

④ Asymptote: $y = 2$

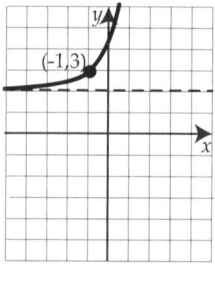

⑤ Asymptote: $y = 1$

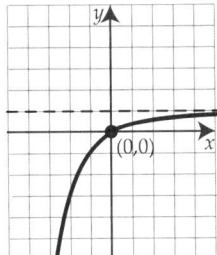

⑥ Asymptote: $y = 1$

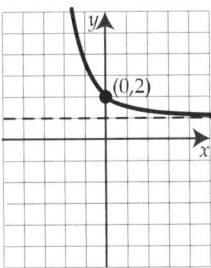

⑦ Asymptote: $y = 0$

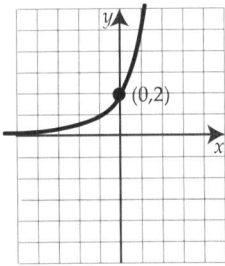

⑧ Asymptote: $y = 0$

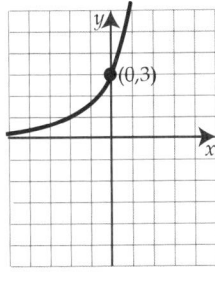

⑨ Asymptote: $y = 0$

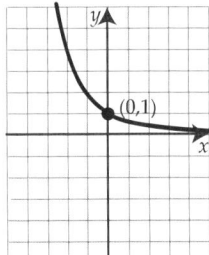

⑩ Asymptote: $y = 1$

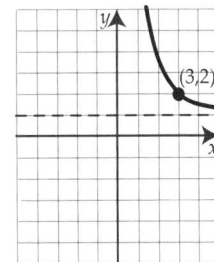

⑪ Asymptote: $y = 1$

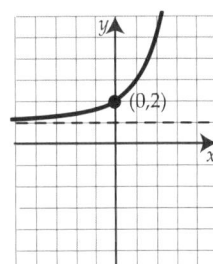

⑫ Asymptote: $y = 0$

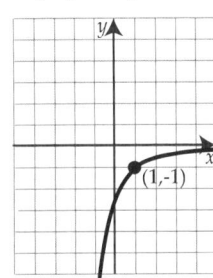

Ex2.

① $y = 5(3)^x$

② $y = -4x - 2$

③ $y = \dfrac{3}{2}x + 7$

	④	$y = 10(2)^x$
	⑤	$y = 8(2)^x$
	⑥	$y = 3(3)^x$
	⑦	$y = 64\left(\dfrac{1}{2}\right)^x$
	⑧	$y = 45\left(\dfrac{1}{\sqrt{3}}\right)^x$
Ex3.	①	linear
	②	linear
	③	exponential
	④	exponential
	⑤	exponential
	⑥	linear
	⑦	linear
	⑧	exponential
	⑨	exponential
	⑩	exponential

8.4 Definition of Logarithm

Ex1.	① $x = 5$	② $x = 5$
	③ $x = -2$	④ $x = -2$
	⑤ $x = -2$	⑥ $x = -1$
	⑦ $x = \dfrac{1}{2}$	⑧ $x = \dfrac{1}{2}$
	⑨ $x = 5$	⑩ $x = \dfrac{1}{4}$
	⑪ $x = 125$	⑫ $x = 4$
	⑬ $x = 6$	

Ex2.	① 0	② 3
	③ 2	④ 0
	⑤ -3	⑥ -4
	⑦ x	⑧ y
	⑨ -2	⑩ -4
	⑪ $\dfrac{1}{2}$	⑫ $\dfrac{1}{4}$
	⑬ $\dfrac{2}{3}$	⑭ $\dfrac{3}{5}$
	⑮ 8	⑯ 5
	⑰ $\sqrt{x}$	⑱ x^2
	⑲ $\dfrac{1}{8}$	⑳ 27

Ex3.	① 6, 7	② 2, 3
	③ 3, 4	④ 9, 10
	⑤ 3, 4	

Ex4.	①	$1000 = 10^3$
	②	$\dfrac{1}{8} = 10^x$
	③	$x = \log_5 4000$
	④	$\dfrac{1}{2} = \log_6 x$
	⑤	$27 = 3^3$
	⑥	$x^2 = 10^a$
	⑦	$x = \log 2$
	⑧	$2z = \log a$
	⑨	$x^2 - x = \log_2 3$
	⑩	$4x^2 = \log_5 7$
	⑪	$x^y = 10^2$

Ex5.	①	$y = 2^x$
	②	$y = 10^x$
	③	$y = 10^{\frac{x+5}{3}} - 1$

	④	$y = 4^{\frac{x-4}{2}} \; (= 2^{x-4})$
	⑤	$y = \log_3 x$
	⑥	$y = \log_8 x + 1$
	⑦	$y = \log_5(x-2) + 1$
	⑧	$y = \log(x-1) - 2$
Ex6.	①	Asymptote: $x = 0$ 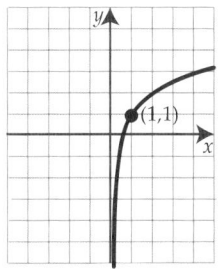
	②	Asymptote: $x = -1$ 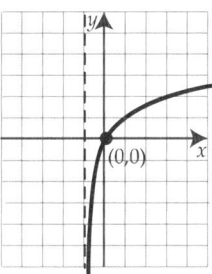
	③	Asymptote: $x = -1$ 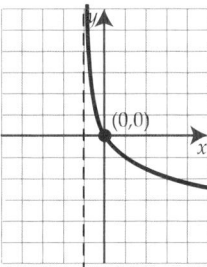

	④	Asymptote: $x = 0$ 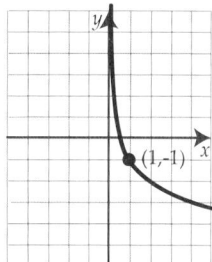
	⑤	Asymptote: $x = 1$ 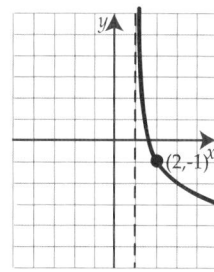
	⑥	Asymptote: $x = -2$ 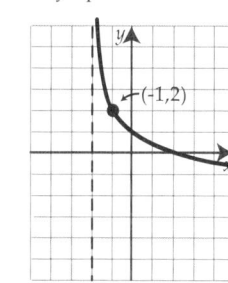
Ex7.	8	
Ex8.	2^{10}	

8.5 Laws of Logarithms

Ex1.	①	1
	②	1
	③	5
	④	2
	⑤	$\log \dfrac{16}{3}$
	⑥	0

Answers 617

	⑦	$\log \dfrac{1}{x^2 y z^4}$
	⑧	$\log \dfrac{xy^2}{z}$
	⑨	$\log_3 \dfrac{x^5}{y^2}$
	⑩	$\log_5 \dfrac{x^2 y^4}{z^6}$
	⑪	$\log \dfrac{\sqrt{xy}}{\sqrt[3]{z^2}}$
	⑫	$\log \dfrac{\sqrt[4]{x^3}}{\sqrt{yz}}$
	⑬	$\log_6 \dfrac{x-1}{x+1}$
	⑭	$\log \dfrac{x-3}{(x+1)^2}$
	⑮	$\dfrac{\log 6}{\log 4}$
	⑯	$\dfrac{\log 5}{\log 2}$
	⑰	25
	⑱	x^3
	⑲	36
	⑳	2
	㉑	$\log 100 x^5$
	㉒	$\log_2 \dfrac{2}{x^3}$
Ex2.	①	$\log x + 3\log y$
	②	$3\log x + 3\log y$
	③	$\dfrac{1}{3}\log x + \dfrac{1}{3}\log y$
	④	$\log x + \dfrac{1}{2}\log y$
	⑤	$\dfrac{1}{2}\log x + \dfrac{1}{4}\log y + \dfrac{3}{4}\log z$

	⑥	$2 + \dfrac{3}{2}\log x + \dfrac{1}{2}\log y$
	⑦	$1 + 2\log y - \dfrac{1}{2}\log z$
	⑧	$\dfrac{2}{3}\log x - 3\log y - \log z$
	⑨	$\dfrac{1}{2}\log x + \dfrac{1}{4}\log y$
	⑩	$-\log x - \dfrac{1}{2}\log y$
Ex3.	① $a+b$	② $2a$
	③ $a-b$	④ $b-a$
	⑤ $2a+2b$	⑥ $2a+b$
	⑦ $\dfrac{1}{3}a$	⑧ $\dfrac{1}{4}b$
	⑨ $-b$	⑩ $-3a$
	⑪ $3a-2b$	⑫ $2a-2b$
	⑬ $\dfrac{2a}{b}$	⑭ $\dfrac{3b}{a}$
	⑮ $\dfrac{a}{2}$	⑯ $2b$
Ex4.	I. False	II. False
	III. True	IV. False
	V. True	VI. False
	VII. False	VIII. True
Ex5.	$\log_3 2 \cdot \log_3 7$	
Ex6.	$\log(x+y) + \log(x-y)$	
Ex7.	6	
Ex8.	10!	

8.6 Log and Exp Equations

Ex1.
① $x = 24$
② $x = 1002$
③ $x = 3^{1024}$
④ $x = \dfrac{1}{100}$
⑤ $x = 27$
⑥ $x = 4$
⑦ $x = 1$
⑧ $x = 4$
⑨ $x = 3^{\frac{4}{3}}$
⑩ $x = \dfrac{1}{4}$
⑪ $x = \dfrac{7}{2}$
⑫ $x = \dfrac{5}{4}$
⑬ $x = 6$
⑭ $x = 1$
⑮ $\varnothing$
⑯ $x = 6$
⑰ $x = \pm\sqrt{3}$
⑱ $x = \pm 1$

Ex2.
① $x = 3$
② $x = -2$
③ $x = 3$
④ $x = -9$
⑤ $x = \dfrac{8}{7}$
⑥ $x = 12$
⑦ $x = \log_2 3 \ \left(= \dfrac{\log 3}{\log 2}\right)$
⑧ $x = \log_3 8 - 1 \ \left(= \dfrac{\log 8}{\log 3} - 1\right)$
⑨ $x = \dfrac{\log 6}{2\log 5}$
⑩ $x = \dfrac{1}{3}\left(\dfrac{\log 8}{\log 7} + 1\right)$
⑪ $x = \dfrac{\log 3 + 2\log 5}{\log 5 - 3\log 3}$
⑫ $x = \dfrac{\log 7 + \log 11}{\log 11 - 2\log 7}$
⑬ $x = \dfrac{\log 7}{2\log 7 + \log 2}$
⑭ $x = \dfrac{3\log 4}{\log 4 - 2\log 6}$

Ex3.
① $x = 10$ or 1000
② $x = 10^{\frac{5}{2}}$ or $\dfrac{1}{10}$

Ex4.
① $x = \log_3 4 \ \left(= \dfrac{\log 4}{\log 3}\right)$
② $x = \log_4 5 \ \left(= \dfrac{\log 5}{\log 4}\right)$
③ $x = 0, \ x = \log_5 4 \ \left(= \dfrac{\log 4}{\log 5}\right)$

8.7 The Natural Logarithm

Ex1.
① 0
② 7
③ -1
④ $-\dfrac{1}{2}$
⑤ $\dfrac{2}{5}$
⑥ $\dfrac{8}{3}$
⑦ $3x$
⑧ 12
⑨ x^2
⑩ $x^{\frac{3}{2}}$

Ex2.
① $20 = e^x$
② $\dfrac{1}{8} = e^x$
③ $x = \ln 4$
④ $\dfrac{1}{2} = \ln x$
⑤ $x^2 = e^y$
⑥ $x + 2 = \ln(y - 8)$

Ex3.
① Asymptote: $y = 0$

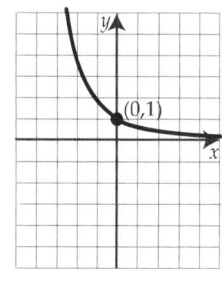

② Asymptote: $y = 1$

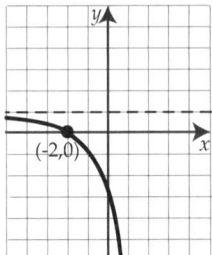

③ Asymptote: $y = -1$

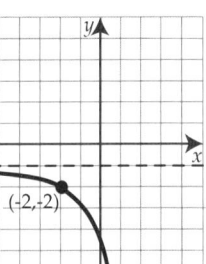

④ Asymptote: $y = -3$

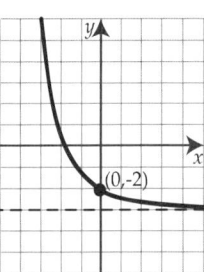

⑤ Asymptote: $x = 0$

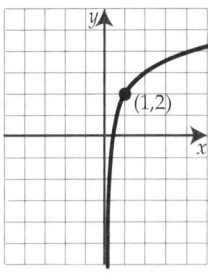

⑥ Asymptote: $x = 0$

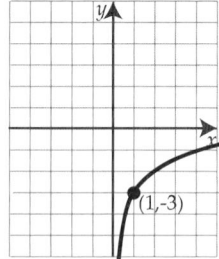

⑦ Asymptote: $x = -2$

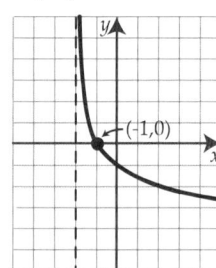

⑧ Asymptote: $x = 3$

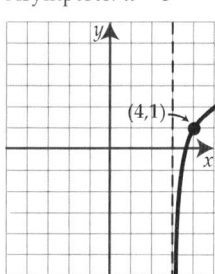

Ex4.

① $x = \ln 10 + 1$

② $x = \dfrac{\ln 9 + 1}{4}$

③ $x = 2\ln 4$

④ $x = \ln \dfrac{1}{2}$

⑤ $x = \dfrac{e^7 - 2}{3}$

⑥ $x = \dfrac{e^4 + 5}{3}$

	⑦	$x = e^e$
	⑧	$x = e^e$
	⑨	$x = e^2, e^{-2}$
	⑩	$x = 1, \dfrac{1}{e^2}$
	⑪	$x = 5$
	⑫	$x = 5$
	⑬	$\varnothing$
	⑭	$x = 2, 4$
Ex5.	① 7 ② x^2
	③ 3	
Ex6.	①	$x = \ln 2$
	②	$x = \ln 7, \ln 8$
	③	$x = 0, \ln 5$
	④	$x = \ln 3$

8.8 Exponential Growth and Modeling

Ex1.	①	$1078(2)^{\frac{t}{8}}$
	②	$420\left(\dfrac{1}{2}\right)^{\frac{t}{26}}$
	③	$416\left(\dfrac{1}{2}\right)^{\frac{t}{23}}$
	④	$1081(2)^{t}$
Ex2.	(a)	$1000(2)^{\frac{t}{3}}$
	(b)	$1000(2)^{5} = 32000$
	(c)	$\dfrac{3\log 200}{\log 2} \approx 22.932\, hrs$

Ex3.	$2^{\frac{t}{9}} = 400$
	$t = \dfrac{9\log 400}{\log 2} \approx 77.795\, days$
Ex4.	(a) $45\left(\dfrac{1}{2}\right)^{\frac{t}{20}}$
	(b) $45\left(\dfrac{1}{2}\right)^{\frac{26}{20}} \approx 18.276$
	(c) $\dfrac{20\log 0.1}{\log 0.5} \approx 66.439\, days$
Ex5.	$\dfrac{7\log 0.2}{\log 0.5} \approx 16.253\, days$
Ex6.	$0.5^{\frac{t}{1900}} = 0.3$
	$t = \dfrac{1900\log 0.3}{\log 0.5} \approx 3300\, years$
Ex7.	(a) $600e^{0.3t}$
	(b) $600e^{3} = 12051.322$
	(c) $t = \dfrac{\ln\dfrac{800}{6}}{0.3} \approx 16.310\, hrs$
Ex8.	$t = \dfrac{\ln 2}{0.1} \approx 6.931\, days$
Ex9.	$Pe^{0.04t} = 3P$
	$t = \dfrac{\ln 3}{0.04} \approx 27.465\, years$

Answers

9. Sequence and Series

9.1 Sequence and Series

Ex1.		
	①	22, 27
	②	$\dfrac{1}{16}, \dfrac{1}{32}$
	③	25, 36
	④	−8, −11
	⑤	1, 1000
	⑥	1, 81
	⑦	$2, 2^{\frac{5}{4}}$
	⑧	$2, 2^7$
Ex2.	①	5, 11, 29, 83
	②	−1, 0, 1, −2
	③	$-1, \dfrac{1}{2}, -\dfrac{1}{4}, \dfrac{1}{8}$
	④	$2, \dfrac{3}{2}, \dfrac{4}{3}, \dfrac{5}{4}$
	⑤	$\log 2, \log 3, \log 4, \log 5$
	⑥	$\log 2, \log 4, \log 8, \log 16$ $(= \log 2, 2\log 2, 3\log 2, 4\log 2)$
Ex3.	①	$a_n = \dfrac{n+1}{n}$
	②	$a_n = \dfrac{n}{n+5}$
	③	$a_n = (-1)^n$
	④	$a_n = (-1)^{n+1}$
	⑤	$a_n = (-1)^{n+1} 7n$
	⑥	$a_n = (-1)^n 2n$
	⑦	$a_n = n(2n-1)$
	⑧	$a_n = 2n(2n-1)$
	⑨	$a_n = \dfrac{1}{n^2}$
	⑩	$a_n = \dfrac{1}{\sqrt{n}}$
	⑪	$a_n = 2^{\frac{n}{4}}$
Ex4.	①	$3+6+9+12+15$
	②	$5^2 + 6^2 + 7^2 + 8^2$
	③	$5+5+5+5$
	④	$\pi + \pi + \pi$
	⑤	$2^2 + 3^2 + 4^2 + 5^2 + 6^2 + 7^2$
	⑥	$4(5)+5(6)+6(7)+7(8)+8(9)+9(10)$
	⑦	$-\dfrac{1}{6^2} + \dfrac{1}{6^3} - \dfrac{1}{6^4}$
	⑧	$\dfrac{5}{4} + \dfrac{5}{4}(2) + \dfrac{5}{4}(2)^2 + \dfrac{5}{4}(2)^3 + \dfrac{5}{4}(2)^4$
	⑨	$x^2 + x^3 + x^4 + x^5 + x^6$
	⑩	$a^2 + \dfrac{a^3}{2} + \dfrac{a^4}{3} + \dfrac{a^5}{4} + \cdots$
Ex5.	①	$\sum_{k=4}^{7} k \quad \left(= \sum_{k=1}^{4} k + 3\right)$
	②	$\sum_{k=4}^{8} 2k$
	③	$\sum_{k=1}^{6} (-1)^{k+1}(2k-1)$
	④	$\sum_{k=1}^{4} (-1)^{k+1} \sin k\pi$
	⑤	$\sum_{k=8}^{12} k^2$
	⑥	$\sum_{k=3}^{10} k^3$
	⑦	$\sum_{k=1}^{\infty} \dfrac{1}{k\sqrt{k}}$

	⑧ $\sum_{k=1}^{\infty} \dfrac{1}{k^2}$
	⑨ $\sum_{k=2}^{\infty} a^{\frac{1}{k}}$
	⑩ $\sum_{k=1}^{\infty} x^k$
Ex6.	① same ② different ③ different ④ same
Ex7.	$a = 15$
Ex8.	54

Ex5.	3367
Ex6.	$\log 3 + (n-1)\log 2$

9.2 Arithmetic Sequence and Series

Ex1.	① $a_n = 2 + (n-1)3 = 3n - 1$
	② $a_n = -6n + 13$
	③ $a_n = 2 + (n-1)\dfrac{1}{2} = \dfrac{1}{2}n + \dfrac{3}{2}$
	④ $a_n = 8 + (n-1)\dfrac{1}{4}$
	⑤ $a_n = (x-1) + (n-1)(-2)$
	⑥ $a_n = (2t+1) + (n-1)(6)$
	⑦ $a_n = 14\sqrt{3} + (n-1)5\sqrt{3}$
Ex2.	① $a_n = 7 + (n-1)2 = 2n + 5$
	② $a_n = 3 + (n-1)5$
Ex3.	① $n = 18$ ② $n = 23$
Ex4.	① -10 ② 590
	③ 120 ④ 20200
	⑤ $\dfrac{363}{2}$ ⑥ 23
	⑦ -5 ⑧ 200
	⑨ -192 ⑩ 672
	⑪ 84

9.3 Geometric Sequence and Series

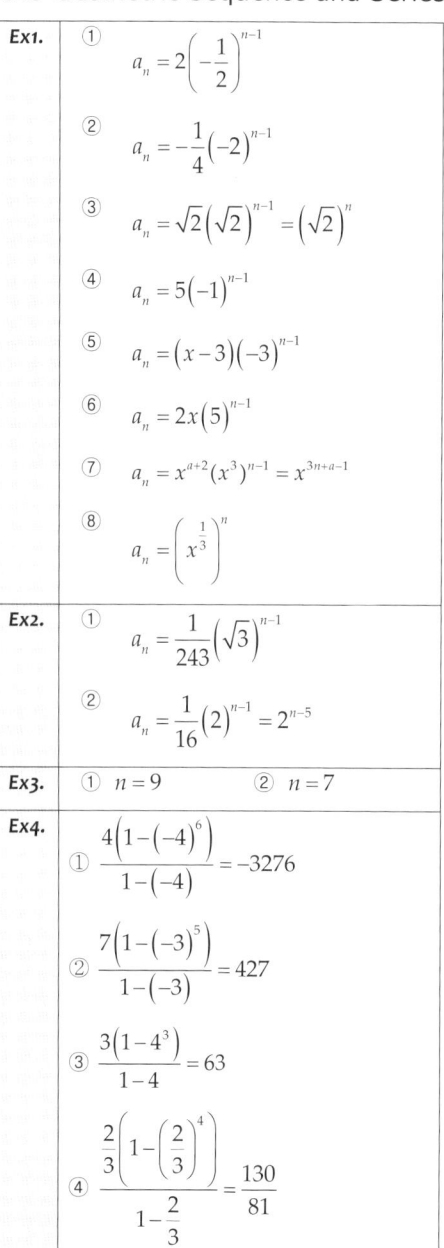

⑤	$\dfrac{10\left(1-\left(\dfrac{1}{5}\right)^6\right)}{1-\dfrac{1}{5}} = 12.4992$
⑥	$\dfrac{0.1\left(1-(0.1)^4\right)}{1-0.1} = 0.1111$
Ex5.	$3^{n-1}\ln 2$
Ex6.	$3^{\frac{1}{2}}\left(3^{-\frac{1}{6}}\right)^{n-1} = 3^{-\frac{1}{6}n+\frac{2}{3}}$

9.4 infinite Geometric Series

Ex1.	① 2	② divergent
	③ divergent	④ 1
	⑤ divergent	⑥ $\sqrt{2}+1$
	⑦ 12	⑧ 2
	⑨ $\dfrac{20}{11}$	⑩ divergent
	⑪ $\dfrac{5}{9}$	⑫ 4
	⑬ divergent	
Ex2.	① $\dfrac{2}{3}$	② $\dfrac{1}{33}$
	③ $\dfrac{234}{999} = \dfrac{26}{111}$	④ $\dfrac{251}{990}$
	⑤ $\dfrac{124}{990} = \dfrac{62}{495}$	
Ex3.	(a) $1.77147\cdots m$	
	(b) $57\ m$	
Ex4.	128	
Ex5.	$\dfrac{1}{3}$	

Answers

10. Coordinate Geometry

10.1 Distance and Midpoint Formulas

Ex1.	① $\left(\dfrac{7}{2}, 3\right)$
	② $(1, 0)$
	③ $(0, 0)$
	④ $\left(\dfrac{1}{2}, \dfrac{3\sqrt{5}}{2}\right)$
	⑤ $(\sqrt{3}, 1)$
	⑥ $(1-5\sqrt{2}, 2\sqrt{5})$
	⑦ $\left(\dfrac{a+b}{2}, 0\right)$
	⑧ (a, a)
Ex2.	$\left(4, \dfrac{1}{2}\right)$
Ex3.	① $\sqrt{13}$ ② 10
	③ $4\sqrt{3}$ ④ $\sqrt{6}$
	⑤ $2\sqrt{11}$ ⑥ $\sqrt{188} = 2\sqrt{47}$
	⑦ $\sqrt{(a+b)^2} = |a+b|$
	⑧ $\sqrt{8b^2} = 2\sqrt{2}|b|$
Ex4.	$\dfrac{\sqrt{65}}{2}$
Ex5.	Since $AB = BC$
	and $AB\sqrt{2} = AC$
	$BC\sqrt{2} = AC$
	So $\triangle ABC$ is isosceles right triangle

10.2 Equation of Circle

Ex1.

① $(1, -3)$, $r = 3$

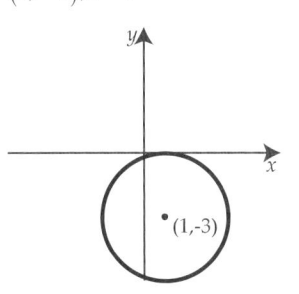

② $(-2, 4)$, $r = 2$

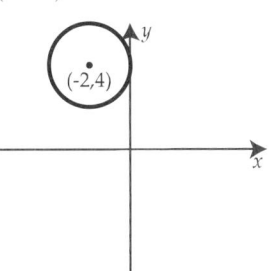

③ $(-2, 0)$, $r = 4$

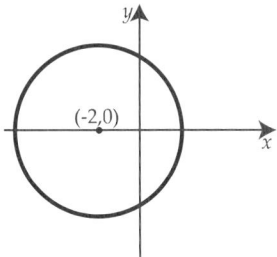

④ $(0, 4)$, $r = 4$

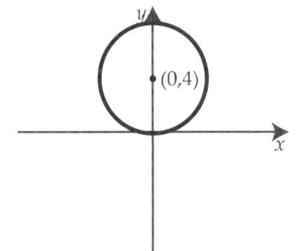

⑤ $(0, 0)$, $r = 3\sqrt{3}$

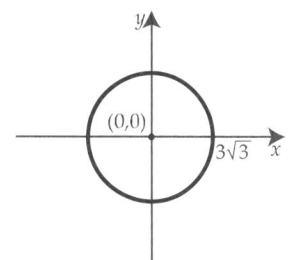

⑥ $(0, -1)$, $r = 2\sqrt{3}$

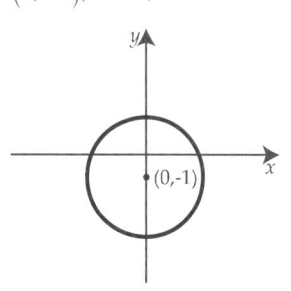

Ex2.

① $(x-3)^2 + (y+7)^2 = 25$

② $x^2 + (y-2)^2 = 9$

③ $x^2 + y^2 = 5$

④ $(x+1)^2 + (y-7)^2 = 2$

⑤ $x^2 + (y+3)^2 = 2$

⑥ $(x+2)^2 + y^2 = 16$

⑦ $(x+2)^2 + (y-3)^2 = 13$

⑧ $(x+5)^2 + (y-2)^2 = 20$

⑨ $(x+4)^2 + (y-2)^2 = 32$

⑩ $(x-2)^2 + (y-2)^2 = 52$

⑪ $(x+8)^2 + (y+5)^2 = 25$

⑫ $(x-5)^2 + (y+4)^2 = 25$

⑬ $(x+7)^2 + (y-3)^2 = 81$

⑭ $(x+3)^2+(y+2)^2=25$

⑮ $(x-4)^2+(y-2)^2=4$ and
$(x-4)^2+(y+2)^2=4$

⑯ $(x+2)^2+(y-2)^2=4$ and
$(x+2)^2+(y+2)^2=4$

⑰ $(x-1)^2+(y-1)^2=1$

⑱ $(x+1)^2+(y-1)^2=1$

Ex3.
① $(5,-4), r=5$
② $(-1,-3), r=2\sqrt{2}$
③ $(3,0), r=\sqrt{21}$
④ $(0,-5), r=\sqrt{11}$
⑤ $(-1,-5), r=\sqrt{23}$
⑥ $(1,4), r=3$

Ex4.

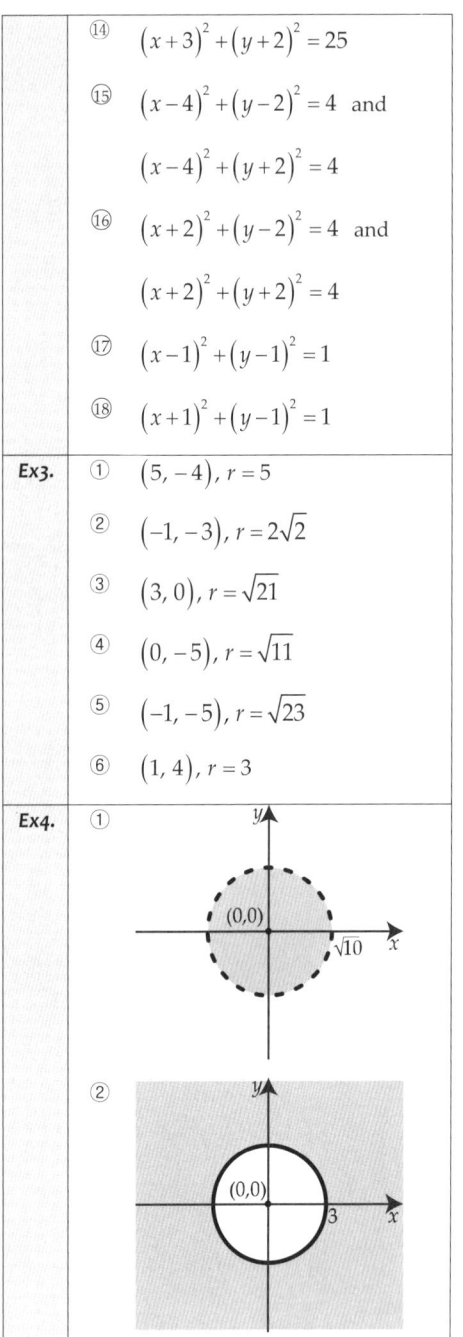

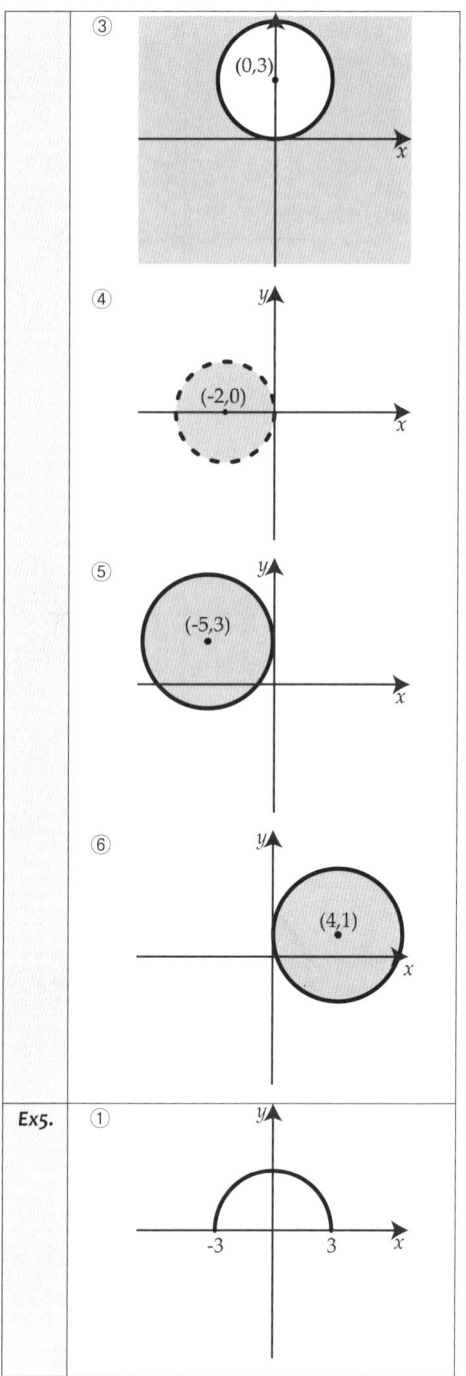

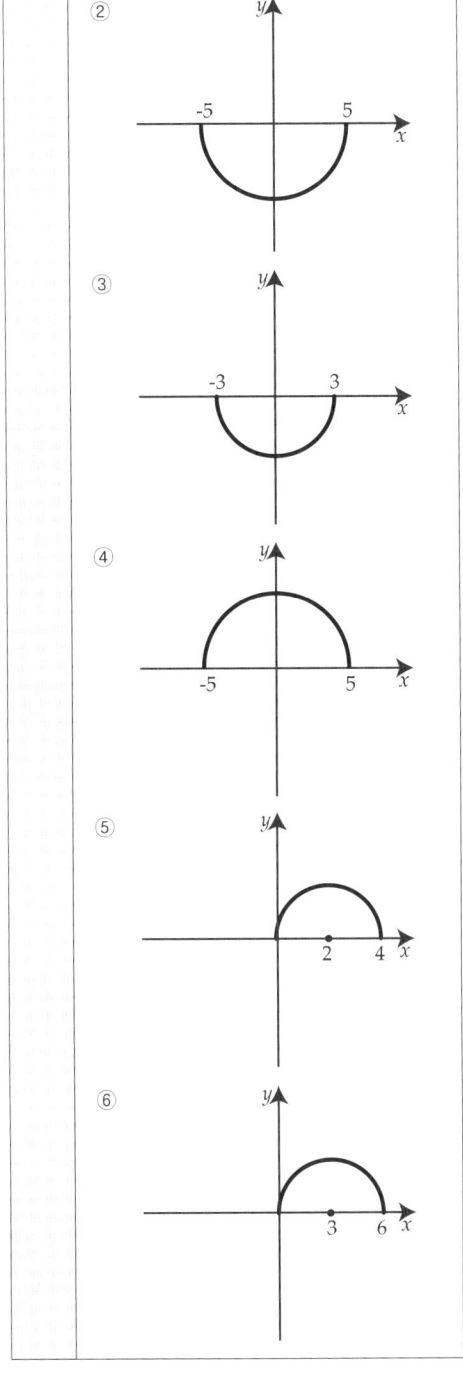

10.3 Basic of Conic Sections

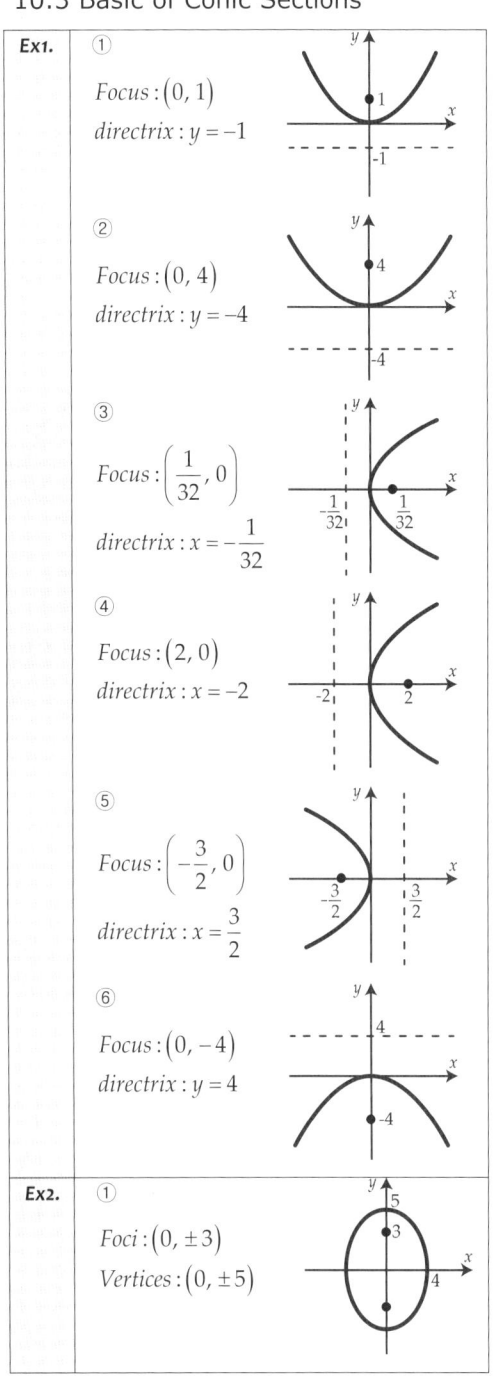

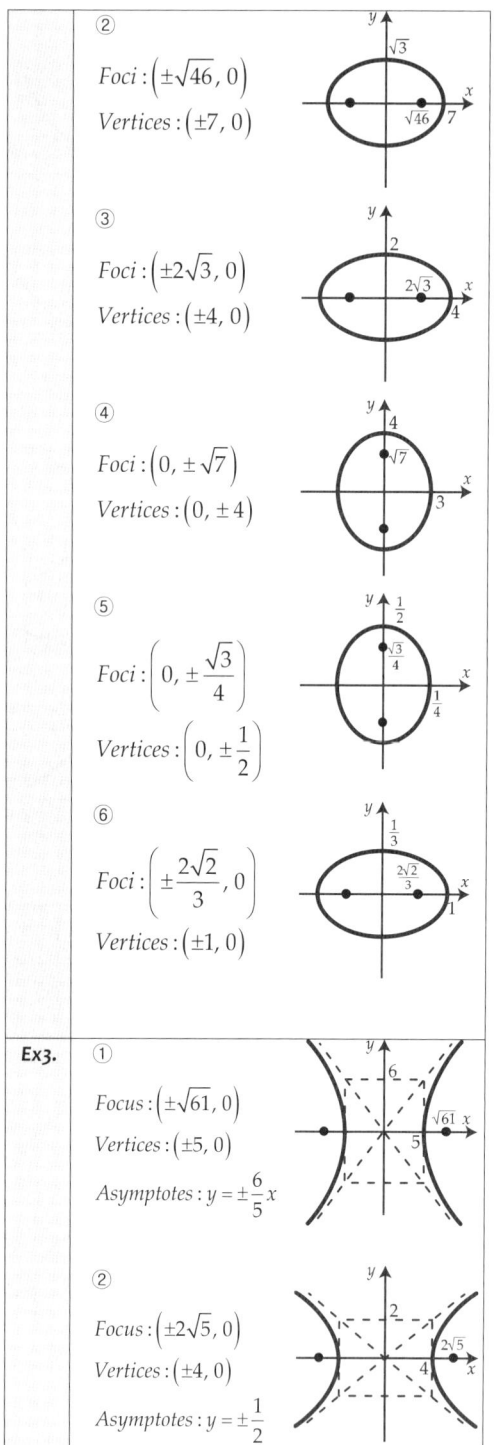
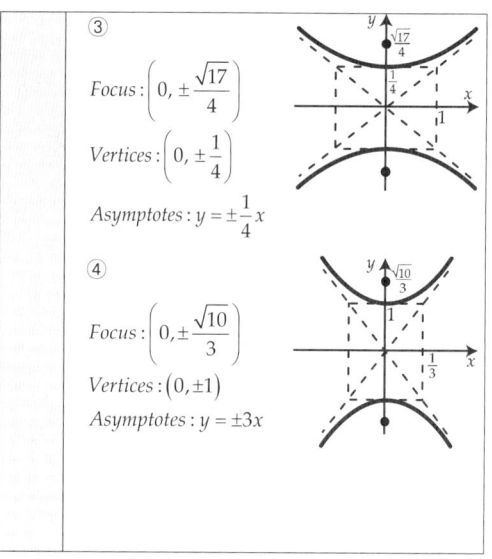

Answers

11. Basic Statistics

11.1 Measuring Center of Data

Ex1.	①	mean : 17.4
		median : 19
		mode : 20
	②	mean : 15
		median : 17
		mode : 17
	③	mean : 15.167
		median : 19.5
		mode : 4, 22 (bimodal)
	④	mean : 29.286
		median : 30
		mode : 30
	⑤	mean : 25.571
		median : 24
		mode : 20
	⑥	mean : 34.625
		median : 32.5
		mode : 50
	⑦	mean : 3.267
		median : 3
		mode : 4
	⑧	mean : 5.2
		median : 5
		mode : 5
	⑨	mean : 237.083
		median : 237.5
		mode : 240
	⑩	mean : 47
		median : 47.5
		mode : 40, 50 (bimodal)
Ex2.	32	
Ex3.	87	
Ex4.	①	skewed to left,
		mean < median
	②	skewed to right
		median < mean
	③	skewed to right
		median < mean
	④	skewed to left
		mean < median
	⑤	symmetry
		median ≈ mean
	⑥	symmetry
		median ≈ mean
	⑦	skewed to right
		median < mean
	⑧	skewed to left
		mean < median
Ex5.	67	

11.2 Measuring Spread of Data

Ex1.

① Min = 5   Q1 = 5.5   Q2 = 8
   Q3 = 12   Max = 17
   range : 12   IQR : 6.5

② Min = 2   Q1 = 10   Q2 = 17
   Q3 = 20.5   Max = 23
   range : 21,   IQR : 10.5

③ Min = 2   Q1 = 4   Q2 = 11
   Q3 = 17   Max = 21
   range : 19   IQR : 13

④ Min = 24   Q1 = 25   Q2 = 30
   Q3 = 33   Max = 37
   range : 13   IQR : 8

⑤ Min = 12   Q1 = 14.5   Q2 = 20
   Q3 = 31.5   Max = 40
   range : 28   IQR : 17

⑥ Min = 20   Q1 = 32.5   Q2 = 42
   Q3 = 49.5   Max = 55
   range : 35   IQR : 17

Ex2.
(a) range : 40
    IQR : 15
(b) (i) 50%   (ii) 25%
(c) I. T   II. F   III. T   IV. T
    V. F   VI. T

Ex3.
(a) range : 2.5
    IQR : 1
(b) (i) 75%   (ii) 25%
    (iii) 50%
(c) I. T   II. T
    III. T   IV. T
    V. T

Ex4.
① Var. = 11.2
   S.D. = $\sqrt{11.2} = 3.347$
② Var. = 13.6
   S.D. = $\sqrt{13.6} = 3.688$

Ex5.
① $A < B$ ② $A < B$
③ $A > B$ ④ $A > B$

Ex6.
mean : $A = B = C$
median : $A = B = C$
range : $A = C > B$
S.D. : $B < A < C$

Ex7.
① mean : 84,   S.D. : 5
② mean : 75,   S.D. : 5
③ mean : 70.2,   S.D. : 4.5
④ mean : 85.8,   S.D. : 5.5
⑤ mean : 156,   S.D. : 10

11.3 Probability

Ex1.
① $\dfrac{2}{4}=\dfrac{1}{2}$ ② $\dfrac{1}{4}$
③ $\dfrac{3}{4}$ ④ $\dfrac{3}{4}$
⑤ $\dfrac{2}{4}=\dfrac{1}{2}$ ⑥ $\dfrac{2}{4}=\dfrac{1}{2}$

Ex2.
① $\dfrac{3}{8}$ ② $\dfrac{3}{8}$
③ $\dfrac{7}{8}$ ④ $\dfrac{7}{8}$
⑤ $\dfrac{6}{8}=\dfrac{3}{4}$ ⑥ $\dfrac{2}{8}=\dfrac{1}{4}$

Ex3.
① $\dfrac{3}{36}=\dfrac{1}{12}$ ② $\dfrac{3}{36}=\dfrac{1}{12}$
③ $\dfrac{3}{36}=\dfrac{1}{12}$ ④ $\dfrac{30}{36}=\dfrac{5}{6}$
⑤ $\dfrac{33}{36}=\dfrac{11}{12}$ ⑥ $\dfrac{33}{36}=\dfrac{11}{12}$
⑦ $\dfrac{33}{36}=\dfrac{11}{12}$ ⑧ $\dfrac{31}{36}$
⑨ $\dfrac{9}{36}=\dfrac{1}{4}$ ⑩ $\dfrac{5}{36}$

Ex4.
① $\{1, 2, 3, 4, 5, 6, 7\}$
② $\{2, 3, 5, 6, 7, 9, 10\}$
③ $\{3, 6, 7\}$
④ $\{3, 4\}$
⑤ $\{2, 3, 4\}$
⑥ $\{1, 2, 3, 4, 6, 7\}$
⑦ $\dfrac{6}{12}=\dfrac{1}{2}$
⑧ $\dfrac{7}{12}$
⑨ $\dfrac{2}{12}=\dfrac{1}{6}$
⑩ $\dfrac{0}{12}=0$
⑪ $\dfrac{7}{12}$
⑫ $\dfrac{10}{12}=\dfrac{5}{6}$
⑬ No
⑭ Yes
⑮ Yes
⑯ No

Ex5.
① 0.1
② 0.3

Ex6.
① 0.9
② 0.4

Ex7.
① 0.6
② 0.6

Ex8.
① $\dfrac{77}{150}$ ② $\dfrac{46}{150}$
③ $\dfrac{14}{150}=\dfrac{7}{75}$ ④ $\dfrac{40}{150}=\dfrac{4}{15}$
⑤ $\dfrac{101}{150}$ ⑥ $\dfrac{113}{150}$
⑦ $\dfrac{59}{150}$ ⑧ $\dfrac{115}{150}=\dfrac{23}{30}$

11.4 Independent & Dependent Event

Ex1.	(a) $\dfrac{12}{50}=\dfrac{6}{25}$	
	(b) $\dfrac{31}{50}$	
	(c) $\dfrac{7}{50}$	
	(d) $\dfrac{7}{12}$	
	(e) $\dfrac{7}{26}$	
Ex2.	① $\dfrac{2}{5}$	② $\dfrac{2}{5}$
	③ $\dfrac{3}{5}$	④ $\dfrac{3}{5}$
	⑤ $\dfrac{2}{4}=\dfrac{1}{2}$	⑥ $\dfrac{3}{5}$
	⑦ $\dfrac{2}{7}$	⑧ $\dfrac{2}{7}$
Ex3.	① $\dfrac{22}{46}=\dfrac{11}{23}$	② $\dfrac{35}{75}=\dfrac{7}{15}$
	③ $\dfrac{22}{77}=\dfrac{2}{7}$	④ $\dfrac{35}{73}$
	⑤ $\dfrac{14}{29}$	⑥ $\dfrac{37}{77}$
	⑦ $\dfrac{59}{121}$	⑧ $\dfrac{37}{75}$
Ex4.	① $\dfrac{17}{50}$	② $\dfrac{13}{50}$
	③ $\dfrac{1}{14}$	④ $\dfrac{7}{24}$
	⑤ $\dfrac{4}{26}=\dfrac{2}{13}$	⑥ $\dfrac{18}{35}$
	⑦ $\dfrac{17}{21}$	⑧ $\dfrac{23}{24}$

Ex5.	① $\dfrac{13}{36}$	② $\dfrac{16}{52}$
	③ $\dfrac{20}{33}$	④ $\dfrac{16}{31}$
	⑤ $\dfrac{23}{52}$	
Ex6.	① $\dfrac{25}{64}$	② $\dfrac{34}{64}=\dfrac{17}{32}$
	③ $\dfrac{30}{64}=\dfrac{15}{32}$	④ $\dfrac{55}{64}$
	⑤ $\dfrac{39}{64}$	
Ex7.	① $\dfrac{20}{56}=\dfrac{5}{14}$	② $\dfrac{26}{56}=\dfrac{13}{28}$
	③ $\dfrac{30}{56}=\dfrac{15}{28}$	④ $\dfrac{50}{56}=\dfrac{25}{28}$
	⑤ $\dfrac{36}{56}=\dfrac{9}{14}$	
Ex8.	① yes	② no
	③ no	④ yes
	⑤ yes	⑥ yes
	⑦ no	
Ex9.	a) 0.5	b) 0.44